For Reference

Not to be taken from this room

Y0-BIM-538

MAGILL'S LITERARY ANNUAL 2021

Essay-Reviews of 150 Outstanding Books Published in the United States During 2020

With an Annotated List of Titles

Volume II
K-Z
Indexes

Edited by
Jennifer Sawtelle

REF.
PN
44
.M351
2021
v.2

SALEM PRESS
A Division of EBSCO Information Services, Inc.
Ipswich, Massachusetts

GREY HOUSE PUBLISHING

Cover photo: Louise Penny, photo by Ian Crysler via Wikimedia.

Copyright © 2021, by Salem Press, a Division of EBSCO Information Services, Inc. All rights in this book are reserved. No part of this work may be used or reproduced in any manner whatsoever or transmitted in any form or by any means, electronic or mechanical, including photocopy, recording, or any information storage and retrieval system, without written permission from the copyright owner. For permissions requests, contact permissions@ebscohost.com.

Magill's Literary Annual, 2021, published by Grey House Publishing, Inc., Amenia, NY, under exclusive license from EBSCO Information Services, Inc.

For information contact Grey House Publishing/Salem Press, 4919 Route 22, PO Box 56, Amenia, NY 12501.

∞ The paper used in these volumes conforms to the American National Standard for Permanence of Paper for Printed Library Materials, Z39.48-1992 (R2009).

Publisher's Cataloging-In-Publication Data
(Prepared by The Donohue Group, Inc.)

Names: Magill, Frank N. (Frank Northen), 1907-1997, editor. | Wilson, John D., editor. | Kellman, Steven G., 1947- editor. | Goodhue, Emily, editor. | Poranski, Colin D., editor. | Akre, Matthew, editor. | Spires, Kendal, editor. | Toth, Gabriela, editor. | Sawtelle, Jennifer, editor. Title: Magill's literary annual.
Description: <1977->: [Pasadena, Calif.] : Salem Press | <2015->: Ipswich, Massachusetts : Salem Press, a division of EBSCO Information Services, Inc. ; Amenia, NY : Grey House Publishing | Essay-reviews of ... outstanding books published in the United States during the previous year. | "With an annotated list of titles." | Editor: 1977- , F.N. Magill; <2010-2014>, John D. Wilson and Steven G. Kellman; <2015>, Emily Goodhue and Colin D. Poranski; <2016>, Matthew Akre, Kendal Spires, and Gabriela Toth; <2017->, Jennifer Sawtelle. | Includes bibliographical references and index.
Identifiers: ISSN: 0163-3058
Subjects: LCSH: Books--Reviews--Periodicals. | United States--Imprints--Book reviews--Periodicals. | Literature, Modern--21st century--History and criticism--Periodicals. | Literature, Modern--20th century--History and criticism--Periodicals.
Classification: LCC PN44 .M333 | DDC 028.1--dc23
ISBN: 97816042657296 (Set) 9781642657302 (Vol. 1) 9781642657319 (Vol. 2)

FIRST PRINTING
PRINTED IN THE UNITED STATES OF AMERICA

CONTENTS

Complete Annotated List of Contents. vii

Kent State—*Deborah Wiles*. 363
Kim Jiyoung, Born 1982—*Cho Nam-joo*. 367
A Knock at Midnight: A Story of Hope, Justice,
    and Freedom—*Brittany K. Barnett* 372

The Last Negroes at Harvard: The Class of 1963 and the 18 Young Men Who
    Changed Harvard Forever—*Kent Garrett and Jeanne Ellsworth*. 377
Leave the World Behind—*Rumaan Alam*. 382
Long Bright River—*Liz Moore*. 387
A Long Petal of the Sea—*Isabel Allende*. 391
The Lost Book of Adana Moreau—*Michael Zapata* 396

Memorial Drive: A Daughter's Memoir—*Natasha Trethewey* 401
Mexican Gothic—*Silvia Moreno-Garcia*. 406
The Mirror & the Light—*Hilary Mantel* 411
Miss Benson's Beetle—*Rachel Joyce*. 416
Moonflower Murders—*Anthony Horowitz* 420
The Mountains Sing—*Nguyễn Phan Quế Mai* 425
My Dark Vanessa—*Kate Elizabeth Russell*. 429

The New Wilderness—*Diane Cook*. 433
The Night Watchman—*Louise Erdrich*. 438
Nobody Will Tell You This but Me:
    A True (as Told to Me) Story—*Bess Kalb*. 442
Not So Pure and Simple—*Lamar Giles*. 447

Obit—*Victoria Chang*. 451
The Office of Historical Corrections—*Danielle Evans* 456
One Mighty and Irresistible Tide: The Epic Struggle over
    American Immigration, 1924–1965—*Jia Lynn Yang* 460
The Only Good Indians—*Stephen Graham Jones* 465
Owls of the Eastern Ice: A Quest to Find and Save the
    World's Largest Owl—*Jonathan C. Slaght* 470

Paying the Land—*Joe Sacco* 475
Pelosi—*Molly Ball* 480
Piranesi—*Susanna Clarke* 485
Postcolonial Love Poem—*Natalie Diaz* 489
The Price of Peace: Money, Democracy, and the Life of
    John Maynard Keynes—*Zachary D. Carter* 494

A Promised Land—*Barack Obama* 499
Punching the Air—*Ibi Zoboi and Yusef Salaam* 504

Race against Time: A Reporter Reopens the Unsolved Murder Cases of the
  Civil Rights Era—*Jerry Mitchell* 508
Reaganland: America's Right Turn 1976–1980—*Rick Perlstein* 513
Real Life—*Brandon Taylor* 518
Recollections of My Nonexistence—*Rebecca Solnit* 523
Ring Shout—*P. Djèlí Clark* 528
The Rise and Fall of Charles Lindbergh—*Candace Fleming* 532

The Searcher—*Tana French* 537
The Second Chance Club: Hardship and Hope after Prison—*Jason Hardy* . . . 541
The Secret Lives of Church Ladies—*Deesha Philyaw* 546
Shuggie Bain—*Douglas Stuart* 550
Sigh, Gone: A Misfit's Memoir of Great Books, Punk Rock,
  and the Fight to Fit In—*Phuc Tran* 554
The Silent Wife—*Karin Slaughter* 559
Sisters—*Daisy Johnson* 564
The Smallest Lights in the Universe—*Sara Seager* 568
Some Assembly Required: Decoding Four Billion Years of Life,
  from Ancient Fossils to DNA—*Neil Shubin* 572
The Southern Book Club's Guide to Slaying Vampires—*Grady Hendrix* 577
The Splendid and the Vile: A Saga of Churchill, Family, and Defiance
  during the Blitz—*Erik Larson* 582
Squeeze Me—*Carl Hiaasen* 587
Stamped: Racism, Antiracism, and You—*Ibram X. Kendi and Jason Reynolds* . . 591
Summer—*Ali Smith* 596
The Sun Down Motel—*Simone St. James* 601
Supreme Inequality: The Supreme Court's Fifty-Year Battle for a
  More Unjust America—*Adam Cohen* 605
Swimming in the Dark—*Tomasz Jedrowski* 610

They Went Left—*Monica Hesse* 615
Those Who Forget: My Family's Story in Nazi Europe—A Memoir, a History,
  a Warning—*Géraldine Schwarz* 620
The Thursday Murder Club—*Richard Osman* 625
Tigers, Not Daughters—*Samantha Mabry* 630
Tokyo Ueno Station—*Yu Miri* 635
Transcendent Kingdom—*Yaa Gyasi* 639
Twilight of the Gods: War in the Western Pacific, 1944–1945—*Ian W. Toll* . . . 643

The Undocumented Americans—*Karla Cornejo Villavicencio*. 648
Untamed—*Glennon Doyle* 653
Unworthy Republic: The Dispossession of Native Americans and
    the Road to Indian Territory—*Claudio Saunt* 657

The Vanished Birds—*Simon Jimenez* 662
The Vanishing Half—*Brit Bennett* 666
Vesper Flights—*Helen Macdonald* 671

We Are Not Free—*Traci Chee* 675
We Are Not from Here—*Jenny Torres Sanchez* 680
We Have Been Harmonized: Life in China's
    Surveillance State—*Kai Strittmatter* 685
Weather—*Jenny Offill*. 690
When Truth Is All You Have: A Memoir of Faith, Justice, and Freedom for the
    Wrongly Accused—*Jim McCloskey with Philip Lerman* 695
Wilmington's Lie: The Murderous Coup of 1898 and
    the Rise of White Supremacy—*David Zucchino* 699

Yellow Bird: Oil, Murder, and a Woman's Search for Justice
    in Indian Country—*Sierra Crane Murdoch* 704

Category Index 709
Title Index. 715

COMPLETE ANNOTATED LIST OF CONTENTS

VOLUME I

The Address Book: What Street Addresses Reveal about Identity,
Race, Wealth, and Power 1
This globe-trotting history of street addresses takes the reader on journeys from ancient Rome to Nazi Germany and modern-day Kolkata, India. Deirdre Mask moves across space and time to introduce the reader to the surprising complexities and social dynamics behind the systematic use of street naming and numbering systems.

Afterlife 6
Antonia Vega, a retired college professor, withdraws from the world after the sudden death of her husband, but a request for help from an immigrant farm worker and the disappearance of her sister Izzy challenge her self-imposed isolation.

Agent Sonya: Moscow's Most Daring Wartime Spy 10
Ben Macintyre offers a thrilling, panoramic look at the life and career of Ursula Kuczynski, also known as Agent Sonya, who is widely considered to have been one of the most successful Soviet spies of the twentieth century. Drawing on exhaustive research, Macintyre brings an informed perspective in chronicling and assessing Kuczynski's place in history.

All the Devils Are Here 15
The sixteenth entry in the best-selling Chief Inspector Armand Gamache mystery series, All the Devils Are Here *finds the detective embroiled in an international intrigue involving his own godfather while visiting Paris. As they search for answers, the whole Gamache family must decide whether they can trust what they think they know about each other, old friends, and even themselves.*

Almost American Girl 20
Almost American Girl, *a graphic memoir by comic artist Robin Ha, explores Ha's teenage years, when she and her mother left their home in South Korea and moved to the United States.*

Anxious People 24
Swedish author Fredrik Backman's Anxious People *is a novel about the importance of compassion that revolves around a bank robbery gone wrong.*

Apeirogon 29
Apeirogon *is an experimental novel told in 1,001 fragmentary chapters exploring the shared grief of two men, one Israeli and one Palestinian, whose lives have been shaped by the Middle Eastern conflict and the deaths of their daughters.*

Apple (Skin to the Core) 34
    Apple (Skin to the Core) *is a poetry collection by Onondaga writer Eric Gansworth that reflects on his family's history and his time growing up on a Tuscarora Nation reservation in New York.*

The Bear. 38
    The Bear, *Andrew Krivak's third novel, is a mythic, lush exploration of the resilience of the natural world and an exploration of love, loss, and harmony at the end of the human species.*

Beowulf: A New Translation 42
    The epic poem Beowulf *is told in a new translation employing twenty-first-century vocabulary that makes the Old English poem accessible to contemporary readers, while taking a feminist perspective to critique the heroic perspective in the original poem.*

Black Sun 47
    In Rebecca Roanhorse's high-fantasy epic Black Sun, *familiar elements of indigenous Mesoamerican mythology coexist with new fantasy elements in a story that moves between time frames and introduces a series of new characters.*

A Black Women's History of the United States. 52
    A Black Women's History of the United States *examines more than five hundred years of North American history through the experiences of the Black women who lived it. Written by historians Daina Ramey Berry and Kali Nicole Gross, the book provides new insights and figures.*

Blacktop Wasteland 57
    In Blacktop Wasteland, *racial and economic tensions underlie an action-packed crime story. Hard-working but financially strapped family man Beauregard Montage, an ex-convict, agrees to act as driver in a jewel heist, but when the caper goes horribly wrong he finds himself involved with powerful, vicious gangsters.*

The Book of Longings 62
    In Sue Monk Kidd's The Book of Longings, *a young woman named Ana works to write the stories of silenced women—including herself—amid political unrest and the foundation of Christianity.*

Brown Album: Essays on Exile and Identity 67
    Brown Album: Essays on Exile and Identity *(2020) is Porochista Khakpour's first essay collection. The book explores Iranian American culture in the United States and what it means to live as an immigrant in a country that often rejects and holds*

down those from other places. The twenty essays are divided into sections focused on the author's coming of age in the United States, her immigrant experience, and her success as a writer.

A Burning..72
    In A Burning, *first-time novelist Megha Majumdar presents a searing indictment of politics and justice in contemporary India through the tale of Jivan, a young Muslim woman jailed for criticizing police inaction after a horrific terrorist attack.*

Caste: The Origins of Our Discontents......................76
    In Caste, *Isabel Wilkerson examines the origins and dynamics of America's race-based social hierarchy and the impact it continues to have on people's lives. She also explores the enduring, global reach of caste through comparisons with other countries and times.*

Cemetery Boys..81
    Aiden Thomas's groundbreaking Cemetery Boys *is a love story between a transgender Latinx boy determined to prove himself to his family and a troublemaking spirit who refuses to leave the world.*

The City We Became...................................85
    In The City We Became, *six people become embodiments of the city of New York, and must band together to defeat a tentacled Enemy bent on destroying the city and everything in it. The novel offers both Lovecraftian fantasy adventure and incisive social commentary particularly attuned to the racial dynamics of New York City.*

Clap When You Land...................................90
    Clap When You Land *tells the story of two half-sisters, Camino and Yahaira, separated by an ocean and the secret of each other's existence. After their father dies in a plane crash, they both struggle with the depth of his secrets and finding each other.*

Cleanness...94
    Cleanness, *Garth Greenwell's follow-up to his 2016 debut novel,* What Belongs to You, *follows an American teacher as he prepares to leave Sofia, Bulgaria, after several years abroad. Told through a series of short-story-like chapters, this novel revisits the territory laid in Greenwell's first effort, exploring desire, masculinity, and detachment against Sofia's post-Soviet setting.*

Code Name Hélène....................................98
    Best-selling author Ariel Lawhon's fourth historical novel, Code Name Hélène, *spotlights the incredible true wartime exploits of a remarkable woman, Nancy Wake, who became a leader of the Resistance, the underground guerrilla movement that helped drive the Nazis from occupied France.*

Conjure Women 103
    Conjure Women is the story of Miss Rue, the conjure woman of a town made of a former slave quarter, and the people she fights to save and the secrets she fights to keep.

Counterpoint: A Memoir of Bach and Mourning 107
    This thought-provoking memoir explores the author's period of grief following the death of his mother, intertwined with his efforts to learn Bach's Goldberg Variations on piano. The book weaves together recollections from Kennicott's difficult childhood, meditations on who his mother was as a person, and deep examination of the power and meaning of great art.

Crooked Hallelujah 112
    Crooked Hallelujah follows a family of four generations of Cherokee women as they seek to persevere through various travails and heartaches. It is Kelli Jo Ford's debut novel.

Dancing at the Pity Party: A Dead Mom Graphic Memoir 116
    In this graphic memoir, Tyler Feder remembers the continuing journey she began as a young college student when her mother became terminally ill. Her honest tale shares the lifetime difficulties caused by the loss of a parent.

Deacon King Kong 120
    An elderly church-going handyman sets off a string of intriguing events in a tight-knit Brooklyn neighborhood when he shoots a young Black drug-pusher in this farcical novel by acclaimed author James McBride.

The Dead Are Arising: The Life of Malcolm X 125
    Thirty years in the making, The Dead Are Arising: The Life of Malcolm X *is an extensive, moving, and, in some respects, explosive new biography of the Black activist who was assassinated in 1965.*

A Deadly Education 130
    In A Deadly Education, *El, a sixteen-year-old sorceress, navigates her junior year at a dangerous and monster-infested school of magic and works to gain the knowledge and allies needed to survive not only her upcoming senior year but also her school's notoriously deadly graduation ceremony.*

Dear Edward 135
    Dear Edward is the story of a young boy who survived a plane crash that killed everyone else on board. The novel shares both the stories of some of the other passengers as it moves between the flight and Edward's life after the tragedy.

Death in Mud Lick: A Coal Country Fight against the Drug Companies
That Delivered the Opioid Epidemic 139
In Death in Mud Lick, *Eric Eyre has turned his Pulitzer Prize–winning coverage of the opioid epidemic in West Virginia into a compelling book that describes both the drug crisis and various threats to independent, small-town journalism.*

The Death of Vivek Oji 144
Akwaeke Emezi's second novel for adult readers, The Death of Vivek Oji *continues the author's exploration of the true self of an individual. Beginning as an investigation by the title character's grieving mother into how her son died, the story evolves into an examination of who he was and how he lived.*

Devolution: A Firsthand Account of the Rainier Sasquatch Massacre 149
Devolution *presents the story of an isolated, eco-friendly community in Washington State that is cut off by an eruption of Mount Rainier and beset by a group of ape-like creatures who are themselves displaced by the disaster. Framed as a work of journalism, the novel weaves timely social criticism into a page-turning monster thriller.*

Dirt: Adventures in Lyon as a Chef in Training, Father, and
Sleuth Looking for the Secret of French Cooking. 154
In Dirt: Adventures in Lyon as a Chef in Training, Father, and Sleuth Looking for the Secret of French Cooking, *Bill Buford chronicles several years spent living and working in Lyon, France, a city with a rich culinary history.*

The Discomfort of Evening 159
Marieke Lucas Rijneveld's debut novel depicts a girl coming of age in a dairy-farming family crumbling under the weight of grief, cattle disease, and strict religious principles.

DMZ Colony 164
Don Mee Choi's National Book Award–winning DMZ Colony *combines poetry, oral history, quotation, photographs, and drawings to, in Choi's words, create "a language of return." Working as a translator, Choi returns to her native South Korea and visits the DMZ, the militarized border with North Korea. She interviews a former political prisoner and meditates on the "forgotten" atrocities of the Korean War. For Choi, translation is both an act of communion and an act of resistance.*

Dragon Hoops 168
In Dragon Hoops, *graphic novelist and former teacher Gene Luen Yang tells the story of the Bishop O'Dowd High School boys' basketball team's 2014–15 season, interspersing basketball history, social issues, and details of his own life.*

The Dragons, the Giant, the Women 173
    The Dragons, the Giant, the Women *is a memoir by Wayétu Moore about her family's escape from Liberia during the Liberian Civil War.*

Eat the Buddha: Life and Death in a Tibetan Town. 177
    In Eat the Buddha, *the distinguished foreign correspondent Barbara Demick presents a penetrating analysis of the Chinese occupation of Tibet. Focusing on the small town of Ngaba, known as a hotbed of Tibetan protest and resistance, Demick traces the effects of Chinese rule on the lives of a diverse group of Tibetans.*

The Eighth Life (for Brilka). 182
    In The Eighth Life, *Nino Haratischvili explores the events of the twentieth century in the country of Georgia through the lens of one family's struggles.*

Entangled Life: How Fungi Make Our Worlds, Change Our Minds &
    Shape Our Futures. 187
    In Entangled Life: How Fungi Make Our Worlds, Change Our Minds & Shape Our Futures, *biologist Merlin Sheldrake explores the complex and interconnected world of fungi and the ways in which such organisms affect the world around them.*

The Evening and the Morning 192
    The Evening and the Morning *is a prequel to Ken Follett's international bestselling Kingsbridge series, including* The Pillars of the Earth. *The story covers a decade at the end of the Dark Ages, with England under siege from both Vikings and the Welsh.*

Fair Warning 196
    Fair Warning *is Michael Connelly's third thriller featuring reporter Jack McEvoy, and the first installment in more than a decade. As in previous series entries, the story revolves around the intrepid investigator's efforts to expose a serial killer, this time one who disguises vicious murders as accidents to escape law enforcement detection.*

Fight of the Century: Writers Reflect on 100 Years of Landmark ACLU Cases . 201
    In the essay collection Fight of the Century: Writers Reflect on 100 Years of Landmark ACLU Cases, *writers explore the most compelling and important cases involving the American Civil Liberties Union (ACLU) since its founding in 1920. The essays' authors are some of the most well-known and respected writers and intellectuals working today, and they offer a range of perspectives covering landmark Supreme Court cases such as* Brown v. Board of Education, Roe v. Wade, *and* Miranda v. Arizona.

Five Days: The Fiery Reckoning of an American City 206
   This book examines the social unrest following the death of Freddie Gray, a Black man who was injured after being arrested in Baltimore, Maryland. Focusing on the five days around Gray's funeral, the authors illustrate the complexity of the situation through the perspectives and actions of eight very different individuals.

A Girl Is a Body of Water. 211
   A Girl Is a Body of Water is an artfully constructed coming-of-age story that examines the intricacies of womanhood and identity with exceptional clarity.

The Glass Hotel 215
   In the novel The Glass Hotel, *characters struggle to rebuild their lives in the wake of falling victim to a Ponzi scheme. In its kaleidoscopic approach to storytelling, the novel serves as a meditation on the nature of memory and truth.*

A Good Neighborhood 220
   In the novel A Good Neighborhood, *a feud between two families in a gentrifying North Carolina neighborhood shines a light on issues of race, religion, and privilege.*

Grown. 225
   Acclaimed author Tiffany D. Jackson examines the impact of misogyny, control, and the exploitation of Black girls and women in this young-adult mystery about an aspiring singer mentored by an abusive music industry star.

Guillotine 230
   In his second collection of verse, prize-winning poet Eduardo C. Corral creates diverse voices and perspectives to explore—usually in stark, dark terms—such issues as the lives of undocumented immigrants and the experiences of gay men.

Hamnet 235
   Maggie O'Farrell's historical novel imagines the lives of the real-life family members of iconic writer William Shakespeare, based around the death of his son Hamnet at age eleven. Relegating the famous dramatist to the periphery, O'Farrell chooses to explore motherhood and grief largely through the lens of Hamnet's mother, Agnes.

Harrow the Ninth 240
   In Harrow the Ninth, *the second novel in Tamsyn Muir's Locked Tomb trilogy, the titular necromancer grapples with Lyctorhood, memory, and her own sanity as a powerful foe draws closer to the Emperor's space station.*

Hench 245
    Natalie Zina Walschots's debut novel, Hench, *imagines a contemporary world inhabited by superheroes and supervillains but takes a different approach by focusing on the henchpeople—hired muscle, data specialists, public relations flaks— who do essential but unappreciated behind-the-scenes work. The result is an effective mix of satire, action, and incisive social commentary.*

Hidden Valley Road: Inside the Mind of an American Family 250
    In Hidden Valley Road, *the distinguished investigative journalist Robert Kolker provides an exhaustive study of a family riven by mental illness. Kolker traces the evolving scientific understanding of schizophrenia while empathetically describing its effects on the Galvins in this* New York Times *Best Seller.*

Hieroglyphics 255
    Frank and Lil, finding that the shared tragedy of losing a parent as a child could provide a strong basis for a lifelong relationship, are married after bonding over their grief. In the empty days of retirement, Frank obsesses over the house where he lived as a child and Lil focuses on their past. Drawn loosely into their lives are Shelley and her son Harvey, who live in Frank's childhood home.

His Very Best: Jimmy Carter, a Life 260
    Journalist and historian Jonathan Alter presents a nuanced view of Jimmy Carter, the much-maligned thirty-ninth US president and celebrated humanitarian, in this first full-length biography.

A History of My Brief Body 265
    A History of My Brief Body, *award-winning poet Billy-Ray Belcourt's memoir in essays, explores love and loneliness through a multi-faceted lens. Incorporating lyric poetry and critical theory, Belcourt's challenging but exhilarating book defies easy categorization.*

Hitler: Downfall 1939–1945 269
    From German historian Volker Ullrich, author of Hitler: Ascent, 1889–1939, *comes a detailed account of the infamous dictator's last years, from the invasion of Poland to the end of the Nazi regime.*

Hitting a Straight Lick with a Crooked Stick 274
    In this new collection of Zora Neale Hurston's short fiction from the Harlem Renaissance, the famed African American author details Black life in both the urban North and the rural South.

Hollywood Park... 279
    Mikel Jollett, front man for the band the Airborne Toxic Event, wrote the biography Hollywood Park *about his experiences escaping rural poverty and addiction and how his turbulent and unconventional upbringing shaped his careers as a writer and musician.*

Home before Dark... 284
    Home before Dark, *a haunted house thriller from best-selling author Riley Sager, takes inspiration from* The Amityville Horror *(1977), a purportedly true story about a family driven from their new home by a poltergeist. In Sager's novel, Maggie Holt, the daughter of famed author Ewan Holt, inherits Baneberry Hall, the Victorian mansion where her father claimed paranormal events took place twenty-five years prior. Grieving her father's death but suspicious of his claims, she returns to Baneberry to uncover the truth.*

Homeland Elegies.. 289
    Pulitzer Prize–winning playwright Ayad Akhtar merges fiction and memoir in this search for the meaning of home for an American son and his Pakistan-born father during the Trump era.

Homie... 294
    Homie *is the third collection by acclaimed poet Danez Smith. Building on a central theme of friendship, in all its complexities, the works especially showcase Smith's vivid exploration of Black and queer identity.*

Hood Feminism: Notes from the Women That a Movement Forgot........ 299
    Hood Feminism *is a collection of essays about the shortcomings of mainstream, White feminism and the need for a more intersectional movement. It is writer and activist Mikki Kendall's second book.*

How Much of These Hills Is Gold............................ 304
    How Much of These Hills Is Gold *is the debut novel of C Pam Zhang. It follows the story of two Chinese American siblings trying to survive in the wild and racist world of the nineteenth-century American West.*

Hurricane Season... 309
    Hurricane Season *is Fernanda Melchor's second published novel and her first to be translated into English. It examines from several different points of view the brutal murder of a notorious person who may have had special abilities in a rural Mexican village.*

I Hold a Wolf by the Ears 314
    I Hold a Wolf by the Ears *is an unsettling and surreal collection of short stories about women who are struggling with their identities, their relationships, and the demands of the men around them.*

If It Bleeds. 319
    Stephen King's 2020 collection of four novellas returns to a form and to characters familiar to his readers. Stories tackle themes of technology, memory, and the Faustian bargains of creative life.

In the Valley. 324
    In the Valley *collects nine short stories and a novella by acclaimed author Ron Rash. Set mostly in Rash's native Appalachia but taking place across more than a century, the works showcase a wide variety of characters and subjects, from intimate depictions of everyday life to almost mythological portrayals of larger-than-life figures.*

Inge's War: A German Woman's Story of Family, Secrets,
    and Survival under Hitler 329
    Svenja O'Donnell's biography of her grandmother's experiences in World War II uncovers dynamics of wartime Europe.

Interior Chinatown 334
    Interior Chinatown *is a parable of pop culture and Asian ambition in America, told in script form, that wrestles with the questions of who can be considered American and how the roles to which Americans are prescribed affect their lives.*

Intimations 338
    Noted writer Zadie Smith examines her experience and chronicles her thoughts during the first months of the pandemic crisis of 2020 in this short volume of six personal essays.

The Invisible Life of Addie LaRue 343
    The Invisible Life of Addie Larue *tells the story of a young woman who promises her soul to an ancient godlike power in exchange for immortality, with unforeseen consequences.*

Is Rape a Crime?: A Memoir, an Investigation, and a Manifesto 348
    Michelle Bowdler advocates for change in the way that rape is treated by police, the criminal justice system, and society as a whole as she recounts the lasting psychological impact of having been raped in the 1980s.

Jack 353
    In this fourth book of the Gilead series, Marilynne Robinson follows Jack, a troubled young man, as he falls in love in segregated St. Louis.

Just Us: An American Conversation 358
    Just Us: An American Conversation *spans multiple genres; it combines poetry with essays and multimedia accompaniments, including social media screenshots and documentary photography. The project offers a conversation between author Claudia Rankine and multiple interlocutors concerning issues of race in contemporary American society.*

VOLUME II

Kent State 363
    Kent State *is a young-adult novel, written in free verse, that recalls the events leading up to the killing of four students by the Ohio National Guard at an antiwar protest at Kent State University in 1970.*

Kim Jiyoung, Born 1982 367
    In the novel Kim Jiyoung, Born 1982, *a young woman begins to experience strange episodes after enduring a lifetime of sexism.*

A Knock at Midnight: A Story of Hope, Justice, and Freedom 372
    A Knock at Midnight *is, in large part, the personal and professional coming-of-age story of Brittany K. Barnett, an attorney who became a prominent national advocate for executive clemency of Black men and women incarcerated under federal drug offenses. Through a powerful account of her own life intertwined with the lives of individuals imprisoned under unjust sentencing laws, Barnett presents an argument for sweeping criminal justice reform in the United States.*

The Last Negroes at Harvard: The Class of 1963 and the 18 Young Men
    Who Changed Harvard Forever 377
    Kent Garrett and Jeanne Ellsworth's The Last Negroes at Harvard *traces the lives and careers of eighteen Black members of the 1963 graduating class at Harvard University. While highlighting many triumphs, it also reveals deep injustices.*

Leave the World Behind. 382
    Leave the World Behind *is a dystopian thriller set in the present that explores race, class, and the limitations of contemporary life.*

Long Bright River. 387
    Long Bright River *is a police procedural thriller set against the backdrop of the opioid epidemic. It is American author Liz Moore's fourth book.*

A Long Petal of the Sea. 391
    In A Long Petal of the Sea, *refugees from the Spanish Civil War find sanctuary in Chile but are forced to flee again after the political coup of 1973.*

The Lost Book of Adana Moreau. 396
    In the novel The Lost Book of Adana Moreau, *a young man is determined to fulfill his recently deceased grandfather's desire to deliver an unpublished manuscript to its rightful owner. With its many references to real and imaginary books, its discussions of parallel universes, and its focus on disasters such as the Great Depression and Hurricane Katrina, the novel muses on the nature of existence and the saving graces of literature and friendship.*

Memorial Drive: A Daughter's Memoir. 401
    In Memorial Drive, *Natasha Trethewey recounts being raised in Mississippi and Georgia following the civil rights movement as the child of a Black mother and a White father and her mother's subsequent abuse and murder at the hands of her second husband. Trethewey writes with lyrical clarity about the loss of her mother and the impact of a Southern childhood and domestic abuse on her growth personally and as a writer.*

Mexican Gothic. 406
    Silvia Moreno-Garcia's Mexican Gothic *follows a young socialite as she investigates her cousin's claims that her new husband is trying to kill her and that her new home is an evil, living being. The novel reframes classic gothic horror tropes in a Latin American setting.*

The Mirror & the Light. 411
    In The Mirror & the Light, *the third installment in the Wolf Hall trilogy, Hilary Mantel brings to life the final years of Thomas Cromwell, adviser to Henry VIII of England.*

Miss Benson's Beetle. 416
    After an incident at the school where middle-aged Margery Benson has taught for years, she decides to embrace a youthful adventure and hires Enid Pretty, a vivacious young woman, as an assistant. The women go on a trip across the world to find an elusive and possibly mythical beetle, developing an unexpected friendship along the way.

Moonflower Murders. 420
    Susan Ryeland, a former editor, investigates the disappearance of a young woman who claims to know the real perpetrator of a crime committed eight years earlier at her family's hotel, having discovered the truth in a novel written by successful mystery writer Alan Conway, one of the authors for whom Ryeland served as editor.

The Mountains Sing. 425
   The Mountains Sing, *Vietnamese poet Nguyễn Phan Quế Mai's debut novel, is a multigenerational saga that explores one family's struggle to survive French and Japanese occupation, a devastating famine, two wars, and brutal political repression. The experiences of the Trần family complicate accepted narratives about Vietnam's recent history and illustrate the importance of preserving the memories of those who lived it.*

My Dark Vanessa 429
   My Dark Vanessa *follows the story of a woman grappling with the long-term effects of sexual abuse. It is American author Kate Elizabeth Russell's debut novel.*

The New Wilderness 433
   Diane Cook's The New Wilderness *imagines a world decimated by climate change, where the only refuge from dangerous pollution is a vast natural preserve called the Wilderness State. Bea and her young daughter, Agnes, are members of a small, nomadic group living in the Wilderness as part of a study to see if humans can exist in nature without destroying it.*

The Night Watchman 438
   Thomas Wazhashk, a Turtle Mountain Chippewa man, fights to stop the termination bill, an attempt to cancel governmental treaties with American Indians. The Night Watchman *tells the story of his family's battle against the senator who proposed the bill.*

Nobody Will Tell You This but Me: A True (as Told to Me) Story 442
   In this unique memoir, author Bess Kalb gives a vivid account of the life of her late grandmother, Bobby Bell, as if narrated by Bobby herself. Both funny and deeply moving, the book probes matrilineal bonds across generations. It also follows the arc of the American Dream, showing how Bobby prospered compared to her Jewish immigrant mother and laid a foundation for Kalb herself.

Not So Pure and Simple. 447
   Not So Pure and Simple *is a comic coming-of-age young-adult novel about navigating faith, sex, and notions of masculinity in small-town America.*

Obit 451
   Victoria Chang's Obit *is a collection of poems that draw on the format of the newspaper obituary to explore feelings of grief, loss, and the idea of how memory functions in people's lives.*

The Office of Historical Corrections 456
    Danielle Evans's second book, The Office of Historical Corrections, *is a collection of six short stories and a novella in which accessible characters explore the past and its impact on the present, grief, and racism.*

One Mighty and Irresistible Tide: The Epic Struggle over
    American Immigration, 1924–1965 460
    Centered on the history of twentieth-century American federal immigration policy, this book studies the politics and personalities behind the legislation. Jia Lynn Yang explores the enduring influence of racist and nationalist biases that drove many politicians' decision-making across this period, as well as the unexpected complications set in play at each attempt at immigration reform.

The Only Good Indians 465
    A suspenseful and gory slasher, at times cerebral but also comedic, The Only Good Indians *uses the storytelling tools of the horror genre to meditate on the meaning of contemporary American Indian life. Ten years after four friends slaughtered a herd of elk on the Blackfeet Indian Reservation, a spirit comes for revenge.*

Owls of the Eastern Ice: A Quest to Find and Save the World's Largest Owl . . . 470
    In Owls of the Eastern Ice: A Quest to Find and Save the World's Largest Owl, *wildlife biologist Jonathan C. Slaght recounts his years of field research in the forests of the Russian province of Primorye, key habitats for the endangered Blakiston's fish owl.*

Paying the Land 475
    Graphic journalist Joe Sacco, known for dynamic reporting from such combat zones as Palestine and Bosnia, takes on a different kind of war in Paying the Land: *the battle for survival of the once-nomadic indigenous peoples of Canada's Northwest Territories in a rapidly changing modern world.*

Pelosi 480
    Political journalist Molly Ball presents a biography of groundbreaking American politician Nancy Pelosi, who became Speaker of the US House of Representatives in 2007 and again in 2019. The book spans from Pelosi's early life and entry into politics to her time as one of the highest-profile—and most polarizing—leaders in the country.

Piranesi 485
    In Piranesi, *Susanna Clarke's long-awaited second novel, the titular narrator inhabits a strange world of endless halls, seemingly empty of almost all other people. As he studies his surroundings he realizes that he has forgotten about his own past, and he begins to unravel the mystery of the place and himself.*

Postcolonial Love Poem 489
Natalie Diaz's collection Postcolonial Love Poem *joins prose poetry with verse, blurring the lines between genre and form. The collection explores violence, desire, and the connections between body and land.*

The Price of Peace: Money, Democracy, and the Life of John Maynard Keynes   494
In The Price of Peace, *journalist Zachary D. Carter presents a highly readable introduction to the life and ideas of the influential economist John Maynard Keynes. Carter does not limit himself to succinctly summarizing Keynes's contributions as a statesman, philosopher, and economic theorist; he also traces the impact of Keynesian economics from Keynes's death shortly after the conclusion of World War II to contemporary times.*

A Promised Land 499
Barack Obama's A Promised Land *is the first of a two-part account of and reflection on the Obama administration, covering his rise to political power and most of his first term in the office of the US presidency.*

Punching the Air 504
National Book Award finalist Ibi Zoboi and Yusef Salaam of the Exonerated Five team up to write a novel-in-verse for young adults. Punching the Air *tells the story of Amal and his experience of being locked up as a Black Muslim teenager, exploring institutional racism and offering a deeply personal look at the dehumanization of incarceration.*

Race against Time: A Reporter Reopens the Unsolved Murder Cases
of the Civil Rights Era. 508
Race against Time *is journalist Jerry Mitchell's account of investigating four unsolved, racially motivated murder cases in a New South grappling with the sins of the past. It is his first memoir.*

Reaganland: America's Right Turn 1976–1980. 513
In Reaganland, *the journalist and popular historian Rick Perlstein concludes his series of books about the development of modern American conservatism. Here he provides a highly detailed narrative of the years 1976 to 1980, which saw an increasingly effective grassroots movement among conservatives challenging a liberal establishment divided and demoralized by domestic problems and foreign embarrassments. The culmination of this conservative resurgence was Ronald Reagan's landslide victory in the presidential election of 1980.*

Real Life. 518
In Real Life, *graduate student Wallace grapples with interpersonal relationships, the trauma of his past, and racism over the course of a late-summer weekend.*

Recollections of My Nonexistence 523
Recollections of My Nonexistence focuses on two intertwined themes: a personal retelling of Rebecca Solnit's professional arc and the internalized reality of gender-based violence and discrimination against women. Solnit weaves a powerful narrative of her own growth as a public intellectual and leading feminist thinker, while laying bare the personal toll of the constant weight of aggression and discrimination.

Ring Shout 528
This novella, set in an alternate 1920s Georgia, imagines a world in which the White supremacist terrorist group the Ku Klux Klan is backed by otherworldly monsters. A team of monster hunters assembles to fight them, leading to a rollicking tale of resistance that combines fantasy, adventure, horror, African and African American folklore, and incisive social commentary.

The Rise and Fall of Charles Lindbergh 532
In this biography for young adults, Candace Fleming focuses on Charles Lindbergh, a flight hero who was also seen as a Nazi sympathizer. She highlights the enigmatic qualities of a person admired and respected by many but who was also deeply flawed.

The Searcher 537
Cal Hooper, a retired Chicago police officer, moves to a small town in Ireland, looking for peace and quiet. After befriending a local child, Hooper becomes involved in a missing persons case that will change his view of his new community and his own life.

The Second Chance Club: Hardship and Hope after Prison 541
This memoir of four years working as a probation and parole officer in New Orleans, Louisiana, takes a critical view of one of the most overlooked parts of the US criminal justice system. Focusing on seven representative cases, it details the challenges and frustrations endured by both parole officers and offenders.

The Secret Lives of Church Ladies 546
Deesha Philyaw's debut collection of short stories, The Secret Lives of Church Ladies, *explores the unseen lives of Southern, Black, church-going women whose stories discuss subjects such as the role of religion, marriage, infidelity, and individuality.*

Shuggie Bain 550
In Douglas Stuart's debut novel, a young boy deals with his mother's alcoholism in the bleak public housing projects of 1980s Glasgow.

Sigh, Gone: A Misfit's Memoir of Great Books, Punk Rock,
and the Fight to Fit In 554
    Sigh, Gone: A Misfit's Memoir of Great Books, Punk Rock, and the Fight to Fit In, *published in 2020, is a coming-of-age memoir of a young Vietnamese American who finds his way in small-town Pennsylvania with the help of great literature and punk rock music.*

The Silent Wife 559
    In The Silent Wife, *Georgia Bureau of Investigations agent Will Trent, medical examiner Sara Linton, and their colleagues investigate a series of disturbing murders that may be the work of a serial killer that they missed eight years earlier.*

Sisters 564
    Daisy Johnson's sophomore novel, Sisters, *is a gothic thriller set in a crumbling seaside cottage called Settle House. July, September, and their mother, Sheela, have fled their home in Oxford after a mysterious and devastating event. As Sheela, deep in the throes of a depressive episode, nurses her grief and rage, the two teenage sisters with an eerie bond explore the old house and test the boundaries of adulthood.*

The Smallest Lights in the Universe 568
    The Smallest Lights in the Universe *is a memoir by astrophysicist Sara Seager that reflects on her search for habitable exoplanets as well as her journey through grief.*

Some Assembly Required: Decoding Four Billion Years of Life,
from Ancient Fossils to DNA 572
    In Some Assembly Required: Decoding Four Billion Years of Life, from Ancient Fossils to DNA, *paleontologist and evolutionary biologist Neil Shubin describes the development of scientific understanding of evolution, genetics, DNA, and the genomes of various forms of life, including human life.*

The Southern Book Club's Guide to Slaying Vampires. 577
    The Southern Book Club's Guide to Slaying Vampires *follows Patricia Campbell, who, in the midst of a changing life, where she feels unneeded by her husband and growing children, is accused of building a fiction around a new neighbor. Nonetheless, with the help of her closest friends, she sets out to defend family and community and takes on the dangers of an unknown entity that attempts to destroy everything she has built.*

The Splendid and the Vile: A Saga of Churchill, Family, and Defiance
during the Blitz 582
The Splendid and the Vile presents a gripping profile of British prime minister Winston Churchill and members of his intimate circle during the intense World War II bombing known as the Blitz.

Squeeze Me 587
In his fifteenth novel about life in Florida, Carl Hiaasen uses the formula of the classic crime story as the framework for a devastating satire on contemporary society.

Stamped: Racism, Antiracism, and You 591
Activists and authors Ibram X. Kendi and Jason Reynolds's Stamped *is an exploration of racism in US history and an examination of how race is constructed and how American society might move toward an antiracist future.*

Summer 596
Summer is the final installment of Scottish author Ali Smith's seasonal quartet of novels exploring the present moment through a kaleidoscopic lens. Smith revisits characters from the previous volumes, interweaving stories across time and space to craft a work that provides both searing sociopolitical commentary and literary reflection on issues such as memory and family.

The Sun Down Motel 601
The Sun Down Motel follows a young woman as she investigates the mystery surrounding the disappearance of her aunt thirty-five years earlier.

Supreme Inequality: The Supreme Court's Fifty-Year Battle for
a More Unjust America 605
Lawyer and journalist Adam Cohen's book Supreme Inequality: The Supreme Court's Fifty-Year Battle for a More Unjust America *traces a half-century of Supreme Court cases that have contributed to the current era of extreme economic disparity. Divided into chapters exploring democracy, poverty, criminal justice, and labor, among others, Cohen makes a powerful argument for adopting a new "blueprint" to repair the damage that the nation has incurred at the hands of the highest court over the past fifty years.*

Swimming in the Dark 610
Tomasz Jedrowski's debut novel, Swimming in the Dark, *is set in Communist Poland in the early 1980s. Addressing his former lover, a young man named Ludwik recounts his coming-of-age in a country where citizens are constricted by authoritarianism and conservative mores; where sex between men is illegal and one must participate in the economy of graft to survive.*

They Went Left 615
    They Went Left *shares the postwar experiences of Zofia Lederman, a Jewish girl from Poland. After recovering from the concentration camps and being released from the hospital, Zofia returns to the apartment where she grew up, searching for her younger brother. When he is not there, she journeys across Europe in search of him.*

Those Who Forget: My Family's Story in Nazi Europe—A Memoir,
    a History, a Warning 620
    Géraldine Schwarz's book combines personal, national, and social history in a complex exploration of her family's—and her nations'—involvement in the rise and remembrance of fascism and nationalism in Europe.

The Thursday Murder Club 625
    Four retirees work together to solve cold cases in The Thursday Murder Club, *but when a local contractor is killed, they become involved in two present-day cases that are closely connected to the retirement village where they live.*

Tigers, Not Daughters 630
    In Samantha Mabry's third young adult novel, three sisters try to cope with the death of their fourth sister, whose ghostly presence haunts their home, as well as with the overbearing men in their lives.

Tokyo Ueno Station 635
    In the novel Tokyo Ueno Station, *a ghostly narrator who haunts a public park tells his life story and sheds light on the economic divide in modern-day Japan.*

Transcendent Kingdom 639
    Transcendent Kingdom *is the story of a Ghanaian American family and their struggles with identity, immigration, addiction, and mental health in Huntsville, Alabama, all told by youngest daughter and narrator, Gifty.*

Twilight of the Gods: War in the Western Pacific, 1944–1945 643
    In the third volume of Toll's masterful narrative history of the Pacific War, he covers the conflict between the Allies and the Empire of Japan in the final years of World War II.

The Undocumented Americans 648
    Karla Cornejo Villavicencio's The Undocumented Americans *is an intimate portrait of the lives of the undocumented in America, especially those who, like Cornejo Villavicencio herself, were brought to the United States as children.*

Untamed. 653
    Untamed *is an intimate memoir of the lessons learned at the end of Glennon Doyle's marriage and the beginning of a new relationship and a new sense of self.*

Unworthy Republic: The Dispossession of Native Americans and
    the Road to Indian Territory. 657
    Claudio Saunt's exhaustively researched Unworthy Republic *details a national shame. An early nineteenth-century campaign, spearheaded by US president Andrew Jackson, resulted in the deportation of thousands of indigenous peoples from ancestral lands in the southeastern United States to wastelands west of the Mississippi River, an action that left permanent stains on American history.*

The Vanished Birds 662
    In The Vanished Birds, *a solitary spaceship pilot adopts a nonverbal young boy with a strange power; the two become close, but their bond is challenged as they are drawn into corporate intrigue with implications for the fate of humanity as a whole.*

The Vanishing Half 666
    The Vanishing Half *relates the story of Black twins born in the fictional town of Mallard, Louisiana, in the mid-twentieth century. After leaving Mallard at sixteen, one twin chooses to live her life passing as a White woman, while the other returns to their hometown, resulting in an exploration of identity and a growing awareness of how their decisions affect the next generation.*

Vesper Flights 671
    Vesper Flights *is a collection of essays on a variety of topics related to the natural world. It is British writer and naturalist Helen Macdonald's second book.*

We Are Not Free 675
    Traci Chee's young adult historical novel We Are Not Free *follows the experiences of Japanese Americans living on the West Coast during World War II. Fourteen young men and women from San Francisco describe what they lost when they were held in internment camps following the Japanese attack on Pearl Harbor.*

We Are Not from Here 680
    A harrowing tale based on contemporary events, We Are Not from Here *tells of three Guatemalan teens who flee the violence of their hometown and head north. Relying on outdated information and rumors, they travel via a network of trains called "La Bestia," hoping for Columbia Books page tracking sheet possible sanctuary in the United States.*

We Have Been Harmonized: Life in China's Surveillance State 685
    Kai Strittmatter's detailed report about life in an increasingly powerful Communist country, with massive access to data about almost all its citizens, is a long-overdue wake-up call about the dangers of surveillance everywhere.

Weather 690
    Weather, *a novel written in fragments, is an exploration of how people love and protect each other during unstable times. Protagonist Lizzie Benson is a university librarian and also works as an assistant for a climate change expert, answering increasingly troubling emails from podcast listeners. While raising her son and supporting her troubled brother, Lizzie attempts to hold onto hope as she deals with the ever-approaching catastrophe of climate collapse and the 2016 US presidential election.*

When Truth Is All You Have: A Memoir of Faith, Justice, and Freedom
    for the Wrongly Accused 695
    When Truth Is All You Have *is a memoir about Jim McCloskey and his efforts with Centurion Ministries, an organization he founded that works to exonerate innocent men and women who have been imprisoned for crimes they did not commit.*

Wilmington's Lie: The Murderous Coup of 1898 and the Rise of
    White Supremacy 699
    This historical investigation by David Zucchino looks at the Wilmington coup, a White supremacist assault on the then majority-Black city of Wilmington, North Carolina, in 1898.

Yellow Bird: Oil, Murder, and a Woman's Search for Justice
    in Indian Country 704
    Investigative journalist Sierra Crane Murdoch's Yellow Bird: Oil, Murder, and a Woman's Search for Justice in Indian Country *is an investigative story about a true crime that took place on an American Indian reservation and the efforts of Lissa Yellow Bird to investigate the crime.*

Kent State

Author: Deborah Wiles (b. 1953)
Publisher: Scholastic Press (New York). 132 pp.
Type of work: Verse novel
Time: May 1–4, 1970
Locale: Kent, Ohio

Kent State is a young-adult novel, written in free verse, that recalls the events leading up to the killing of four students by the Ohio National Guard at an antiwar protest at Kent State University in 1970.

As award-winning author Deborah Wiles explains in the prelude to her powerful novel-in-verse, *Kent State*, the United States first sent troops to Vietnam in 1964. By 1968, more than 500,000 Americans, most of them young men, were stationed there, and over 40,000 had died. Many Americans opposed the war. Vietnam, an ancient country with more recent ties to imperial France, was fighting for its political future—one in which Americans played no discernable part. Students and young people were at the forefront of the antiwar movement. In the spring of 1970, President Richard Nixon invaded neutral Cambodia, Vietnam's neighbor. News of the escalation roiled college campuses across the nation, including Kent State University, a university in rural northeastern Ohio.

Wiles's novel describes the days leading up to May 4, 1970, the day Ohio National Guard, called in to quell growing protests, shot and killed four students—Sandy Scheuer, Bill Schroeder, Jeff Miller, and Allison Krause—and wounded nine others. Wiles notes that the shooting at Kent State was not the first time the National Guard had clashed with civilian students, nor the only such incident in which people were killed. (Ten days after Kent State, police officers at Jackson State College, a predominantly Black university in Mississippi, shot and killed students Phillip Lafayette Gibbs and James Earl Green.) But the violence at Kent State captured national attention, becoming an important and disturbing emblem of an era marked by state violence. Musicians Crosby, Stills, Nash & Young immortalized Scheuer, Schroeder, Miller, and Krause, in their 1970 song "Ohio," which begins: "Tin soldiers and Nixon's coming / We're finally on our own / This summer I hear the drumming / Four dead in Ohio."

Wiles was a sixteen-year-old high school student in 1970, and in her author's note, she writes that the horror of the Kent State shooting became part of "the fabric of my coming of age." Wiles, who was raised in Mississippi, is best known for the juvenile fiction novel *Each Little Bird That Sings* (2005), which was a finalist for the National

Book Award for Young People's Literature, and the Sixties Trilogy, which includes the novels *Countdown* (2010), *Revolution* (2014), and *Anthem* (2019). The trilogy explores defining moments of the era, such as the Cuban Missile Crisis and the civil rights movement. *Revolution*, which follows the story of two teenagers living in Mississippi during the Freedom Summer campaign in 1964, was also a finalist for the National Book Award. The Sixties Trilogy combines primary source material with a fictional narrative.

While *Kent State* can also be considered historical fiction like Wiles's earlier works, its form is harder to define. The book is written in free verse. Competing, disembodied voices—distinguished by typeface—attempt to describe the events leading up to the killings. Sections are organized in musical terms: prelude, lament, and elegy. The terms are fitting; *Kent State* reads like music, with moments of both harmony and discord. One voice offers a steady refrain: "They did not have to die." The dialogue incorporates material from oral histories, interviews, and newspaper articles. The voices frequently disagree, arguing about everything from the chronology of events— were there helicopters on Saturday night or only on Sunday?—to the value of the protests themselves. No character has a name, but each can be vaguely identified as students, townspeople, and National Guard members. This multiplicity of view energizes Wiles's tale, bringing the action alive in a way that is difficult to convey through an entirely fictional story. In her concluding author's note, which is itself a highlight of the book, Wiles explains that she chose the format to reflect the fact that history does not belong to any one perspective. There are "as many versions of the truth as there are people who lived it," she writes. As Jennifer Hubert Swan wrote in her review for *Horn Book* magazine, the book is "full of fascinating research forays and information about 1960s protest songs" and "should not be skipped."

As important to the book as its players is its audience. Wiles specifically addresses a new generation of young people, most of them unfamiliar with Kent State and the larger protest movement of which it was a part. "You are new here," the book begins, "and we don't want to scare you away, but we want you to know the truth." The concept of the truth offers plenty of fodder for the characters, who begin their story on May 1, 1970. On that day, a group of students, angry about Nixon's invasion of Cambodia, organized a protest in which they ceremonially buried a copy of the United States Constitution. One student, or so it was rumored, burned a copy of his draft card—a serious offense. Another, a veteran, burned his discharge papers. The next day, a campus building housing the Army Reserve Officer Training Corps (ROTC)—representing "Nixon and his evil, Vietnam and all the senseless killing, killing, killing"— was torched. As these events are described, new voices appear—naysaying adults and townspeople—to lay blame for the demonstration, citing "outside agitators" and the influence of radical groups like the Weather Underground and Students for a Democratic Society (SDS). The Weather Underground and SDS were militant leftist student groups, associated in the popular imagination with violence. *Kent State* is a short book, and it is impressive how much complicated and complex history Wiles is able to bring into it. Mention of the Weather Underground and SDS is an early indication of the host of adversarial relationships at play: between young people and their parents; rural sensibilities and urban; Ivy League schools and public; and Black and White students.

Wiles incorporates the collective voice of a campus group called Black United Students (BUS). BUS held a separate rally on May 1, 1970. A group of BUS students from the Ohio State University was there, and they told how the Ohio National Guard had been called to stop their protest in Columbus days before. Guard members shot seven people, but the story did not appear in the press. After the rally, BUS instructed Black students at Kent to stay away from the protests that weekend, knowing it was likely that the guard would be called and that they would be carrying live ammunition. The detail demonstrates the racial divisions among the larger campus antiwar movement, which was most visibly led by White men, but also the ways in which Black activists, all too familiar with state violence, anticipated the strength of their adversaries in a way that young White activists did not. "We didn't believe they had real bullets," one voice says, later. Another replies: "If you were white, you had the privilege of believing that." Later in the book, Wiles invokes Black activists in Oakland and Huey Newton, a founder of the Black Panther Party. The voices of Black activists chide White students for the naivete, their failure to see the systems of injustice that undergird their grievances.

The inclusion of the voice of Black students is one of the most successful parts of the novel, as critics have widely acknowledged. A review in *Kirkus* noted that the words of the Black students were "especially compelling," and the anonymous *Publishers Weekly* reviewer wrote: "The black students' voice proves particularly poignant in its depiction of long-standing institutionalized racism, and Wiles effectively portrays the combustible and enduring controversies that led to this tragedy."

Wiles also incorporates the collective voice of the National Guard members, some of whom were also students at Kent, and the friends of the four people who were killed. The youth of the victims is striking. Sandy Scheuer kept scrapbooks with photographs, movie tickets stubs, and cute quotations like "2 nice 2 be 4 gotten." Allison Krause was from Maryland but chose to attend Kent because of her fond childhood memories visiting family and eating at the Robin Hood restaurant in town. Bill Schroeder, a drummer in a band, began protesting the war when he was sixteen, while Jeff Miller, who was in the US Army Reserve, was obsessed with the Rolling Stones. Wiles does not soften the gruesome violence of their deaths. Readers will feel the shock and confusion of the melee, in which sixty-seven shots were fired in thirteen seconds. The guard was ordered to reload their weapons, and they would have continued to shoot had a professor not begged protestors to disperse to save their lives.

Wiles published *Kent State* in 2020, the fiftieth anniversary of the Kent State killings. In her author's note, she writes movingly of attending a vigil at Kent on a past anniversary, mourning "lives forever altered" and a "country forever scarred." Wiles, like most Americans, could not have foreseen the historic uprisings that began after the murder of George Floyd in May 2020. Given those events, elements of her story will be more familiar to contemporary young people than Wiles might have guessed. They may recognize the exhilaration of mass protest, but also the frustration of harnessing its unwieldy power; the inherent messiness of political action, but also its necessity.

(The Kent State shootings marked a major turning point in American support for the war.) The voices of the opposition might also sound chillingly familiar, from accusations of "outside agitators," to another president exercising military might under the banner of "law and order." There is also the shocking venom of everyday people. In the book, one voice says of the guard: "They should have killed more of them [students]!" In her author's note, Wiles reveals that the line comes from a letter to a local Kent newspaper. Similarly, when one reads a voice use the acronym SDS as an epithet, one just as easily imagines the same voice decrying "BLM" (Black Lives Matter). Wiles directly addresses the reader as "you," urging them to action. (Less successfully, in the book's climax, she implores the reader to "insert your name here.") "We hope you're on fire for change," Wiles writes. As a reviewer for *Publishers Weekly* aptly described, her words are "both timely and timeless."

Author Biography
Deborah Wiles, a young-adult novelist and picture book author, is best known for *Each Little Bird That Sings* (2005), part of the Aurora County series; the award-winning picture book *Freedom Summer* (2001); and the Sixties Trilogy (2010–19). Wiles has twice been a finalist for the National Book Award for Young People's Literature.

Molly Hagan

Review Sources
Cary, Alice. Review of *Kent State*, by Deborah Wiles. *BookPage*, 5 May 2020, bookpage.com/reviews/25112-deborah-wiles-kent-state-ya#.X48JLGhKiUk. Accessed 20 Oct. 2020.
Hubert Swan, Jennifer. Review of *Kent State*, by Deborah Wiles. *Horn Book*, 4 May 2020, www.hbook.com/?detailStory=review-of-kent-state. Accessed 11 Oct. 2020.
Review of *Kent State*, by Deborah Wiles. *Kirkus*, 19 Jan. 2020, www.kirkusreviews.com/book-reviews/deborah-wiles/kent-state-wiles. Accessed 11 Oct. 2020.
Review of *Kent State*, by Deborah Wiles. *Publishers Weekly*, 12 Mar. 2020, www.publishersweekly.com/978-1-338-35628-1. Accessed 11 Oct. 2020.
Westmoore, Jean. "Books in Brief: *We Dream of Space* by Erin Entrada Kelly; *Kent State* by Deborah Wiles." Review of *Kent State*, by Deborah Wiles. *The Buffalo News*, 15 May 2020, buffalonews.com/entertainment/books/books-in-brief-we-dream-of-space-by-erin-entrada-kelly-kent-state-by-deborah/article_621bfc5c-263d-51f7-8b5c-cda8ec1d09d1.html. Accessed 11 Oct. 2020.

Kim Jiyoung, Born 1982

Author: Cho Nam-joo (b. 1978)
First published: *Palsip yi nyeon saeng Kim Jiyeong*, 2016, in South Korea
Translated from the Korean by Jamie Chang
Publisher: Liveright (New York). 176 pp.
Type of work: Novel
Time: 1982–2016
Locale: South Korea

In the novel Kim Jiyoung, Born 1982, *a young woman begins to experience strange episodes after enduring a lifetime of sexism.*

Principal characters
KIM JIYOUNG, the protagonist, a young woman who has begun to experience strange episodes in which she takes on the personalities of other individuals
JUNG DAEHYUN, her husband, an information technology professional
JUNG JIWON, her young daughter
OH MISOOK, her mother, a former aspiring teacher
JIYOUNG'S FATHER, a civil servant who later goes into the restaurant business
KIM EUNYOUNG, her older sister
JIYOUNG'S BROTHER, the baby of the family and the favored child
KOH BOONSOON, her paternal grandmother, a resident of Jiyoung's parents' household
KIM EUNSIL, the team leader at Jiyoung's workplace
THE PSYCHIATRIST, a male specialist who evaluates Jiyoung

In many countries around the world, the second decade of the twenty-first century was marked by an increased cultural focus on issues related to gender inequity, including sexual harassment and assault, educational and economic disparities, and the systemic misogyny underlying numerous areas of society. A reckoning in that regard began in South Korea late in the decade, and the 2016 publication of the novel *Palsip yi nyeon saeng Kim Jiyeong* both drew on and further fueled this broad social reflection. The third novel by author Cho Nam-joo, the work shed light on cultural pressures and practices detrimental to women as well as the microaggressions and greater injustices experienced by women throughout the country but rarely discussed publicly. Having proven relevant worldwide, the novel was widely translated and published outside of South Korea in the years following its debut. In 2020, the novel became the first work by Cho to be published in the United States, appearing under the title *Kim Jiyoung,*

Born 1982. The English translation was the work of Jamie Chang, a South Korea–based literary translator and teacher.

Written as a case study of sorts, *Kim Jiyoung, Born 1982* begins in the year 2015. The novel recounts the beginning of a strange ailment that has afflicted the title character, a thirty-three-year-old woman who the previous year had become the mother of a baby girl named Jiwon. Jiyoung has quit her job at a marketing agency in order to care for the child, while her husband, Jung Daehyun, has maintained his career in the information technology industry. Jiyoung's life is seemingly average and unremarkable. However, it does not take long for a more unusual side to emerge. In September 2015, Jiyoung began to experience strange episodes in which she would take on the personality and mannerisms of people other than herself. These were not mere imitations: rather, she would fully embody the individuals in question and, still more concerning, seemed to have no awareness of the fact that she was doing so.

Cho Nam-joo

Initially, the individuals being embodied included Jiyoung's mother, Oh Misook, as well as a deceased woman, Cha Seungyeon, with whom Jiyoung and Daehyun had both been friends in college. In the latter case, Jiyoung appeared to have knowledge of an event for which only Daehyun and Seungyeon were present. In addition, the persona of Seungyeon told Daehyun that Jiyoung was "having a hard time" with the "emotionally draining" work of raising a child and that he needed to express his appreciation for his wife more often. Though disturbed by those incidents, Daehyun did not take action until after the autumn Chuseok holidays, during which the couple visited Daehyun's parents in Busan. During the visit, Jiyoung once again took on the personality of her mother and in doing so angered Daehyun's father, who felt her behavior to be disrespectful. Much like during the Cha Seungyeon incident, Jiyoung-as-Misook spoke out about the difficulties Jiyoung had been experiencing and chastised Daehyun's father for monopolizing the holidays, as Jiyoung had been unable to visit her family due to her visits with her husband's family. Following that incident, Daehyun approached a psychiatrist and arranged a first appointment for Jiyoung, who remained unaware of her strange episodes but agreed to see the psychiatrist to discuss a possible case of postpartum depression.

The remainder of the novel tells the chronological story of Jiyoung's life, as told to and subsequently reported by the psychiatrist. In addition to detailing notable incidents in her life, the narrative delves into her family background, which offers a degree of historical perspective. For example, the hardships Jiyoung's grandparents endured to support their families come into focus. A nuanced picture also emerges of Jiyoung's mother, Oh Misook, who spent her teen years and early adulthood working arduous, low-paying jobs in order to fund her brothers' educations. Facing substantial pressure to have a son after giving birth to Jiyoung and her older sister, Eunyoung, Misook had an abortion after learning that her third pregnancy would result in another daughter. She subsequently gave birth to a son, who became the favored child of the family.

As the novel reveals, Jiyoung was acutely aware of that gender-based favoritism as a child. While she and her sister had to share bedrooms, treats, and everything else, her brother was not required to share. Upon enrolling in school, she found that boys experienced similar favoritism there, including being allowed to eat lunch first and to wear less restrictive uniforms. When a teacher stepped in to stop a boy from repeatedly bullying Jiyoung, the school environment initially seemed to be becoming less hostile. However, the teacher went on to tell Jiyoung that the boy had been bullying her because he liked her, a statement that Jiyoung immediately recognized as incorrect. As she grew older, Jiyoung faced blatant sexual harassment and in one incident was harassed by a fellow cram school student, who attempted to follow her home. While she escaped harm thanks to the assistance of a sympathetic older woman, her father later implied that the incident was in part Jiyoung's fault for attending a cram school so far from home.

The narrative relates how Jiyoung continued to encounter microaggressions and systemic misogyny throughout her years in college and early adulthood. After multiple potential employers passed her over in favor of male applicants, she secured a job at a marketing agency where she worked under a female team leader who sought to attain equitable treatment for her employees. Upper management, however, deliberately excluded female employees from long-term projects and required them to work for the most demanding clients, in keeping with the prevailing belief that women would soon leave the company to start families and thus did not need to worry about professional burnout. When Jiyoung herself became pregnant, she and Daehyun indeed decided that she would leave her job to care for the child. Although Daehyun attempted to be helpful and understanding of the substantial changes Jiyoung would be going through and the responsibilities of raising a child, he characterized himself as "helping out" with home and childcare responsibilities rather than as being an active participant in caring for his daughter and home, an attitude that angered Jiyoung.

After leaving her job, Jiyoung struggled not only with the loss of a career she enjoyed and the intense responsibility of being her daughter's primary caretaker, but also with disparaging views of stay-at-home mothers, who were at times painted as freeloaders who lived lavishly while spending their husbands' money. The buildup of such pressures culminated in the beginning of Jiyoung's episodes, the precipitating event of the novel. The narrative concludes in 2016, as the psychiatrist Jiyoung has been seeing reflects on her case and his own changing opinions regarding her diagnosis. While he claims to have gained a greater understanding of women's experiences through both his observations of his own wife, a doctor turned stay-at-home mother, and his work with Jiyoung, it is clear that he still harbors serious biases against working mothers, which signals that the problems explored throughout the novel are far from resolved.

In keeping with its in-universe status as a psychiatrist's report, *Kim Jiyoung, Born 1982* features a notably straightforward and clinical writing style that presents the events as they occurred while expressing relatively little emotion. Claims made throughout the work are supported by footnotes, which reference real-life statistics and studies. At the end of the chapter dealing with Jiyoung's life between 1982 and 1994, for instance, the novel cites a statistical report on sex ratio at birth and a publication dealing with the part-time jobs available to middle-aged, married Korean women, among other sources. Though the footnotes can be distracting, as they are unusual in the context of a novel, they effectively emphasize the scholarly nature of the psychiatrist's report while also providing interesting insight into the broader social issues at play.

The detached, academic tone of the novel provides an intriguing contrast with the decidedly unfair, objectifying, and at times degrading and frightening treatment that Jiyoung and other girls and women face over the course of the narrative. This allows the events depicted to stand on their own, existing simply as examples of incidents that could take place in the life of any woman. Indeed, though the events that occur and the pressures that build up over the course of her life prove profoundly damaging to Jiyoung, they are by no means out of the ordinary or fringe incidents. Rather, the novel presents a highly realistic portrait of an average woman's first thirty-three years of life—and the mistreatment Jiyoung experiences is all the more disturbing for its sheer mundanity. The shift in focus to the psychiatrist for the final portion of the novel further emphasizes the inescapable presence of gender bias, demonstrating how even purportedly enlightened individuals can uphold and reinforce the patriarchal systems they claim to recognize as detrimental. For readers already well aware of the manifestations of systemic misogyny, portions of *Kim Jiyoung, Born 1982* may come off as a bit obvious. However, the novel serves as a valuable and necessary addition to the body of literature dealing with that topic and offers particular insight into the ways in which patriarchal systems intersect with historical, cultural, and economic facets of life in South Korea and beyond.

A best seller in South Korea following its initial release there, *Kim Jiyoung, Born 1982* went on to be adapted into a successful film released in 2019. The novel's great popularity and social resonance led to translations in numerous languages, and critical reception was positive in many other countries as well. The US publication was included in the longlist for the National Book Award in the category of translated literature. Reviewers of the English translation generally praised the novel's depiction of life in an unjust society. Writing for the *New York Times*, Euny Hong recognized that the work is, at its heart, "about the banality of the evil that is systemic misogyny," a deep-rooted problem in South Korean society but an issue in many cultures around the world. In a review for the *Guardian*, Sarah Shin called attention to the novel's "claustrophobic" style, which she suggested not only befits the work's in-universe existence as a psychiatric case study but also succeeds in "creating an airless, unbearably dull world in which Jiyoung's madness makes complete sense." The anonymous reviewer for *Publishers Weekly* specifically highlighted the novel's conclusion, writing that the ending "demonstrates Cho's mastery of irony."

Though the novel was well-received overall, some reviewers did find faults. Most notably, several critics noted that for all its social commentary, the work offers little new insight into the problem of systemic misogyny. The anonymous reviewer for *Kirkus* wrote that *Kim Jiyoung, Born 1982* is "basically feminism 101 but in novel form" and also noted that the book does not acknowledge any alternative to a binary understanding of gender. However, they also commented approvingly on the novel's depiction of the intersection between patriarchy and capitalism and described the work as a whole as "compelling." Ultimately, Cho chooses an incisive focus on one central theme rather than complexity, an approach that is effective if not groundbreaking. Readers may find this story familiar, but that does not make it any less important.

Author Biography
Kim Jiyoung, Born 1982 is Cho Nam-joo's first novel to be translated into English. She previously worked as a scriptwriter for television.

Translator Jamie Chang is a Seoul-based literary translator and university teacher.

Joy Crelin

Review Sources
Hong, Euny. "In This Korean Best Seller, a Young Mother Is Driven to Psychosis." Review of *Kim Jiyoung, Born 1982*, by Cho Nam-joo. *The New York Times*, 14 Apr. 2020, www.nytimes.com/2020/04/14/books/review/kim-jiyoung-born-1982-cho-nam-joo.html. Accessed 20 Nov. 2020.

Review of *Kim Jiyoung, Born 1982*, by Cho Nam-joo. *Kirkus*, 14 Apr. 2020, www.kirkusreviews.com/book-reviews/cho-nam-joo/kim-jiyoung-born-1982/. Accessed 20 Nov. 2020.

Review of *Kim Jiyoung, Born 1982*, by Cho Nam-joo. *Publishers Weekly*, 16 Dec. 2019, www.publishersweekly.com/978-1-63149-670-7. Accessed 20 Nov. 2020.

Mond, Ian. Review of *Kim Jiyoung, Born 1982*, by Cho Nam-Joo. *Locus*, 22 July 2020, locusmag.com/2020/07/ian-mond-reviews-kim-jiyoung-born-1982-by-cho-nam-joo/. Accessed 20 Nov. 2020.

Ratcliffe, Sophie. "*Kim Jiyoung, Born 1982* by Cho Nam-joo Review: Is This South Korea's #MeToo Moment?" *The Telegraph*, 2 Mar. 2020, www.telegraph.co.uk/books/what-to-read/kim-yiyoung-born-1982-cho-nam-joo-review-south-koreas-metoo/. Accessed 20 Nov. 2020.

Shin, Sarah. "*Kim Jiyoung, Born 1982* Review—South Korean #MeToo Bestseller." *The Guardian*, 19 Feb. 2020, www.theguardian.com/books/2020/feb/19/kim-jiyoung-born-1982-cho-nam-joo-bestseller-review. Accessed 20 Nov. 2020.

A Knock at Midnight
A Story of Hope, Justice, and Freedom

Author: Brittany K. Barnett (b. 1984)
Publisher: Crown (New York). 336 pp.
Type of work: Memoir, sociology, law
Time: 1984–the present day
Locale: Largely Texas

A Knock at Midnight is, in large part, the personal and professional coming-of-age story of Brittany K. Barnett, an attorney who became a prominent national advocate for executive clemency of Black men and women incarcerated under federal drug offenses. Through a powerful account of her own life intertwined with the lives of individuals imprisoned under unjust sentencing laws, Barnett presents an argument for sweeping criminal justice reform in the United States.

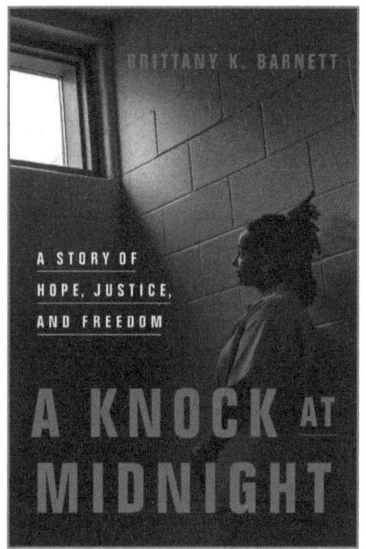

Principal personages

BRITTANY "BRITT" K. BARNETT, the author, an attorney
EVELYN FULBRIGHT, her mother, an addict imprisoned for drug offenses
DONEL CLARK, a man who was imprisoned and sentenced to serve thirty-five years after a federal drug and conspiracy conviction
LORETTA DE-ANN COFFMAN, a woman who was imprisoned for eight years on drug charges, with a sentence of life without parole, before receiving clemency in 2001 from President Bill Clinton
COREY "BUCK" JACOBS, a man convicted of conspiracy to distribute crack cocaine and imprisoned on sixteen life sentences
ALICE JOHNSON, a woman imprisoned on a life sentence for a drug offense
SHARANDA JONES, a woman imprisoned on a life sentence for conspiracy to distribute crack cocaine
MIKE WILSON, a man who was sentenced to life in prison without parole for drug charges
WAYLAND WILSON, the older brother of Mike Wilson, imprisoned for federal drug and conspiracy conviction
CHRIS YOUNG, a man who was incarcerated for drug charges, serving life without parole

In *A Knock at Midnight: A Story of Hope, Justice, and Freedom* (2020), Brittany K. Barnett recounts the personal and professional journey that brought her to the exceptional position of successfully representing seven cases of executive clemency.

Brittany K. Barnett

She grew up in rural East Texas, the child of teenage parents who separated before either had reached the age of twenty. She and her younger sister, Jazz, were raised primarily by their mother, Evelyn Fulbright, with support from extended family. As a child, Barnett witnessed the impact of drugs and drug addiction on her family. Ultimately, the experience of her mother's addiction to drugs would set Barnett on her future professional course. From age ten until her graduation from the University of Texas at Arlington, Barnett witnessed her mother's worsening addiction. Her mother attended Barnett's college graduation "gaunt and deep in the throes of addiction."

Earlier in the book, upon beginning to describe her mother's lengthy struggle with addiction, Barnett recounts that her family faced a difficult period similar to so many other Black families who found themselves in the vice of the national War on Drugs. "When the drug war came for us, it came with a vengeance," she poignantly writes. "When the drug war came for us, it came straight for my mom." During the two-year long incarceration of her mother that began in the year after her undergraduate graduation, Barnett, along with her sister, experienced tremendous emotional suffering. She also got firsthand exposure to the traumatic conditions of inmates and their families as they were often held under seemingly unjust circumstances in an undignified, inhumane environment. This personal journey, which makes up the first part of the book, was intertwined with the start of Barnett's professional career. This experience became the catalyst for the tremendous efforts in legal and social advocacy that would become Barnett's primary focus, illustrated in her powerful reflection and emphasis on how her mother had been punished instead of treated for her illness of addiction. The second and third parts of the book are dedicated to telling the story of Barnett's growth into a career as a clemency advocate. As she details the arc of her own professional journey, she blends her story with the traumatic and compelling narratives of key individuals whom she has represented.

Barnett's personal story is exceptional for the tremendous professional success that she obtained, but she goes to great lengths to use her own life as a window into the routine systematic oppression faced by the Black community as a whole in the United States. Although she was always a strong student, and graduated in the top 10 percent of her high school class, Barnett had been socially conditioned to think small about her future. Despite her father urging her to attend the flagship state university of Texas, she instead went to the regional branch university. Similarly, she downsized her life's dreams to fit an aspiration that seemed more realistic. At the University of Texas at Arlington she pursued a business degree in accounting with the intention of working in a local bank branch. She recounts this slow reduction in her dreams, stating that until junior high she "never wavered from wanting to be a lawyer, but as you get older your dreams begin to shrink, narrowed by what's around you."

Drug culture also surrounded Barnett and threatened to ensnare her. Indeed, as her mother's addiction spiraled out of control, Barnett was cohabiting with a boyfriend named Red who was enmeshed in the drug world. As Red became violently abusive, Barnett first hid the abuse from her family but, ultimately, sought her father's help in escaping the relationship. Her emergence from this relationship—stronger, and more sure of her self—is the first example of the adult persona that Barnett compellingly weaves for herself throughout the text. Although she was only nineteen, Barnett comments, "I emerged from the confusion and despair of that experience with a strong sense of power and purpose. I knew who I was and what I would not tolerate."

In a relatively short but intense amount of time, Barnett escaped an abusive relationship, endured her mother's imprisonment, launched a successful career as an accountant, and decided that her real professional ambition lay in the powerful world of corporate law. Fortunately, another young, Black lawyer named Christa Brown-Sanford offered Barnett mentorship as she applied to law school. Brown-Sanford helped her to channel this newborn sense of power and purpose, while using her personal experience "as a source of strength, power, and wisdom—not a weakness." Although she aspired to a career in corporate law, her law school application contained the germ of her first major social justice initiative: a project called Girls Embracing Mothers, which would seek to offer support to girls with imprisoned mothers. As the story unfolds, Barnett builds a successful corporate law career but almost as quickly lets it fall by the wayside as her passion and success grow in the area of social justice and clemency.

Some of the most compelling storytelling in *A Knock at Midnight* comes when Barnett retells the stories of the incarcerated clients for whom, up to the point of the publication of her book, she had sought sentence reductions and/or clemency. These finely tuned narratives are closely related to the legal arguments she had to construct to win these individuals back their freedom. Because of the relationships that Barnett developed with these clients, these stories are also closely tied with her own. As with her own autobiographical material, she goes to great lengths to emphasize that while these are individual stories, they are also simply examples of the unjust American system of crime and punishment by which many Black Americans have been entrapped. Even as some of the nation's leaders—including former president Barack Obama and his attorney general Eric Holder—sought to reduce or eliminate many of the practices that resulted in exorbitant "mandatory minimum" sentences for drug-related crimes, even for first-time offenders, these incarcerated individuals had little recourse under past or future law. *A Knock at Midnight* unfolds a compelling, very human argument for systematic change in the nation's legal system and in its system of incarceration. However, Barnett also sets herself apart from other advocates in that she is not concerned only with top-down change at the level of government and law. She proposes that a new perspective on freedom and justice must additionally harness the minds and energy—what she calls "the world-changing impact"—of those who were once imprisoned.

The central and best-known figure among Barnett's clemency stories is Sharanda Jones. At the time of her arrest, Jones was a single mother and successful small business owner. Although she had not been active in drug-related circles for several years, in the past she had transported drugs from a major regional distributor to local dealers. She was arrested, and ultimately convicted to life without parole, while the major players with whom she had been involved received much more lenient sentences. Barnett felt an immediate connection to her when she became familiar with the case. Although Jones was the first clemency case on which Barnett began to work, her case would take longer to resolve than some others discussed in the book. Barnett details the close relationship she developed with Jones while working on her case pro bono on top of her developing career. Barnett would travel routinely to visit Jones in prison, and the two women became deeply involved in each other's lives, building a near-family connection.

In discussing her relationship with Jones, and, later, with Corey Jacobs, Barnett spends a great deal of time highlighting the ways in which these individuals enriched her life. Jones is presented as a paragon of positive thinking, a mentor, and even a maternal figure for Barnett. Jacobs, meanwhile, coaches her in meditation, resilience, and even in her career path. Unstated within Barnett's memoir, though clear from the larger web of her narrative, is that these relationships also play a vital role in her personal journey of recovering from the traumas of her own childhood and early adult years. She did not even begin to admit these traumas until she worked on her law school application's personal statement. Her social justice work is interlocked with her personal biography from its earliest stages, and her deeply personal relationship with her clients seems to be a genuine reflection of this, not merely a legal strategy.

A Knock at Midnight is a profound and affecting condemnation of the legal and political systems in place in the United States that have allowed so many individuals to receive disproportionate sentences and to be incarcerated for addiction rather than receive treatment. Barnett's memoir works within this system and highlights its realities. While she criticizes the Obama administration for not reaching the full potential of its clemency initiative, she recognizes and celebrates the achievement of freedom for several of her own clients under the initiative. Similarly, while she celebrates Alice Johnson's receipt of executive clemency from the administration of President Donald Trump, she mourns the lack of further movement on such initiatives.

As Barnett is a practicing lawyer, it is perhaps understandable that her political criticisms are fairly measured, to avoid any disruption that might hamper her career progress. Some reviewers of the book took some issue with her tempered approach, as well as the boundaries she draws in exploring her own traumatic past, but these seem both wise and strategic decisions for an author still very much engaged in such important and public work. Most importantly, Barnett lays bare the essential truth at the heart of her project—that her own life, and those of every member of the Black American community—is closely bound to the unjust structures of American society. While she became successful despite many traumas, few achieve the same result. She closes with the story of her client Chris Young, whose youthful brilliance could not uplift him from the web of poverty, chronic illness, and addiction into which he was born. Still incarcerated under a mandatory sentence so unjust that it triggered the resignation of the judge who oversaw his trial, Barnett concludes that Young never had a free life. Instead, he experienced "a suffocating socioeconomic environment that offered no access to channels of opportunity."

Author Biography
Brittany K. Barnett is an attorney and social justice activist. She worked in accounting and corporate law but ultimately shifted her focus to advocacy. She is a founder of several nonprofit endeavors, including the Buried Alive Project and Girls Embracing Mothers.

Julia A. Sienkewicz, PhD

Review Sources
Butler, Paul. "A Young Lawyer Battling for Women Caught Up in Mass Incarceration." Review of *A Knock at Midnight: A Story of Hope, Justice, and Freedom*, by Brittany K. Barnett. *The Washington Post*, 16 Oct. 2020, www.washingtonpost.com/outlook/a-young-lawyer-battling-for-women-caught-up-in-mass-incarceration/2020/10/15/4df77418-041a-11eb-a2db-417cddf4816a_story.html. Accessed 14 Dec. 2020.
Review of *A Knock at Midnight: A Story of Hope, Justice, and Freedom*, by Brittany K. Barnett. *Kirkus*, 15 Mar. 2020, www.kirkusreviews.com/book-reviews/brittany-k-barnett/a-knock-at-midnight/. Accessed 18 Dec. 2020.
Review of *A Knock at Midnight: A Story of Hope, Justice, and Freedom*, by Brittany K. Barnett. *Publishers Weekly*, 17 Apr. 2020, www.publishersweekly.com/978-1-9848-2578-0. Accessed 18 Dec. 2020.
Murdoch, Sierra Crane. "The Injustice Deep within the Justice System." Review of *A Knock at Midnight: A Story of Hope, Justice, and Freedom*, by Brittany K. Barnett. *The New York Times*, 8 Sept. 2020, www.nytimes.com/2020/09/08/books/review/a-knock-at-midnight-brittany-k-barnett.html. Accessed 14 Dec. 2020.

The Last Negroes at Harvard
The Class of 1963 and the 18 Young Men
Who Changed Harvard Forever

Authors: Kent Garrett (b. 1942) and Jeanne Ellsworth (b. 1951)
Publisher: Houghton Mifflin Harcourt (Boston). 320 pp.
Type of work: Biography, memoir, history, education
Time: 1963–the present
Locales: Cambridge, Massachusetts; various other places around the world

Kent Garrett and Jeanne Ellsworth's The Last Negroes at Harvard *traces the lives and careers of eighteen Black members of the 1963 graduating class at Harvard University. While highlighting many triumphs, it also reveals deep injustices.*

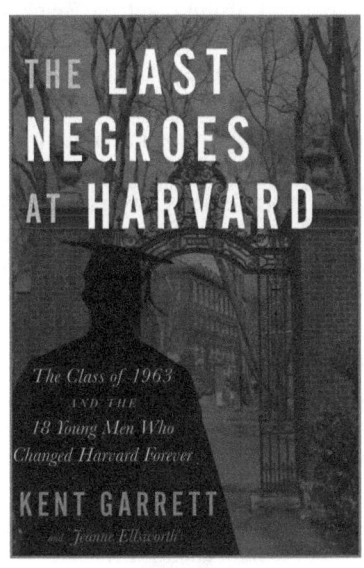

Principal personages
KENT GARRETT, the author, a member of the 1963 class at Harvard University
LOWELL JOHNSTON, his classmate, who went on to a career as a civil rights lawyer
EZRA GRIFFITH, his classmate, who became a psychiatry professor
WILLIAM HENRY EXUM, his classmate, who became a scholar of African American studies and sociology
JACK BUTLER, his classmate, founder of Harvard's first Black student organization and later a businessperson and professor
FRED EASTER, his classmate, who built a career working with at-risk youth

The Last Negroes at Harvard (2020) is a subtle and complex history tracing the lives of eighteen men who became part of the Harvard University graduating class of 1963. Though coming from a diverse range of backgrounds, they are all Black—or Negro, in the language of the time. Indeed, they made up the largest cohort of Black students in Harvard's long history up to that point, though still constituting just a tiny fraction of their overall class. Kent Garrett, one of the authors of the book, was a member of this group. Aided by his partner Jeanne Ellsworth, herself an experienced college educator, he relates his own story as well as those of his peers in a unique biographical history.

Garrett lays out the genesis of the book in the preface. He spent decades as a television journalist and producer before becoming a dairy farmer in 1997, all the while harboring ambivalent feelings about his prestigious alma mater. Around 2007, as he planned to retire from farming, he happened to read an obituary of a fellow Black Harvard alumnus, igniting a curiosity about the fates of the other Black members of the

1963 class. Soon after he met Ellsworth, and together they embarked on a documentary video project on the subject. After interviewing fourteen of the eighteen Black students who were part of the class, Garrett and Ellsworth decided they wanted to write a book to provide deeper detail, both as a memoir and in the broader context of the civil rights movement.

The record-setting diversity of the 1963 Harvard class was the result of an early form of affirmative action, though that term would not become popularized until after the class's four years at the institution. While the school's racial barrier had been broken with the class of 1870, Black students remained few and far between into the mid-twentieth century. But as the civil rights movement began to take off, Garrett explains, a few forward-thinking Harvard administrators essentially decided that the university needed to be more proactive in finding Black enrollees to help change the racial composition of the university. Garrett estimates that about half of the eighteen Black students selected for admission in 1959 were there in part because of their racial heritage, though each also represented the educational elite of their community.

Kent Garrett and Jeanne Ellsworth

The backbone of the book is Garrett's personal experience, which is related in clear first-person narration. Though he was raised in the Brooklyn borough of New York City, most of his family hailed from Edgefield, South Carolina, their lives directly overshadowed by Jim Crow laws and the pervasive impact of institutionalized racism. As Garrett describes arriving at Harvard in 1959, he acknowledges that not long before his family members had been sharecroppers working cotton fields, facing the threat of violence by terrorists such as the Ku Klux Klan. The serene world of the famed university seems completely different, filled with hope and promise. But Garrett admits to thinking little about such historic progress that first day, preoccupied instead with the typical anxieties of any new student.

Garrett's freshman year roommate, Ezra Griffith, was another of the eighteen Black members of the class of 1963. Griffith's story helps relay the diversity of Black experience even within such a small group. In some ways the two came from a very similar background: they were classmates at New York's Boys High, a highly selective public school, where they were nearly the only two Black students on the scholarship track. But Griffith had been born and raised in Barbados, immigrating to the United States while in high school. Though his home country was long shaped by oppression and racism much like in the American South, it developed a culture quite different from that of the Garrett family. Even as a teen in the melting pot of New York City, Griffith's friendships reflected a tapestry of West Indian Blackness. Garrett and

Ellsworth similarly include family histories for the other classmates, which range from upper-class comfort to poverty. Beyond providing interesting context, this crucially helps reject the notion of a single Black experience and provides perspective into how society was changing during this tumultuous period in history.

The Last Negroes at Harvard has an overall chronological progression, documenting each semester of the class's undergraduate years. Along the way it builds profiles of each of the eighteen central figures, all unique yet bonded by shared experience. Though not all remained friends in their later lives, there was a clear sense of community among them as they settled in and adapted to a historically White institution. Common memories relayed in the book include everything from good-natured but awkward interactions with White students interested in their "black experience" to feeling unable to fully integrate with a student population who saw them as curiosities rather than true peers. Through their discussions and shared meals at the "Black Table," many of the eighteen began to become more active on a political level, though doing so was often a balancing act to avoid overly highlighting their racial difference. In interviews, several members of the class express feeling pressure to avoid any confrontation or controversy that might provide evidence for those who did not believe Black people belonged in institutions like Harvard. Despite the challenges, they pressed on in many ways. For example, Jack Butler led the push to form Harvard's first Black student group, eventually succeeding after an early effort failed due to administration resistance.

As the book explores the unique experiences of the class of 1963, Garrett and Ellsworth also provide an interesting look at the broader evolution of Harvard culture and society in general. They point out how the university long stood as a prime example of a kind of elite White culture that was only just beginning to show signs of change as the 1960s dawned. Harvard had once assigned each student a Black valet, banned Black students from dorms and fraternities, and hosted a chapter of the Ku Klux Klan, for example. Even to the present, Garrett admits, the school's reputation for exclusiveness is problematic. Yet outside of the Ivy League, the push for civil rights was even more fraught. Garrett effectively compares and contrasts national events during the time with the experiences of the 1963 class, for instance noting the struggles of James Meredith, who legally challenged segregation in Mississippi to become the first Black student at the University of Mississippi, and had to be escorted to his first classes by armed guards to protect him from violent protestors.

The post-Harvard fates of the eighteen Black members of the class of 1963 are arguably just as interesting as their college days. They are again highly diverse, ranging from elite achievement to tragedy. Some of the historical class had died by the time Garrett and Ellsworth conducted their interviews. These include North Carolina native Travis Williams, who died in 1968 and was described by friends as volatile and troubled, with his racially divided upbringing making it difficult for him to adjust to life at Harvard. In contrast, Lowell Davidson was a successful athlete, biochemist, and pianist in his university days, later becoming a student of famed jazz saxophonist Ornette Coleman and producing an album before his death in 1990.

Perhaps unsurprisingly given the social climate of the day, many members of the 1963 class were drawn one way or another into political activism, social service, or education. Several are among the most prominent figures in the book, with noted careers. Oklahoma native William Exum went on to receive a PhD in sociology from New York University and worked as a professor of African American studies at Northwestern University until his death in 1986, authoring the respected history *Paradoxes of Protest* (1985) about the Black students protest movement of the 1960s. Lowell Johnson, who grew up in an upper-middle-class family in Washington, DC, took part in the 1963 March on Washington and other civil rights activities. He returned to Harvard to attend law school and spent much of his career working for the NAACP Legal Defense Fund. Fred Easter would spend his life after Harvard in San Francisco and New York working with inner city at-risk youth. Jack Butler, who came from Pittsburgh, Pennsylvania, went on to become an activist helping to build housing in Africa before returning to the United States to teach business and finance. Griffith left Harvard for the US Army, serving in Vietnam before studying medicine in France and returning to the United States as a professor of psychiatry at Yale University. By following their cohort to the present day, Garrett and Ellsworth ably demonstrate the scope and power of history, merging individual and universal experiences.

The Last Negroes at Harvard won much praise from critics, with many reviewers calling it an important contribution to fields such as African American studies, civil rights literature, and the history of higher education. It earned starred reviews from *Library Journal*, *Kirkus*, and *Publishers Weekly*, with the latter capturing the general consensus: "this outstanding retrospective deserves to be widely read." Indeed, it will be an eye-opening read for many audiences. The book does not hide the challenges that its subjects experienced in college and beyond, or the fact that many of the same obstacles remain in place for Black Americans; the diverse perspectives presented in its pages include degrees of anger and frustration. Yet it also a celebratory work, revealing a group of people who together represent one positive step in the long struggle against racial prejudice. As the title hints, Garrett and company were the last generation of students who would accept the term "Negro," as over the course of their time as Harvard undergraduates they witnessed the beginnings of a national shift in race relations. Though there may still be much progress to be made, trailblazers such as the class of 1963 deserve to be recognized.

Author Biography
Kent Garrett had a lengthy career as a television journalist and producer, including stints at CBS News and NBC News. He later worked as an organic dairy farmer. *The Last Negroes at Harvard* is his first book.

Jeanne Ellsworth is an educator with decades of experience, including more than twenty years in the State University of New York network.

Micah L. Issitt

Review Sources

Connor, Elizabeth. Review of *The Last Negroes at Harvard: The Class of 1963 and the 18 Young Men Who Changed Harvard Forever*, by Kent Garrett and Jeanne Ellsworth. *Library Journal*, 1 Oct. 2019, www.libraryjournal.com/?reviewDetail=the-last-negroes-at-harvard-the-class-of-1963-and-the-18-young-men-who-changed-harvard-forever. Accessed 12 Jan. 2021.

Hughey, Aaron W. Review of *The Last Negroes at Harvard: The Class of 1963 and the 18 Young Men Who Changed Harvard Forever*, by Kent Garrett and Jeanne Ellsworth. *Bowling Green Daily News*, 21 June 2020, www.bgdailynews.com/community/book-review-the-last-negroes-at-harvard/article_039aa929-1abb-57e7-9c43-74f406418c54.html. Accessed 12 Jan. 2021.

Kennedy, Randall. "What Harvard Was Like for a Black Freshman in 1959." Review of *The Last Negroes at Harvard: The Class of 1963 and the 18 Young Men Who Changed Harvard Forever*, by Kent Garrett and Jeanne Ellsworth. *The Washington Post*, 19 Mar. 2020, www.washingtonpost.com/outlook/what-harvard-was-like-for-a-black-freshman-in-1959/2020/03/19/ab3ccee2-5e53-11ea-9055-5fa12981bbbf_story.html. Accessed 12 Jan. 2021.

Review of *The Last Negroes at Harvard: The Class of 1963 and the 18 Young Men Who Changed Harvard Forever*, by Kent Garrett and Jeanne Ellsworth. *Kirkus*, 23 Oct. 2019, www.kirkusreviews.com/book-reviews/kent-garrett/the-last-negroes-at-harvard/. Accessed 12 Jan. 2021.

Review of *The Last Negroes at Harvard: The Class of 1963 and the 18 Young Men Who Changed Harvard Forever*, by Kent Garrett and Jeanne Ellsworth. *Publishers Weekly*, 2 Dec. 2019, www.kirkusreviews.com/book-reviews/kent-garrett/the-last-negroes-at-harvard/. Accessed 12 Jan. 2021.

Nathans-Kelly, Steve. Review of *The Last Negroes at Harvard: The Class of 1963 and the 18 Young Men Who Changed Harvard Forever*, by Kent Garrett and Jeanne Ellsworth. *New York Journal of Books*, www.nyjournalofbooks.com/book-review/last-negroes-harvard. Accessed 12 Jan. 2021.

Leave the World Behind

Author: Rumaan Alam (b. 1977)
Publisher: Ecco (New York). 256 pp.
Type of work: Novel
Time: Present day
Locale: The Hamptons

Leave the World Behind is a dystopian thriller set in the present that explores race, class, and the limitations of contemporary life.

Principal characters
AMANDA, a forty-three-year-old marketing executive on vacation with her family in the Hamptons
CLAY, her husband, a tenured professor of media studies at City College
ARCHIE, her fifteen-year-old son
ROSE, her thirteen-year-old daughter
GEORGE, a.k.a. *G. H.*, a financial analyst in his sixties who owns the Hamptons house that Amanda and Clay have rented
RUTH, G. H.'s wife

Throughout his career as a novelist, Rumaan Alam has defied American readers' expectations of him. The son of Bengali immigrants, he began his career as a writer who often felt tokenized because of his family's background. He subsequently worried that White editors were not hiring him for the quality of his work but because they assumed that he could provide their publications with a diverse perspective. As a result of this fear, Alam quit several coveted literary jobs before pushing back against the publishing world's perception of him with a debut novel that focuses on characters who, ostensibly, were dramatically different from him. *Rich and Pretty* (2016) follows the friendship of two privileged White women and was praised for the deft way that it captures the female perspective. Alam continued to challenge mainstream expectations of what an author of Indian descent "should" write about in his next novel, *That Kind of Mother* (2018), which depicts the experience of a White woman adopting a Black son.

Alam's 2020 novel *Leave the World Behind* feels like a perpetuation of his previous works in the best possible way. Like Alam's first two books, the novel explores the themes of race and class by focusing primarily on the experiences of privileged White Americans. Specifically, it follows a Brooklyn family of four who have traveled out to Long Island for a week-long summer vacation. These characters comprise many attributes that have become synonymous with upper-middle-class White people in New York City. In other words, they are organic-food-buying, sunscreen-wearing liberals with a cursory awareness of America's racial injustices. The mother, Amanda, works

Rumaan Alam
Courtesy HarperCollins Publishers

in advertising while her husband, Clay, is a professor who writes book reviews for the *New York Times*. Meanwhile, their children, Archie and Rose, are awkward young adolescents more concerned with staying in touch with their friends on their smartphones than anything else. For some readers, this cast may feel stereotypical; for others, they will simply seem familiar—like neighbors. However they might come across on the page, what is most important about them is the fact that they are the type of people who, while not supremely wealthy, still feel entitled to the beautiful house in the Hamptons that they are renting from Airbnb.

One of the most fascinating aspects of *Leave the World Behind* is how difficult it is to classify the central narrative. This is because Alam utilizes the plot to continuously subvert his readers' expectations. When the novel begins, it appears to be a kind of social comedy of manners. Late on their second night at the rental house, Amanda and Clay hear a knock on the door. When they open it, they find a Black couple in their sixties who introduce themselves as the house's owners and explain that they are there seeking shelter because a mysterious blackout has taken over New York City. It is a tense, darkly satirical scene that kicks off the entire narrative as Amanda and Clay doubt whether these people, G. H. and Ruth, are actually the owners but reluctantly let them in so that they do not appear racist. Here, Alam provides readers with a window into the psyche of some privileged White Americans. Despite being liberal, educated, and well intentioned, Amanda and Clay are still quite racist. They struggle to believe that these Black people have more claim to the house they are staying in than them—even when it becomes clear that they are not lying about their identity. It is through these actions that Alam skewers contemporary White "wokeness" by demonstrating its lack of depth. At the end of the day, when faced with helping Black people at the expense of their own comfort, Amanda and Clay are reluctant to act.

While *Leave the World Behind* could easily stay in this lane and become a piece exclusively about race and class in contemporary America, Alam quickly shifts its focus to something much more ambitious. It gradually becomes clear that G. H. and Ruth's initial instincts that something is terribly wrong in New York City and across the eastern seaboard are correct. The television stops working as well as all of the characters' cell phones. In turn, these two families have no way to get news from the outside world. In a pace that feels like a crawl over the next day, the familiar, modern life that Alam has depicted in the earlier chapters begins to shift into a dystopian nightmare. To successfully create this effect, he utilizes some of the genre's most familiar visual touchpoints. There are no other people on the roads. Animals start acting strangely.

And, perhaps most disturbingly, one of the children starts developing scary physical symptoms. The four adult characters are subsequently forced to come together to try and figure out what is going on and what actions they must take to survive.

As a storyteller, Alam excels at providing readers with insight into who his characters really are. One subtle, indirect way he accomplishes this is by continuously detailing his characters' actions. In an early scene, for example, he spends an entire paragraph making note of all the specific groceries that Amanda is buying for her family. Surprisingly, this act of describing all the snacks and meals they will be eating in the upcoming week proves to be a simple, effective way to give his audience a better example of exactly who these people are. Internal dialogue is another tool that Alam successfully employs to create fully fleshed-out characters. As he pivots to follow each of these characters at different times throughout the novel, Alam provides their innermost thoughts on both the situation at hand and each other. In addition to creating a sense of familiarity with the characters, this tactic prevents readers from making assumptions about what any of them think or feel. It is immediately clear what all of the characters' true motivations are.

Due to its focus on issues like race and class, *Leave the World Behind* is comparable to many contemporary works of popular culture. Specifically, the socioracial tension that initially builds between the four main characters is reminiscent of films such as *Get Out* (2017) and *Parasite* (2019). However, it can be argued that it also belongs in the genre of dystopian literature alongside books like Ray Bradbury's *Fahrenheit 451* (1953) and Cormac McCarthy's *The Road* (2004). Perhaps what makes *Leave the World Behind* powerful as a work of dystopian literature is just how much it feels like the present day. Rather than speculate about the near future, Alam sets the story in the present. As a result, the world that the characters live in is recognizable and the sudden challenges that they face feel especially terrifying. For example, when the characters are unable to use the television and their cell phones, they become completely immobilized. At one point, Clay tries to drive to a nearby store to get information on the blackout but immediately gets lost without a GPS. It is a reminder of just how unprepared people of the modern world are for any sort of catastrophe.

Reception of *Leave the World Behind* was overwhelmingly positive, with many publications calling it one of the best books of 2020. Critics were quick to note how relevant the novel is as a result of the fact that it was published during a tumultuous year defined by a pandemic as well as sociopolitical unrest. Maureen Corrigan wrote in her National Public Radio (NPR) review, "*Leave the World Behind* is atmospheric and prescient: Its rhythms of comedy alternating with shock and despair mimic so much of the rhythms of life right now." Mary Ann Gwinn made a similar comment in her review for the *Los Angeles Times* by observing that "what might have been a suspenseful and socially realistic piece of dystopian fiction has become something far more resonant, a vision of an entirely plausible future." Although Alam wrote the novel back in 2019 and had no idea what a tragically historic year 2020 would be, he still somehow captured how quickly the world can be turned upside down by unexpected events.

Beyond its relevance to the time in which it was published, *Leave the World Behind* was also commended by critics for the quality of its writing. In her review for the *New Yorker*, Hillary Kelly called Alam's novel "enthralling" and extolled the way that the author created narrative suspense. Similarly, Alex Preston's glowing review for the *Guardian* deemed it an "extraordinary book, at once smart, gripping and hallucinatory." While almost all critics were in agreement on the novel being an exceptional piece of dystopian literature, it is important to note that not everyone felt it achieved its goals. In his review for the *New York Times*, Afia Atakora stated, "Alam's early tragicomedy-of-manners approach to race falters." Atakora is not wrong here—the novel does set up racial tension between the two primary couples that it ultimately abandons for the sake of the larger story. In turn, readers who wanted something comparable to the work of author Colson Whitehead or filmmaker Jordan Peele will be disappointed. The novel is better suited for those who are looking for a story that addresses the many different issues of modern life—from race, to class, to global warming, to technology and parenthood. Ultimately, it is a gripping, well-written examination of today's world that successfully addresses people's deepest fears.

Author Biography

Rumaan Alam is a novelist and literary critic. His work has appeared in the *New York Times*, the *Wall Street Journal*, *New York*, and the *New Republic*. His novels include *Rich and Pretty* (2016), *That Kind of Mother* (2018), and *Leave the World Behind* (2020).

Emily E. Turner

Review Sources

Atakora, Afia. "What Happens When a Vacation Goes Wrong—And Not in a Funny Way?" Review of *Leave the World Behind*, by Rumaan Alam. *The New York Times*, 6 Oct. 2020, www.nytimes.com/2020/10/06/books/review/rumaan-alam-leave-the-world-behind.html. Accessed 7 Dec. 2020.

Corrigan, Maureen. "'Leave the World Behind' Is a Signature Novel for This Blasted Year." Review of *Leave the World Behind*, by Rumaan Alam. *NPR*, 29 Sept. 2020,www.npr.org/2020/09/29/915978294/leave-the-world-behind-is-a-signature-novel-for-this-blasted-year. Accessed 10 Dec. 2020.

Gwinn, Mary Ann. "Review: Apocalypse Now: A Funny, Terrifying End-Of-The-World Novel Is As 2020 As It Gets." Review of *Leave the World Behind*, by Rumaan Alam. *Los Angeles Times*, 2 Oct. 2020, www.latimes.com/entertainment-arts/books/story/2020-10-02/rumaan-alam-leave-the-world-behind-review. Accessed 7 Dec. 2020.

Kelly, Hillary. "'Leave the World Behind': A Novel About the Disaster That Won't End." Review of *Leave the World Behind*, by Rumaan Alam. *The New Yorker*, 5 Oct. 2020, www.newyorker.com/books/page-turner/leave-the-world-behind-a-novel-about-the-disaster-that-wont-end. Accessed 7 Dec. 2020.

Preston, Alex. "Leave the World Behind by Rumaan Alam Review—Breathtaking and Prescient." Review of *Leave the World Behind*, by Rumaan Alam. *The Guardian*, 9 Nov. 2020, www.theguardian.com/books/2020/nov/09/leave-the-world-behind-by-rumaan-alam-review-breathtaking-and-prescient. Accessed 7 Dec. 2020.

Long Bright River

Author: Liz Moore (b. 1983)
Publisher: Riverhead Books (New York). 496 pp.
Type of work: Novel
Time: Present day
Locale: Philadelphia

Long Bright River is a police procedural thriller set against the backdrop of the opioid epidemic. It is American author Liz Moore's fourth book.

Principal characters
MICHAELA "MICKEY" FITZPATRICK, a police officer who is searching for her sister while a serial killer is at large
KACEY FITZPATRICK, her sister, who struggles with addiction, lives on the streets, and has been missing for months
THOMAS, her highly intelligent but sensitive four-year-old son
TRUMAN DAWES, her mentor, an older policeman
GEE, her emotionally abusive grandmother who raised her and Kacey
SIMON CLEARE, Thomas's estranged father, a police officer

Liz Moore's *Long Bright River* examines the opioid epidemic and its impact on the families of opioid users through the lens of fiction. Using a mystery to frame her narrative, the author introduces readers to a world where multi-generational families are devastated by narcotics both directly and indirectly. The novel is an unwavering, compelling look at the familial cost of addiction and the corrupt systems that uphold it.

Perhaps one of the most impressive qualities of *Long Bright River* is how it cannot be easily categorized. The novel feels like a crime thriller, a family drama, and a piece of journalism all at once. Moore's ability to successfully blend these elements can be attributed both to her skills as a writer and her extensive research into the world about which she writes. Some of this research came through real-life experience. As a creative writing teacher at a women's day shelter, Moore came in contact with many different types of people involved in the opioid epidemic, including addicts, the family members of addicts, social workers, dealers, sex workers, and police officers. The knowledge she subsequently gained allowed her to capture the complex world of addiction and highlight how neither side of the law is definitively "good" or "bad."

Moore draws readers into this difficult issue through the Trojan horse of a murder mystery. The novel follows the story of thirty-three-year-old Michaela "Mickey" Fitzpatrick as she searches for her missing sister while a serial killer terrorizes the same neighborhood where she was last seen months earlier. For Mickey, finding her sister Kacey proves to be an emotionally conflicted endeavor. The two grew up close. They were each other's support after their mother died from an overdose and they were sent to live with their emotionally abusive grandmother. As teenagers, however, a rift grew between them as Kacey experimented with drugs and Mickey began dating a police officer named Simon. From that point on, their paths diverged. Kacey became a sex worker to fund her addiction, while Mickey went into law enforcement. In a twist that feels melodramatic but ultimately works, their only interactions as adults are when Mickey arrests Kacey for solicitation or drug possession. When Kacey goes missing, Mickey has not truly spoken to her for years. She worries she will never get the chance to reconnect as the serial killer is targeting women like Kacey.

Liz Moore

While most of the characters that populate *Long Bright River* are well-crafted and compelling, none demonstrate Moore's skill for nuance better than Mickey. At first glance, she appears to be the kind of stereotypical female law enforcement agent found in so many crime novels—a tough, intelligent loner with colleagues who dismiss her because of her gender. As the narrative continues, however, Moore pulls back the layers to reveal a much more realistic person. Although Mickey is tough, she is also extremely vulnerable. In addition to Kacey, she worries constantly about her young, sensitive son, Thomas, who she has to leave with a babysitter all day. Furthermore, she is a good police officer but by no means an exceptional one. Mickey does not have the savant-like intuition that so many female detectives in the crime genre have and instead relies on her training and practical advice from her mentor, Truman Dawes.

One of the most compelling details about Mickey is that she never wanted to be a cop. As an intelligent young woman with academic promise who happened to be stuck in an impoverished, unsupportive family, she was easily convinced to join the force by her ex-boyfriend Simon. Simon is an unusual antagonist in that he really only exists in flashbacks to Mickey's past, and yet he still has an enormous impact on her present. When Mickey first met Simon, she was a high school freshman and he was a twenty-seven-year-old police officer who was working as a counselor at the after-school program that she attended. She gravitated towards him because he was the kind of paternal figure that she lacked in her life and he made her feel important. It was not until she was in her twenties that she realized that Simon was a dangerous predator and left him. Still, his presence in her life is inescapable—in addition to being the father of her son, he is the reason she is a police officer. He also played a role in the disintegration of Mickey and Kacey's relationship.

A large part of what makes Mickey's journey so absorbing is Moore's depiction of the setting. *Long Bright River* takes place predominantly in the Philadelphia neighborhood of Kensington. As Moore demonstrates, Kensington is a poor area with high crime rates. Many of the people Mickey encounters there are addicts and sex workers. While such characters could easily come across as one-dimensional stereotypes, Moore humanizes them in such a way that readers become aware of how much value they add to their community. Specifically, these characters look out for and support one another. This community also includes the ward-like figures of corner store workers, church volunteers, former addicts, and even police officers like Mickey and Truman. While it is clear that narcotics are destructive to families and society as a whole, the way in which people struggling with addiction try to help one another so that they can all carve out a life together is heartening.

Although the novel reveals the reality of the opioid epidemic, *Long Bright River* never feels didactic. It is primarily a thriller where addiction happens to exist around the edges of the protagonist's life. Still, Moore makes it clear through her characters' experiences how this national crisis came to fruition. Mickey is similar to many Americans in that she is from a poor family that has been undermined by a lack of job opportunities and the ubiquity of narcotics. As her parents both succumbed to addiction, it is not surprising that her sister, Kacey, faced similar struggles. While Moore never points fingers, the story also shows how many civil services are ineffective. The police do not help the people of Kensington by arresting them. Furthermore, there is no government-funded assistance to help addicts get and stay sober. Through a dynamic, character-driven story, Moore quietly demonstrates how the crumbling civic foundations of cities can fail citizens.

The critical reception of *Long Bright River* was overwhelmingly positive. After much online pre-publication buzz, the novel quickly became a *New York Times* best seller. Initially, much of the critical praise was directed toward the book's superbly crafted, suspenseful plot. In his review for *Oprah Magazine*, Hamilton Cain wrote, "it's got all the ingredients that make for an unputdownable mystery, but it's got something more, a narrator who leads you into unexpected places, and keeps surprising you until the end." Indeed, Moore is adept at keeping readers on their toes. She creates this suspense by alternating between two storylines: "Then" and "Now." The "Then" chapters move chronologically through Mickey's childhood, adolescence, and adulthood, while the "Now" chapters follow her in the present day as she searches for Kacey. What is surprising about these storylines is how they make the novel's biggest mystery not who the serial killer is but rather why Mickey and Kacey are no longer speaking to one another.

While many critics were quick to point out Moore's talents as a writer, not everyone found her prose and storytelling to be enjoyable. For example, the anonymous reviewer for *Kirkus Reviews* concluded, "With its flat, staccato tone and mournful mood, it's almost as if the book itself were suffering from depression." There is some truth to this critique. The novel's somber atmosphere is largely due to the fact that Mickey exists in a gritty world populated by tragic figures. This feeling is elevated by the fact that it is set in the year's darkest months of November, December, and January.

Additionally, the novel's "staccato tone" is a result of its unusual literary style, which comprises short sentences and paragraphs.

Arguably the most ubiquitous point of praise among critics has been for what the novel achieves as a whole. Maureen Corrigan wrote for the *Washington Post* that *Long Bright River* is, "a sweeping, elegiac novel about a blighted city" and that the author successfully "excavates Kensington and surround areas in Philadelphia, illuminating the rot, the shiny facades of gentrification and the sturdy endurance of small pockets of community life." As Corrigan suggests, the novel takes readers by the hand and leads them into America's darkest corners in a way that is both informative and entertaining. Those interested in getting a sense of the ravages the opioid crisis will not be disappointed, while readers who simply want a hardboiled crime thriller will surely be satisfied. Moore strikes a balance between these two elements by creating a hero who defies tropes. The end result is a smart, engaging, and original work of fiction that will keep audiences on the edge of their seats.

Author Biography

Novelist Liz Moore is the critically acclaimed author of *Heft* (2012) and *The Unseen World* (2016). She earned the Medici Book Club Prize and the 2014 Rome Prize in Literature.

Emily E. Turner

Review Sources

Cain, Hamilton. "Liz Moore's Long Bright River is a Page-Turning Mystery About the Opioid Epidemic." Review of *Long Bright River*, by Liz Moore. *Oprah Magazine*, 15 Jan. 2020, www.oprahmag.com/entertainment/books/a30473458/long-bright-river-liz-moore-review. Accessed 10 Nov. 2020.

Corrigan, Maureen. "Long Bright River is that Wonderful Thriller that Subverts Your Expectations till the Very Last Page." Review of *Long Bright River*, by Liz Moore. *The Washington Post*, 3 Jan. 2020, www.washingtonpost.com/entertainment/books/long-bright-river-is-that-wonderful-thriller-that-subverts-your-expectations-till-the-very-last-page/2020/01/03/72a24f50-2da0-11ea-bcb3-ac6482c4a-92f_story.html. Accessed 10 Nov. 2020.

Review of *Long Bright River*, by Liz Moore. *Kirkus Reviews*, 15 Sept. 2019. *Literary Reference Center Plus*, search.ebscohost.com/login.aspx?direct=true&db=lkh&AN=138870143&site=lrc-plus. Accessed 10 Nov. 2020.

Merritt, Stephanie. "Long Bright River by Liz Moore—Startlingly Fresh." Review of *Long Bright River*, by Liz Moore. *The Guardian*, 3 Feb. 2020, www.theguardian.com/books/2020/feb/03/long-bright-river-by-liz-moore-review. Accessed 10 Nov. 2020.

A Long Petal of the Sea

Author: Isabel Allende (b. 1942)
First published: *Largo pétalo de mar*, 2019, in Spain
Translated from the Spanish by Nick Caistor and Amanda Hopkinson
Publisher: Ballantine Books (New York). 336 pp.
Type of work: Novel
Time: 1938–94
Locales: Primarily Catalonia, France, and Chile

In A Long Petal of the Sea, *refugees from the Spanish Civil War find sanctuary in Chile but are forced to flee again after the political coup of 1973.*

Principal characters

VICTOR DALMAU, a medic in the Republican Army
CARME DALMAU, his mother
GUILLEM DALMAU, his younger brother, a soldier killed by a Nazi bomber
ROSER BRUGUERA, his wife, a gifted pianist who was his father's student and his brother's girlfriend
MARCEL DALMAU BRUGUERA, his nephew, Guillem and Roser's son
OFELIA DEL SOLAR, his love interest
ISIDRO DEL SOLAR, Ofelia's father, the patriarch of a prominent aristocratic family in Chile
LAURA DEL SOLAR, Ofelia's mother, a descendant of an old and powerful Chilean family
FELIPE DEL SOLAR, Ofelia's wayward, socially conscious older brother
PABLO NERUDA (1904–73), an ambassador, politician, and poet, based on the historical personage of the same name
SALVADOR ALLENDE (1908–73), the first socialist Chilean president, based on the historical personage of the same name; the author's father's first cousin

Chilean poet Pablo Neruda once described his country, named for its resemblance to a chili pepper, as a "long petal of the sea" (in Spanish, *largo pétalo de mar*). Novelist Isabel Allende, who grew up in Chile and became a well-known television personality there, uses Neruda's metaphor as the title of her 2020 novel, *A Long Petal of the Sea*. She also uses a few lines of Neruda's poetry to introduce each chapter of the novel and Neruda's efforts to save refugees after the Spanish Civil War forms the basis of her story. Like her semiautobiographical first novel, *The House of the Sprits* (1982),

Long Petal is both a celebration of her native country and a lament for what it lost with the military uprising against her father's cousin Salvador Allende in 1973.

"War and Exodus," the first part of *A Long Petal of the Sea*, is set in Catalonia in 1938, just as the Spanish Civil War is ending. The protagonist, Victor Dalmau, comes from a family of Republicans who support Spain's first elected government. Committed to the Roman ideal of a republic where all citizens are represented, as opposed to a monarchy or dictatorship, they are fighting to protect their modern democracy against Nationalists who want to preserve Spain's feudal aristocracy and the church that supports it. Though the Republicans have the backing of idealists from many foreign countries, including the Lincoln Brigade from the United States, the Nationalists have military support from the fascist regimes of Adolf Hitler's Germany and Benito Mussolini's Italy. Thousands of surviving Republicans escape to France, knowing they will receive no mercy from General Francisco Franco and the Nationalists. Once there, however, many refugees, including Victor and Roser, the heavily pregnant girlfriend of his deceased brother, are incarcerated in a French concentration camp before they can escape once more.

Isabel Allende

Meanwhile, Chile's right-leaning aristocracy, who are themselves descendants of Spanish settlers, debate whether to allow the Spanish Republican refugees entry. Neruda, as he did in real life, persuades the Chilean government he serves to let him identify more than two thousand Spanish refugees who can contribute to the country's future. Victor, Roser, and his newborn nephew, Marcel—now legally husband, wife, and son to improve their chances of immigration—are among the lucky ones Neruda chooses to voyage to Chile on the *Winnipeg*, a nine-ton cargo ship chartered for the rescue.

When the Spanish refugees arrive in Chile in part 2, "Exile, Loves, and Misunderstandings," they are met with mixed responses. People of the working class, especially those who support the county's first democratic government, welcome them with great enthusiasm, while people with nationalistic and anti-Semitic sentiments strongly object to their presence in a country still recovering from the worldwide economic depression of the 1930s. There are even divisions within families. The affluent and influential Isidro del Solar will have no "Reds" in his house, while his rebellious son, Felipe, welcomes Victor, Roser, and Marcel into his nearby dwelling. It takes Felipe's old nanny to persuade Isidro that he should invite the three refugees to his Christmas Eve dinner, at which the talented mother and her son charm everyone.

In time Victor earns his medical degree, and Roser becomes the pianist of the Santiago orchestra. Marcel grows into a healthy youth who speaks Spanish with a strong

Chilean accent and declines to speak the native Catalan of his parents. Because Chile does not recognize divorce, Victor and Roser remain a couple in name only, though they are both equally committed to Marcel. Then, one day, they receive a message from Victor's mother, Carme, from whom Roser was separated while fleeing from Spain to France. Having supposed Carme to have died, Victor and his family are delighted to bring her to Chile.

The novel's third part, "Returns and Roots," is the longest. Whereas part 1 covers the last years of the Spanish Civil War and part 2 covers the decade during which refugees establish new lives in Chile, part 3 traces the larger picture of political tensions within Chile during five decades after World War II. These tensions force some émigrés and native Chileans into exile, but the potential for return and reconciliation always arises. Part 3 is full of surprises, as old characters reappear and new ones turn up to convince Victor that his family is larger than he ever imagined.

With its combination of history and fiction, spreading across several countries, the novel needs an omniscient narrator, much like Leo Tolstoy's narrator in *War and Peace* (1869). Unlike Tolstoy's narrator, however, Allende's never intrudes on the reader, never expresses a private opinion. Only in the acknowledgments that follow the last chapter does Allende explain that she heard about the shipload of refugees as a child but did not think about the significance of Neruda's action until she was forced to leave Chile and go into exile in Venezuela in the 1980s. In Venezuela, she met Victor Pey Casado (1915–2018), who had traveled with his family on the cargo ship that Neruda commissioned to bring refugees to Chile. Allende's novel has a double dedication, first to her brother Juan Allende, who offered constructive criticism as she wrote, and then to "Victor Pey Casado and other navigators of hope."

Like Victor Pey Casado, Allende's protagonist, Victor Dalmau, grew up in Barcelona, the capital of the autonomous community of Catalonia. Dalmau studied medicine, whereas Pey Casado studied engineering. But both Victors experienced the mutations in government as Chile went from being a democracy to having various political identities: as a military dictatorship, a transitional government, and a democracy once more.

As Victor stoically braves the challenges he faces, much of the novel's drama revolves around Roser and his unobtainable love interest in Chile, Ofelia del Solar. Roser and Ofelia are as different in their origins, talents, and personal beliefs as two characters could be, but readers come to appreciate their individuality and their common humanity even before Victor finally does. Readers see the full variety of human life in women like Victor's mother, Carme, and Ofelia's mother, Laura. The mothers' attitudes toward religion and life are quite different; nevertheless, they have produced principled children because of their convictions and, sometimes, despite them.

Because there is no single character from whose point of view the story is presented, readers are left to decide which characters they admire and, with some characters, under what circumstances. Allende's two historical characters, Pablo Neruda and Salvador Allende, hew closely to their known public and private statements. Meanwhile, her fictional characters' thoughts and dialogue give meaning to the novel. At one point, Victor is able to return the kindness that Neruda showed to him, by sheltering the poet when he has fallen out of favor with those in power. Victor tells the distressed Neruda, "Governments come and go, but poets remain."

Nick Caistor and Amanda Hopkinson's English translation reads quite smoothly. The pair had translated two of Allende's previous novels, *The Japanese Lover* (*El amante japonés*, 2015) and *In the Midst of Winter* (*Más allá del invierno*, 2017). The Spanish custom of writing a person's full name with the father's surname preceding the mother's is replaced by the standard usage in English-speaking countries. Words with special historical significance for Spanish readers—words like *la Retirada* ("the Retreat") for the Republican exodus to France—are given the context that readers of the English translation will need.

Most early reviews were quite positive. In England, where the English-language version was prepared, the reviewer for the *Guardian* stressed the novel's emphasis on the displacement of whole populations as well as individuals and on the human capacity for survival. In the United States, the reviewer for the *New York Times* sounded a similar note, noting Allende's established reputation for creating characters who manage to survive and live their lives under the most daunting conditions. The long, reflective review in the *Los Angeles Review of Books* turns to George Orwell's *Homage to Catalonia* (1938) for the prescient observation that the Spanish Civil War exposed what would prove to be the nature of many twentieth-century wars, pitting human beings against "the capitalist machine." Allende's genius, the reviewer says, is to show how "love awakens feelings that make us human even as war and exile work to destroy them." On a contrary note, a reviewer for the *Harvard Crimson* suggests that the sheer profusion of detail, especially about the competing forces that govern the countries where the action occurs, makes the novel both "undeniably brilliant and rich" and a "war of attrition" to read. Most readers will find themselves somewhere between these two positions, depending on their interest in the larger historical issues that shape personal responses.

Author Biography
Isabel Allende is the award-winning author of twenty novels and several works of nonfiction. Her first novel, *The House of the Spirits* (1982), became a successful film (1993). She has received several prestigious honors, including the Presidential Medal of Freedom in 2014 and the National Book Foundation Medal for lifetime achievement in 2018.

Nick Caistor is a British journalist, translator, and two-time winner of the Premio Valle Inclán for translations of literary works from Spanish to English (2008 and 2014). Amanda Hopkinson is a photography writer, scholar, and literary translator with a PhD from Oxford. Their translations of Allende's work include the English editions of *The Japanese Lover* (2015) and *In the Midst of Winter* (2017).

Thomas Willard

Review Sources

Anderson, Hephzibah. "Love on the Run from Franco." Review of *A Long Petal of the Sea*, by Isabel Allende. *The Guardian*, 2 Feb. 2020, theguardian.com/books/2020/feb/02/a-long-petal-of-the-sea-isabel-allende-review. Accessed 14 Oct. 2020.

Avilés, Marcela Davison. Review of *A Long Petal of the Sea*, by Isabel Allende. *NPR*, www.npr.org/2020/01/27/799345645/a-long-petal-of-the-sea-finds-love-in-a-time-of-chaos. Accessed 14 Oct. 2020.

Buckland, Sam. "Love and Solitude in Exile: Isabel Allende's 'A Long Petal of the Sea'." Review of *A Long Petal of the Sea*, by Isabel Allende. *Los Angeles Review of Books*, 12 Mar. 2020, lareviewofbooks.org/.article/love-and-solitudein-exile-isabel-allendes-a-long-petal-of-the-sea. Accessed 14 Oct. 2020.

Chen, Kelsey. "'A Long Petal of the Sea': Another Long Tale of Gut-Wrenching Events." Review of *A Long Petal of the Sea*, by Isabel Allende. *The Harvard Crimson*, 26 Feb. 2020, www.thecrimson.com/anicle/2020/2/27/loPng-petal-of-the-sea-review. Accessed 14 Oct. 2020.

McLain, Paula. Review of *A Long Petal of the Sea*, by Isabel Allende. *The New York Times Book Review*, 1 Feb. 2020, www.nytimes.com/2020/01/20/books/review/a-long-petal-of-the-sea-isabel-allende.html. Accessed 14 Oct. 2020.

The Lost Book of Adana Moreau

Author: Michael Zapata
Publisher: Hanover Square Press (New York). 266 pp.
Type of work: Novel
Time: Largely 1920s–30s and 2004–05, with flashbacks set in other times
Locales: Primarily New Orleans and Chicago

In the novel The Lost Book of Adana Moreau, *a young man is determined to fulfill his recently deceased grandfather's desire to deliver an unpublished manuscript to its rightful owner. With its many references to real and imaginary books, its discussions of parallel universes, and its focus on disasters such as the Great Depression and Hurricane Katrina, the novel muses on the nature of existence and the saving graces of literature and friendship.*

Principal characters

ADANA MOREAU, a.k.a. *the Dominicana*, a woman originally from the Dominican Republic who settles in New Orleans and writes a science-fiction novel that becomes a cult classic. She dies before her second novel can be published
MAXWELL MOREAU, her son, who becomes a theoretical physicist
TITUS MOREAU, a.k.a. *the pirate*, her husband and Maxwell's father, a smuggler
SAUL DROWER, a man who has come into possession of the lost manuscript of Adana Moreau, and travels to New Orleans to find Maxwell and give him his mother's manuscript
BENJAMIN DROWER, Saul's grandfather
JAVIER, Saul's best friend, a reporter who has extensive experience covering disasters

The Lost Book of Adana Moreau (2020) is a novel about disaster, exile, friendship, and the enduring power of literature to connect people and speak the truth. In his ambitious debut novel, Michael Zapata takes a maximalist approach, discoursing on speculative concepts such as parallel universes, allowing any number of characters to tell stories of their own, and peppering his narrative with literary references and lists of books real and imagined. With his many references to lost books and to labyrinths, Zapata wears his love of writers such as Jorge Luis Borges on his sleeve. Latin American magical realism, the metafictional works of Umberto Eco, and classic science-fiction novels are other ready influences on the book. Yet Zapata synthesizes all of these influences to create something new and original. Despite its many references to previous works

Michael Zapata

of literature, his novel is ultimately about real, difficult contemporary times and about the enduring power of friendship and storytelling to help one make sense of a chaotic world.

The action of the book primarily shuttles between two settings. In the late 1910s, Adana Moreau, referred to with creative strategic effect in the book's initial pages as "the Dominicana," survives a US invasion of the Dominican Republic in which her parents are killed by soldiers. She meets an American smuggler, described initially by Zapata only as "the pirate" and later named as Titus Moreau, moves to New Orleans, and has a son. For several years, this new family lives a modest but idyllic existence. Moreau learns to read, and after consuming any number of novels at her local library, begins writing herself. Her first novel, *Lost City*, is a tale of exiles trying to reconnect across parallel universes. The book is published and becomes a cult classic.

Although she writes a sequel, "A Model Earth," Moreau's health fails her, and on her deathbed she tells her publisher that she had burned the manuscript. She leaves behind her husband and her young son, Maxwell. After he receives a letter from his father, who had gone north to find work, that establishes a plan for them to meet in Chicago, thirteen-year-old Maxwell sets out to find him. Riding the rails and walking the streets of America during the Great Depression, Maxwell risks his life to try to reunite with his father.

The other main plotline of the novel takes place between 2004–05, at the time of the Iraq War and Hurricane Katrina. Saul Dower, a man whose parents were killed in a terrorist attack in Israel when he was around five, was brought up in Chicago by his grandfather, Benjamin. Before Benjamin dies, he arranges for Saul to mail a package for him that is intended to reach Maxwell Moreau, a theoretical physicist at a university in Chile. When the package is sent back to Benjamin's house unreceived by Maxwell and unopened not long after Benjamin's death, Saul himself opens it and finds the unpublished manuscript of Adana Moreau's second novel, "A Model Earth." Having read the manuscript and summarized it for his friend Javier, Saul determines that he must track down Maxwell and deliver it to him in person. As they had learned that Maxwell's last known address was in New Orleans, Javier and Saul drive to a city that has just been hit particularly hard by Hurricane Katrina. Javier, who has spent the last several years as a reporter covering various injustices and events in Latin America, fears he has become addicted to disaster. The friends embark on a journey that will take them into the heart of an American catastrophe and that will teach them more about their own lives and fates.

As the novel progresses, these two story lines ultimately come together. While part of this convergence is literal, it is thematic as well: these characters have all been buffeted and shaped by loss, exile, and disaster. A long list of historic events and catastrophes make it into this novel: the Russian Revolution, the Great Depression, European anti-Semitism, American racism, the Chilean Dirty War, the Iraq War, and the US government's appalling response to Hurricane Katrina. Yet this slim novel is not swamped by the weight of history. As reviewer Will Chancellor put it for the *New York Times*, at the many points during which Zapata "favors people over events, their stories come alive." There is a leisurely pace to this novel, in that the main action of the plot can always be put on pause for a character to share their reminiscences, to tell a story, or to create a list of favorite books. This form of storytelling is, in many respects, the theme of the book. Characters are shaped by the historical forces around them, and their own individuality and humanity are thrown into sharp relief by the brutal events that they have lived through and the stories they tell.

There is an inherent risk to writing a novel that involves two time frames and two different sets of characters: one may prove more compelling than the other. Fortunately, the two sections of Zapata's novel are well matched, with neither of them feeling like a lesser half or like a mere frame story for the other. The novel is propelled forward by Zapata's tact of leaving one of the stories at a suspenseful moment to turn his attention to the other. Furthermore, the connections between the two stories prove increasingly more complex and satisfying as the novel progresses. Maxwell's journey during the Depression and Saul and Javier's during Hurricane Katrina illuminate each other and underscore the ways in which people's lives are shaped by the larger forces of history.

While *The Lost Book of Adana Moreau* is not a science-fiction novel, Zapata himself is clearly steeped in the genre. He includes long lists of science-fiction authors and novels in his book, and several characters refer to the influential pulp publication *Weird Tales*. Maxwell's research as a theoretical physicist focuses on the existence of parallel universes. His life's work has essentially been to prove and to make possible the imaginary worlds of his mother's novels. The multiverse becomes a powerful trope for understanding the intersection of choice and chance in one's life. In this novel, so many characters' futures turn on a seemingly random act. Saul, for example, thinks about what his life might have been like had his parents not boarded the particular bus in Tel Aviv that terrorists targeted. If each choice that one makes leads to ramifying parallel universes, then in some alternate reality Saul and his parents are living together happily. The whole concept can, in turns, bedevil or console. Is it better, ultimately, to accept that the arrow of time moves in one direction and that the past is irredeemable, or to imagine worlds in which one has suffered less? Science fiction writes large the latter impulse: the human capacity for speculation and for imagining different worlds.

Another powerful element in this novel is the library of audio tapes that Benjamin leaves behind. A historian, Benjamin was more concerned with people than events, and over the course of his life he conducted extensive interviews with ordinary people on a great range of subjects. In his own way, Benjamin also discovered the principle of the multiverse: "To him, a narrative path was to be followed even if it split off into another path and then another. After all, each path carried the probability of all the others." With his seemingly infinite patience for and interest in other people's stories, Benjamin becomes a stand-in for Zapata and an embodiment of the organizing principle of this novel. Here, too, is another Borges-like library and another garden of forking paths. Benjamin's library of past voices, like the lists of novelists real and imagined that are interspersed across this novel, speak to Zapata's interest in how storytelling can recapture lost lives and silenced voices.

The Lost Book of Adana Moreau was well received by critics overall. Writing for National Public Radio (NPR), Jason Heller said, "Zapata tackles huge feelings and ideas in *Lost Book*, but he makes it look effortless." He considered the novel "a gripping, lyrical narrative full of eerie parallels and profound connections." In a review for the *Washington Post*, Paul Di Filippo wrote, "Zapata's carefully crafted prose oscillates between matter-of-fact and lyrically poetic, a tonal range that provides a very pleasant reading experience." Despite its pivoting around brutal historical events, the book is "about taking steps to create the world you wish to inhabit," he added. According to Chancellor, Zapata's narrative trope of the multiverse allows him to successfully explore "the gulf between universes of human experiences."

Zapata's ambitious first novel is a gripping tale of loss and reconciliation and a powerful meditation on the ways in which an individual's life is shaped by history.

Author Biography

Michael Zapata is an educator and one of the founders of *MAKE*, a literary magazine. *The Lost Book of Adana Moreau* is his first novel.

Matthew J. Bolton

Review Sources

Chancellor, Will. "Generations of Exiles Collide in Post-Katrina New Orleans." Review of *The Lost Book of Adana Moreau*, by Michael Zapata. *The New York Times*, 31 Jan. 2020, www.nytimes.com/2020/01/31/books/review/michael-zapata-the-lost-book-of-adana-moreau.html. Accessed 22 Dec. 2020.

Di Filippo, Paul. "Bibliophiles Love the Mystery of a Missing Manuscript. 'The Lost Book of Adana Moreau' Is Just What They're Looking For." Review of *The Lost Book of Adana Moreau*, by Michael Zapata. *The Washington Post*, 2 Feb. 2020, www.washingtonpost.com/entertainment/books/bibliophiles-love-the-mystery-of-a-missing-manuscript-the-lost-book-of-adana-moreau-is-just-what-theyre-looking-for/2020/02/02/2cffc7d0-436b-11ea-b503-2b077c436617_story.html. Accessed 22 Dec. 2020.

Heller, Jason. "Multiple Universes Fill the Pages of 'The Lost Book of Adana Moreau.'" Review of *The Lost Book of Adana Moreau*, by Michael Zapata. *NPR*, 5 Feb. 2020, www.npr.org/2020/02/05/802654221/multiple-universes-fill-the-pages-of-the-lost-book-of-adana-moreau. Accessed 22 Dec. 2020.

Review of *The Lost Book of Adana Moreau*, by Michael Zapata. *Kirkus*, 11 Nov. 2019, www.kirkusreviews.com/book-reviews/michael-zapata/the-lost-book-of-adana-moreau/. Accessed 22 Dec. 2020.

Review of *The Lost Book of Adana Moreau*, by Michael Zapata. *Publishers Weekly*, 25 Sept. 2019, www.publishersweekly.com/978-1-335-01012-4. Accessed 22 Dec. 2020.

Memorial Drive
A Daughter's Memoir

Author: Natasha Trethewey (b. 1966)
Publisher: Ecco (New York). 224 pp.
Type of work: Memoir
Time: Largely 1960s–the 2010s
Locales: Mississippi; Atlanta, Georgia

In Memorial Drive, *Natasha Trethewey recounts being raised in Mississippi and Georgia following the civil rights movement as the child of a Black mother and a White father and her mother's subsequent abuse and murder at the hands of her second husband. Trethewey writes with lyrical clarity about the loss of her mother and the impact of a Southern childhood and domestic abuse on her growth personally and as a writer.*

Principal personages

NATASHA TRETHEWEY, a poet and the daughter of Gwendolyn Turnbough and Eric Trethewey
GWENDOLYN TURNBOUGH, her mother, a social worker killed in 1985 by her second husband
ERIC TRETHEWEY, her father, a poet and teacher
JOEL GRIMMETTE, her stepfather, a Vietnam War veteran

Natasha Trethewey's powerful book *Memorial Drive: A Daughter's Memoir* (2020) is partly a reflective tribute to her murdered mother, partly an analysis of the American South colliding with the civil rights era and its aftermath, and partly a story of coming of age as an artist. Trethewey weaves these threads together seamlessly, offering not only a loving and moving portrait of her mother, who was killed in her prime at the age of forty, just as she was beginning to achieve some of her hard-won career goals as a social worker, but also an account of how she learned to process the trauma of this profound loss and cope with survivor's guilt. Trethewey deftly draws connections between this tragedy, the ensuing trauma, and the oppression and racial injustice of the lingering "Old South" mentality, and then transforms them through the power of art. Additionally, Trethewey puts her significant gifts as a writer on display, particularly through her vivid and lyrical prose, her perceptive shifts in writing style, and her use of metaphor to enhance the story. By the end of *Memorial Drive*, she has provided a full and vibrant portrait of her mother and has lit the way forward for those who have suffered trauma and severe loss.

To tell her story, Trethewey chose to organize the events in a broadly chronological way while dividing the memoir into two parts and then sections, each with its own unique focus. Thus, after the prologue, she begins by depicting her birth and childhood while reflecting on her parents' loving but complicated relationship. She relates that she was born in Mississippi in 1966 to a Black mother, Gwendolyn Turnbough, and a White, Canadian father, Eric Trethewey. They were college sweethearts, but due to the existence of laws that did not allow people of different races to marry, they had to cross state lines into Ohio to wed legally. As a child, Trethewey recognized that she was treated differently in the community when she was with her Black mother as opposed to her White father, who was treated with much more respect; yet when she was in the cradle of her family home with her parents and her mother's extended family who lived within walking distance, she felt safe and deeply loved. However, when she was six, her parents divorced, and her mother moved the two of them to Atlanta, Georgia, to pursue her independence and continue with her career goals. It was a difficult adjustment for Trethewey, made more difficult when her mother began a relationship with Joel Grimmette, a troubled Vietnam War veteran who was jealous and abusive. Poignantly, she clearly notes in her descriptions of the early days of his presence in their lives that she had felt something unsettling about him. They all moved into a house together, where the abuse escalated. After her mother had finally managed to get Trethewey and her half brother, Joey, out of the house and into an apartment on Memorial Drive, as established in the prologue, she was shot and killed at the complex by Grimmette, whom she had divorced by that point. As the large chronological arc of the story unfolds, Trethewey also includes affecting sections recounting her first meaningful efforts as a writer and the influence and implications of living, for a time, near the base of Stone Mountain, with its relief carvings of Jefferson Davis, Robert E. Lee, and Stonewall Jackson serving as a memorial to Confederate leaders during the Civil War who fought for the right to keep African Americans as slaves; she writes that her mother had been "murdered in the shadow" of that landmark.

Natasha Trethewey

Although the chronology of events is clearly established, Trethewey further organizes the many specific instances of racial prejudice or trauma by dividing the memoir into two parts. Part 1, after the short prologue in which she discusses her mother's death and why she chose to return decades later to examine it more directly, focuses on her childhood and the growing abuse against her mother. In part 2, the abuse escalates, Trethewey shares the events that led to her possession of her mother's police file, and she includes transcripts of phone conversations, recorded with equipment installed by the local police department, between her mother and stepfather. These transcripts concretely document her stepfather's psychological abuse and the physical harm he promises to inflict while also allowing readers to know and more deeply understand Trethewey's mother through her actual determined, careful, yet almost empathetic responses. Interspersed between subsections of titled chapters are bracketed sections in which the space between the brackets is blank. In these sections, Trethewey includes dream sequences and personal insights. Thus, while the memoir is largely chronological, Trethewey enriches the content and structure by skillfully intertwining seemingly disparate events and varying the writing styles and perspective.

Trethewey's decision to change the writing style at different points in the memoir, including switching from first person to writing in second person for a chapter midway through, signals her shifts in thinking and represents her long struggle to cope as she progresses through topics and events while also showing her mother fully as a parent, spouse, and professional as well as a Black woman suffering from extensive domestic abuse. Through these shifts, Trethewey portrays her mother's multifaceted personality and struggles as well as her own. Although Trethewey addresses themes of abuse, power, and racial prejudice with depth and imagination, one of the most inventive elements of the memoir is her use of language. As a renowned poet, she has received many accolades for her poems, but her prose is equally riveting. The first section of the book is especially lyrical. Here, she writes in poetic detail of her idyllic early childhood with her extended family. In the following example, she reminisces about her Aunt Lizzie and her Uncle Son, a local night club owner:

> Unlike most other houses in the neighborhood, theirs was fully air-conditioned, and Aunt Lizzie kept it cold as a funeral parlor, the lace curtains drawn against the afternoon heat. A large Bible lay open on a reading stand beneath portraits of Jesus, Kennedy, and King. When Son sat with my father some evenings in the front room, the women in the back of the house laughing around the kitchen table, I would lie at his feet taking in the heady scent of his cigars, the glow of bourbon swirled in a cut crystal glass, and the sound of his voice, low and lilting.

Trethewey's writing is elegant, and her astute use of details sets a scene that is relaxed, yet illustrates the sociopolitical landscape through the description of the pictures prominently displayed together of President John F. Kennedy, civil rights leader Martin Luther King Jr., and Jesus Christ.

In addition to the lyrical nature of the first section, Trethewey also includes some dreamlike passages throughout the memoir and heightens the language of other passages with metaphor. A dream sequence opens and closes the memoir, and depicts a dream Trethewey has often about meeting and walking with her mother on a path and then being interrupted by an outsider:

> It's then that my mother turns to me, then that I see it: a hole, the size of a quarter, in the center of her forehead. From it comes a light so bright, so piercing, that I suffer the kind

of momentary blindness brought on by staring at the sun—her face nothing but light ringed in darkness when she speaks: "Do you know what it means to have a wound that never heals?"

The "wound that never heals" is literal and figurative, and it is an image Trethewey effectively returns to often in *Memorial Drive* as she continues to grieve and work toward healing. In terms of metaphor, she applies that concept through the book's title, *Memorial Drive*, which was both the literal street they lived on in Atlanta and figurative in the sense that the book is a memorial to her mother. Trethewey also aptly and movingly compares her mother to a bird after her stepfather is sent to prison, writing, "My mother is flying. She is smiling, her slender arms undulating as if they are wings, as if she is a bird." For the first time, Trethewey sees her mother as free.

From the middle part of the memoir until the end, Trethewey's writing is more expository in its depiction of abuse. In the middle section, especially, she details her mother's and her own abuse at the hands of her stepfather. The writing crackles here with vibrant details, particularly when her stepfather breaks the lock on her diary, a gift from her mother on her twelfth birthday to support her writing efforts. Once Trethewey is aware of the violation, she responds by writing entries she knows her stepfather will read, addressing him directly. She is free to express her anger since she knows if her stepfather complains to her mother, his crime will be revealed. Not only is writing in her diary one of the first commitments she makes to writing, but her entries give her an unexpected and powerful way to respond to an abuser.

In the last section of the book, Trethewey shifts yet again to include not only her own writing about the escalation of abuse, but also numerous passages from transcripts in the police file and excerpts from police reports her mother filed. Trethewey allows her mother to speak for herself, thereby allowing readers to hear her mother's voice directly rather than through Trethewey's interpretation or description of her. In these transcripts, Gwendolyn Turnbough emerges fully, displaying caring and kindness but also making it quite clear that she will not continue to be a victim.

Critics overwhelmingly applauded Trethewey's efforts in *Memorial Drive*, with Ann Levin for *USA Today* calling it "an exquisitely written, elegiac memoir" and Imani Perry, in a review for the *Boston Globe*, describing it as "a luminous and searing work of prose." While some labeled *Memorial Drive* as true crime, most critics recognize that it is much more than that. The memoir does offer some details of the abuse and murder of Trethewey's mother, but it also explores Trethewey's trauma and how it shaped how she began to see herself as a writer. It is as much about healing as it is about loss. In *Memorial Drive*, Trethewey investigates, with raw insight and vivid, elegant writing, grief and how to survive it.

Author Biography
Poet Natasha Trethewey won the 2007 Pulitzer Prize in Poetry for her collection *Native Guard* (2006) and served as Poet Laureate of the United States for two consecutive terms (2012 and 2013). *Memorial Drive* is her first memoir.

Marybeth Rua-Larsen

Review Sources

Laymon, Kiese Makeba. "In 'Memorial Drive' a Poet Evokes Her Childhood and Confronts Her Mother's Murder." Review of *Memorial Drive: A Daughter's Memoir*, by Natasha Trethewey. *The New York Times*, 30 July 2020, www.nytimes.com/2020/07/30/books/review/memorial-drive-natastha-trethewey.html. Accessed 3 Nov. 2020.

Levin, Ann. "'Memorial Drive': A Former Poet Laureate Tries to Make Sense of a Beloved Mother's Slaying." Review of *Memorial Drive: A Daughter's Memoir*, by Natasha Trethewey. *USA Today*, 26 July 2020, www.usatoday.com/story/entertainment/books/2020/07/26/memorial-drive-poet-tries-make-sense-her-mothers-murder/5482277002/. Accessed 3 Nov. 2020.

Page, Lisa. "In 'Memorial Drive,' Natasha Trethewey Reclaims Her Mother's Life from the Man Who Took It." Review of *Memorial Drive: A Daughter's Memoir*, by Natasha Trethewey. *The Washington Post*, 17 Aug. 2020, www.washingtonpost.com/entertainment/books/in-memorial-drive-natasha-trethewey-reclaims-her-mothers-life-from-the-man-who-took-it/2020/07/31/7fabc8bc-d006-11ea-8d32-1ebf4e9d8e0d_story.html. Accessed 3 Nov. 2020.

Perry, Imani. "Living with Woundedness." Review of *Memorial Drive: A Daughter's Memoir*, by Natasha Trethewey. *The Boston Globe*, 27 July 2020, www.bostonglobe.com/2020/07/23/arts/living-with-woundedness/. Accessed 3 Nov. 2020.

Wabuke, Hope. "A Daughter Unearths and Remembers Trauma in 'Memorial Drive.'" Review of *Memorial Drive: A Daughter's Memoir*, by Natasha Trethewey. *NPR*, 27 July 2020, www.npr.org/2020/07/27/895146831/a-daughter-unearths-and-remembers-trauma-in-memorial-drive. Accessed 3 Nov. 2020.

Mexican Gothic

Author: Silvia Moreno-Garcia (b. 1981)
Publisher: Del Rey (New York). 320 pp.
Type of work: Novel
Time: 1950s
Locale: Mexico

Silvia Moreno-Garcia's Mexican Gothic *follows a young socialite as she investigates her cousin's claims that her new husband is trying to kill her and that her new home is an evil, living being. The novel reframes classic gothic horror tropes in a Latin American setting.*

Principal characters

NOEMÍ TABOADA, a wealthy socialite who aspires to be an anthropologist
CATALINA DOYLE, her cousin, a young woman suffering from a mysterious illness
VIRGIL DOYLE, Catalina's husband, the son of an English expatriate who once owned a silver mine
HOWARD DOYLE, Virgil's father, a tyrannical old man in poor health
FLORENCE DOYLE, Virgil's cousin, a stern woman tasked with caring for Catalina
FRANCIS DOYLE, Florence's son, a shy young man who seems to want to help Noemí

The title of *Mexican Gothic* (2020) boldly states the book's intentions: to take what has historically been a very Anglo genre and reimagine it in a Mexican context. Dominated by authors like Ann Radcliffe, the Brontë sisters, Daphne du Maurier, and Shirley Jackson, the gothic novel has mostly been the domain of White British and, occasionally, American authors. In transplanting the conventions of the genre to 1950s rural Mexico, Silvia Moreno-Garcia finds new resonances in the familiar tropes of once illustrious, now impoverished families and mysterious, brooding men hiding dark secrets, living in decaying manors.

The novel follows Noemí Taboada, the daughter of a wealthy Mexico City family. Her father expects her to devote her time to searching for a suitable husband, but Noemí has other ideas; she wants to attend university and study anthropology. As the story begins, her father summons her home from a party to relay some concerning family news. Her cousin Catalina, who married the Englishman Virgil Doyle after a very short courtship, has written a frantic letter begging for help. The letter talks about ghosts and speaks of the Doyles' house, High Place, as if it is a living—and malicious—entity. Noemí's father believes that Catalina may be mentally ill and wants Noemí to visit her and, if necessary, make discreet arrangements with a psychiatrist.

Silvia Moreno-Garcia

He offers his daughter an unexpected deal: if she goes to High Place to find out what is happening to Catalina, he will allow her to enroll at the university.

Noemí obliges—as much out of concern for Catalina as out of self-interest—and travels to the remote mountainside where the Doyles live. Catalina seems strangely placid most of the time but has strange outbursts in which she insists that she sees ghosts and that the house is trying to take over her mind. Virgil assures Noemí that this is merely a symptom of Catalina's struggle with a case of tuberculosis, and the family doctor backs him up, but Noemí, who has seen the disease before, is not convinced.

Noemí has few allies in High Place. Virgil behaves oddly toward her, sometimes friendly and sometimes antagonistic. His father, Howard, is a eugenicist who seems to delight in forcing Noemí to defend her value as a member of an ethnic group he considers inferior, under the guise of discussing anthropology. He brags that he has kept his own bloodline "pure" through inbreeding: Virgil's mother was his cousin. Virgil's cousin, Florence, who is the main person responsible for caring for Catalina, is cold and strict. She rarely allows Noemí to see her cousin, insisting that Catalina needs rest.

The only member of the family who seems sympathetic is Florence's son, Francis, a shy and awkward young man with an interest in mycology. With his help, Noemí travels to the nearby village to speak to the local doctor and a folk healer about Catalina's condition. From the latter, she learns that many of the workers in the Doyle family's now-defunct silver mine died of an illness with symptoms strangely similar to Catalina's. She also learns that Virgil's older sister, Ruth, went on a murderous rampage shortly before her planned wedding, shooting many of her relatives and then herself. Howard, Virgil, Florence, and Francis are the sole survivors of this massacre.

As Noemí spends more time in the house, she begins to have strange dreams of festering sores on the walls and a woman whose face is obscured, or perhaps replaced, by golden light. She sleepwalks and wakes up in strange places. She remains determined, however, to discover the secrets of the Doyle family's bloody history and, hopefully, rescue Catalina.

The gothic is a genre that deals heavily in metaphor, with supernatural aspects standing in for real-life horrors that are, perhaps, difficult to talk about directly. In *Mexican Gothic*, the true horror at the root of the story is colonialism. The Doyles, a European family, came to Mexico to benefit from the land's riches and brought with them sickness, decay, and death. Virgil, in particular, has a superficial glamor that is seductive to Catalina and Noemí, much in the way that the culture of the colonizer and the things it seems to offer may hold some fascination for the colonized. But, underneath his veneer of charm, there is only violence and the desire to control others. This subtext gives *Mexican Gothic* freshness, originality, and relevance despite its use of stock characters and plot points that are, in some cases, centuries old.

There are also feminist themes. Noemí's desire to get an education rather than pursue marriage is underscored by the consequences of Catalina's marriage. Marrying Virgil has left her trapped—she is confined to her room, and even if she could escape from it, she could not get down the mountain on her own. She no longer has any control over her own life; she seems listless, resigned to her situation. It is no coincidence that Noemí's attempt to help her is in part motivated by the bargain with her father to allow her to pursue her studies—in rescuing Catalina, she hopes to also rescue herself from the same fate. The book nods to an older gothic take on this theme: Catalina's belief that there are "people in the walls" and Noemí's dream, or hallucination, of kaleidoscopic shifting patterns on the wallpaper are reminiscent of Charlotte Perkins Gilman's "The Yellow Wallpaper" (1892), a short story about a woman who has been confined to her room by her husband and eventually comes to believe that there is a woman trapped in the wall.

Critical response to *Mexican Gothic* was largely positive. Many compared the book favorably to Charlotte Brontë's *Jane Eyre* (1847) and Daphne du Maurier's *Rebecca* (1938), arguing that *Mexican Gothic* reinvigorates these novels' somewhat dated narrative of a young woman learning the secrets of an old manor house and its mysterious and sometimes frightening owner.

A key difference, most reviewers agreed, is the character of Noemí, who is neither mousy like Jane Eyre nor naive and easily intimidated like the narrator of *Rebecca*. Rather, she is intelligent and filled with determination. Maureen Corrigan, for NPR, praised her "fight-or-flight feminist resolve," while Ian Mond and Paula Guran, for *Locus*, wrote, "Noemí is the perfect gothic heroine: beautiful, smart, and spunky but hardheaded enough to ignore all the signs to escape when she can." To call someone a gothic heroine calls to mind a character who is passive, merely reacting to whatever happens to her, but Noemí is proactive, despite the Doyles' attempts to limit what she is able to do.

Reviewers were also nearly unanimous in their appreciation for the novel's themes of colonialism, racism, and sexism. For example, Laura Miller, reviewing the book for *Slate*, wrote that "while sustaining the gothic's old-fashioned appeal, Moreno-Garcia converts its motifs into a supple metaphor for colonialism." Corrigan wrote that the novel "isn't simply escapist" and "explores how, for its independent female characters, marriage threatens to be a premature burial."

Most reviewers also took note of another departure from the conventions of the gothic novel, in that while the early parts of the book lean mainly on a foreboding atmosphere and suggestions of darkness just beneath the surface, later parts delve into a more gory and visceral form of horror. Mond and Guran noted that the simmering tension of the earlier chapters "comes to a ferocious boil with a memorable, albeit stomach-churning, climax that nearly put me off a certain food." About the novel as a whole, Corrigan wrote that "if you don't mind some gore, it's inventive and smart, injecting the Gothic formula with some fresh blood." Miller, meanwhile, compared the later parts to the work of acclaimed Mexican director Guillermo del Toro, creator of such films as *Pan's Labyrinth* (2006) and *The Shape of Water* (2017), as well as the gothic *Crimson Peak* (2015). The shift in style is, Miller wrote, "an audacious and satisfying move," because Moreno-Garcia's "skill with the baroque and hallucinatory is peerless."

Classic gothic works are often characterized by heightened descriptive language, and reviewers felt that Moreno-Garcia created a successful pastiche of this style in *Mexican Gothic*, particularly in her descriptions of High Place and its inhabitants. In her original letter, Catalina writes that the house is "sick with rot, stinks of decay, brims with every single evil and cruel sentiment." Upon seeing it, Noemí compares it to "a great, quiet gargoyle" and "the abandoned shell of a snail." She describes Virgil as hiding his true nature behind "a veneer of wretched civility," Howard as "a corpse, afflicted by the ravages of putrefaction," and Francis as having the face of "a plaster saint haunted by his impending martyrdom." "Moreno-Garcia has a sharp ear for the slightly antiquated and sinister language of the Gothic," Corrigan concluded.

Most of all, critics agreed that the novel is a gripping read. "It's as if a supernatural power compels us to turn the pages," Carol Memmott wrote for the *Washington Post*, while Guran and Mond called the book "a dark and delectable concoction readers can't help but relish." It is no easy feat to combine a thrilling plot with insightful social commentary; it is *Mexican Gothic*'s deft interweaving of these two aspects that makes it one of the most significant speculative fiction novels of 2020.

Author Biography

Silvia Moreno-Garcia is the best-selling author of *Signal to Noise* (2015), *Certain Dark Things* (2016), *The Beautiful Ones* (2017), and *Gods of Jade and Shadow* (2019). She is also the editor of the World Fantasy Award–winning horror anthology *She Walks in Shadows* (2015).

Emma Joyce

Review Sources

Corrigan, Maureen. "'Jane Eyre' Meets 'Dracula' in This Sharp, Inventive 'Mexican Gothic' Tale." Review of *Mexican Gothic*, by Silvia Moreno-Garcia. *Fresh Air*, NPR, 9 July 2020, www.npr.org/2020/07/09/889365673/jane-eyre-meets-dracula-in-this-sharp-inventive-mexican-gothic-tale. Accessed 16 Nov. 2020.

Guran, Paula, and Ian Mond. Review of *Mexican Gothic*, by Silvia Moreno-Garcia. *Locus*, 5 July 2020, locusmag.com/2020/07/ian-mond-and-paula-guran-review-mexican-gothic-by-silvia-moreno-garcia. Accessed 16 Nov. 2020.

Memmott, Carol. "'Mexican Gothic' Is a Creepy, Intoxicating Mystery That's Almost Impossible to Put Down." Review of *Mexican Gothic*, by Silvia Moreno-Garcia. *The Washington Post*, 30 June 2020, www.washingtonpost.com/entertainment/books/mexican-gothic-is-a-creepy-intoxicating-mystery-thats-almost-impossible-to-put-down/2020/06/30/e6f974f2-ba02-11ea-8cf5-9c1b8d7f84c6_story.html. Accessed 16 Nov. 2020.

Review of *Mexican Gothic*, by Silvia Moreno-Garcia. *Kirkus Reviews*, 1 May 2020. *Literary Reference Center Plus*, search.ebscohost.com/login.aspx?direct=true&db=lkh&AN=143001418&site=lrc-plus. Accessed 16 Nov. 2020.

Miller, Laura. "This Haunting New Bestseller Is Part du Maurier, Part del Toro." Review of *Mexican Gothic*, by Silvia Moreno-Garcia. *Slate*, 27 July 2020, slate.com/culture/2020/07/mexican-gothic-book-review-silvia-moreno-garcia-novel.html. Accessed 16 Nov. 2020.

The Mirror & the Light

Author: Hilary Mantel (b. 1952)
Publisher: Henry Holt (New York). 784 pp.
Type of work: Novel
Time: 1536–40
Locale: England

In The Mirror & the Light, *the third installment in the* Wolf Hall *trilogy, Hilary Mantel brings to life the final years of Thomas Cromwell, adviser to Henry VIII of England.*

Principal characters
THOMAS CROMWELL, a trusted adviser to Henry VIII, the Lord Privy Seal and Viceregent in Spirituals; based on the historical personage of the same name
HENRY VIII, the king of England and a member of the House of Tudor; based on the historical personage
JANE SEYMOUR, the third wife of Henry VIII, an English noblewoman; based on the historical personage
ANNA OF CLEVES, the fourth wife of Henry VIII, a German noblewoman; based on the historical personage
MARY, the eldest daughter of Henry VIII, the sole surviving child of former queen Katherine of Aragon; based on the historical personage
GREGORY CROMWELL, Cromwell's son; based on the historical personage

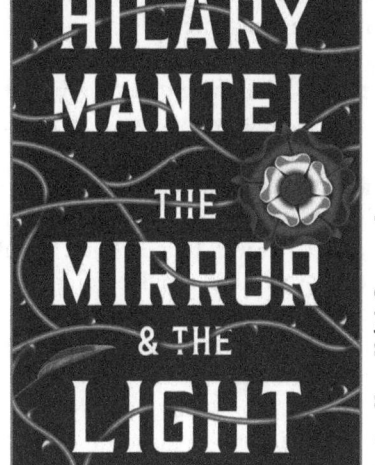

Hilary Mantel, an accomplished writer since the 1980s, gained further widespread acclaim beginning in the year 2009, which saw the publication of her ambitious novel *Wolf Hall*. The first work in a trilogy, *Wolf Hall* delves into the life and career of Thomas Cromwell, an adviser to King Henry VIII of England who was infamous both during and long after his lifetime. Popular among both readers and critics, *Wolf Hall* and its sequel, *Bring Up the Bodies* (2012), earned widespread recognition, winning Mantel two prestigious Booker Prizes and inspiring an award-winning 2015 television adaptation and a Broadway play. Works of historical fiction, both novels focus heavily on real-world events and Cromwell's involvement in them; *Wolf Hall*, for instance, covers a large swath of Cromwell's life but focuses especially on the 1520s and early 1530s, a significant period in which Cromwell, the common-born son of a tradesman, rose to prominence thanks in part to his association with then-cardinal Thomas Wolsey. He subsequently became a key adviser to Henry VIII and helped to facilitate the annulment of Henry's marriage to Katherine of Aragon, which in turn allowed Henry to marry his second wife, Anne Boleyn. All the while, he encouraged Henry's break with the Catholic Church, an act that ushered in the English Protestant Reformation. Mantel's second book about Cromwell, *Bring Up the Bodies*, covers a period that is far shorter but no less significant, spanning the years 1535 and 1536. During that period, Cromwell was once more called upon to help rid Henry of an unwanted wife, as Anne, much like Katherine before her, had failed to produce a male heir. Turning against the woman whose marriage to the king he had once supported, Cromwell framed Anne for infidelity and treason. This provided Henry with the grounds to annul the marriage, marry his third wife, Jane Seymour, and execute Anne for her purported crimes. With her 2020 novel, *The Mirror & the Light*, Mantel returns to the Tudor-era England of *Wolf Hall* and *Bring Up the Bodies* for a third and final time, completing the trilogy with a work chronicling the downfall and death that have long awaited Cromwell.

Hilary Mantel

Both picking up where *Bring Up the Bodies* left off and foreshadowing the bloody fate awaiting Cromwell himself several years in the future, *The Mirror & the Light* begins just after Anne Boleyn's execution, carried out by a hired swordsman brought in from France. That event is effectively the culmination of Cromwell's months of effort to dispose of Anne on Henry's behalf, and for Cromwell and other close allies of the king, Anne's death should be a triumph. Yet, the moment is an unprecedented one—Cromwell's son, Gregory, inquires after the event if a queen of England had ever been executed before—and appears to leave many who witnessed it feeling conflicted or uneasy. While Cromwell later muses about whether the execution of Anne was right in the moral sense, he is steadfast in his belief that it was the right course of action in light of its benefit to England, as it enabled Henry to marry his third wife, Jane Seymour, and attempt once again to produce a son to serve as his heir. As the novel progresses, that long hoped-for event does come to pass, as Jane gives birth to Henry's sole surviving male heir, the future King Edward VI. However, Jane dies from complications related to childbirth not long afterward, a result that is tragic for Henry and the members of the Seymour family while also representing an unseen threat toward Cromwell, setting in motion the series of events that will lead to his downfall.

In addition to advising Henry on matters related to his marriages, Cromwell engages in a number of different projects over the course of the novel. Among them are efforts to further the spread and acceptance of the Protestant Reformation in England by arranging for the creation of an English-language translation of the Bible, a work that would have been considered heretical under the Catholic Church. He likewise dedicates himself at times to assisting Henry's eldest daughter, Mary, the sole surviving child from the king's first marriage to Katherine of Aragon, prompting some around them to believe that the widowed Cromwell aspires to marry Mary and thus tie himself to the royal family. While his true intentions are often difficult for others to ascertain, and easy for his enemies to misinterpret willfully, Mantel gives readers perhaps the closest view into the man's thoughts possible, presenting the narrative in a third-person, present-tense point of view that places the reader almost within Cromwell's mind, forcing the reader to perceive events largely as he does. One particularly intriguing facet of the novel's style is the infrequency with which the narration mentions Cromwell by name: Cromwell is typically referred to as simply "he" or "him," and on occasion as "he, Cromwell." While that stylistic choice can at times render sentences confusing, as Cromwell often participates in conversations with others to whom the pronoun "he" could refer, it ultimately contributes to the distinctive style and tone that pervades all three books in Mantel's trilogy, *The Mirror & the Light* included.

While Cromwell's interactions with a number of characters prove crucial to the novel, no relationship is more important than his relationship with Henry, for whom he has served as a trusted adviser for some time. His success in accomplishing desired tasks for the king, however, has made him enemies. Others around Henry desire the king's favor and resent Cromwell for possessing it, while some nobles oppose Cromwell because of actions he has taken against members of their families. Indeed, in an era in which strategic intermarriages bind many of England's aristocratic families together, targeting any one individual or family seems a risky prospect: for every queen who is executed, countless relatives remain alive to hold a grudge. All of those factors appear to play a role in Cromwell's fall from grace, an apparently inevitable event that begins in earnest following the death of Jane Seymour. After her death, Cromwell is tasked with helping Henry find yet another wife, ideally one who would both birth additional heirs and—particularly important to Cromwell—further solidify England's religious separation from the Church in Rome. He supports Henry's betrothal to Anna of Cleves, a noblewoman from a German region with Protestant sympathies, whom Henry soon marries. Displeased with his new wife, however, Henry swiftly has the marriage annulled and visits much of his displeasure on Cromwell. Cromwell's enemies spread accusations regarding his loyalty, turning Henry away from his former adviser for good. The novel concludes with Cromwell's execution for treason he did not commit, a death that mirrors those he imposed on Anne Boleyn and others.

As a work of historical fiction, *The Mirror & the Light* is rich with historical detail, reflecting years of extensive research and worldbuilding that Mantel put into each novel in her Cromwell trilogy. The novel's extensive cast of characters is made up largely of real people, and even some of the few original characters—such as Cromwell's illegitimate daughter, Jenneke—are based loosely on individuals thought to have existed. While the historical Cromwell's own story ended at the moment of his death, the stories of those around him did not, and a concluding author's note reflects that, recounting the real-world fates of many of the individuals who appear in Mantel's work. Of particular interest are the portions of the author's note concerning Henry's family and that of Cromwell himself. Mantel points out that following the death of Henry's younger daughter, Queen Elizabeth I, in 1603, the Tudor line died out. The Cromwell line, however, continued on through both Cromwell's son, Gregory, and his nephew

Richard, to oddly fitting results: a great-grandson of Richard was Oliver Cromwell, who ruled England as lord protector during the 1650s, following the English Civil War. Thomas Cromwell, despite the insistence of some of his enemies, did not aspire to overthrow the monarchy and claim power for himself, but his distant relative Oliver went on to do just that.

Highly anticipated prior to its publication, *The Mirror & the Light* received largely positive reviews and became an international best seller upon its release. Many critics identified the novel as a strong follow-up to Mantel's earlier Cromwell novels, and the anonymous critic for *Publishers Weekly* suggested, in a starred review, that the third installment in the trilogy might be "even better" than *Wolf Hall* and *Bring Up the Bodies*. Writing for *Kirkus*, another anonymous critic described the novel as "brilliant" and characterized its opening sentence dealing with Anne Boleyn's execution as "perfect." The *Kirkus* reviewer likewise commented approvingly on the novel's distinctive narrative voice, a facet that also appealed to *Atlantic* reviewer Judith Shulevitz. In addition to highlighting the novel's narration, which adheres closely and powerfully to Cromwell's point of view, Shulevitz wrote that Mantel succeeded in turning Cromwell into a "tragic hero" in the classical mold. Writing for the *Guardian*, Stephanie Merritt noted that as Cromwell was a historical figure whose downfall and death were widely documented, the events depicted in *The Mirror & the Light* are inevitable and expected, yet Mantel "creates suspense and apprehension where none should exist," constructing a lyrical yet muscular narrative that is "shaped as meticulously as any thriller." *New Yorker* critic Daniel Mendelsohn expressed appreciation for the novel's "sumptuous prose"' and "swoony passages."

While most professional reviews of the novel were positive, critics were divided over its pacing and scope. The reviewer for *Kirkus*, for instance, commented that the momentum falters at times and the novel "does occasionally idle." Mendelsohn similarly critiqued the novel's length, describing the work as "bloated and only occasionally captivating," and lamenting that intriguing themes of the novel, such as Cromwell's hubris, were ultimately "too submerged beneath the exhausting accumulation of events and details." By contrast, Genevieve Valentine remarked for NPR that the storytelling of the final installment was indeed slower than its predecessors "but no less effective for it." Fans of Mantel's previous Wolf Hall entries and lovers of the Tudor period will likely find Mantel's latest tome a satisfying read, whether for its language or its action.

Author Biography

Hilary Mantel is the author of more than a dozen books, including the Booker Prize–winning historical novels *Wolf Hall* (2009) and *Bring Up the Bodies* (2012). Prior installments in the Wolf Hall trilogy proved immensely popular, appearing in dozens of languages and selling millions of copies.

Joy Crelin

Review Sources

Mendelsohn, Daniel. "Great Matter." Review of *The Mirror & the Light*, by Hilary Mantel. *The New Yorker*, vol. 96, no. 4, 16 Mar. 2020, pp. 80–86. *Literary Reference Center Plus*, search.ebscohost.com/login.aspx?direct=true&db=lkh&AN=142158780&site=lrc-plus. Accessed 15 Feb. 2021.

Merritt, Stephanie. "*The Mirror and the Light* by Hilary Mantel Review—a Shoo-In for the Booker Prize." *The Guardian*, 1 Mar. 2020, www.theguardian.com/books/2020/mar/01/the-mirror-and-the-light-hilary-mantel-review-thomas-cromwell. Accessed 15 Feb. 2021.

Review of *The Mirror & the Light*, by Hilary Mantel. *Kirkus Reviews*, vol. 88, no. 7, Apr. 2020. *Literary Reference Center Plus*, search.ebscohost.com/login.aspx?direct=true&db=lkh&AN=142488844&site=lrc-plus. Accessed 17 Feb. 2021.

Review of *The Mirror & the Light*, by Hilary Mantel. *Publishers Weekly*, 5 Mar. 2020, www.publishersweekly.com/978-0-8050-9660-6. Accessed 15 Feb. 2021.

Shulevitz, Judith. "Hilary Mantel Takes Thomas Cromwell Down." Review of *The Mirror & the Light*, by Hilary Mantel. *The Atlantic*, vol. 325, no. 3, Apr. 2020, pp. 80–83. *Literary Reference Center Plus*, search.ebscohost.com/login.aspx?direct=true&db=lkh&AN=142095419&site=lrc-plus. Accessed 17 Feb. 2021.

Valentine, Genevieve. "'The Mirror & the Light' Is a Triumphant End to a Spellbinding Story." Review of *The Mirror & the Light*, by Hilary Mantel. *NPR*, 2 Mar. 2020, www.npr.org/2020/03/02/809727472/the-mirror-the-light-is-a-triumphant-end-to-a-spellbinding-story. Accessed 15 Feb. 2021.

Miss Benson's Beetle

Author: Rachel Joyce
Publisher: Dial Press (New York). 368 pp.
Type of work: Novel
Time: 1914–83
Locales: London and New Caledonia

After an incident at the school where middle-aged Margery Benson has taught for years, she decides to embrace a youthful adventure and hires Enid Pretty, a vivacious young woman, as an assistant. The women go on a trip across the world to find an elusive and possibly mythical beetle, developing an unexpected friendship along the way.

Principal characters
MARGERY BENSON, a forty-six-year-old teacher who leaves London to embark on a scientific adventure
ENID PRETTY, her assistant
MUNDIC, a former soldier and prisoner of war (POW)
GLORIA, Enid's daughter
VICTORIA POPE, the wife of the British consul in New Caledonia
DOLLY WIGGS, the wife of a British miner in New Caledonia

In Rachel Joyce's *Miss Benson's Beetle* (2020), at ten years old, Margery Benson's life changes forever. First, she is introduced to the "golden beetle of New Caledonia" when her father shows her a book titled *Incredible Creatures*. She quickly determines to find the beetle. "It was that simple. She would go to wherever New Caledonia was, and bring it home." Just as Margery makes this declaration, her father receives the news that all four of her older brothers have been killed in a World War I battle. Unable to deal with the news, Tobias Benson takes a gun from his desk, steps outside the door of the room where his daughter sits, and shoots himself.

Over thirty years later, Margery's life is stuck in a rut. She is teaching domestic science at a girls' school. She not only hates it, but her students neither like nor respect her, and she is not even good at cooking. She lives alone in an apartment left to her by two spinster aunts, a place that had become a haven for her mother and herself after her father's death. Her life is a drudgery until one day her students pass around a caricature of her titled "The Virgin Margery." She is so devastated by the betrayal of her authority, she flees the school, mindlessly snatching the school deputy's new boots on her way out.

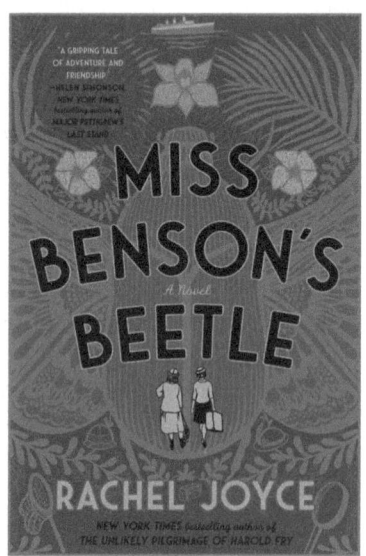

This act of unintentional thievery seems to set her free from the limitations of her ordinary life, and she determines to finally grasp her childhood dream of seeking out the golden beetle. The adventure that ensues is full of humor, frustration, growth, and friendship. Once determined to fulfill her lifetime dream, Margery sets out to hire an assistant, and she receives four responses to her ad. The first she meets is a former soldier named Mr. Mundic. Both Margery and Mundic are awkward, and their meeting is "like a dance that had already gone wrong." The second interview is with a widow who does not want to travel, and the third is with a retired teacher, Miss Hamilton. This bodes well until Miss Hamilton is informed that Margery is being investigated for the theft of the boots. That leaves Margery with only the fourth option: Mrs. Enid Pretty. Margery's first introduction to Enid is at the docks, while waiting to depart on the RMS *Orion* bound for New Caledonia, a French-speaking island off the coast of Australia. She is far from impressed with the bold, brassy woman; however, the two seem destined to be tied together.

Rachel Joyce

As the story plays out, there are several themes that drive the action and characterization. Unexpected friendship is the most significant of the thematic ideas. Margery is a large woman, tall and overweight. She sees herself as unattractive, something reinforced by the students she teaches, and in most cases, she prefers to blend into the background where she will not be noticed. Her one outstanding trait is her fascination with beetles of all kinds, and she can talk about them for hours. She knows how to properly collect, kill, pin, and record them; thus, she believes that with help from an outdated book, *The Pocket Guide to New Caledonia*, by the Reverend Horace Blake, she knows what she is doing as she sets off to discover the golden beetle. Margery's social awkwardness and physical attributes are a direct contrast to the vivacious Enid. While Margery's clothing is dull and colorless, Enid appears on the dock in a bright pink suit with bleached blond hair that floats around her head like a cloud. She is loud, funny, and flirtatious, drawing attention to herself at every turn, especially the attention of men. She, too, has an obsession, but unlike Margery's scientific interest in the beetle, Enid's is an emotional obsession with having a child.

While traveling, the two clash more than they get along. Margery's immediate seasickness makes her voyage miserable for both herself and Enid since she is confined to their small, shared cabin, vomiting relentlessly. In contrast, Enid flaunts around the ship, socializing and becoming involved with a man. When she is finally able to function, Margery covers herself in tent-like dresses, while Enid bares her body to the sun in an animal-print bikini. Despite the seemingly shallow qualities of Enid's character, she sticks with Margery even through her sickness. The two form an unlikely bond, and after arriving in New Caledonia, they work together to hunt for Margery's golden bug.

New Caledonia presents a number of new problems. Margery feels she must follow all of the appropriate steps to ensure that her discovery of the beetle will be sanctioned by the Natural History Museum, and Enid falsely tells everyone that Margery works for the institution. As a result of Margery's desire to follow the rules, the women end up at a party hosted by the British consulate and his wife, Mrs. Victoria Pope. (Mrs. Pope's snooty attitude will later cause problems for the women.) In addition, Margery's luggage, containing her clothing and her scientific supplies, has been lost, so she is stuck with a recovered suitcase full of men's clothing and supplies Enid steals from a local high school. Adding to their challenges, Mundic, who has convinced himself that he must lead Margery's expedition, has secretly followed Margery from London, stowing away on the RMS *Orion* and later stealing passage to reach the remote island. The setting of the island itself presents further problems for the women. Reverend Horace Blake's guide is so romanticized that the geography is unrecognizable. The hut Margery rented is in terrible condition. The weather and topography cause even more difficulties as they must survive a cyclone, biting insects, and unrelenting jungle.

The theme of loss also plays prominently throughout the novel. Margery's whole life has been filled with loss, and from childhood on, she has not learned to deal with or accept death. Though she was a witness to her father's suicide and learned of the deaths of her older brothers, she had convinced herself that they would return some day. Her mother's ensuing withdrawal, sitting in a chair in the apartment of Margery's paternal aunts, neither living nor dying for the next several years, does not help Margery come to terms with their shared tragedy. By the time she is a young woman, Margery has lost her mother, both of her aunts, and the elderly housekeeper who took care of the women. Left alone, she continues to deny her very aloneness and seeks out the only thing that has captured her attention since childhood. Enid has also experienced loss. She is most affected by the loss of several infants due to miscarriage. Her only desire is for a baby to survive. She is also affected by the loss of her husband, a man with whom she had lived in a platonic relationship. Unlike Margery, however, Enid openly grieves, dealing much better with the deaths in her life and teaching the older woman a lesson in love and grief.

The issue of post-traumatic stress disorder (PTSD) is also explored in the novel. This is most obvious in the character of Mundic, who had been a prisoner of war. Most of Mundic's actions center around his time as a soldier, and memories of being a prisoner of war plague him, making him not only mentally unstable but dangerous as well. Enid's husband, Perce, has also been affected by war, having lost a leg during a training exercise. His entire existence revolved around the ensuing invalidism, and Enid cared for him in every way possible even to the point when his mental instability left her in a precarious position. Not all is negative, though. Joyce infuses the novel with a sense of hope and humor. Margery and Enid become inseparable friends. Both learn the value of loving someone, and humor is found even as the duo face their many challenges.

One more significant aspect of the novel is the narrative formatting. The book is broken into five sections. The introductory chapter from Margery's childhood, set in 1914, begins the tale. Following that are sections taking place in early September 1950, late November 1950, 1951, and a closing chapter from 1983. Though the main plotline follows Margery and Enid on their quest to find the golden beetle, there are several side plots that enhance the action and character. The most important of these is the British criminal hunt for a woman named Nancy Collette, who is wanted for the murder of her husband. Mundic's obsession with Margery's expedition becomes meaningful to the central story as well as he stalks the women across the world. Even Mrs. Pope's dissatisfaction with life serves as a minor diversion.

The critical reception for the novel was mostly positive and many applauded Joyce's well-developed and richly imagined characters. The reviewer for *Publishers Weekly*, for instance, praised "Joyce's graceful touch and cutting humor [that] undercut[s] the potential for mawkishness and give[s] the characters a rich complexity and depth." Writing for the *Guardian*, Katy Guest faulted the novel's predictability but commented favorably on its "insight into the lives of women, the value of friendship and the lasting effects of war." Likewise, the *Kirkus* reviewer pointed out that the characters "are set on a collision course teeming with screwball comedic scenes deftly choreographed by Joyce." That reviewer also commented on the success of the book's themes of "women's friendship and the triumph of outrageous dreams." In addition, critics praised Joyce's work for its joyful escape from reality and the pleasure of following the two women on their exciting adventure.

Author Biography

Rachel Joyce is an award-winning author of plays, novels, short stories, and radio adaptations. She previously worked as an actor. Several of her books have become international best sellers, and two were being considered for film versions.

Theresa L. Stowell, PhD

Review Sources

Crow, Sarah McCraw. Review of *Miss Benson's Beetle*, by Rachel Joyce. *BookPage*, Nov. 2020, bookpage.com/reviews/25630-rachel-joyce-miss-bensons-beetle-fiction. Accessed 11 Dec. 2020.

Guest, Katy. "Miss Benson's Beetle by Rachel Joyce Review—The Value of Friendship." Review of *Miss Benson's Beetle*, by Rachel Joyce. *The Guardian*, 1 Aug. 2020, www.theguardian.com/books/2020/aug/01/miss-bensons-beetle-by-rachel-joyce-review-the-value-of-friendship. Accessed 29 Dec. 2020.

Review of *Miss Benson's Beetle*, by Rachel Joyce. *Kirkus*, 19 Aug. 2020, www.kirkusreviews.com/book-reviews/rachel-joyce/miss-bensons-beetle/. Accessed 11 Dec. 2020.

Review of *Miss Benson's Beetle*, by Rachel Joyce. *Publishers Weekly*, 17 Aug. 2020, www.publishersweekly.com/978-0-5932-3095-4. Accessed 11 Dec. 2020.

Moonflower Murders

Author: Anthony Horowitz (b. 1955)
Publisher: Harper (New York). 608 pp.
Type of work: Novel
Time: 1953, 2008, and 2016
Locales: Crete, Greece; Suffolk County, England

Susan Ryeland, a former editor, investigates the disappearance of a young woman who claims to know the real perpetrator of a crime committed eight years earlier at her family's hotel, having discovered the truth in a novel written by successful mystery writer Alan Conway, one of the authors for whom Ryeland served as editor.

Principal characters

SUSAN "SUE" RYELAND, a book editor turned hotelier
ANDREAS PATAKIS, her partner
LAWRENCE TREHERNE, an owner of Branlow Hall, a boutique hotel
PAULINE TREHERNE, Lawrence's wife, the other owner of Branlow Hall
CECILY TREHERNE MACNEIL, the Trehernes' missing daughter
AIDEN MACNEIL, Cecily's husband
LISA TREHERNE, the Trehernes' other daughter, who works at Branlow Hall and who has reason to dislike Cecily
FRANK PARRIS, a guest murdered at Branlow Hall eight years earlier
STEFAN CODRESCU, a hotel employee convicted of Parris's murder
ALAN CONWAY, a deceased mystery novelist
ATTICUS PÜND, a detective created by Conway

"It is a riddle wrapped in a mystery inside an enigma." This clever phrase, coined by British politician Winston Churchill to describe the undecipherable behavior of Soviet Russia in October 1939, has been used to describe all manner of particularly complicated situations, when the outcome seems nearly impossible to foretell. With some variation, it may be applied to *Moonflower Murders* (2020), Anthony Horowitz's second mystery novel featuring Sue Ryeland. Like its predecessor, *Magpie Murders*, *Moonflower Murders* wraps a contemporary mystery around a classic detective novel that is presented in full as a kind of interpolated tale. The result is that readers get the pleasure of reading two mysteries within a single book. Additionally, as the plots of the two novels unfold, Horowitz incorporates into his narratives a web of allusions and adaptations of earlier examples of mystery and detective fiction, offering a critique of the genre.

Horowitz introduced readers to Sue Ryeland in *Magpie Murders*. In that novel Ryeland is an editor at Cloverleaf Books, where her duties include production of a successful series of mystery novels by Alan Conway featuring his fictional detective, Atticus Pünd. In *Magpie Murders* Ryeland is chagrined when she is given a copy of what Conway says is his ninth and final Atticus Pünd novel—also titled *Magpie Murders*—only to discover that the final chapters are missing. She soon finds herself embroiled in a "real" murder mystery, and her search for the killer almost leads to her own death.

The sequel, *Moonflower Murders*, is as complex and intellectually stimulating as its predecessor. In his *Washington Post* review, Michael Dirda described the novel as "a super Mobius strip, interlacing multiple degrees and levels of fictiveness." Some sense of its many layers can be seen in a brief plot summary. The novel opens on the isle of Crete, where Ryeland now runs a small hotel with her partner Andreas Patakis. Ryeland is visited by Lawrence and Pauline Treherne, owners of Branlow Hall, a boutique hotel in Suffolk, England. Branlow Hall served as the model for the setting of *Atticus Pünd Takes the Case*, the third of Alan Conway's novels (Conway takes the name of his fictional hotel from the Moonflower wing at Branlow Hall). Conway's book, set in the early 1950s, is a fictional account of the murder of a film star, but it is based on the murder of ad executive Frank Parris. He was killed at Branlow Hall on the weekend of the wedding of the Trehernes' daughter Cecily to Aiden MacNeil some eight years prior to the action of *Moonflower Murders*. A quick investigation led to the conviction of Stefan Codrescu, an immigrant working at the hotel. Conway visited Branlow Hall after Codrescu's conviction and shortly thereafter remarked cryptically that he knew who the real murderer was. Rather than revealing his discovery, however, he inserted a clue about the killer's identity in *Atticus Pünd Takes the Case*.

Eight years later Cecily Treherne MacNeil reads *Atticus Pünd Takes the Case* and announces to her family that she has discovered the clue in the novel and is ready to reveal Parris's murderer—but she disappears mysteriously. The Trehernes have traveled to Crete to ask Ryeland to help find their missing daughter. They are aware that Conway has died by this point and believe that since Ryeland edited Conway's novels, she might be able to identify the killer and discover Cecily's whereabouts. Ryeland, stressed from running her hotel and missing the publishing world, agrees to assist the Trehernes.

The majority of the frame novel is taken up with Ryeland's attempts to track down Cecily and discover the real murderer of Frank Parris. On returning to England, she takes up temporary residence at Branlow Hall, where she begins to systematically

Anthony Horowitz

Courtesy HarperCollins Publishers

interview a slew of potential suspects who might have murdered Parris eight years earlier and who may have wanted Cecily to disappear. Among them are members of the Treherne family, the night manager at Branlow Hall, and Conway's ex-wife, who is living in the area. Ryeland's presence at Branlow Hall infuriates the Trehernes' other daughter, Lisa, who works at the hotel, and Ryeland receives only minimal help from Cecily's husband, Aiden. Her investigation does uncover an important fact about Parris and Conway, however.

Looking for the clue Cecily mentioned before her disappearance, Ryeland rereads *Atticus Pünd Takes the Case*, which is reproduced in its entirety (title page, copyright, dedication, and text) to track down the clue. As one might expect in a detective novel, the information is there for her to discover once she has gained a better sense of the "real" people on whom Conway based his fiction. *Moonflower Murders* ends with Ryeland unmasking the murderer of Frank Parris and solving the mystery of Cecily's disappearance. As with most good mystery novels, the resolution leaves readers with a sense of satisfaction.

Of course, as one might expect from Horowitz, *Moonflower Murders* offers readers a sense of enjoyment on various levels. The novel provides lovers of mysteries the opportunity to travel imaginatively with two detectives as they examine the evidence and follow leads that eventually unmask the guilty parties in murders that occurred in the past and in the present. Additionally, the two mysteries in *Moonflower Murders* provide good examples of the differences between classic mysteries and contemporary ones—and also highlight the many similarities, demonstrating the essential continuity of conventions within the genre. The Conway novel at the center of *Moonflower Murders* is a clever example of the traditional cozy mystery. Horowitz displays exceptional familiarity with the conventions of the genre and employs many of them in *Atticus Pünd Takes the Case*. This novel-within-the-novel is set in a secluded location where, by convention, however unusual the circumstances in which a murder is committed, the murderer must be one of a limited number of suspects. Readers are distanced from the action by having the story set in the 1950s and told in third person (with limited omniscience, of course, as secrets must be kept from readers lest the illusion of mystery be destroyed). Most notably, Pünd is modeled quite closely on Agatha Christie's Hercule Poirot. He is an outsider—a German Jewish refugee who fled to England—whose eccentricities are exceeded only by his exceptional skills as a sleuth.

The frame tale—the mystery Ryeland must solve—is decidedly postmodern. The story is told in the first person and set in contemporary times, creating a sense of intimacy between narrator and reader. Ryeland is a twenty-first-century woman approaching middle age, with all the anxieties that come with the crises she is undergoing as she tries to determine where her professional and personal future lies. Although dead, Alan Conway is a central figure in *Moonflower Murders*; not only is one of his novels at the center (both literally and figuratively) of the contemporary story, his lifestyle as an author and a gay man plays a prominent role in the narrative. Conway seems modeled in part on Sir Arthur Conan Doyle. Conan Doyle was chagrined at the success of his Sherlock Holmes stories because the time he took to write them was time away from more serious literary work. Like Conan Doyle, Conway claims to hate his detective and considers his mystery novels mere potboilers designed to earn money so that he can turn his attention to more serious fiction.

By making Ryeland exceptionally self-aware, Horowitz is able to use her as a mouthpiece to critique the kind of fiction he is writing. For example, when discussing the murder of Frank Parris with one witness, she asks, "Can you tell me what happened on the night of the murder?" Immediately she thinks to herself that the question was so clichéd that had she been a character in a text, as an editor she would have eliminated the banal and overused query.

Avid readers of mysteries dating back to the nineteenth century will also recognize many allusions to classic detective fiction, which Horowitz makes clever use of. Perhaps the most obvious is the repeated reference in *Moonflower Murders* to the dog that barked in the night. The allusion is to the observation made by Sherlock Holmes in the story "Silver Blaze" of "the curious incident of the dog in the night-time." In Conan Doyle's tale, the dog did nothing—"that," says Holmes, "was the curious incident." Holmes surmises that because the dog, who lives at the stables from which the prize racehorse Silver Blaze is abducted, did not bark out a warning, it must have known person who stole the horse. The allusion points to an important clue here as well. At another point in the novel, Ryeland calls attention to Agatha Christie's frequent use of allusions in her fiction, particularly to fairy tales and to works by William Shakespeare—mirroring Horowitz's own effective use of allusions to other literary works and television series. For example, more than once Horowitz mentions the popular, long-running British television series *Midsomer Murders*, whose title recalls that of Horowitz's two mysteries featuring Sue Ryeland. Adding another layer, those familiar with *Midsomer Murders* know that Horowitz had a hand in creating the series, which is based on a series of novels by British mystery writer Caroline Graham.

One of the great joys in reading mystery and detective fiction comes from the pleasure experienced in solving the crime along with the protagonist. Unfortunately, the intellectual satisfaction that readers get when the perpetrator is finally revealed is often a one-time experience. On occasion, however, an interesting backstory for the detective-protagonist or some wider commentary on political, social, cultural, or literary matters allows a mystery novel to rise above the limitations of the genre and provide satisfaction on repeated readings. *Moonflower Murders* is such a novel.

Author Biography
Anthony Horowitz is an acclaimed novelist and screenwriter, author of a series of young-adult novels, mysteries, and thrillers, including ones featuring iconic characters Sherlock Holmes and James Bond. He has adapted Agatha Christie's Hercule Poirot novels for television, helped develop the long-running series *Midsomer Murders*, and created the award-winning series *Foyle's War.*

Laurence W. Mazzeno

Review Sources

Dirda, Michael. "Agatha Christie Fans, Take Note: Anthony Horowitz Has a Clever New Twist on the Classic Whodunit." Review of *Moonflower Murders*, by Anthony Horowitz. *The Washington Post*, 11 Nov. 2020, www.washingtonpost.com/entertainment/books/agatha-christie-fans-take-note-anthony-horowitz-has-a-new-twist-on-the-classic-whodunit. Accessed 5 Jan. 2021.

Kanell, Beth. Review of *Moonflower Murders*, by Anthony Horowitz. *New York Journal of Books*, www.nyjournalofbooks.com/book-review/moonflower-murders-novel. Accessed 5 Jan. 2021.

Lyall, Sarah. "One Whodunit Nests Inside Another in 'Moonflower Murders.'" Review of *Moonflower Murders*, by Anthony Horowitz. *The New York Times*, 2 Dec. 2020, www.nytimes.com/2020/12/02/books/review-moonflower-murders-anthony-horowitz.html. Accessed 5 Jan. 2021.

Nolan, Tom. "Mysteries: Double Dealing." Review of *Moonflower Murders*, by Anthony Horowitz. *The Wall Street Journal*, 6 Nov. 2020, www.wsj.com/articles/mysteries-double-dealing-11604678419. Accessed 5 Jan. 2021.

Pierce, J. Kingston. Review of *Moonflower Murders*, by Anthony Horowitz. *January Magazine*, 19 Nov. 2020, januarymagazine.com/wp/crime-fiction-moonflower-murders-by-anthony-horowitz/. Accessed 5 Jan. 2021.

The Mountains Sing

Author: Nguyễn Phan Quế Mai (b. 1973)
Publisher: Algonquin Books (Chapel Hill, NC). 352 pp.
Type of work: Novel
Time: 1930–2012
Locale: Northern Vietnam

The Mountains Sing, Vietnamese poet Nguyễn Phan Quế Mai's debut novel, is a multigenerational saga that explores one family's struggle to survive French and Japanese occupation, a devastating famine, two wars, and brutal political repression. The experiences of the Trần family complicate accepted narratives about Vietnam's recent history and illustrate the importance of preserving the memories of those who lived it.

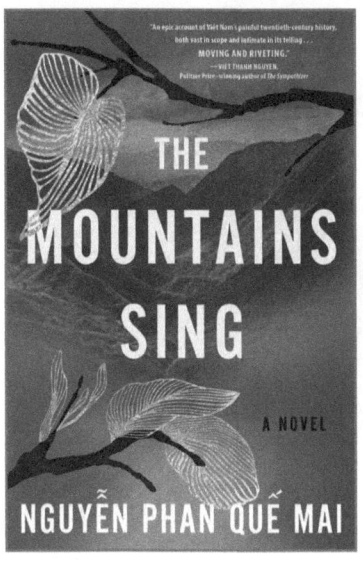

Principal characters
Hương "Guava" Trần, a young Vietnamese girl, the narrator
Diệu Lan, her grandmother, a teacher
Ngọc, her mother, a medic during the war
Tam, her classmate and love interest

In *The Mountains Sing* (2020), the debut novel of Vietnamese poet Nguyễn Phan Quế Mai, three generations of women tenaciously struggle to survive colonization, occupation, famine, and war. The book begins near the present day in 2012. A grown-up Hương, or Guava as she is affectionately known to family members, conjures the memory of her beloved grandmother, Diệu Lan, at her family altar. Guava was a child during the height of the Vietnam War, or the Resistance War against America to Save the Nation, as it is known in Hanoi where Guava was born and raised. Her memories of this time serve as the book's anchor. With her parents and uncles serving on the front lines, Guava and her grandmother must fend for themselves. Near constant bombings drive them from their home in the city to a small, mountain village whose name means "peace." Guava is forced to leave her treasured book collection behind.

The sadness of parting is compounded by the sadness of return; when Guava and her grandmother come down from the mountains, they discover that the family house has been leveled by bombs. None of their possessions remain. Guava and Diệu Lan set up camp in what was once their yard, doing their best to feed and shelter themselves on food coupons distributed by the ruling Communist Party and Diệu Lan's meager wages as a teacher. To buoy Guava's spirits, Diệu Lan tells her stories about her own childhood and describes the twisting path that led her to Hanoi as an adult. Critics

Nguyễn Phan Quế Mai

noted that Nguyễn's honest depiction of Diệu Lan's life breaks powerful taboos about how Vietnam engages with its own history. For instance, Gaiutra Bahadur, who reviewed *The Mountains Sing* for the *New York Times*, described how the novel suggests "what history might look like when written from people's memories rather than enshrined in textbooks that silence or distort the truth." As Diệu Lan tells Guava, "We're forbidden to talk about events that relate to past mistakes or the wrongdoing of those in power, for they give themselves the right to rewrite history. But you're old enough to know that history will write itself in people's memories, and as long as those memories live on, we can have faith that we can do better."

The Mountains Sing is not an autobiographical novel, but author Nguyễn's own story is integral to its telling. Born in North Vietnam in 1973 and raised in poverty in a small village in the South, Nguyễn's earliest memories were colored by the horrors of war. An uncle, who fought for the North Vietnamese, suffered from severe post-traumatic stress disorder (PTSD). Further back in her family's history, Nguyễn's paternal grandmother died in the devastating famine known as the Great Hunger, and her grandfather died during the brutal land reforms of the 1950s. She weaves their stories, and the stories of other people she interviewed, into the experiences of the Trần family at the heart of her novel. *The Mountains Sing* is Nguyễn's fiction debut; she was previously best known as a poet, and several of her poems have been turned into popular Vietnamese songs. Her collection of poems *The Secret of Hoa Sen* was published in 2014. Pulitzer Prize–winning novelist Viet Thanh Nguyen was instrumental in the publication of *The Mountains Sing*, his support stemming from his commitment to presenting Vietnamese history in its full complexity. Such stories about Vietnamese history are often discouraged within Vietnam; in fact, Nguyễn wrote her book in English to evade censorship and to ensure a global readership. Still, as Bahadur wrote, she is part of a growing movement of Vietnamese writers, if not Vietnamese historians, who seek to grapple with the country's complicated past, "drawing on personal experience and oral histories to tell the tale from the points of view" of peasants, women, and others.

Like Guava, her grandmother was lucky enough to grow up in a family that encouraged women to read and study. Diệu Lan's parents were wealthy landowners in the Nghệ An province in North Vietnam during the French occupation. But even in happy times, bad omens abound. As France continues to exploit Vietnam for profit, a resistance movement that will blossom into the Việt Minh grows. Meanwhile, a fortune teller tells a ten-year-old Diệu Lan that she will "lose everything and become a wandering beggar in a faraway city." World War II comes and, with it, Japanese colonial rule. For Diệu Lan, this new occupation is an abstraction until she, her brother, and her father embark on a journey to Hanoi to visit her old tutor. They are stopped by Japanese soldiers, and Diệu Lan's father is beheaded. It is a startling image and a portent of the profound violence that the family will face in the coming years. Fighting among the Japanese, the French, and the Việt Minh intensifies through the war and the Great Hunger, a famine that killed two million Vietnamese people in 1945. During the Great Hunger, Diệu Lan can barely summon the strength to care for her children, much less her aging mother. As Nguyễn writes in Diệu Lan's voice, "Rather than being a vicious tiger gobbling us down, the hunger was a python that squeezed our energy until there was nothing left of us except skin and bones." Nguyễn's prose is simple, but not simplistic. Her background as a poet is obvious in her careful arrangement of images, lending the story the air of a myth or fable. Take for instance one passage during the Great Hunger, in which Diệu Lan and her mother must venture into the forest to look for food. Bodies, living and dead, litter the road, grasping at their ankles, but in the forest, a miracle: a secret field of corn. As they gorge themselves on sweet kernels, they are brought down by the whip of a character called Wicked Ghost.

Wicked Ghost is a tax man that collects on behalf of the French, robbing men of property and lashing their wives when they cannot pay. But his name also hints at a larger idea Nguyễn appears to be grappling with through the structure of *The Mountains Sing*. Chapters alternate between Diệu Lan, whose story spans the 1930s through the 1960s, and Guava's coming of age in the 1970s. But the past is never safely behind either of them. Through the plot—driven by scenes of separation and reunion in both timelines—Nguyễn evocatively illustrates the entanglement of past and present. Like Guava's uncle, a veteran whose wife gives birth to a stillborn child because he was exposed to Agent Orange during the war, each generation of the Trần family is indelibly marked by the experiences of their ancestors.

The crux of the story, the center from which all plot points radiate, is the land reform movement of 1955. After the war and the Great Hunger, Diệu Lan and her family rebuilt their home and farm, prospering as the Communist Party rose to power. In 1955, the party issued a policy of wealth distribution; its implementation was swift and brutal, with landless peasants killing traders and landlords, or anyone perceived to be part of the bourgeois class. Driven by greed and violence, the realities of the land reform campaign contradicted the ideology of North Vietnam and the Communist Party—thus, to this day, it is a traumatic history that many would prefer to leave unexamined. But Nguyễn is unsparing. She describes how land reform tears the Trần family apart. Diệu Lan's brother is viciously killed, and her oldest son, Minh, fleeing his torturers, is lost. Diệu Lan escapes with her other five children, though she is forced to leave them with various strangers as she tries to make her way to Hanoi.

The book is also partially set during, and in the immediate aftermath of, the Vietnam War, during which conflict, Nguyễn writes, the United States dropped seven million tons of bombs on Vietnam. (A staggering number, even amidst countless scenes of explosions.) After Diệu Lan and Guava lose their home, Diệu Lan makes the difficult decision to quit her Party-sanctioned teaching job and become a trader on the black market. The family suffers the social stigma of her choice, losing both friends and family members, but at last they are able to eat. Much of Guava's story involves her mother, Ngọc, a doctor who served as a medic in the war. Ngọc returns to Hanoi deeply traumatized. Her experiences force young Guava to grapple with the depth of suffering wrought by the war. Guava also longs for the return of her father, who served in the North Vietnamese army. Her uncle, also a soldier, returns with a small, wooden bird, carved for her by her father. The bird is a symbol of immortality whose name means "mountains sing," giving the book its title. "The challenges faced by the Vietnamese people throughout history are as tall as the tallest mountains," Diệu Lan tells Guava. "If you stand too close, you won't be able to see their peaks. Once you step away from the currents of life, you will have the full view."

The Mountains Sing received starred reviews from both *Kirkus* and *Publishers Weekly*, and the novel became a New York Times Best Seller. In her enthusiastic review for NPR, Thúy Đinh lamented the instinct to suppress difficult history and the hurdles that the book would likely face in Vietnamese translation, poignantly asking, "Can Nguyễn Phan Quế Mai's message be heard in her homeland, where the mountains of Vietnam are still a fortress silencing the sounds of birds?"

Author Biography
Nguyễn Phan Quế Mai has published eight books of poetry, as well as short fiction and nonfiction, in Vietnamese, and was the recipient of the Poetry of the Year Award from the Hanoi Writer's Association in 2010. *The Mountains Sing* is her first novel and first full-length English work.

Molly Hagan

Review Sources
Bahadur, Gaiutra. "A Stirring Family Saga Tells a Taboo History of Vietnam." Review of *The Mountains Sing*, by Nguyễn Phan Quế Mai. *The New York Times*, 17 Mar. 2020, www.nytimes.com/2020/03/17/books/review/the-mountains-sing-nguyen-phan-que-mai.html. Accessed 17 Mar. 2021.
Đinh, Thúy. "'The Mountains Sing' a Song of Many Voices." Review of *The Mountains Sing*, by Nguyễn Phan Quế Mai. *NPR*, 19 Mar. 2020, www.npr.org/2020/03/19/817857822/the-mountains-sing-a-song-of-many-voices. Accessed 17 Mar. 2021.
Review of *The Mountains Sing*, by Nguyễn Phan Quế Mai. *Kirkus*, 23 Dec. 2019, www.kirkusreviews.com/book-reviews/qu-mai-phan-nguyn/the-mountains-sing/. Accessed 17 Mar. 2021.
Review of *The Mountains Sing*, by Nguyễn Phan Quế Mai. *Publishers Weekly*, 16 Dec. 2019, www.publishersweekly.com/978-1-61620-818-9. Accessed 17 Mar. 2021.
Wallace, Jane. Review of *The Mountains Sing*, by Nguyễn Phan Quế Mai. *Asian Review of Books*, 31 July 2020, asianreviewofbooks.com/content/the-mountains-sing-by-nguyen-phan-que-mai/. Accessed 17 Mar. 2021.

My Dark Vanessa

Author: Kate Elizabeth Russell (b. ca. 1985)
Publisher: William Morrow (New York). 384 pp.
Type of work: Novel
Time: 2000–2017
Locale: Maine

My Dark Vanessa *follows the story of a woman grappling with the long-term effects of sexual abuse. It is American author Kate Elizabeth Russell's debut novel.*

Principal characters

VANESSA WYE, a thirty-two-year-old woman struggling to confront the relationship she had with her high school English teacher as accusations against him begin to emerge

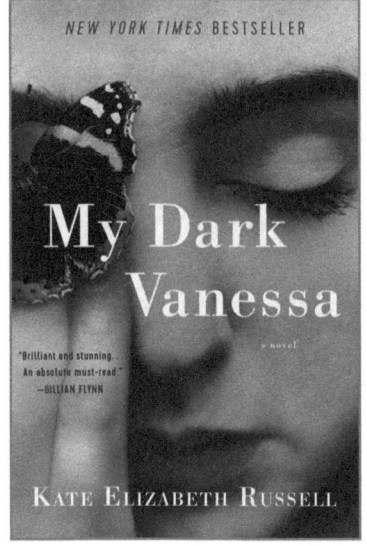

JACOB STRANE, her high school English teacher who began a sexual relationship with her when she was fifteen years old

TAYLOR BIRCH, another student from her high school who publicly accuses Strane of having sexually abused her

In interviews, author Kate Elizabeth Russell stated that it took her approximately two decades to write her debut novel, *My Dark Vanessa* (2020). The reason for this was not due to inexperience or a prolonged bout of writers' block but because the book tackled a subject largely considered repugnant by others. In fact, most people encouraged her to drop the project altogether once they learned that she was writing about the romantic relationship between a teenage girl and her teacher. While working on *My Dark Vanessa* as a part of her dissertation for her creative writing PhD program, Russell even had a professor tell her to refrain from submitting it any more. After it was rejected by over sixty agents, however, the author's luck began to change. In 2018, having landed representation, her manuscript sparked a bidding war that earned her a seven-figure deal with the publisher William Morrow. *My Dark Vanessa* would then go on to become one of the most anticipated and controversial books of 2020.

Arguably Russell's eventual success is due in part to her work happening to align with the #MeToo movement, one of the most important cultural moments of the first two decades of the twenty-first century. In its simplest description, *My Dark Vanessa* is about a woman navigating the aftermath of years of sexual abuse. More specifically, it follows, through shifts in time, protagonist Vanessa Wye from the time she is fifteen years old and begins a relationship with her forty-two-year-old English teacher to when she is thirty-two and learns that another former student is accusing him of

Kate Elizabeth Russell

being a sexual predator. Vanessa's struggle to recognize that she was a victim of a man who abused his authority to engage in a sexual relationship with her is reminiscent of America's growing awareness of the sexual abuse that women have often suffered in the workplace.

What makes *My Dark Vanessa* such an important book is the way in which it examines the nebulous dynamics of consent in sexually abusive relationships. Vanessa is a more unusual heroine in that she continuously defends her former teacher, Jacob Strane. While other women start speaking out about Strane to the media, Vanessa refuses to corroborate their stories. Despite what everyone around her says, she cannot let go of the idea that her relationship with him was a consensual love affair. Furthermore, she believes that he is the victim in their relationship and that she is to blame for the destruction of his reputation. Because of this misguided perspective, some readers might find that Vanessa occasionally proves an unlikeable character. This would be problematic if the book were tackling a lighter subject matter. However, Russell's decision to put a flawed protagonist at the center of a story about sexual abuse ultimately is a powerful one. Readers quickly realize that Vanessa's denial of what Strane did to her is an authentic coping mechanism. She has framed their relationship as a love story because it is less upsetting than the truth. This provides greater insight into and empathy for other survivors of sexual abuse.

My Dark Vanessa has rightfully drawn comparisons to Vladimir Nabokov's *Lolita* (1955). Nabokov's seminal novel is omnipresent throughout Russell's book. Beyond the narrative setup of exploring a forbidden relationship between a child and an adult man, *My Dark Vanessa* also addresses *Lolita* directly by having the protagonist become obsessed with its story. Published to scandalous acclaim, *Lolita* is told from the perspective of thirty-seven-year-old Humbert Humbert, who kidnaps and rapes his twelve-year-old stepdaughter, Dolores. In the decades following its publication, *Lolita* has, in some cases, been touted as one of the greatest love stories of all time. In part, this can be attributed to Nabokov's prose, which is so beautiful and acrobatic that some readers can forget that the narrator is in fact a pedophile.

One major reason that *My Dark Vanessa* is such a powerful read is that Russell tells the same story as Nabokov but from the perspective of the Dolores character. In this way, she challenges the patriarchal fetishization of pubescent girls. When Strane gives Vanessa a copy of *Lolita*, it is part of his ritualistic grooming of her. He wants her to see an example of how love can exist between an adult man and a girl. Like many readers, Vanessa mistakes the book to be about forbidden love. By following Vanessa into adulthood, Russell showcases just how much long-term psychological damage this type of relationship can have on women. At thirty-two, Vanessa is working a dead-end job at a hotel in Portland, Maine. Depressed and unable to move on from her past, she self-medicates with alcohol and drugs. No matter how much she tries to claim her relationship with Strane was a love story, the quality of her life demonstrates otherwise.

Russell's prose throughout the novel is both florid and elusive. Writing in the first-person present tense from Vanessa's point of view, an effective choice to convey the lasting impact of the character's past, the author alternates between two story lines. The first of these is set in 2017, when adult Vanessa learns that Taylor Birch, a former student from her boarding school, has come forward to accuse Strane of being a sexual predator. As Taylor's accusations gain media attention and more women come forward, Vanessa is forced to reexamine her past. The second story line begins in 2000, when Vanessa is fifteen and first meets Strane. It unfolds over the next seven years, following Vanessa as she continues her relationship with Strane through the rest of high school and college. There is a certain patchiness to Vanessa's narration that implies that she does not fully understand what is happening to her. This creates an engaging feeling of suspense as the mystery of how Vanessa will grapple with the truth about Strane hangs over the story.

Strane is an unusual antagonist simply by how ordinary he comes across due to perspective. Neither particularly handsome nor charming, he is an academic who is highly knowledgeable about literature, but beyond that, there are few desirable traits. Russell carefully demonstrates through several different scenes that Vanessa's attraction to him is based almost entirely on the way that he makes her feel. When they first meet, Vanessa is a normal, albeit lonely, teenager trying to find her place in the world. From a working-class family, she often feels as though she does not belong at the elite Maine boarding school she attends. Most of the other students there are from wealthy families, but she is on a scholarship. When Strane singles her out, he goes to great lengths to highlight how intelligent, beautiful, and talented she is. He compliments her hair, comparing it to maple leaves, and constantly reminds her of the power she has over him. It is because Vanessa wants to feel special and powerful that she is drawn to Strane and confuses these feelings for adult love.

As a whole, *My Dark Vanessa* can best be described as an engaging, disturbing, and necessary book. Reviews proved largely positive, with most critics praising Russell's skilled depiction of the complex thinking of an abuse victim living in a post–#MeToo society. For the *Guardian*, Sofka Zinovieff wrote that *My Dark Vanessa* is a "fast-paced, intelligent novel" that "encapsulates the current zeitgeist in which earlier sexual mores are being re-evaluated and clearer boundaries laid down. It also shows how social media plays a vital role in uniting survivors and advocating justice." Indeed, Russell's debut succeeds in capturing the way in which modern society is letting go of long-held ideas of what is acceptable when it comes to sex and power. Until the eruption of #MeToo in 2017, men who abused their positions of authority to sexually harass and abuse women rarely faced serious consequences. Strane's trajectory throughout the novel illustrates this cultural trend. When the boarding school first finds out about his relationship with Vanessa in 2001, she lies for him and gets kicked out while he is allowed to keep his job. In the years that follow, other students like

Taylor Birch launch complaints against Strane's inappropriate behavior, but nothing ever happens. It is not until 2017, when the country collectively begins high-profile outings and punishment of accused sex offenders, that Strane's career and freedom become jeopardized.

Not all critics have been warmly receptive to *My Dark Vanessa*, however. Its release was marred by an online controversy when a Latinx writer named Wendy Ortiz argued that the novel's critical acclaim was due largely to the author being White. Ortiz had written a memoir titled *Excavation* (2014) about the relationship she had with her eighth-grade English teacher. While both books share a similar narrative, only Russell was offered a seven-figure deal. As a result, the conversation surrounding *My Dark Vanessa* transitioned from anticipation to one about racial bias in the publishing industry.

Most other criticisms of Russell's debut novel were aimed at the book's prose. For example, *New York Times* critic Katie Roiphe remarked that the author's writing style very occasionally "veers toward clunkiness or overexplication." It is true that some readers may find parts of the novel to be awkward or in need of editing. Furthermore, the story sometimes feels too long and repetitive—especially toward the end. Perhaps the most significant criticism of *My Dark Vanessa*, however, was that it requires readers to become submerged in a very disturbing subject. In a review for the *Atlantic*, Sophie Gilbert wrote, "To spend substantial time—roughly 350 pages—in the mind of a person defending the assault of an underage girl isn't particularly pleasant." Although *My Dark Vanessa* is most certainly not an easy read, it is an important one. Those who engage in Russell's intelligent narrative will likely gain a better understanding of sexual abuse survivors and the long-term challenges they face.

Author Biography

My Dark Vanessa (2020) is Kate Elizabeth Russell's first novel. She holds a master of fine arts degree from Indiana University and a doctorate in creative writing from Kansas State University.

Emily E. Turner

Review Sources

Gilbert, Sophie. "The Controversial Novel That Immerses Readers in Teen Abuse." Review of *My Dark Vanessa*, by Kate Elizabeth Russell. *The Atlantic*, 25 Mar. 2020, www.theatlantic.com/culture/archive/2020/03/my-dark-vanessa-not-quite-contemporary-lolita/608641/ Accessed 5 Oct. 2020.

Roiphe, Katie. "Girl, Interrupted." Review of *My Dark Vanessa*, by Kate Elizabeth Russell. *The New York Times*, 6 Mar. 2020, www.nytimes.com/2020/03/06/books/review/my-dark-vanessa-kate-elizabeth-russell.html. Accessed 5 Oct. 2020.

Zinovieff, Sofka. "My Dark Vanessa by Kate Elizabeth Russell Review—a Powerful, Shocking Debut." Review of *My Dark Vanessa*, by Kate Elizabeth Russell. *The Guardian*, 4 Apr. 2020, www.theguardian.com/books/2020/apr/04/my-dark-vanessa-kate-elizabeth-russell-review-debut-novel. Accessed 5 Oct. 2020.

The New Wilderness

Author: Diane Cook (b. 1976)
Publisher: Harper (New York). 416 pp.
Type of work: Novel
Time: The future
Locale: The Wilderness State

Diane Cook's The New Wilderness *imagines a world decimated by climate change, where the only refuge from dangerous pollution is a vast natural preserve called the Wilderness State. Bea and her young daughter, Agnes, are members of a small, nomadic group living in the Wilderness as part of a study to see if humans can exist in nature without destroying it.*

Principal characters

BEA, a young mother who lives with a group called the Community in the Wilderness State
AGNES, her daughter
GLEN, her husband, Agnes's stepfather
CARL, the leader of the Community, Glen's former student
RANGER BOB, one of the keepers of the Wilderness State

In late 2020, the *New York Times* published an article warning of the long-term health effects of pollution and wildfire smoke on children living in California. The danger of a child developing asthma, respiratory infections, or a compromised immune system are proportionate to a family's means, the authors wrote. Wealthier children, who live in more desirable zip codes and have access to better care, are equipped to combat these effects; poorer children are not. Climate change is a dire and imminent threat to everyone, but as the planet ambles toward catastrophe, its effects will be meted out disproportionately. In her new novel, *The New Wilderness*, Diane Cook explores the raw urge to survive amid the effects of dangers such as climate change and pollution and the lengths to which one parent will go to save her child by any means necessary.

Set in the near future, the book follows the story of a woman named Bea and her young daughter, Agnes. Several years before the story begins, Bea is forced to flee the City, "where the air was poison to children, the streets were crowded, filthy, where rows of high-rises sprawled to the horizon and beyond." Agnes cannot breathe in the polluted metropolis, but escape is nearly impossible. The continent has been divided into various sections, each with their own purpose: the City, the Manufacturing Zone, the Woodlots, and the Server Farms. (Abandoned lands include the Heat Belt and the New Coast.) There are rumors of a kind of fresh-air paradise known as the Private Lands, but if they exist at all, they are the realm of the wealthy and well-connected. Bea and Agnes are luckier than others, though. Glen, Bea's husband and Agnes's stepfather, works for a university and has special access to a scientific study taking place in the continent's last nature preserve, the Wilderness State. The family joins a small group of people—there are twenty of them, in all—who leave the City behind, striking out into the heart of the Wilderness State to live as nomads. The study, strictly regulated by a dense book of rules called the Manual, seeks to determine whether or not human beings can live in nature without destroying it. In its execution, the study becomes far more complicated, testing the limits of its participants in unforeseen ways. As Bea muses early on: "When they first arrived in the Wilderness, they imagined living there might make them more sympathetic, better, more attuned people. But they came to understand there'd been a great misunderstanding about what *better* meant."

Diane Cook

Cook's debut, a collection of short stories called *Man v. Nature* (2014), explores similar thematic territory. That book also grapples with the overwhelming power of nature, the uncertainty of the future in a rapidly changing world and, as one reviewer darkly put it, the "anxiety of oblivion." Some stories depict various apocalyptic scenarios, including a September 11–like attack. Other stories depict the end of the world, symbolically. In one, a man serially kidnaps infants in a small town. Years later, the children are returned, and their mothers must confront a different kind of loss. *The New Wilderness*, Cook's first novel, depicts an apocalypse happening in slow motion. It is fairly realistic speculative fiction, rooted in a world similar to our own. Before she joined the Community—the name for the group of volunteers who move to the Wilderness—Bea worked as an interior decorator. In a familiar cave in the Wilderness State, she has squirreled away a ragged copy of a design magazine and a molding pillow to remind her of her former life. (These talismans are profoundly comforting to Bea, but they are, unsurprisingly, against the rules.) Bea's daughter, Agnes, has no so such attachment to the City or any of the recognizable trappings of human civilization—a harsh reality (for Bea, at least) that informs the tension between them.

The New Wilderness begins with a miscarriage. Bea, alone, births and buries a stillborn child named Madeline. Bea grieves the loss, but also wrestles with the guilt of having been wary about the pregnancy in the first place, wondering if it is fair to introduce a child into such a harsh world. Ironically, the brutal Wilderness is the only place Agnes can live—and, indeed, thrive. Agnes, once a frail and sickly five-year-old, flourishes in the Wilderness. She relishes the freedom of nomadic life, even if the eating is crude. The Community subsists on foraged plants and the occasional deer or rabbit. When Agnes is surreptitiously given a sugary lollipop, the taste is so overwhelming that she gives it to Glen, who, like Bea, never lost his taste for manmade treats. Agnes develops a keen sense of the environment, tracking prey and finding water. She is particularly attuned to the behaviors of wildlife. Whenever the group struggles to consult a map, Agnes beseeches them to "follow the animals." Her judgement is nearly always sound. While Agnes excels at reading her surroundings, she is less adept at reading her mother. She is not alone. The first half of the book is written from Bea's perspective. The second half centers on Agnes. Though the reader is given omniscient access to Bea's secret thoughts, she remains a bit of a mystery. In Cook's telling, the slog of survival dulls one's emotions. Bea's true feelings occasionally bubble to the surface—as when she must account for Madeline's death at one of the Community's infrequent check-ins with the outside world. When a ranger shows more concern for an adult member of the group who drowned crossing a river, Bea explodes with fury. The scene, as novelist Téa Obreht wrote in her review for the *Guardian*, is one of "the novel's most poignant." Elsewhere, Bea's motivations are less clear, or rather, less precise. Unlike her daughter, Bea never fully embraces the Wilderness as her home. Her actions, seemingly random, are united by a wild desperation that is implied but never truly seen.

Agnes proves to be a more engaging protagonist. Her coming-of-age is expressed through her maturation as one of the group's leaders. When the Community is forced to take on new members—all of them as clueless and unskilled as the original Community members had once been—Agnes forms relationships with people her own age. Their oddball personalities and humorous interactions are illuminating and delightfully strange. Jake is a smirking, floppy-haired teen heartthrob. Agnes is livid upon seeing him for the first time, fuming that he will never be able to survive with hair in his eyes. Patty and Celeste call themselves the Twins, though they are not twins or even related. When they ask Agnes how old she is, she guesses thirty; they decide she is eleven. (The Wilderness seems to warp one's sense of time; another child tells Agnes that her age is "three plus.") The Twins, who upon arrival touted their most prized possession as a small pot of neon pink nail polish, catch on to Wilderness living quicker than one might expect, becoming the Community's most lethal hunters. Like Agnes—like all adolescents—they straddle two worlds: the world of their parents and their own. In the Wilderness, the trials and tribulations of being a teen are magnified; Agnes astutely observes the ways in which her new companions are like animals for their strategic ambivalence and their sudden and ferocious emotional outbursts. The Community is more compelling as seen through their eyes. The young people see the Wilderness as a place to make a future; the Community elders, absorbed in petty politicking, are blinded by the demands of the endless present.

As if nature were not enough of a foe, there are also human villains in *The New Wilderness*. Among them are the Gestapo-like rangers, who tend to the Wilderness from posts stationed along its perimeter. Bea tries her best to charm them, forming a kind of friendship with Ranger Bob, who appears to be the most humane. Bea does not understand that the rangers all serve a larger system, whose control is absolute. When the rangers tell the Community to move to a new settlement—they are supposed to be nomads, after all—the Community must do it, or face eviction. As the book progresses, the rangers' demands become more erratic and confusing, and their enforcement, more brutal. Comparisons to settlers and American Indians are inevitable, though the novel is curiously apolitical. Cook hints at a "new Administration" behind these policy changes, and also, through talk of the Private Lands, of the extraordinary privilege of the wealthy, but she never directly engages with these ideas, or how they shape her world. Bea, Agnes, and their Community compatriots are individuals vying for survival, and the rangers are villains trying to thwart them. Because the human forces beyond the Wilderness are ill-defined, the rangers are robbed of their metaphorical teeth. They are a useful device, but disappointingly wanting in terms of their meaning.

Despite its flaws, *The New Wilderness*, which was short-listed for the Booker Prize, is a unique and exciting work, exploring familial love in a dying world. Its critical reception was largely positive, with reviewers highlighting the story's unsettling timeliness in today's uncertain climate. A review in *Publishers Weekly* remarked that the novel "explores maternal love and man's disdain for nature with impressive results." Writing for *USA Today*, Eliot Schrefer commented positively on Cook's "masterful" writing, noting that the "ever-surprising relationship between Bea and Agnes . . . breaks and mends in remarkable and moving ways."

Author Biography

Diane Cook, formerly a producer for the NPR radio show *This American Life*, published *Man v. Nature*, her debut short story collection, in 2014. *The New Wilderness* is her first novel. It was short-listed for the Booker Prize in 2020.

Molly Hagan

Review Sources

Review of *The New Wilderness*, by Diane Cook. *Kirkus*, 18 May 2020, www.kirkusreviews.com/book-reviews/diane-cook/the-new-wilderness/. Accessed 23 Nov. 2020.

Review of *The New Wilderness*, by Diane Cook. *Publishers Weekly*, 28 Feb. 2020, www.publishersweekly.com/978-0-06-233313-1. Accessed 23 Nov. 2020.

Obreht, Téa. "The New Wilderness by Diane Cook Review—A Dazzling Debut." Review of *The New Wilderness*, by Diane Cook. *The Guardian*, 4 Sept. 2020, www.theguardian.com/books/2020/sep/04/the-new-wilderness-by-diane-cook-review-a-dazzling-debut. Accessed 23 Nov. 2020.

Schrefer, Eliot. "'The New Wilderness': Humanity Returns to Nature in Diane Cook's Timely Ecological Tale." Review of *The New Wilderness*, by Diane Cook. *USA Today*, 10 Aug. 2020, www.usatoday.com/story/entertainment/books/2020/08/09/the-new-wilderness-humanity-returns-nature-diane-cook-debut/3306196001/. Accessed 23 Nov. 2020.

Temple, Emily. "Diane Cook's 'The New Wilderness' Is Accidentally Timely but Also Timeless." *The Washington Post*, 17 Aug. 2020, www.washingtonpost.com/entertainment/books/diane-cooks-the-new-wilderness-is-accidentally-timely-but-also-timeless/2020/08/17/1cbca6f6-db1c-11ea-b205-ff838e15a9a6_story.html. Accessed 23 Nov. 2020.

The Night Watchman

Author: Louise Erdrich (b. 1954)
Publisher: Harper Perennial (New York). 432 pp.
Type of work: Novel
Time: 1953–54
Locales: Turtle Mountain Reservation, North Dakota; Minneapolis, Minnesota; Washington, DC

Thomas Wazhashk, a Turtle Mountain Chippewa man, fights to stop the termination bill, an attempt to cancel governmental treaties with American Indians. The Night Watchman tells the story of his family's battle against the senator who proposed the bill.

Principal characters
THOMAS WAZHASHK, a night watchman and tribal leader
PATRICE "PIXIE" PARANTEAU, his younger niece
VERA PARANTEAU, his older niece
RODERICK, his childhood friend
WOOD MOUNTAIN, a local boxer
LLOYD BARNES, the White math teacher at the local school
MILLIE CLOUD, the educated daughter of Thomas's friend Louis

Louise Erdrich's *The Night Watchman* (2020) is the fictionalized story of Erdrich's grandfather, Patrick Gourneau (Thomas Wazhashk in the novel), a member of the Turtle Mountain Band of Chippewa who worked as a night watchman while fighting for the rights of American Indians. She opens the novel with an author's note stating:

> On August 1, 1953, the United States Congress announced House Concurrent Resolution 108, a bill to abrogate nation-to-nation treaties, which had been made with American Indian Nations for 'as long as the grass grows and the rivers flow.' The announcement called for the eventual termination of all tribes, and the immediate termination of five tribes, including the Turtle Mountain Band of Chippewa.

What follows is the fictional depiction of real events. Thomas fights against the termination bill from home by writing letters, and later travels to the Washington, DC, to make his case to protect American Indian rights in person. While Thomas is based on Erdrich's grandfather, however, the rest of the characters were created for the novel. Alongside Thomas's quest are the stories of members of his community,

Louise Erdrich

people who fight every day to survive on an impoverished reservation.

Like many of Erdrich's previous novels, *The Night Watchman* switches point of view from chapter to chapter. Thomas and his niece Patrice "Pixie" Paranteau are the main narrators, but a variety of side personalities also provide insight into the issues dealt with by the community. As the novel begins, Thomas has been hired as the night watchman at the local Jewel Bearing Plant, which creates jewel bearings with precious stones used by the Defense Department and the watch maker Bulova. Patrice is the plant's best worker. Thomas spends his work hours watching over the buildings and grounds. In between his rounds, he writes letters to his family and to the government, which is trying to break treaties with the American Indian tribal nations. In contrast, Patrice works days in the factory, excelling at the detailed work required by the jewels. When she goes home at night, she cares for her aging mother and younger brother, chops wood to warm their home, and traps animals for their food. The main narrative thread of the novel follows these two characters on their different but intersecting journeys.

Erdrich uses Thomas to share the story of the fight against the termination bill that has been presented by Senator Arthur V. Watkins, a real governmental official who proposed that the American Indian nations in North Dakota needed neither governmental aid nor the land that had been promised to them in treaties signed generations earlier. Watkins argues that the bill "was supposed to emancipate Indians," however, the tribes that would be affected see it as a way to further erase them. Thomas and several other people in the community stand up to protect their land and their existence. They know that "every so often the government remembered about Indians. And when they did, they always tried to *solve* Indians. . . . They solve us by getting rid of us." Thomas and the others understand the absurdity of this bill. He explains just how harmful the bill would be, stating,

> *Emancipated.* But they were not enslaved. Freed from being Indians was the idea. Emancipated from their land. Freed from the treaties that Thomas's father and grandfather had signed and that were promised to last forever. So, as usual, by getting rid of us, the Indian problem would be *solved.*

Fortunately for the Turtle Mountain Band, one of the specific tribes that the bill targets, Thomas does not stop his campaign for American Indian rights until he reaches Washington, DC, to fight for the cause in person.

Patrice fights a different—but no less important—battle involving human trafficking. When Patrice's sister, Vera, who has moved to the nearby city to find a job and better life off the reservation, does not send word of her wellbeing home, Patrice travels to Minneapolis to find her. While there, the younger woman is manipulated into working in a club where men gawk at her as she swims in a tank of water wearing a blue diving suit. The diving suit, however, has been dyed with coloring that poisons the wearer. When Patrice discovers that her predecessors died after prolonged exposure to the suit, she flees the job and renews her efforts into finding her lost sister. As she looks for Vera, she discovers a house with chains and collars. She knows something is wrong with this place, but it is not until later that she learns that her sister has been held captive and forced into sex work.

While Thomas and Patrice provide the two main point of views, Erdrich frames their journeys with interspersed perspectives on the daily lives and struggles of the Turtle Mountain Band. Erdrich presents the tribe's fight to retain their identity with honest portrayals of the problems faced in the community, and the story reveals a variety of issues found in the fictional families of her reservation. Poverty is one issue highlighted particularly with Patrice's family. This is first introduced when Patrice's lunch bucket is found to hold uncooked dough. The other women share their food, but Patrice's former best friend Valentine loudly points out that Patrice's usual meal is "lard on bread," which is "poor people food." The home where she lives with her mother and brother is "a simple pole and mud rectangle, unimproved, low and leaning" with a "slop pail where they pissed on winter nights." Another problem showcased through Patrice's family is alcoholism. At the beginning of her novel, her father has shown up begging for money so he can drink. Patrice and her mother, Zhaanat, take turns sitting up all night to make sure he does not return to rob them. One more dilemma faced by families is the number of young people who leave the reservation, going to the nearby cities to find jobs and abandoning the reservation.

In contrast to the current everyday issues that Patrice's family faces, Thomas also struggles with issues from the past. Years in a Catholic boarding school gave him an education that he uses to help his community, but also left him with the ghost of Roderick, a childhood friend who died after being beaten and starved for a minor infraction committed by another child. Religion is also brought into the story with the introduction of two Mormon missionaries who attempt to convert the people in the tribe to their thinking despite the reality of their founder's prejudice against anyone with darker skin.

As Erdrich tells her story, she brings the people of the Turtle Mountain Reservation to life. Some of them speak English, but others only speak their native language. Some of them are educated, but most are illiterate. All of them, however, are human, and Erdrich makes readers see their humanity. Juggie Blue, the caretaker and cook at the barracks where the local schoolteachers live, routinely stays late and keeps food warm for Lloyd Barnes, the White math teacher and boxing coach. Barnes works with Wood Mountain, Juggie's son, teaching the young man to box in his hours after work. Wood Mountain's generosity and kindness are seen when he follows Patrice to Minneapolis to make sure she is safe. Other characters include Thomas's elderly father, Biboon, who had served as a tribal leader in the past, including helping negotiate government treaties; Thomas's wife, Rose, who runs a daycare out of their home; Zhaanat, Thomas's cousin and Patrice's mother; Louis, who owns and races horses; Grace, Louis's teenage daughter, who rides the horses and has a crush on Wood Mountain; Millie, the scholar; LaBatte, a childhood friend of Thomas, haunted by Roderick's death; and many others whose lives revolve around the reservation.

Reviews of the novel have largely been positive and emphasized the character development in it. The *Publishers Weekly* review commented on the author's ability to create a reality that pulls readers into the story with its "durable network of families, friends, and neighbors, alive or dead." The review continued, "Erdrich's inspired portrait of her own tribe's resilient heritage masterfully encompasses an array of characters and historical events." Donna Seaman's *Booklist* review also praised Erdrich, saying, "Through the personalities and predicaments of her many charismatic characters, and through rapturous descriptions of winter landscapes and steaming meals, sustaining humor and spiritual visitations, Erdrich traces the indelible traumas of racism and sexual violence and celebrates the vitality and depth of Chippewa life." The *Library Journal* review, written by Sally Bissell, continued the praise with the verdict that "Erdrich once again calls upon her considerable storytelling skills to elucidate the struggles of generations of Native people to retain their cultural identity and their connection to the land."

Author Biography

Louise Erdrich is an Ojibwe author of novels, poetry, and children's books. She won the 1984 National Book Critics Circle Award for Fiction for *Love Medicine* (1984), the 2006 Scott O'Dell Award for Historical Fiction for the children's book *The Game of Silence* (2005), and the 2012 National Book Award for Fiction for *The Round House* (2012).

Theresa L. Stowell, PhD

Review Sources

Bissell, Sally. Review of *The Night Watchman*, by Louise Erdrich. *Library Journal*, vol. 145, no. 2, Feb. 2020, p. 78. *Literary Reference Center Plus*, search.ebscohost.com/login.aspx?direct=true&db=lkh&AN=141333213&site=lrc-plus. Accessed 2 Nov. 2020.

Review of *The Night Watchman*, by Louise Erdrich. *Kirkus Reviews*, 15 Jan. 2020. *Literary Reference Center Plus*, search.ebscohost.com/login.aspx?direct=true&db=lkh&AN=141173502&site=lrc-plus. Accessed 2 Nov. 2020.

Review of *The Night Watchman*, by Louise Erdrich. *Publishers Weekly*, 16 Dec. 2019, p. 88. *Literary Reference Center Plus*, search.ebscohost.com/login.aspx?direct=true&db=lkh&AN=140369039&site=lrc-plus. Accessed 2 Nov. 2020.

Seaman, Donna. Review of *The Night Watchman*, by Louise Erdrich. *Booklist*, 1 Jan. 2020, p. 48. *Literary Reference Center Plus*, search.ebscohost.com/login.aspx?direct=true&db=lkh&AN=141181475&site=lrc-plus. Accessed 2 Nov. 2020.

Nobody Will Tell You This but Me
A True (as Told to Me) Story

Author: Bess Kalb (b. 1987)
Publisher: Alfred A. Knopf (New York). 224 pp.
Type of work: Memoir, biography
Time: ca. 1926–2017
Locales: Brooklyn, New York; Westchester, New York; Palm Beach, Florida; Los Angeles, California

In this unique memoir, author Bess Kalb gives a vivid account of the life of her late grandmother, Bobby Bell, as if narrated by Bobby herself. Both funny and deeply moving, the book probes matrilineal bonds across generations. It also follows the arc of the American Dream, showing how Bobby prospered compared to her Jewish immigrant mother and laid a foundation for Kalb herself.

Principal personages
BARBARA "BOBBY" DOROTHY BELL [NÉE OTIS], the narrator, the author's deceased grandmother
BESS KALB, her granddaughter, the author
HAROLD "HANK" BELL, her husband and Kalb's grandfather
ROBIN BELL, her daughter and Kalb's mother
ROSE OTIS, her mother

With *Nobody Will Tell You This but Me: A True (as Told to Me) Story* (2020), Bess Kalb produces an imaginative work that bridges the genres of memoir and oral history. After the death of her grandmother, Barbara "Bobby" Dorothy Bell, Kalb sets out to capture her grandmother's spirit and her stories. But most of all, she seems intent on paying tribute to the strength of their grandmother-granddaughter bond. This focus captures both the great joy of love and memories and the profound sadness of loss.

Bobby's cutting wit and overbearing affection give the memoir its spice. The book is written in first person, with the voice of Bobby speaking from the grave (and in snippets from real voicemails and reconstructed conversations) to Kalb—and, thus, also to the reader. This format gives the narrative an informal, intimate, and irreverent tone, quite literally picking up the conversation from grandmother to granddaughter cut short by death. This is established from the outset; in the prologue, when recounting her own funeral, Bobby remarks, "It's a terrible thing to be dead. Oh, how boring. How maddening. Nothing to do. Nothing to read. No one to talk to. And everyone's a mess. Thank God for that, at least." But there are also more somber interludes along with the cutting humor. Many of these darker moments derive from Bobby's Jewish family's immigration story, or dance around Kalb's grief and other moments of family trauma. From this family lore come the words of wisdom that Bobby shares from her own grandfather (her *zayde*): "when the earth is cracking behind your feet, you go forward. One foot in front of the other. One foot in front of the other." These words, often repeated throughout, serve both as a metaphor for Kalb's personal grief and as the underlying impetus for the multigenerational story at the heart of the memoir.

Bess Kalb

Nobody Will Tell You This but Me is divided into three main parts, as well as a shorter fourth section and a prologue and epilogue. The first main part is labeled "My Mother," and indeed focuses on Bobby's mother, Rose, from her own background through Bobby's childhood and early adult years. The second section, "Your Mother," is organized around Bobby's complicated relationship with her own daughter (and Kalb's mother), Robin. The third section, "Our Life Together," focuses on the relationship between Bobby and Kalb. This organizational structure makes the matrilineal focus of the text self-evident. Rose, Bobby, and Robin each have only one daughter (though they all have sons as well), and the angst of their troubled mother-daughter bonds is a recurring cadence. Kalb positions her own affectionate relationship as her grandmother's "pet" in contrast with these strained mother-daughter bonds, though even here some more tense strains emerge, as Bobby seeks to control many aspects of Kalb's lifestyle and image into adulthood.

Many critics have found the first part of the book dealing with Rose's life story and Bobby's childhood particularly compelling. At age ten, Bobby almost dies of an infection. Her mother sits by her bedside and recounts the tragic story of her own childhood in Pinsk, a village in modern-day Belarus, then part of the Russian Empire. It is the only time that she speaks to her daughter of her life before America and of the family she was forced to leave at age twelve. Rose's father had already fallen victim to the anti-Semitic pogroms, and her brothers had been conscripted into the Russian army. Her mother insisted that young Rose raise money and leave for what the villagers called "the Goldene Medinah, the Promised Land, flowing with milk and honey"— the United States. The description of Rose's departure from Pinsk is one of the most poignant moments of the book. The terrified young girl "considered taking her cloth bunny rabbit; she picked it up and stared at it. She was too scared to kiss her mother goodbye so she kissed the rabbit instead and left it on the bed. She said she regretted kissing the rabbit instead of her mother every second of every day."

Rose's traumatic experience of childhood, her dangerous and solitary escape to the United States, and her endurance of extreme poverty and deprivation all shine a telling light on her hands-off relationship with Bobby, who seems to have perceived her as aloof. Yet Bobby also remembers her mother as supporting her brothers' education (and her own) and managing to provide home-cooked meals to unpredictable throngs on a shoestring budget. Rose's resilience and strength is evident. Her story is significant for readers interested in tracing the Jewish diaspora, and her survival can be celebrated even as it helps recover some memory of many others who perished.

Also contained in the first section of the book is the story of Bobby's early years of marriage to Hank Bell. While their marriage begins in poverty, the two soon develop financial security through real estate development in the postwar housing boom of New York City and its environs. Although it is not a major theme of the book, the account of Hank's work in New York real estate provides another layer of historical interest. Further, Bobby's shift from an urban tenement to a sprawling suburban ranch is representative of both the period of economic prosperity following World War II and the more timeless ideal of the so-called American Dream, an archetypal concept that intersects in many interesting ways with the arc of Bobby's life. Kalb effectively communicates the optimism in Bobby's rags-to-riches story as a first generation American but also recognizes the specific conditions that made it possible and are not in fact available to all.

The wealth generated by the Bells' real estate investments also permeates the later sections of the book. These parts have fewer intersections with major historical events or tragedies, focusing more on the personal experiences of Bobby, Robin, and Kalb in their comfortable upper-middle-class lives. Several reviewers noted that this may be less compelling to many general readers, but the innovative writing style sustains interest, and the humor and deeply felt emotions remain strong. One fascinating larger-scale theme that does surface in the "Your Mother" section is the tension surrounding Robin's initiative to explore her Jewish roots more deeply. Rose, having escaped persecution, never abandoned her faith but avoided its most visible traditions. Bobby's faith is not overtly discussed within the book, but her reaction to Robin's trip to a *kibbutz* in Israel is vocal incredulity. Fully integrated into upper-class suburban society, Bobby seems less interested than her daughter in delving into the family's past and its cultural traditions. She perceives keenly how easy it would be to return to poverty and persecution.

If "My Mother" has a historical focus and "Your Mother" looks at transition, "Our Life Together" is the heart of *Nobody Will Tell You This but Me*. Above all, it permits Kalb to memorialize her relationship with her grandmother, which is, of course, the entire reason behind the book. It is here that author and narrator unite, though Kalb maintains the structure in which Bobby speaks in first person, while Kalb remains the "you." Sweet memories and childhood anecdotes come to the forefront, though Kalb also recounts a few moments of pain and strife. As other reviewers have noted, Kalb is perhaps too focused on a positive accounting of her grandmother, avoiding digging deeper into the more negative or complex memories that could make her appear more well rounded to a reader. But the humanity of grief is on full display and readers may appreciate the presentation here as they weigh their own losses. Kalb shares the deepest moments of her grief in losing her grandmother and the rituals she followed attempting to reconcile herself to the loss. She also shares her recognition of the seismic shifts this loss caused for her whole family—she lost a grandmother, but her mother lost a mother, and these losses are not equivalent.

Kalb's account of the poignant nature of love and loss also reflects the role of mementos and documentation in keeping the memory of a person alive. The author's recollection of phone conversations with her grandmother are central to the narrative—and many of these offer the best humor and moments to which many readers might feel a connection. But even more immediate, and haunting, are the many voicemails from Bobby that Kalb has kept over the years. Transcriptions of some of these allow the most direct window into Bobby's true voice. But the recorded messages are both sweet and painful; a year after her grandmother's death, Kalb is reluctant to listen to them even as she feels that she is losing the ability to conjure Bobby's voice in her head. While the voicemails show the impact of modern technology on grief and memory, the inclusion of photographs throughout the book highlights a more traditional aid to remembering. The images of Bobby and the other subjects of the book are enriching, giving anchor to the thoughts and emotions within and allowing the reader to develop a fuller understanding of these people.

Nobody Will Tell You This but Me is ultimately built on both the power and the slippage of memory, particularly regarding those we have loved and who have passed away. The unusual but effective narrative structure acknowledges this in all its complexity. In the epilogue, Bobby and her granddaughter have a dialogue about the authorship of the book at hand—Kalb denies writing it and attributes the words to her grandmother until Bobby corrects her sharply: "Of course I'm not. I'm in a box in the ground. You're putting words in my mouth. In a dead woman's mouth." Kalb is aware that this could potentially be problematic, but the voice she gives her grandmother waves off any worry. The book, no matter who the true author, is a fitting tribute, an honor not only to Bobby but also to the very idea of family bonds across generations.

Critical reception to *Nobody Will Tell You This but Me* was largely positive. Writing for the *New York Times*, Miranda Popkey noted she was moved to tears more than once in her reading and praised the "conversational but always assertive narration," though she also found that "one longs for a still more fully rounded portrait" of Bobby. *Kirkus* gave a starred review, calling the book "endearing, bittersweet, and entertainingly fresh." The critic for *Publishers Weekly* gave a deft summary of the work's appeal, stating, "This is a fun, touching tribute to family, and the perfect book for anyone who treasures their domineering, spirited grandmother."

Author Biography
Bess Kalb is an essayist and screenwriter. She won a Writer's Guild Award for her writing for the television program *Jimmy Kimmel Live!* and has published essays in outlets such as the *New Yorker*, the *New Republic*, *Wired*, and *The Nation*.

Julia A. Sienkewicz, PhD

Review Sources

Irvine, Artemis. Review of *Nobody Will Tell You This but Me: A True (as Told to Me) Story*, by Bess Kalb. *The Palatinate*, 22 Apr. 2020, www.palatinate.org.uk/review-nobody-will-tell-you-this-but-me/. Accessed 8 Nov. 2020.

Review of *Nobody Will Tell You This but Me: A True (as Told to Me) Story*, by Bess Kalb. *Kirkus*, 3 Dec. 2019, www.kirkusreviews.com/book-reviews/bess-kalb/nobody-will-tell-you-this-but-me/. Accessed 10 Nov. 2020.

Review of *Nobody Will Tell You This but Me: A True (as Told to Me) Story*, by Bess Kalb. *Publishers Weekly*, 26 Nov. 2019, www.publishersweekly.com/978-0-525-65471-1. Accessed 10 Nov. 2020.

Popkey, Miranda. "The Ghost Writer: An Author Imagines a Letter From Her Late Grandmother." Review of *Nobody Will Tell You This but Me: A True (as Told to Me) Story*, by Bess Kalb. *The New York Times*, 17 Mar. 2020, www.nytimes.com/2020/03/17/books/review/bess-kalb-nobody-will-tell-you-this-but-me.html. Accessed 8 Nov. 2020.

Tolchin, Edith G. Review of *Nobody Will Tell You This but Me: A True (as Told to Me) Story*, by Bess Kalb. *New York Journal of Books*, 17 Mar. 2020, www.nyjournalofbooks.com/book-review/nobody-will-tell-you. Accessed 8 Nov. 2020.

Not So Pure and Simple

Author: Lamar Giles (b. ca. 1979)
Publisher: HarperTeen (New York). 400 pp.
Type of work: Novel
Time: Present day
Locale: Green Creek, Virginia

Not So Pure and Simple *is a comic coming-of-age young-adult novel about navigating faith, sex, and notions of masculinity in small-town America.*

Principal characters

DEL RAINEY, a teenager who ends up joining a Purity Pledge program at his church in an effort to be with a girl he has long had an interest in
KIERA WESTING, his crush
CRESSIE RAINEY, his older sister
JAMEER SESAY, his church friend
SHIANNE GRIFFITHS, a friend with whom he shares a secret

Del Rainey, the teenage protagonist and narrator of Lamar Giles's 2020 young-adult novel *Not So Pure and Simple*, is a master of what he has termed covert "Prayer Peeking." Del does not come from a family of "hard-core Church People," as he puts it, but his mother's recent interest in attending services at the First Missionary House of the Lord has taught him skills of disengagement any long-suffering church kid could appreciate. With Pastor Newsome, whom he sees as a bit of an extravagant showman, on a prayer tear, Del sneaks a longing look at his longtime crush, Kiera Westing. Kiera is smart, beautiful, popular, and, to Del's chagrin, perpetually involved with someone else. Her most recent beau was Colossus Turner, a state champion wrestler with a dubious reputation. On the day the novel begins, Del's Prayer Peeking confirms a rumor he had desperately hoped to be true: no promise ring is encircling Kiera's delicate finger; she and Colossus are over. Dreams of wooing Kiera after the service carry Del far away from the church proceedings, so much so that when Kiera rises from her pew to volunteer for a teen church group, he, blinded by love and lust, unthinkingly does so as well. Del's seemingly harmless leap of faith backfires, at least as far as romance is concerned, for he has unwittingly pledged to protect his virginity and remain "pure" until marriage.

"Because I love God," Del tentatively answers when a beaming Sister Vanessa—leader of the Purity Pledge group—proffers a microphone, asking him why he has freely chosen to make such a serious commitment to his faith. Del knows this is always an appropriate answer within church walls. "When you did something good, and someone asked why you did it: 'Because I love God,'" he explains. "If you did something bad, and someone asked why you shouldn't do it again: 'Because God loves me.'"

Exemplified by this scene, Giles, writing in Del's humorously flippant voice, easily pokes fun at and, later, offers criticism of church ritual and doctrine without making it the book's focus. *Not So Pure and Simple* is more expansive than its first few chapters let on, juxtaposing various thought-provoking ideas about sex and gender, rather than sex and faith. Throughout, Giles maintains an engaging, comedic tone that only occasionally slips into didacticism. His ease with humorous teen parlance belies the fact that he is best known for writing mysteries and thrillers, though also for young-adult readers. His 2014 debut, *Fake ID*, is a murder mystery featuring a teenager in the witness protection program. Other novels, including *Endangered* (2015), *Overturned* (2017), and *Spin* (2019) are of a similar genre. *Not So Pure and Simple* is his first novel centered on realism.

Lamar Giles

Courtesy HarperCollins Publishers

Though Del is now an official member of the church's Purity Pledge group, his desire for Kiera has only intensified. Another pledger, the quiet and meticulously groomed Jameer Sesay, somewhat suspiciously offers his assistance. Jameer, the only child of exceedingly strict parents, is a veteran church kid. He is also Kiera's neighbor and confidante. He offers to help Del win her heart in exchange for an unusual favor: answers to a list of uncomfortable questions about sex. Jameer's request is one of the few moments in *Not So Pure and Simple* that strains plausibility. While the idea that Jameer—and, later, multiple curious teens—would be so thoroughly blocked from using the internet seems hard to believe, it does not detract from the overall impact of the story and prose. Jameer is not asking Del directly, though Del does have an unmerited reputation for being a player; he is asking Del to convey his questions to MJ, the friendly teacher tasked with leading the local high school's Healthy Living class. Of course, Healthy Living is just an obfuscating title for sexual education—a class that Jameer's parents, like all Purity Pledge parents except for Del's, have forbidden him to take. It could be considered a bit of a clumsy narrative tie, having Jameer ask Del to give voice to his most embarrassing, private thoughts, but it is an important one. *Not So Pure and Simple* explores the competing narratives offered by Purity Pledge and Healthy Living, but as his title suggests, Giles compellingly complicates his theme further with the introduction of the "Baby-Getters Club."

The Baby-Getters Club, Del wearily explains, is not a real club. In 2012 national media reported on a real-life case in which a group of students in Le Roy, New York, began experiencing bizarre tics and spasms. The mysterious affliction seemed to strike at random, felling sufferers like an uncontrollable plague. *Not So Pure and Simple*'s Baby-Getters Club is presented with a similar aura of myth. Nine young women in Del's school became pregnant around the same time. Del attributes the "phenomenon" to a snowstorm that stranded teenagers at home and parents at work, but the local media was quick to offer a more conspiratorial explanation. As a joke, a classmate told a news crew that the girls had made a pact to get pregnant and called themselves the Baby-Getters Club. The unfortunate name and story stuck. Purity Pledge and Healthy Living are both direct responses to the Baby-Getters Club, two bumbling attempts by adults to talk to their children about sex.

But as Giles writes, the young people have plenty to say themselves. Giles demonstrates a firm grasp on how contemporary teenagers use social media and the internet to advocate for themselves. One so-called Baby-Getter named Taylor ultimately identifies the father of her young son. In a brazen Instagram story, she expresses frustration that she and the other girls are experiencing a kind of social death, while their unnamed partners remain under the radar, unscathed. Del's older sister, Cressie, a first-year college student, reaches out to Taylor. Though the Raineys live in a small Virginia town called Green Creek, Cressie attends a school in nearby Richmond, and her removal from the town offers her a sobering look at its social mores. Therefore, she attempts to cut through the noise with a social media project of her own.

It turns out that Del is close with another Baby-Getter named Shianne. During their first year of high school, it was rumored that Del and Shianne had had sex at an infamous basement party. He reveals fairly early that the story is a lie, an agreed-upon fiction that results in the book's only real pact. Del and Shianne, like the other characters in the story also generally considered, including by critics, to be well-rounded and authentic, present the reader with effective opposing views of adolescence. Their imaginary basement escapade made Del's reputation, just as it ruined Shianne's. Giles forces the reader to reckon with this disparity, impactfully highlighting the ways in which sex is often socially encouraged and celebrated for young men while young women are shamed and reviled for it. This is one of the book's central achievements. For example, Del's father offers his son condoms and a cursory explanation of birth control. He encourages Del to enjoy his sexuality but also, to Del's embarrassment, suggests that his son maintains a sex life that is beyond his actual experience. There is also Qwan, Del's best friend. Qwan takes pride in being a serial dater until he meets Angie, who foils his credo of never becoming too attached to any one girl. Still, he retains certain potentially harmful ideas about how men should behave. Further contributing to the realism successfully conveyed through the book's characters, writing, and plot, there are no clear-cut villains in *Not So Pure and Simple*. Giles offers plenty of evidence that Del's father and Qwan are "good guys," while simultaneously illustrating their flaws. A look, a comment, an outdated piece of advice—these are the scraps of experience that undergird a world in which toxic masculinity causes serious harm.

Del has his own difficult lessons to learn. His thoughtful—if narratively convoluted—act of self-reflection feels in tune with a generation focused on accountability for past harm. It is refreshing to see a young-adult novel about sex and abstinence tackle gender (and, if not as rigorously, sexuality) in this way. It would be unrealistic to assume that Kiera, Del, Shianne, and Jameer perceive the Purity Pledge, Healthy Living, and the Baby-Getters Club through the same lens. Critics were in agreement about the book's merits in this regard. A reviewer for *Kirkus* gave the book a starred review, writing, "The novel takes on teen attitudes toward sex and relationships and gender power dynamics in a way that is appealing and thought provoking." Reviewing the novel for *School Library Journal*, in another starred review, Carla Riemer wrote, "Without being didactic, this story explores expectations around gender roles and calls out toxic behaviors that even 'good guys' are guilty of." There is an unprintable phrase Del and Qwan use that refers to what is, in their view, a cardinal teenage sin: lying about one's sexual escapades. As the book progresses, the phrase comes to encompass a serial dishonesty about sex and relationships. If Qwan were honest about how he felt about Angie, if Jameer were honest about his questions, if Del were honest about his lack of experience, if sexual education were both teen friendly and genuinely informative—would not everyone benefit? As the teenagers in the story reckon with radical honesty, adults like Del's father, MJ, and even Pastor Newsome demonstrate that it is never too late to embrace personal growth.

Author Biography
Novelist Lamar Giles is a two-time Edgar Award finalist. His young-adult books include *Fake ID* (2014), *Endangered* (2015), *Overturned* (2017), and *Spin* (2019). He has also authored middle-grade mystery novels. He is also a founding member of the organization We Need Diverse Books.

Molly Hagan

Review Sources
Harris, Monique. Review of *Not So Pure and Simple*, by Lamar Giles. *The Horn Book*, 13 Feb. 2020, www.hbook.com/?detailStory=review-of-not-so-pure-and-simple. Accessed 16 Oct. 2020.
Review of *Not So Pure and Simple*, by Lamar Giles. *Kirkus*, 13 Oct. 2019, www.kirkusreviews.com/book-reviews/lamar-giles/not-so-pure-and-simple. Accessed 16 Oct. 2020.
Review of *Not So Pure and Simple*, by Lamar Giles. *Publishers Weekly*, 30 Oct. 2019, www.publishersweekly.com/978-0-06-234919-4. Accessed 16 Oct. 2020.
Riemer, Carla. Review of *Not So Pure and Simple*, by Lamar Giles. *School Library Journal*, 1 Nov. 2019, www.slj.com/?reviewDetail=not-so-pure-and-simple. Accessed 16 Oct. 2020.

Obit

Author: Victoria Chang (b. 1970)
Publisher: Copper Canyon (Port Townsend, WA). 120 pp.
Type of work: Poetry

Victoria Chang's Obit *is a collection of poems that draw on the format of the newspaper obituary to explore feelings of grief, loss, and the idea of how memory functions in people's lives.*

Those familiar with American poet Victoria Chang's previous works, particularly the 2017 collection *Barbie Chang* and her 2013 collection *The Boss*, will enjoy a new side to the artist's oeuvre with *Obit* (2020). Readers who are new to Chang, too, will likely find much to appreciate in this soulful, meditative collection. The work both challenges and intrigues with its unique structure and its focus on difficult emotional concepts. As the title suggests, the obituary format is central to the poems in the collection, but while death is a central theme, Chang expands her scope considerably through her masterful command of language.

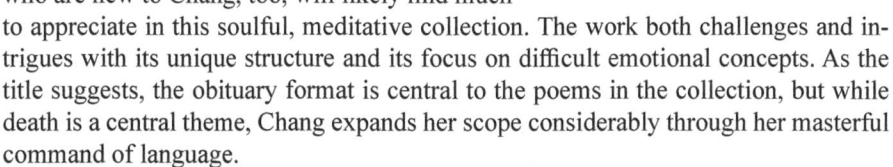

In many ways *Obit* represents a natural step in Chang's career, both building on her established style and continuing her tendencies to experiment and examine key themes in new ways. Widely recognized as a notable figure in modern poetry, Chang has been published in literary journals including the *Kenyon Review*, *Slate*, the *Nation*, and the *Paris Review*, as well as anthologies such as *Best American Poetry 2005*. She received a number of awards and recognitions for her work, including a California Book Award and a PEN Center USA Literary Award for *The Boss*. Yet perhaps unlike many poets, she also earned a business degree and had a career in banking and consulting. This diversity in experience and perspective is informative to the complexity and diversity that Chang demonstrates in her poetry.

Many poetry critics have noted that Chang became more experimental in her work over the course of her writing career. Her first poetry collection, *Circle* (2005), and her second, *Salvinia Molesta* (2008), both focused in slightly different ways on the construction of identity, the experience of women, and on Asian and Asian American life. Reviewers appreciated Chang's evocative language and the emotional depth of her work, but many also noted the first hints at the use of experimental linguistic and structural techniques to highlight or contrast with the messages contained within her poems. By the time Chang published *The Boss*, experimentation had become a more central focus of her writing. That collection continued to showcase her ability to provide a wealth of perspectives through a diverse array of characters, while using more challenging structures such as run-on sentences and sentence fragments. Chang's use of unusual linguistic constructions to experiment with the physical form of the poem expanded in *Barbie Chang*, which further explored concepts of identity, including femininity, masculinity, and marginalization.

With *Obit*, Chang once again experiments with structure and format to deepen and reflect upon the themes explored in the collection. Many of her familiar themes of identity are also carried over, but here the concepts of death and grief are the overarching focus. Chang, who stated in interviews that she was inspired in part by her mother's death in forming these poems, provides readers with poetic obituaries for all the things she has lost in the world. The poems are not elegies, which are intended to celebrate and immortalize a person who has died, but rather they are obituaries, in that they express the feelings of those left alive after someone—or, at times, something—has died or otherwise been somehow lost. More specifically, most of the poems in *Obit* emulate the style of the common newspaper obituary, stating the name of the deceased and the date of death before a relatively brief description. Some are more straightforward reflections on the death or loss of an individual, but others provide an unusual perspective, presenting obituaries of ideas, concepts, items, and memory itself. The poem "Secrets" provides an example of how the works are not always directly about people or even objects, yet even the most abstract losses relate back to human relationships:

> Secrets—died on August 7, 2015 and
> they were relieved to die. No one at the
> funeral had known about my mother's illness. No one had known how fiercely my
> mother and father fought.

Overall, the obituary structure helps make the work experimental as a whole and at the level of each poem, and also on the emotional level by transforming what might be marginal or tangential reflections on grief and loss into fully realized statements on the many dimensions of grief.

At times, Chang's poems range into dark humor, with at times caustic and sarcastic verse. A prime example can be found on the cover of the book itself, which features repeated images of an obituary for the author herself, telling readers:

> CHANG–Victoria.
> Died unknowingly on June 24,
> 2009 on the I-405 freeway.
> Born in the Motor City, it is
> fitting she died on the freeway.
> When her mother called about
> her father's heart attack, she
> was living an indented life, a
> swallow that didn't dip. This
> was not her first death.

Readers may find that Chang's unusual approach invites them to reconsider two separate genres, the poem and the newspaper obituary. It is a purposeful choice that the work was entitled *Obit*, rather than obituary, because the truncated structure of the poems are part of the artistic thrust of the work, not only reflecting ruminations on death and loss, but also forcing those reflections into a familiar structure designed for brevity and practicality rather than emotional heft. Chang's stanzas are forced into a column format, cleaving words and sentences in half and creating mental spaces where there might otherwise be a clean transition from thought to thought. In choosing to structure her work in this way, Chang not only provides the poem with a new, yet familiar, framework, but also reorganizes the thoughts, sounds, and syllables to create different meanings and different inflection points for the reader's mind.

The fragmentary nature of the obit column also provides a structural reflection of the fragmentary nature of memory and one's emotional reactions to the persons, ideals, and ideas that one loses throughout one's life. This is seen in the obituary for Chang's mother, which is perhaps the most central to the work as a whole. It is actually spread throughout the book, captured in snippets directly about her death, but also in poems about the loss of artifacts and memories of her life. Chang's father is the other central figure, as several poems reflect on the slow deterioration of his health and its impact on Chang and her mother. Both large and small losses ultimately combine to create an entire picture, that of Chang's loss of her parents as people and of her memories of them.

A good example of this interconnection comes in the poem "Hands," which relates how Chang's mother's hands grew shaky and her handwriting declined. Chang compares hands to other parts of the body, noting how they are used to "enhance language" and complete hugs. This emphasizes how if one part of a person stops performing as it should, communication and emotional connection can suffer. Shaky hands may not be as tragic as an actual death, but Chang suggests these kinds of losses still touch not only the person specifically affected but also those around them. In addition, the language of grief itself is a key concern, and Chang skillfully shows how in some ways it is impossible to fully express the depth and variety of grief.

Similar ideas emerge as Chang considers her father's declining mental state in "The Clock," writing:

> I think about my father and
> his lack of first thoughts, how every
> thought is a second or third or fourth
> thought, unable to locate the first most
> important thought.

This excerpt shows Chang's ability to craft both poignant remembrances and philosophical, deeply literary reflections at the same time. These poems are personal and often heartfelt, but also incisive comments on the nature of memory, language, and other complex themes. Again, the structure is important to this dual nature, as Chang is able to both explore the potential depth that an obituary might contain and subvert the traditional form. Taking on universal human concepts such as aging, death, and grief may be fairly expected in poetry, and in a different way is central to the typical obituary, yet combining the two forms brings unexpected power and reveals Chang's mastery of her craft. While each poem is short, each carefully chosen word and purposefully crafted break contributes to the emotional depth of the piece.

Obit, like most of Chang's previous works, received rave reviews from numerous critics. In the *Los Angeles Review of Books*, Carol Muske-Dukes found Chang's *Obit* a deeply moving and essential work, stating, "Perhaps the poet's most startlingly precise and original observation about grief in *Obit* is this: 'Sadness is plural, but grief is singular.'" This observation reflects on one of the ways that *Obit* plays with familiar forms in unexpected ways. Grief is the internal reflection on loss, necessarily subjective and filtered through a person's individual and independent lens, while the obituary is a public expression of loss, often containing only the most superficial reflections of the emotional impact of the death being described. Chang upends this traditionalism, presenting pieces that express the depth of the personal in the format of public discourse.

Many other reviewers were equally complimentary. Writing for the *Kenyon Review*, Dean Rader noted, "That these poems do such complete work with so few tools from the poetry toolbox is humbling. Each poem is a masterwork of compression and compassion." In the *New Republic*, Megan Evershed wrote, "for all the failures of language, Chang's employment of it is beautiful and resonant." *Obit* was named a notable book of the year by publications including the *New York Times*, and was longlisted for the prestigious National Book Award in Poetry. Considering its effective use of experimental structures as a poetic medium, the book is a notable success. Yet it is ultimately as a work of emotional significance, reflecting Chang's own experience as well as themes common to the human condition, that *Obit* makes its deepest mark. For many readers, it may be impossible to see an obituary in the same way ever again.

Author Biography
Writer Victoria Chang has received many honors for her work, including a Guggenheim Fellowship, a MacDowell Fellowship, and a Pushcart Prize. In addition to several poetry collections, she authored the children's picture book *Is Mommy?* (2015) and the middle-grade verse novel *Love, Love* (2020).

Micah L. Issitt

Review Sources
Evershed, Megan. "Reading the Literature of Grief during a Pandemic." Review of *Obit*, by Victoria Chang, and *Scorpionfish*, by Natalie Bakopoulos. *Critical Mass*, 9 July 2020, newrepublic.com/article/158413/reading-literature-grief-pandemic Accessed 14 Oct. 2020.

Muske-Dukes, Carol. "'Grief Is Singular': On Victoria Chang's 'Obit'." Review of *Obit*, by Victoria Chang. *Los Angeles Review of Books*, 15 Apr. 2020, lareviewofbooks.org/article/grief-is-singular-on-victoria-changs-obit/. Accessed 14 Oct. 2020.

Review of *Obit*, by Victoria Chang. *Publishers Weekly*, 17 Jan. 2020, www.publishersweekly.com/978-1-55659-574-5. Accessed 14 Oct. 2020.

Rader, Dean. "Victoria Chang and the Elegy/Anti-Elegy: On Obit." Review of *Obit*, by Victoria Chang. *Kenyon Review*, kenyonreview.org/reviews/obit-by-victoria-chang-738439/. Accessed 14 Oct. 2020.

The Office of Historical Corrections

Author: Danielle Evans (b. 1983)
Publisher: Riverhead Books (New York). 288 pp.
Type of work: Short fiction, novella
Time: Present day
Locale: The United States

Danielle Evans's second book, The Office of Historical Corrections, *is a collection of six short stories and a novella in which accessible characters explore the past and its impact on the present, grief, and racism.*

Principal characters

LYSSA, a Black woman working at a novelty banquet hall who is mourning the death of her mother
RENA, a photographer who attends the wedding of a White male acquaintance
CLAIRE, a young White woman who becomes a divisive figure at her small liberal arts college when a photo of her wearing a Confederate-flag bikini goes viral
VERA, a young woman who decides to adopt a toddler whom she finds on a bus
CASSIE, a government employee whose job is to correct American history in public records
GENIE, Cassie's lifelong rival who is also a colleague at the Office of Historical Corrections

In interviews, American fiction writer Danielle Evans has stated that she loves short story collections because they provide writers with the opportunity to ask the same question and give different answers. This sentiment is evident in Evans's debut collection, *Before You Suffocate Your Damn Fool Self* (2010), which comprises eight short stories. While the protagonists in these stories are distinctly different from one another in their backgrounds and journeys, each serves as the catalyst of their own undoing. In this way, *Before You Suffocate* explores the cause and effects of self-destruction from multiple angles.

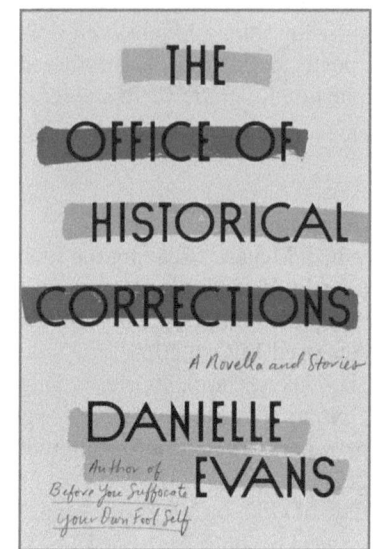

As in her first collection, Evans uses unconnected stories to explore connected themes in her second collection of short fiction, *The Office of Historical Corrections* (2020). In its simplest description, *The Office of Historical Corrections* asks questions about the nebulous nature of history and its impact on the present day. Throughout the superb six short stories and novella, Evans successfully demonstrates both how subjective history can be as well as how much its impact can linger over time. As such, the cast of characters found within the stories are all haunted by the past in some capacity—whether it is their own personal pasts, the country's, or both.

As a writer, Evans has a talent for crafting characters who feel like everyday, relatable people. She accomplishes this by anchoring most of them in seemingly universal experiences, which in turn makes them more accessible to readers. Lyssa, the protagonist from "Happily Ever After," is stuck in a dead-end retail job. Rena in "Richard of York Gave Battle in Vain" is obligated to endure a tacky, over-the-top wedding of someone who can be best described as an acquaintance. And Vera of "Anything Could Disappear" is a college dropout traveling on a Greyhound bus to start a new life in New York City. What makes Evans' stories so powerful is the fact that she takes people who would likely be background characters in other stories and puts them front and center in unexpected situations. This makes for exciting, fresh narratives.

Beyond the dynamic storytelling, *The Office of Historical Corrections* is a fulfilling read thanks to its smart, resonant social commentary. Most of the stories explore the issue of race in some capacity, but not in a direct manner or a didactic one. Instead, Evans presents racism as something that exists continuously within her characters' other experiences. Lyssa, for example, endures aggressions simply for being a Black woman. She has never worked as a princess at any of the children's birthday parties hosted at the banquet hall where she works, and "the one time anyone bothered to give her an explanation for this (she hadn't asked), it was a supervisor who mumbled something about historical accuracy, meaning no Black princesses." In a later scene, her boyfriend, Travis, tries to do her a favor and pick up her mother's prescription, but is accused of having a fake ID and physically accosted by her pharmacy's security because he is "a man and a good three shades darker than she was." Ultimately, Lyssa's story is also one about familial grief as she grapples with both losing her mother to cancer and learning that she may not be able to have children.

The stories in *The Office of Historical Corrections* that do focus primarily on the issue of racism in America are deftly written. "Boys Go to Jupiter" is one such example of how brilliant Evans is at crafting narratives that are both searing and engaging in their message. The story follows a young White woman named Claire who is caught on social media wearing a Confederate-flag bikini that her boyfriend gifted her for spring break. She returns to her small liberal arts college to find most of her peers and the staff are outraged. Despite the fact that she wore the bikini to annoy her stepmother rather than make any kind of political statement, Claire does not take ownership for her actions and becomes defensive, leading to a chain reaction of disheartening events. What makes "Boys Go to Jupiter" such a remarkable read is the fact that Evans tries to understand Claire and the complex forces behind her behavior. Through flashbacks, readers are provided with insight into her relationship with a Black family growing up and how several tragedies led her to become bitter towards them. While this provides insight into Claire, it does not foster empathy for her character.

Arguably the best piece found within *The Office of Historical Corrections* is the titular novella, which also happens to be the story that addresses the issue of racism most directly. It is the story of a Black professor named Cassie who left academia to work for the government as a factchecker of the public record. Cassie is interested in making the world better for Black people but believes the best way to do this is as nonconfrontationally as possible. Meanwhile, her childhood rival and government colleague Genie unapologetically seeks to hold White people accountable. When Genie fixes a sign that marks the site of a historical hate crime in Wisconsin so that it does not state just the name of the victim but the perpetrators' names as well, several of the descendants of the White people listed become enraged. Cassie must travel there to learn the truth behind the history of the sign and what it should say to the world. "The Office of Historical Corrections" is a gripping read that borrows elements from the mystery and speculative fiction genres but is firmly rooted in reality. Evans uses the contrasting characters of Cassie and Genie to make commentary about different paths that Black people can choose when seeking racial justice. More than anything, however, the novella succeeds in illustrating the tenuous relationship between history and the truth. As the story makes clear, sometimes White people tend to separate the two because erasing racism from the past absolves them of taking any corrective or restorative actions in the present.

Reviews of *The Office of Historical Corrections* were overwhelmingly positive, with most critics praising Evans' talent for writing short stories. Jane Hu touched on this in her review for the *New York Times*, writing that, "Evans's propulsive narratives read as though they're getting away with something, building what feel like novelistic plots onto the short story's modest real estate." Indeed, one of the most enjoyable aspects of *The Office of Historical Corrections* is the way which Evans packs a lot of dynamic storytelling into just a few pages. In some ways, however, it could also be argued that is a detriment as it often leaves readers wanting more. Several of the short stories as well as the novella are so excellent that it is hard not to feel that they are deserving of many more pages. Bethanne Patrick commented on this in her review for the *LA Times* when she wrote that the book's short stories "risk being given short shrift" as they essentially function as a preamble to the novella. Yet although the length of these superb pieces may be frustrating to some, they should not deter readers from picking up the book.

Most other reviews have extolled the book for its well-crafted characters. In her review for *USA Today*, Ann Levin noted that Evans studied both anthropology and African American studies in college and that her subsequent observational skills have allowed her to bring an "anthropologist's eye to the material conditions of her characters' lives." It is true that a large part of what makes stories of *The Office of Historical Corrections* work is how nuanced and real the characters are. Through each of her protagonists, Evans succeeds in providing poignant insights about race and identity in late capitalist America.

Perhaps the most common point of praise among critics has been how relevant the stories of *The Office of Historical Corrections* are to the issues that the country faces today. The reviewer for *Publishers Weekly* wrote that it was "a timely, entertaining collection from a talented author who isn't afraid to take chances," while the *Kirkus Reviews* critic concluded that it comprised "necessary narratives, brilliantly crafted." In the 2010s and early 2020s, with the rise of the Black Lives Matter movement, conversations about how whitewashed American history has perpetuated anti-Black racism have come to the forefront of the national conversation in the mainstream media. Through the exceptionally engaging stories of *The Office of Historical Corrections*, Evans pushes this discussion into new and necessary directions.

Author Biography

A 2020 National Endowment for the Arts fellow, Danielle Evans is the author of the short story collection *Before You Suffocate Your Own Fool Self* (2010). Honors for that book included the PEN America PEN/Robert W. Bingham Prize for Debut Short Story Collection and the Hurston/Wright Legacy Award.

Emily E. Turner

Review Sources

Hu, Jane. "New Story Collections Reconsider History and Upend Tradition." Review of *The Office of Historical Corrections*, by Danielle Evans. *The New York Times*, 10 Nov. 2020, www.nytimes.com/2020/11/10/books/review/danielle-evans-office-historical-corrections.html. Accessed 7 Jan 2021.

Levin, Ann. "Danielle Evans' New Collection of Stories is Exhilarating and Timely." Review of *The Office of Historical Corrections*, by Danielle Evans. *USA Today*, 8 Nov. 2020, www.usatoday.com/story/entertainment/books/2020/11/08/review-danielle-evans-office-historical-corrections-exhilarating/6094851002/. Accessed 7 Jan. 2021.

Review of *The Office of Historical Corrections*, by Danielle Evans. *Kirkus Reviews*, 2 Sept. 2020, www.kirkusreviews.com/book-reviews/danielle-evans-46646/the-office-of-historical-corrections/. Accessed 7 Jan. 2021.

Review of *The Office of Historical Corrections*, by Danielle Evans. *Publishers Weekly*, 18 Aug. 2020, www.publishersweekly.com/978-1-59448-733-0. Accessed 7 Jan. 2020.

Patrick, Bethanne. "Blistering Stories of Black Lives That Set the Record Straight." Review of *The Office of Historical Corrections*, by Danielle Evans. *LA Times*, 10 Nov. 2020, www.latimes.com/entertainment-arts/books/story/2020-11-10/review-blistering-stories-that-set-the-record-striaght. Accessed 7 Jan. 2021.

One Mighty and Irresistible Tide
The Epic Struggle over American Immigration, 1924–1965

Author: Jia Lynn Yang
Publisher: W. W. Norton (New York). 336 pp.
Type of work: History
Time: 1924–65
Locale: United States

Centered on the history of twentieth-century American federal immigration policy, this book studies the politics and personalities behind the legislation. Jia Lynn Yang explores the enduring influence of racist and nationalist biases that drove many politicians' decision-making across this period, as well as the unexpected complications set in play at each attempt at immigration reform.

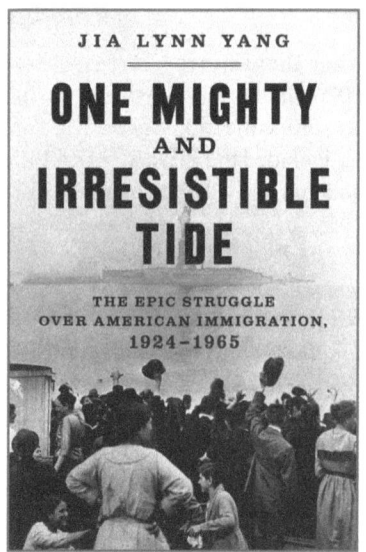

Principal personages

EMANUEL "MANNIE" CELLER, a member of the US House of Representatives
MICHAEL FEIGHAN, a member of the US House of Representatives
LYNDON JOHNSON, the thirty-sixth US president
JOHN F. KENNEDY, the thirty-fifth US president
ROBERT KENNEDY, a US senator
EDWARD "TED" KENNEDY, a US senator
PAT MCCARRAN, a US senator

In *One Mighty and Irresistible Tide: The Epic Struggle over American Immigration, 1924–1965* (2020), Jia Lynn Yang offers a detailed political history of immigration in the United States that is bookended by the passage of the Johnson-Reed Act of 1924 and the Immigration and Nationality Act of 1965. The Johnson-Reed Act, created in tandem with the prevalent isolationist and racist tendencies of its period, established a limited quota system for immigration to the United States that was specifically designed to privilege immigrants arriving in the country from western and northern Europe and to maintain a majority Anglo heritage in the United States. By contrast, the 1965 legislation spearheaded and signed by President Lyndon Johnson sought to eliminate discrimination as a factor in immigration and was perceived by supporters as a legislative accomplishment in line with the Civil Rights Act he had signed a year earlier. In between the passage of the 1924 and 1965 laws, Yang's narrative focuses chronologically on arguments at the federal level over immigration in the intervening years, teasing out a complex story of politics, personalities, racism, and international relations.

Some reviewers of the book observed that Yang produces a compelling, big-picture story about immigration but can sometimes be weighed down by the inclusion of the many political players involved in these four decades of arguments over legislation. The structure of the book allows Yang to engage with well-known historical figures (such as Presidents Lyndon Johnson and John F. Kennedy) from interesting perspectives that are infrequently associated with their legacies. More importantly for the historical record, Yang's text introduces myriad lesser-known historical figures (such as the anti-immigration senator Pat McCarran and the pro-immigration representative Mannie Celler). Through her deep research into the complex workings of congressional committees and the actions of individual members of Congress, Yang foregrounds the outsized significance that individual lawmakers can have in advancing and revising proposed legislation. Equally interesting is the manner in which this historical approach allows Yang to consider the push and pull between presidential, congressional, and bureaucratic power. Although most readers will be more familiar with the presidents who played a role in tipping the scales significantly, there have been many others in government influencing the inclusivity or exclusivity of immigration laws. Further, employees in the US Department of State and other federal offices could hold powerful influence over how aspects of the legislation were implemented, in some cases shaping the form of a bill's impact for decades. It can be challenging to follow these many lesser-known personages through Yang's narrative, but it is worth the attempt, as her approach offers readers many opportunities to consider the workings of government at multiple levels.

Jia Lynn Yang

Both the Johnson-Reed Act and the Immigration and Nationality Act emerge from Yang's narrative as fundamentally flawed legislation—though the first was flawed for its explicit racism, and the second for consequences of the legislation with respect to immigration from within the Western Hemisphere. In her discussion, Yang intriguingly demonstrates that the failures of these laws were a product of racist actors in Congress, a lack of focus on immigration patterns, and unintended consequences of components of the legislation. The stark impact of these legislative failures extends well beyond direct issues of immigration and hits on the vaunted moral character of the United States. While it took legislators four decades to replace the Johnson-Reed Act, the Immigration and Nationality Act was still the keystone of federal immigration policy more than fifty years later, with a significant impact on arguments over policing the southern border between the United States and Mexico and increased tensions focused on the Latino community as a result.

It is well-known that the United States failed to open its borders to European Jews as Nazi power rose in Germany and beyond. Yang's narrative digs deeply into how the racist and xenophobic aspects of the Johnson-Reed Act contributed to the nation's later failure to save thousands of innocent lives. Equally troubling is the alignment of the legislation with fascist thinking. Those who framed the legislation sought expert witnesses involved in eugenics. This pseudoscience reinforced existing racist thinking, purporting to offer a scientific framework to justify sharp changes in immigration policy. Many ascribed to an "America first" mentality that privileged ancestry of Anglo-Saxon descent. The legislation not only established quotas for (and in some cases, bans on) immigration, but blocked individuals with mental or physical disabilities. Seeking to reverse the population trends of immigrants from southern and eastern Europe who arrived in large numbers in the United States in the late nineteenth and early twentieth centuries, the 1924 legislation deliberately established the national immigration quotas on fictional percentages from a historical moment in which the population was "purer" in its Anglo-Saxon descent. Yang effectively, chillingly notes that Adolf Hitler himself was inspired by the immigration policy of the United States, praising the country for the racist structure of immigration it had set in place. While attempts were made by some leaders during World War II to circumvent these ethnic and racial quotas or to find an end-around within which the system could be manipulated to save more lives, the Johnson-Reed Act was stubbornly successful in maintaining a nationalist immigration structure despite rising awareness of the humanitarian crisis in Europe.

When Lyndon Johnson made immigration reform a priority of his presidency, he sought to eliminate racism as a factor in immigration, turning the tide of four decades of flawed national policy via an explicitly racist quota system. Yang follows Johnson's proposed legislation through congressional committees and party politics to explain how changes were made that ultimately significantly hampered the egalitarian ideal that motivated Johnson. Most important in this regard was the fundamental change that the 1965 legislation made to immigration from within the Americas. Before 1965, immigration from within the Americas had not been subject to the quotas imposed on arrivals from other countries. The longstanding porous nature of the southern border was a policy built on largely positive international relations with neighboring nations as well as a practical benefit for agriculture and industry in the United States. But, as Johnson's administration worked to increase the inclusivity of immigration policy, Congressman Michael Feighan pushed to impose a "radical idea—one that had never been carried out before" in the form of a cap on immigration from the Western Hemisphere. Despite strong opposition from Johnson and from many congressional leaders, Feighan was successful in adding this cap as an addendum to the legislation from within a congressional committee. Yang's narrative follows the process by which this alteration was made to the legislation, the machinations through which Celler and others sought to defeat Feighan's change, and the ultimate political pragmatism that drove Johnson to support the legislation despite this concerning addition.

Also laid bare in Yang's narrative is the reality that congressional arguments leading up to the 1965 bill were blatant in their racism and xenophobia. Yang clearly shows that there were still some in government who sought to ensure that any legislation reinforced the nation's supposed Anglo-Saxon heritage. Even Dean Rusk, secretary of state for Johnson's administration, balked at testifying to Congress in support of the legislation, stating to a State Department colleague, "You don't really think we should let in people . . . on a world-wide competitive basis, do you? After all, we are an Anglo-Saxon country." Although Rusk did, ultimately, testify for the Johnson administration, Yang records his comment to powerful effect, underlining the depth to which the myth of an Anglo-Saxon origin and future for the country drove many decisions concerning immigration. Ultimately, the 1965 legislation would fundamentally alter the system of immigration in the United States, privileging professionally skilled immigrants and the close family members of US citizens. Importantly, this legislation would reverse previous draconian policies concerning immigration from Asia, but it would also institute the Western Hemisphere caps that would precipitate many of the darkest crises of immigration related to undocumented immigrants crossing the southern border in the final decades of the twentieth century and into the twenty-first century.

Ultimately, Yang concludes that the 1965 legislation "deserves a place in history alongside this country's most significant civil rights breakthroughs" and that the legislation "helped define America as a multicultural nation." In her epilogue, which pushes into the twenty-first century, she also underlines that members of the Donald Trump administration were explicit in seeking to essentially reverse the effects of the 1965 bill and, as much as possible, to return to the framework of the Johnson-Reed Act. Mindful of the prominent crises concerning immigration that were brought to the forefront during the Trump administration, Yang concludes the book with a call for a true reexamination of the nation's immigration system—one that takes a hard look at how the nation sets priorities for who can enter the country and why. Importantly, she also calls on the nation's diverse citizenry to help the country to establish ethnic pluralism as "a foundational value of their nation," lest the countervailing voices for Anglo-Saxon heritage dominate the political discourse. As a child of immigrants herself, a personal fact that she discusses poignantly in her book, she speaks to those whose families have succeeded in coming to the United States since 1965 and, more profoundly, to all Americans who uplift the history of the United States as a "nation of immigrants." She concludes, "Not one of us deserves to be here. So what difference is there between us, with our precious papers, and the people we see at our border who are dying to come in? There is none." Yang urges those who have benefited from or believe in this principle of ethnic pluralism to help define a "new vision for the current era, one that embraces rather than elides how far America has drifted from its European roots." *One Mighty and Irresistible Tide* lays bare how US immigration policy, even at its most liberal, has been shaped and distorted by the forces of nationalism and White supremacy. While it remains to be seen whether Yang's vision for a policy that embraces and reinforces the nation's ethnic pluralism can be made a reality, her book and perspective are valuable for consideration regarding an ongoing and prominent societal issue.

Author Biography
Jia Lynn Yang is an editor and journalist who, after working for the *Washington Post*, became the deputy national editor for the *New York Times* in 2017.

Julia A. Sienkewicz, PhD

Review Sources
Nasaw, David. "America's Immigration Paradox." Review of *One Mighty and Irresistible Tide: The Epic Struggle over American Immigration, 1924–1965*, by Jia Lynn Yang, and *The Deportation Machine: America's Long History of Expelling Immigrants*, by Adam Goodman. *The New York Times*, 19 May 2020, www.nytimes.com/2020/05/19/books/review/one-mighty-and-irresistible-tide-jia-lynn-yang-the-deportation-machine-adam-goodman.html. Accessed 21 Jan. 2021.

Shribman, David M. "Battles over Borders in 'One Mighty and Irresistible Tide.'" Review of *One Mighty and Irresistible Tide: The Epic Struggle over American Immigration, 1924–1965*, by Jia Lynn Yang. *Boston Globe*, 14 May 2020, www.bostonglobe.com/2020/05/14/arts/battles-over-borders-one-mighty-irresistible-tide. Accessed 21 Jan. 2021.

Terzian, Philip. "'One Mighty and Irresistible Tide' Review: How They Became Us." Review of *One Mighty and Irresistible Tide: The Epic Struggle over American Immigration, 1924–1965*, by Jia Lynn Yang. *The Wall Street Journal*, 19 May 2020, www.wsj.com/articles/one-mighty-and-irresistible-tide-review-how-they-became-us-11589927080. Accessed 21 Jan. 2021.

Wides-Muñoz, Laura. "The Long Fights—and Hasty Decisions—That Shape Immigration Policy." Review of *One Mighty and Irresistible Tide: The Epic Struggle over American Immigration, 1924–1965*, by Jia Lynn Yang. *The Washington Post*, 31 July 2020, www.washingtonpost.com/outlook/the-long-fights--and-hasty-decisions--that-shape-immigration-policy/2020/07/30/183a91c8-c524-11ea-a99f-3bbdffb1af38_story.html. Accessed 21 Jan. 2021.

The Only Good Indians

Author: Stephen Graham Jones (b. 1972)
Publisher: Saga Press (New York). 320 pp.
Type of work: Novel
Time: Unspecified, likely late twentieth century
Locales: Great Falls, Montana; Browning, East Glacier, and other locales on the Blackfeet Indian Reservation; Williston, North Dakota

A suspenseful and gory slasher, at times cerebral but also comedic, The Only Good Indians *uses the storytelling tools of the horror genre to meditate on the meaning of contemporary American Indian life. Ten years after four friends slaughtered a herd of elk on the Blackfeet Indian Reservation, a spirit comes for revenge.*

Principal characters
LEWIS A. CLARKE, a Blackfeet man who has left the reservation
PETA, his White wife
SHANEY, his new coworker, a Crow
CASSIDY "CASS" SEES ELK, one of Lewis's childhood friends, who still lives on the reservation
JOLENE, a.k.a. *Jo*, Cass's partner, another Crow
GABRIEL "GABE" CROSS GUNS, another one of Lewis's old friends and hunting buddies
DENORAH CROSS GUNS, Gabe's fourteen-year-old daughter, a basketball prodigy
DENNY PEASE, the reservation game warden and Denorah's stepfather
VICTOR YELLOW TAIL, a tribal cop on the Blackfeet reservation
NATHAN YELLOW TAIL, Victor's fourteen-year-old son
RICKY BOSS RIBS, another member of Lewis's old friend group
ELK HEAD WOMAN, an elusive and supernatural figure bent on revenge

In *The Only Good Indians* (2020), the old racist adage "The only good Indians are dead Indians" is a constant, looming threat. While dead bodies do begin to pile up, this is just one of the many ways that author Stephen Graham Jones—who is Blackfeet—skillfully subverts tropes of all kinds. On one hand, he crafts a story that gleefully embraces standard elements of the horror genre: the awakening of something otherworldly and angry, dogged stalking and gaslighting, creeping paranoia, and slasher levels of bloodshed. On the other hand, he elevates things to a higher literary level with crisp prose, flavors of Shakespearean tragedy, and keen insight into the complexity of the modern American Indian experience. The result is a gripping novel that will please many horror fans but defies simple categorization.

The events of the book all stem from a hunting trip a decade earlier. Lewis, Ricky, Cass, and Gabe, four friends living on the Blackfeet Reservation in Montana, trespassed on the tribal elders' hunting ground and killed a herd of elk. One of the animals turned out to be a pregnant female, which Lewis shot several times before it died. He extracted and buried the fetus once he discovered it, a memory that has haunted him ever since. Significantly, it is a female spirit who ten years later seeks revenge on the four men.

Stephen Graham Jones

The book opens with a prologue detailing the death of Ricky Boss Ribs. He has left the reservation weeks after his brother's overdose death and has taken up a job in South Dakota on his way to Minnesota. One night he heads out of a bar packed with rather hostile White men to urinate. In the parking lot, he encounters a strangely belligerent elk that charges him and damages several parked trucks. He grabs a wrench to defend himself, but when other people emerge from the bar, the elk is gone, leaving them to conclude that a drunk Ricky has smashed all the vehicles to get back at someone. The racial dynamics are clear as a White mob attacks him, leading to the first of several terse headlines for the victims of the vengeful spirit: "Indian Man Killed in Dispute Outside Bar."

The first third of the book goes on to tell Lewis's story. He and his wife, Peta, who is White, have just moved into a new house in Great Falls, Montana. They have been together for ten years, which also how long Lewis has lived off reservation. He is somewhat proud to have made it out and to have reached his mid-thirties "having avoided all the car crashes and jail time and alcoholism on his cultural dance card." A postal worker, Lewis is training his new coworker, Shaney, who is Crow and the only other American Indian on staff. There is a hint of a flirtation between them.

Some strange things begin to happen around the new house that Lewis and Peta have moved into. While on a ladder fixing a light, Lewis has an unnerving vision of a dead elk through the spinning arms of the ceiling fan, leading to a fall that could have been fatal if not for Peta's intervention. Their dog, Harley, has also been mysteriously getting out, over the fence and into the street. Then, when Lewis invites his coworkers over to see the new house, they discover Harley hanging from the fence by the chain Lewis used to tie him up, near dead. They save the dog, but a coworker is bitten in the process, and only a few days later Harley is hanged once again and dies. These ominous events send Lewis on a downward spiral of fear and paranoia. He calls Gabe and Cass for the first time in years to ask if they still think of the elk they slaughtered. He also confesses what happened on the hunting trip to Shaney before he tells Peta, and Peta catches them in a compromising position. Lewis becomes obsessed with the idea that the vengeful elk is haunting him; he stops going to work and his tether on reality loosens as he suspects both Peta and Shaney of being the elk.

Back on the reservation, Cass and Gabe prepare for a sweat lodge ceremony in honor of a fallen friend and to help Nathan, the son of tribal cop Victor, get a sense of perspective. Cass feels as though he is finally getting his own life together, thanks in large part to his partner, Jo. Gabe, by contrast, has little stability in his life other than his love for his daughter, Denorah. Although he has been forbidden to see her by his ex-wife, he is fiercely proud of Denorah's basketball skills and goes to watch her practice before going to the sweat lodge. Once at the lodge, Gabe, Cass, and Nathan sit naked while Victor provides fresh fire-heated rocks and water to create steam. In the sweat-induced trance, it is easy for the three not to realize that Cass's dogs have been oddly quiet or that Victor has not responded to their calls for a long time. As the Elk Woman strikes again, more and more people are drawn into the cycle of violence, building the tension toward an action-packed conclusion.

Alongside the page-turning suspense, one of the book's biggest strengths is its reckoning with American Indian identity. Amid the supernatural and thriller elements of the story, Jones paints a vivid picture of contemporary Indian life, from the struggles of life on the reservation to the feeling of being an "other" off reservation. All four men at the center of the story are lost in some way and frame themselves largely in a sense of absence or opposition. Lewis's internal monologue makes this very clear, for example, as he frequently thinks of himself in terms of being Indian or losing some of his Indianness, and of Peta's Whiteness or moments of being like an Indian. All four of the Blackfeet men often consider what it would they would have been like a hundred years ago and hold some connections to tradition. Yet they also recognize the "three-braid days are over and done with," lost to colonialism, stereotyping, and cultural appropriation. Their lived experience is that being an Indian is to be constantly reminded that they are not White—and therefore always under threat.

For Jones's characters, their connections to tradition and nature are both crucial and dangerous. This is perhaps at the root of the vengeful spirit they face. Supporting this complex underlying theme, Jones draws on the Blackfeet spiritual tradition. For example, Nathan is at times compared to the Blood-Clot Boy hero. More overtly, Elk Head Woman shows the connection the Blackfeet have with the elk.

Jones's language is simple, colloquial, and effective throughout *The Only Good Indians*. In between the gore and paranoia, he nestles moments of comedy, but the humor often appears a way to hide deep-rooted pain. In one of the most viscerally horrifying scenes of the book (a murder involving a motorcycle), for example, Lewis makes jokes to himself as he unravels. Gabe, arguably the most broken of the four friends, makes jokes constantly. This helps make the darker parts of the book all the more impactful. As Gabino Iglesias noted in a review for NPR, "the horror is unlike anything you've read before. It goes from disturbing flashes of thing that may or may not be there to in-your-face explosions of gore and violence tinged with supernatural elements."

Iglesias was not alone in praising Jones's knack for horror, as many reviewers highlighted the book's blend of psychological tension and outright violence, as well as the incorporation of both classic horror setups and more original ideas. However, some dedicated horror fans may find the action at times hews too closely to genre clichés. Mike Ramberg, writing for the science fiction/fantasy outlet *Three Crows Magazine*, voiced these concerns: "As suspenseful as the narrative goes . . . *The Only Good Indians* can't help stumbling over tropes." He specifically pointed to the book's final sequences as problematic in this sense and further suggested that some of the narrative's deeper social themes are not ultimately fleshed out enough. Yet despite such quibbles, Ramberg concluded that the novel was "a great read at a great pace," echoing the overall strong critical reception.

There are few other complaints to be made about *The Only Good Indians*. The first part of the book starts somewhat slowly, though this can be justified as it takes a little while for Jones to sow the seeds of Lewis's undoing. Occasionally, the choreography of the action-heavy scenes is difficult to follow, especially if the reader is not especially familiar with trucks, motorcycles, or the slang that accompanies these vehicles. The ending, too, as Ramberg noted in his review, might drag a bit. Yet none of this can derail a book that, as a reviewer for *Kirkus* put it, is "scary good." The novel earned starred reviews in *Kirkus* and *Publishers Weekly* and was named a best or most anticipated book of the year by numerous publications. Several critics called it one of Jones's best works, and it is a worthy read even for those not normally interested in horror fiction.

Author Biography

Stephen Graham Jones is a prolific writer of novels and short fiction, known especially for his horror and crime work. He has received numerous honors, including the Texas Institute of Letters Award for Fiction, a Bram Stoker Award, multiple This is Horror Awards, and a National Endowment for the Arts fellowship.

Meaghan O'Brien

Review Sources

González, Rigoberto. "A Native Horror Story Re-appropriates a Racist Trope: The 'Indian Curse.'" Review of *The Only Good Indians*, by Stephen Graham Jones. *Los Angeles Times*, 15 July 2020, www.latimes.com/entertainment-arts/books/story/2020-07-15/the-only-good-indians-by-stephen-graham-jones-review. Accessed 4 Jan. 2021.

Iglesias, Gabino. "Grief and Guilt Spawn Horrors in *The Only Good Indians*." Review of *The Only Good Indians*, by Stephen Graham Jones. *NPR*, 16 July 2020, www.npr.org/2020/07/16/891433693/grief-and-guilt-spawn-horrors-in-the-only-good-indians. Accessed 4 Jan. 2021.

Miller, Max. Review of *The Only Good Indians*, by Stephen Graham Jones. *Columbia Journal*, 18 May 2020, columbiajournal.org/review-the-only-good-indians-by-stephen-graham-jones. Accessed 4 Jan. 2021.

Review of *The Only Good Indians*, by Stephen Graham Jones. *Kirkus*, 2 Mar. 2020, www.kirkusreviews.com/book-reviews/stephen-graham-jones/the-only-good-indians. Accessed 4 Jan. 2021.

Ramberg, Mike. Review of *The Only Good Indians*, by Stephen Graham Jones. *Three Crows Magazine*, 29 July 2020, threecrowsmagazine.com/the-only-good-indians. Accessed 4 Jan. 2021.

Owls of the Eastern Ice
A Quest to Find and Save the World's Largest Owl

Author: Jonathan C. Slaght (b. ca. 1976)
Publisher: Farrar, Straus and Giroux (New York). 368 pp.
Type of work: Nature
Time: 2005–18
Locale: Primarily Primorye, Russia

In Owls of the Eastern Ice: A Quest to Find and Save the World's Largest Owl, *wildlife biologist Jonathan C. Slaght recounts his years of field research in the forests of the Russian province of Primorye, key habitats for the endangered Blakiston's fish owl.*

Principal personages

JONATHAN C. SLAGHT, the author, a wildlife biologist who was a doctoral student at the University of Minnesota
SERGEY SURMACH, an ornithologist based in Vladivostok, Russia
SERGEY AVDEYUK, a longtime colleague of Surmach and an experienced leader of field research teams
TOLYA RYZHOV, a member of the expedition team, a photographer and videographer
SHURIK POPOV, a field assistant who aided with nest access and banding
ANATOLIY YANCHENKO, a falconer, a member of a later expedition
ANDREY KATKOV, a field assistant who aided with traps and monitoring
KOLYA GORLACH, another field assistant

While the average American might be able to name some of the endangered animals of eastern Russia, such as the Siberian tiger and Amur leopard, few would probably mention the Blakiston's fish owl—or have even heard of that species, perhaps best known for being the largest variety of owl in the world. For wildlife biologist Jonathan C. Slaght, however, the Blakiston's fish owl has long been a source of both personal fascination and scientific curiosity. The child of a diplomat, he was drawn as a teenager to the Russian Far East and particularly to the region of Primorye, known more formally as Primorsky Kray and a primary site of fish owl habitats. He subsequently spent several years in that region as a member of the Peace Corps, during which time he spotted and photographed his first Blakiston's fish owl.

Fascinated by the owls and concerned about the prospects of the endangered species, Slaght chose to focus on the Blakiston's fish owl while pursuing doctoral studies at the University of Minnesota, centering his research on the habitats and natural resources key to the birds' survival. He sought to gather data on the owls' behaviors and

Jonathan C. Slaght

needs, analyze that data, and create a conservation plan that would protect the owls from threats such as habitat loss due to logging or a decline in food supply from overfishing. At the same time, his plan would also consider the needs of other wildlife in the area as well as the humans of Primorye, many of whom rely on hunting, fishing, and logging to survive in the region's remote villages. Carried out largely during the first decade of the twenty-first century, Slaght's expeditions into the field and efforts to locate, capture, and track fish owls form the basis of *Owls of the Eastern Ice: A Quest to Find and Save the World's Largest Owl* (2020), the author's first book. Chronicling his years of fieldwork and some of the results of his analysis, *Owls of the Eastern Ice* is not only an entertaining travel memoir but also a compelling work of nature writing that renders Slaght's enthusiasm for the Blakiston's fish owl both understandable and contagious.

Slaght explores the origins of his interest in the Blakiston's fish owl in a prologue. He then begins his account in the year 2005, when he traveled to Russia to meet with the ornithologist Sergey Surmach. Based in Vladivostok, the largest city in Primorye, Surmach was accustomed to leading research teams in the region and was already involved in efforts to assess the environmental needs of fish owls and determine where to build new roads in the region so as not to harm the owls. Slaght and Surmach developed a partnership in which Surmach provided staff and resources like vehicles for Slaght's proposed expeditions, while Slaght himself obtained grant funding and developed processes for collecting and analyzing the desired data. Fieldwork in Primorye could be challenging at any time of year due to the remoteness of many of its communities and the inconsistent presence of infrastructure such as roads and bridges. Slaght's expeditions would be particularly challenging, though, because they would be carried out in late winter, the best time to identify fish owl habitats due in part to the characteristic tracks the birds leave in the snow.

As Slaght recounts, his work in Primorye began in earnest in early 2006, when he and a small team led by experienced expedition leader Sergey Avdeyuk made their first trip into the wilderness to locate owls. While later steps of the project would entail capturing and placing trackers on the birds, Slaght makes it clear that the team's initial focus was simply to determine where the owls could be found, following clues such as shed feathers, tracks in the snow, and the distinctive "duet" vocalizations performed by fish owl pairs. Although the owls themselves are a primary focus of *Owls of the Eastern Ice*, the book also deals extensively with the decidedly unglamorous realities of fieldwork, providing readers with minimal experience in field research a far greater understanding of the amount of work and dedication that goes into multiyear research projects like Slaght's. Over the course of the narrative, he often delves into the challenging logistics of traveling throughout the Russian Far East in winter; he recounts that during the first winter in the field, for instance, a severe storm prevented a key helicopter trip from taking place, thus delaying the start of the expedition. When traveling by snowmobile on frozen rivers, Slaght and his companions found that spring had come unexpectedly early, causing the ice to melt around them and presenting a new threat: *naleds*, a slushy mixture of water and ice that forms atop the solid ice. In later winters, the team continued to reckon with blizzards that delayed their plans and at times left them stranded or forced them to abandon their vehicle on the side of the road. Yet, while the remoteness and harsh weather of Primorye presented a host of challenges for Slaght and his colleagues, area residents often helped to counteract those challenges, offering lodging and assistance to the team despite being little more than acquaintances. Slaght's depictions of his interactions with the members of his team and with memorable locals—including hard-drinking hunters and a hermit who believes in teleportation—are both entertaining and informative, shedding light on life in Primorye and on Slaght and his colleagues as individuals.

As his narrative progresses, Slaght recounts the subsequent stages of his research project, conducted largely during the winters of the next several years. After identifying the territories in which fish owl pairs could be found, he and his colleagues worked to trap the birds. This difficult process required a great deal of trial and error, as few people had ever intentionally captured a live Blakiston's fish owl. After trying several common raptor traps, to little success, the team devised a means of repeatedly luring the owls to a specific hunting location, where they would eventually place a trap. As owls kept escaping the traps before Slaght or his colleagues could collect them, members of the team went on to spend significant periods of time waiting in concealed tents near the trap locations, enduring the bitter cold and a loss of sleep—and at times the nonstop chattering of a particularly talkative team member—in order to achieve their goal. Indeed, such portions of *Owls of the Eastern Ice* call significant attention to the dedication of Slaght and his team members, all of whom are willing to put up with numerous discomforts, and even life-threatening conditions, to see the project through. Slaght goes on to reveal that their trapping efforts ultimately proved successful, and the team was able to fit a number of owls with tracking devices, first radio-based devices that the owls swiftly dismantled and later Global Positioning System (GPS) trackers capable of recording and storing location data. The limited storage space in the GPS trackers required Slaght and his teammates to recapture each owl on various occasions over the next years to download the data. This would prove crucial to his efforts to understand the extent of fish owl territories, their hunting habits, and their connections to the rivers where they hunt. While much of that fieldwork took place during the winter, Slaght writes that he also traveled to Primorye in the summer of 2009 and returned to some fish owl territories he had previously visited to gather information about the vegetation present in those areas and assess the number and species of fish present in the rivers.

Having dedicated much of *Owls of the Eastern Ice* to his work in the field, Slaght concludes the book with several chapters dealing with his analysis of the collected data and the events of the following years. After processing the location data collected with the GPS trackers, he was able to map the extent of the fish owl territories, taking note of the distances the birds were willing to travel as well as their movement over the course of the year. Based on his findings, Slaght theorizes that fish owls move to various points within their territories because they are following the movements of fish that travel through and spawn in the rivers, thus highlighting the interconnected nature of the different fauna living within a single area. He goes on to explore the results of his work, noting that his research had persuaded logging companies operating in Primorye to cease their practice of cutting down potential fish owl nest trees for use in bridges. Not all of the follow-up details he provides are positive: he reports, for example, that a typhoon devastated much of the fish owl habitat in Primorye, snapping or uprooting trees throughout the region and destroying nests at multiple of the sites Slaght had surveyed. Upon returning to one such site in 2018, however, he found that the birds themselves had survived the loss of their nest and had simply relocated, building a new home base elsewhere in their territory. That revelation ends *Owls of the Eastern Ice* on a hopeful note, demonstrating both the adaptability of the Blakiston's fish owl and the potential for the continued survival of the species.

The critical response to *Owls of the Eastern Ice*, which was long-listed for the 2020 National Book Award for Nonfiction, was highly positive, with reviewers praising not only the work's intriguing subject matter but also Slaght's compelling prose. The anonymous critic for *Kirkus* commented on the work's "vivid language and tight storytelling" and called particular attention to Slaght's ability to create "an intimate sense of place," while the reviewer for *Publishers Weekly* described the book as "detailed and thrilling." The *Publishers Weekly* critic further took note of Slaght's focus on the work of his colleagues in Russia, including the field assistants who helped make much of his research possible. Indeed, Slaght's emphasis on the challenges and rewards of fieldwork appealed to many reviewers, including fellow nature writer Helen Macdonald, who commented positively on that focus in a review for the *Guardian* and likewise wrote that the book "reads like a modern-day grail quest." Locating *Owls of the Eastern Ice* firmly within the genre of nature writing, *Wall Street Journal* critic Heller McAlpin praised the work as a whole, describing Slaght's debut as "a stellar example of the fruitful intersection of scientific inquiry, conservation advocacy and wilderness adventure."

Author Biography

Jonathan C. Slaght holds the position of Russia and Northeast Asia coordinator for the Wildlife Conservation Society. *Owls of the Eastern Ice* (2020) is his first book.

Joy Crelin

Review Sources

Macdonald, Helen. "*Owls of the Eastern Ice* by Jonathan C. Slaght Review—An Extraordinary Quest." *The Guardian*, 22 July 2020, www.theguardian.com/books/2020/jul/22/owls-of-the-eastern-ice-by-jonathan-c-slaght-review-an-extraordinary-quest. Accessed 15 Feb. 2021.

Malarkey, Tucker. "Through the Russian Wilderness in Search of the World's Largest Owl." Review of *Owls of the Eastern Ice: A Quest to Find and Save the World's Largest Owl*, by Jonathan C. Slaght. *The New York Times*, 29 Jan. 2021, www.nytimes.com/2020/08/04/books/review/owls-of-the-eastern-ice-jonathan-slaght.html. Accessed 15 Feb. 2021.

McAlpin, Heller. "'Owls of the Eastern Ice' Review: The Salmon Eaters." Review of *Owls of the Eastern Ice: A Quest to Find and Save the World's Largest Owl*, by Jonathan C. Slaght. *The Wall Street Journal*, 31 July 2020, www.wsj.com/articles/owls-of-the-eastern-ice-review-the-salmon-eaters-11596207020. Accessed 15 Feb. 2021.

Review of *Owls of the Eastern Ice: A Quest to Find and Save the World's Largest Owl*, by Jonathan C. Slaght. *Kirkus*, 9 Feb. 2020, www.kirkusreviews.com/book-reviews/jonathan-c-slaght/owls-of-the-eastern-ice/. Accessed 15 Feb. 2021.

Review of *Owls of the Eastern Ice: A Quest to Find and Save the World's Largest Owl*, by Jonathan C. Slaght. *Publishers Weekly*, 20 Feb. 2020, www.publishersweekly.com/978-0-374-90384-8. Accessed 15 Feb. 2021.

Paying the Land

Author: Joe Sacco (b. 1960)
Publisher: Metropolitan Books (New York). 272 pp.
Type of work: Graphic nonfiction, current affairs, history, environment
Time: Primarily 2015–16, with flashbacks to the twentieth century
Locale: Northwest Territories, Canada

Graphic journalist Joe Sacco, known for dynamic reporting from such combat zones as Palestine and Bosnia, takes on a different kind of war in Paying the Land: *the battle for survival of the once-nomadic indigenous peoples of Canada's Northwest Territories in a rapidly changing modern world.*

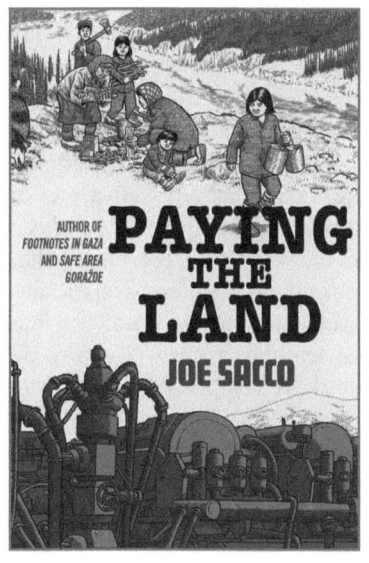

Principal personages

JOE SACCO, a veteran graphic journalist, a Maltese American
SHAUNA MORGAN, his guide and driver, a White resident of Yellowknife
PAUL ANDREW, a Dene elder
WILLARD HAGEN, head of the Mackenzie Valley Land and Water Board
RENÉ FUMOLEAU, a French-born Catholic priest, a missionary to the Northwest Territories
MARIE WILSON, a White former journalist and Truth and Reconciliation commissioner
STEPHEN KAKFWI, a Dene elder, a former activist and premier of the Northwest Territories
JIM ANTOINE, a Dene elder, another former activist and premier
PATRICK SCOTT, a former cameraman turned negotiator, the White spouse of a Dene woman
MARGARET JUMBO, a Dene boarding school survivor
HARRY DENERON, chief of Acho Dene Koe First Nation
EUGENE BOULANGER, a young Dene man from Tulít'a

History is a "tableau of crimes and misfortunes," to paraphrase the French philosopher Voltaire, in which strife stimulates the imagination more than peace. Joe Sacco, as he has throughout his career, captures three basic levels of conflict—personal, national, and universal—in his eleventh major publication, *Paying the Land* (2020). As usual, his work is unlike conventional recounts of the past, the sweeping overviews written by winners. Instead, his focus is on the impact of history on powerless and vulnerable human beings who get caught up in inexorable events beyond their control.

Though Sacco is usually labeled a "comics journalist" or a "cartoonist-reporter," the designations can be somewhat misleading for those who are unfamiliar with graphic media apart from Saturday morning cartoons or newspaper funny pages. Certainly, the author-illustrator occasionally employs irony, satire, exaggeration, self-deprecation, in-jokes, and cultural references, plus other devices and techniques common to the contemporary comic-book and graphic media. But his subject matter is deadly serious. Sacco consistently balances well-drawn pictures—critics have compared his visual storytelling abilities to such luminaries as Pieter Bruegel the Elder, R. Crumb, Francisco Goya, William Hogarth, and Art Spiegelman—with well-chosen words. Together, they show and tell about specific examples of injustice or exploitation. They illuminate the heights of humanity and plumb the depths of inhumanity.

Joe Sacco

Courtesy Henry Holt & Company

Sacco's books are up-close-and-personal examinations of the causes and effects of ethnic clashes. Representatives from the ranks of the competing parties are coaxed to articulate what they knew or saw, what they felt or believed, how they interpret what happened during the crisis under study. Their collective accounts define traumatic experiences that would be understandable to fellow humans in any time or place. Amazingly detailed black-and-white ink renderings—sweeping panoramas and cityscapes, dynamic action sequences, historical vignettes, portraits that range from realistic to caricature (particularly of himself)—work to help untangle complicated human issues of global consequence. While historical facts or highlights are woven into the narrative to provide necessary background for readers unfamiliar with the territory in question, the bulk of the story is always presented from the perspective and in the words of recognizable people. Some are well-known figures. A few may be criminals. Most are ordinary people—working folk, children, elderly people—who have become victims, through no fault of their own, of the destructive nature of conflict. Sacco immerses himself in combat zones, questioning, observing, and documenting interactions—including his own thoughts and emotions. Like other war correspondents before him, Sacco routinely risks health, life, and freedom following elusive leads in the pursuit of truth. He chases rumors, visits hot spots, and meets in secret with shady characters. Persistent, he secures interviews with scared eyewitnesses, confused bystanders, and frightened survivors, then displays his impressions in stylish panel art that freezes stunning images in the memory. In his *Palestine* (1994) and *Footnotes in Gaza* (2009), for example, Sacco dives into the complex, long-standing, continuing violent dispute between Palestinians and Israelis. *Safe Area Goražde: The War in Eastern Bosnia 1992–1995* (2000), *The Fixer: A Story from Sarajevo* (2003), and *War's End: Profiles from Bosnia, 1995–96* (2005) all deal with aspects of the disintegration of Yugoslavia, the Third Balkan War, and the vicious ethnic cleansing that occurred in Bosnia during the 1990s.

While all the elements Sacco is known for are present in *Paying the Land*—a story of humans in dispute with other humans, superb draftsmanship and composition, compelling layouts, uncomplimentary self-portrayal—this book is a slight departure for him. Though the subject matter is still war, it is a different type of battle. The drawn-out, albeit bloodless, conflict is being waged between the indigenous peoples of Canada's Northwest Territories (NWT) and the territorial and national governments, operating under the influence of capitalism. The conflict, as the title suggests, is over the control and proper use of the land. In this case, the territory spans more than a half-million square miles, "the size of France and Spain combined," occupied by fewer than forty-five thousand people. It is a land of hidden riches. Vast deposits of crude oil, natural gas, gold, and diamonds have been discovered, and great wealth is being extracted. It is the profit motive at the heart of the matter that Sacco explores.

Most of those who inhabit the NWT are the Dene, whose name means "the people." Part of the Athabascan linguistic group scattered up and down North and South America, in Canada the Dene live in six regions: Inuvialuit, Gwich'in, Sahtú, Dehcho, Tłįchǫ, and Akaitcho and NWT Métis Nation. Sacco begins *Paying the Land* with a documentary-style section highlighting the traditional lifestyle of the close-knit, self-contained indigenous communities. Dialogue for the entire opening chapter consists of statements from Paul Andrew, a middle-aged man born and raised "in the bush." He answers periodic questions asked by Sacco, who, aside from speech balloons, is not yet seen or identified. The Dene are shown living in harmony with the land, as they have for time out of mind. In the bush, they hunt, fish, and trap animals for their pelts. The Dene built temporary shelters and efficiently crafted moose-skin canoes. Nomads with teams of sled dogs, they moved with the changing seasons across the Mackenzie River Valley. They met annually with other families to socialize and exchange information.

At the outset of chapter 2, in a foreshadowing for the inevitable clash that will upset that indigenous way of life described in chapter 1, Sacco shows up in Yellowknife, the territorial capital, arranging to journey north on his quest. A renowned war correspondent and cartoon artist, he is famous for bold excursions into dangerous situations, so savvy readers familiar with his work will know trouble will start soon after he appears. Typically, the author's self-portrayal is unflattering and unheroic. Here he appears small and slight, a sensitive, easily embarrassed nebbish. His drawn profile shows an advancing nose and retreating chin, a wide mouth, prominent lips, and teeth as square as Chiclets. His round glasses turn his eyes into unreadable blanks, like a comic-strip Little Orphan Annie. Also introduced at this point is Shauna Morgan, Sacco's no-nonsense guide. She serves as Sacco's driver for the entire project. Sacco may be fearless, but he cannot operate the stick shift of the lightweight two-wheel-drive pickup they will use to negotiate about a thousand perilous miles of narrow, snow-clogged winter road that snakes across the rugged Canadian wilderness.

Despite giving himself a significant role in the drama he presents, told from the viewpoint of the sufferers among whom he eats and drinks and shelters, Sacco ultimately remains a hopeful but nonjudgmental presence. A professional journalist who enhances his research with distinctive sequential artwork, he always maintains a discreet reportorial distance. He presents neutral facts, records the blunt opinions of hurt individuals, and lets readers decide which, if any, side to take in the arguments he outlines over the fate and future of the Dene.

The road trip provides an excellent opportunity to establish a major theme of the book: how the intrusion of modern technology is ending a millennia-long way of life. The upheaval caused by the advance of industrial resource extractors incorporates many related issues. The toxicity of hydraulic fracturing, or fracking, for example, is a major health concern. Another worry is the environmental disruption of a pristine ecosystem through the clearing of land by heavy machinery for roads, well pads and pipelines, mining operations, and personnel support facilities.

An even larger consideration in *Paying the Land* is the deleterious effect of modernization and assimilation on the psyche of the Dene. Their culture and language and sacred traditions are disappearing. Their long, intimate connection with the land has been broken. Societal ills such as alcohol and drug use, prostitution, abuse, and suicide have begun to plague their communities and even cost lives as individuals often drown or freeze to death when intoxicated, for example. As usual, the details of this broad aspect of the story are related in blunt, bitter words that issue from the mouths of the several dozen affected people, both White and Dene, whom Sacco interviewed. Some dwell upon the Dene spirituality. They are supposed to treat their land gently. Out of respect for the bounty they have always received from nature, they are required to "pay the land," to give something back, with an item such as "a bullet, water, tobacco or tea," as Dene elder Frederick Andrew explains.

Another crucial portion of the narrative comes midway through, when multiple witnesses reflect on their upbringing and the impacts that mandatory education in government-supported residential mission schools had on their own lives and on their families and communities. Boys were shorn of their hair, and children wore uniforms and responded to numeric identifiers. Their languages and traditions and beliefs were stripped away in the process of colonization. This section, as with some others, might seem a tangent or detour but ultimately helps give readers a clearer picture of the drivers behind some of the political and economic changes that have occurred in the Northwest Territories since the early twentieth century.

Those stories, reinforced by elements such as hand-drawn maps and diagrams, are explosive salvos throughout the saga of the Dene. Through them, Sacco explains how, within decades, the indigenous peoples both lost and willingly gave up their independence. As multiple informants demonstrate, working for a wage pays better than wringing a living off the land. So many traded freedom, along with its vagaries, to enter a world controlled by incomprehensible government policies filtered through a complex legal system that does not always act in their best interests.

As other reviewers have noted, what makes *Paying the Land* relatively unique is Sacco's portrayal of the conundrums now facing the Dene in light of those historic and ongoing injustices, which can never really be undone, and the multiplicity of views within their communities about the best course forward. Here, as in his previous publications, Sacco excels at humanizing individuals within a broader cultural context through their speech and expressive line-drawing portraits. He also succeeds in rendering a sense of place as strong as any he has conveyed, perhaps more so. Much of the history described in *Paying the Land* may be foreign to non-Canadians but seem familiar to students of American history. The government's attempts at forced assimilation and the exploitation of indigenous people for mineral wealth in particular are strikingly similar to what has happened to American Indians in the United States. Even those well-versed in these colonial histories may learn a great deal and find themselves moved by Sacco's book.

Author Biography

Comics journalist Joe Sacco founded *Yahoo*, an alternative comic in the mid-1980s, before becoming an independent war correspondent. His numerous honors include an American Book Award (1996), two Eisner Awards (2001 and 2010), a Harvey Award, and the Ridenhour Book Prize (2010). *Paying the Land* is his eleventh full-length book.

Jack Ewing

Review Sources

Batten, Thomas L. Review of *Paying the Land*, by Joe Sacco. *Library Journal*, 1 Apr. 2020, www.libraryjournal.com/?reviewDetail=paying-the-land. Accessed 25 Oct. 2020.

Edemariam, Aida. "Paying the Land, by Joe Sacco Review—A Triumph of Empathy." Review of *Paying the Land*, by Joe Sacco. *The Guardian*, 2 July 2020, www.theguardian.com/books/2020/jul/02/paying-the-land-by-joe-sacco-review-. Accessed 25 Oct. 2020.

Kelly, Alice. "Detailed Comics Journalism about the Remote Canadian Northwest Territories." Review of *Paying the Land*, by Joe Sacco. *Times Literary Supplement*, 1 May 2020, www.the-tls.co.uk/articles/paying-the-land-joe-sacco-graphic-novel-review-alice-kelly. Accessed 25 Oct. 2020.

Review of *Paying the Land*, by Joe Sacco. *Kirkus Reviews*, 7 July 2020, www.kirkusreviews.com/book-reviews/joe-sacco/paying-the-land. Accessed 25 Oct. 2020.

Pierce, Leonard. Review of *Paying the Land*, by Joe Sacco. *The Comics Journal*, 9 July 2020, www.tcj.com/reviews/paying-the-land. Accessed 25 Oct. 2020.

Woodend, Dorothy. "Joe Sacco Shows What's Been Taken from the North—and What Remains." Review of *Paying the Land*, by Joe Sacco. *The Tyee*, 12 Aug. 2020, thetyee.ca/Culture/2020/08/12/Joe-Sacco-North-What-Remains-Paying-Land. Accessed 25 Oct. 2020.

Pelosi

Author: Molly Ball
Publisher: Henry Holt (New York). 368 pp.
Type of work: Biography
Time: 1940–present
Locales: Baltimore, Maryland; San Francisco, California; Washington, DC

Political journalist Molly Ball presents a biography of groundbreaking American politician Nancy Pelosi, who became Speaker of the US House of Representatives in 2007 and again in 2019. The book spans from Pelosi's early life and entry into politics to her time as one of the highest-profile—and most polarizing—leaders in the country.

Principal personages
NANCY PELOSI, Democratic member of the US House of Representatives for California, who has served stints as House minority leader and Speaker of the House
PAUL PELOSI, her husband
THOMAS D'ALESANDRO JR., her father
ANNUNCIATA LOMBARDI D'ALESANDRO, her mother
DONALD TRUMP, US president elected in 2016 and a key political enemy of Pelosi
BARACK OBAMA, US president from 2009 to 2017
GEORGE W. BUSH, US president from 2001 to 2009

Journalist Molly Ball built a reputation for strong political reporting, winning numerous awards with her work for outlets such as *Politico* and the *Atlantic* before becoming the national political correspondent for *Time* magazine. She also honed her expertise as a political analyst for CNN and a commentator on various television and radio programs. With her debut book, *Pelosi*, Ball turns her trained political lens on one of the most revered and reviled figures in American politics: Speaker of the House Nancy Pelosi.

Though a fixture in American politics since the 1980s, Pelosi truly became a national figure in 2003, when she made history as the first woman leading a party in Congress. Her profile was raised even further in 2007, when she took office as the first female Speaker of the House. While the groundbreaking achievement made her one of the most powerful people in the United States, it also made her the object of intense attacks from Republicans. Pelosi's polarizing public image is a core part of the biography, and Ball highlights both the ways the political veteran embraced controversy and remained a pragmatist willing to compromise to get things done. Throughout, Ball

Molly Ball

also dedicates considerable analysis to the ways in which Pelosi's gender informed this and other aspects of her career. Misogyny is presented as one of the many obstacles Pelosi worked to overcome, and the sexist elements of many attacks on her and female politicians in general are clearly laid out.

While Pelosi's position as a Democratic Party power broker during the Democratic administration of President Barack Obama had her in the spotlight, her subsequent role as a key opponent of Republican president Donald Trump arguably brought her even more attention. Acting as one of Trump's most visible critics heightened Pelosi's status, making her a hero to some and a villain to others. In this way Ball's biography benefits from its release in the build up to the 2020 presidential election, with many Americans closely following a deeply divided political situation. *Pelosi* is a timely portrait of an important figure in US politics and provides insights into a fascinating life. While Ball does not shy away from addressing shortcomings and missteps in Pelosi's long career, the account is ultimately celebratory, depicting a public servant who struggled against the political boys' club to become one of the most powerful women in American political history.

In many ways the book is a standard biographical treatment, beginning with Pelosi's childhood and family influences and extending to her present-day battles against the Trump administration. Along the way, Ball highlights Pelosi's resolve, dedication, intelligence, and savvy, as well as her flaws and mistakes. The writing is clear and engaging, providing an excellent portrait of an unintentional rise to the political front page. Yet the work is not an insider's view of Pelosi's mind and emotions. Pelosi, famously circumspect about revealing her inner life and thoughts, provided Ball with little material from which to construct a more intimate portrait ,and so Ball's book is a history of Pelosi's actions more than her feelings.

Pelosi's eventual interest in politics was, as it turns out, something of a family tradition. Her father, Thomas D'Alesandro Jr., was a Democratic politician who served in Congress and as mayor of Baltimore, Maryland, where Pelosi grew up. Her mother, Annunciata Lombardi D'Alesandro, was an immigrant who, according to Ball, was perhaps the most political minded in the family, though she was the only one who never had the opportunity to pursue politics herself and had to be content serving as chief strategist to her husband. There is a fair amount of detail dedicated to Pelosi's early life, including her father's rise to prominence, his fall amid a criminal investigation, and his failed return to politics. Pelosi herself was often involved in her father's campaigns, and her brother eventually followed in his footsteps to become mayor of Baltimore.

Pelosi's decision to dedicate her own life to politics was not completely straightforward, however. She obtained a degree in political science from Trinity College in Washington, DC, and interned for US senator Daniel Brewster. But then Pelosi's life took a more domestic turn. After marrying banker Paul Pelosi, she relocated to San Francisco, where the couple had five children. It took some time for her to return to political activity, initially as a volunteer. She was eventually appointed by San Francisco mayor Joseph Alioto to the city's public library commission, and from there, she began playing a more important role in local affairs. Pelosi became one of the strongest and most effective supporters of California governor Jerry Brown in his 1976 bid for the presidency, a role that helped transform her from a minor figure in Democratic California politics to a rising star in the field of political strategy.

In 1981 Pelosi experienced another major leap forward in prominence, becoming chair of the California Democratic Party. From this seat she racked up some significant accomplishments, including leading a voter registration drive that increased registration by over 100,000. It was in 1987 that Pelosi decided to pursue elected office herself. She won a special election to succeed her friend Sala Burton, a US representative from California who died in office. In 1988 she was reelected to a full term and went on to win her deeply liberal district handily in every election over the next few decades.

In the House of Representatives, Pelosi quickly established herself as a serious political fighter by making the AIDS crisis a primary focus. Despite resistance from conservatives who attempted to portray the disease as something that happened only to the degenerate, Pelosi was instrumental in turning public opinion and garnering federal funding for support and research. She also built a reputation as a champion of human rights issues early in her career. One notable episode came in 1989, when she criticized China over the Tiananmen Square massacre and proposed legislation to allow pro-democracy Chinese students to remain in the US despite lapsing visas. President George H. W. Bush vetoed the successful bill, preferring to avoid risking trade relations with China, but eventually he signed an executive order to the same effect, showing the impact of Pelosi's pressure.

Pelosi continued to rise through the ranks of the House Democrats, earning the minority whip position in 2002. The following year she became minority leader and, in Ball's account, began to temper her strong liberal positions somewhat to appeal to more moderate and conservative Democrats. Still, as the Iraq War developed, she was among the most outspoken critics of Republican president George W. Bush. She also distinguished herself as skilled in the nuances of playing politics. Pelosi's savvy maneuvering is outlined through examples such as her response when Representative John Murtha—a relatively conservative Democrat and a veteran—openly criticized the Bush administration's war effort in 2005. She declined to support Murtha publicly, resulting in some backlash from liberals. As Ball describes the situation, "Pelosi let them criticize her even though she knew the truth: she and Murtha had orchestrated the whole thing, and agreed that it had to look like a one-man crusade." She had known that such an attack would simply be portrayed as anti-American and weak if it came from her or the party overall, and indeed, Murtha's independent criticism proved highly influential.

Though an excellent example of Pelosi's strong political instincts, the Murtha episode also demonstrates another key theme in Ball's biography: the unique challenges facing women in leadership roles. Part of the reason Pelosi felt the need to remain behind the scenes in that case was the sexism she regularly faced. Pelosi understood the nuances of attempting to exist in the male-dominated world of politics, and she learned to deprive her potential enemies of ammunition. She avoided discussing her family or children with male colleagues, and she purposefully pushed for being placed on the "hard" congressional committees to earn a reputation as a politician who would not shy away from the serious, tough issues. Yet Ball also shows how Pelosi did not simply adapt to a flawed system; many times she sacrificed the potential of a "likable" image in order to achieve her legislative goals.

Pelosi's willingness to take unpopular stances helped make her a key target of Republicans during the Obama administration. After Democrats lost control of the House in the 2010 midterm elections, she faced opposition within her own party as well, even fending off a challenge for the minority leadership. Yet she remained in power following the election of President Trump and quickly emerged as one of his chief opponents. Pelosi often bluntly criticized Trump's false claims, earning much media attention along with new fans and detractors. Along the way she regained the Speaker post after helping guide the Democrats to electoral gains in 2018. Importantly, Ball examines Pelosi's shift from opposing the idea of impeaching Trump to leading the effort to remove him from office. Though the Republican-led Senate ultimately acquitted Trump, Ball frames Pelosi's successful impeachment effort as one of the most telling achievements of her political career.

Pelosi was generally well received by critics, though most noted that it would be mainly appreciated by readers who, like Ball, who are generally sympathetic to the subject's political views. Reviewers appreciated Ball's engaging writing style and her resistance to pure hagiography. Many also praised the insights not only into Pelosi's life, but also into the general workings of the American political system. In the *New York Times*, for example, Michelle Greenberg described the book as a thorough exploration of political effectiveness through compromise. The *Washington Post*'s Joe Klein called it a "smart, solid biography with a lesson: Despite our current fixation on political showmanship, politics works best in a complicated democracy like ours when its practitioners can navigate their way through the byzantine cloakrooms of power." Ultimately a wide swath of American political history comes into focus through Ball's eye on Pelosi. Yet the biography is also in a way unfinished, as it concludes with Pelosi still in power and poised before an election widely characterized as crucial for the future of the United States.

Author Biography

Molly Ball is a journalist who has covered politics for *Time*, the *Atlantic*, *Politico*, and other outlets. She earned the Gerald R. Ford Prize for Distinguished Reporting on the Presidency and the Society of Professional Journalists Sigma Delta Chi Award, among other awards. She also served as a political analyst for CNN.

Micah L. Issitt

Review Sources

Goldberg, Michelle. "Nancy Pelosi's Brilliant Career." Review of *Pelosi*, by Molly Ball. *The New York Times*, 5 May 2020, www.nytimes.com/2020/05/05/books/review/pelosi-molly-ball.html. Accessed 9 Oct. 2020.

Green, Lloyd. "Pelosi Review: The Speaker, Her Rise and How She Came to Rend Space in Donald Trump's Brain." Review of *Pelosi*, by Molly Ball. *The Guardian*, 17 May 2020, www.theguardian.com/us-news/2020/may/17/pelosi-review-speaker-donald-trump-brain. Accessed 9 Oct. 2020.

Kelley, Kitty. Review of *Pelosi*, by Molly Ball. *Washington Independent Review of Books*, 5 May 2020, www.washingtonindependentreviewofbooks.com/index.php/bookreview/pelosi. Accessed 9 Oct. 2020.

Klein, Joe. "Nancy Pelosi Is an Anachronism—in a Good Way." Review of *Pelosi*, by Molly Ball. *The Washington Post*, 8 May 2020, www.washingtonpost.com/outlook/nancy-pelosi-is-an-anachronism--in-a-good-way/2020/05/07/340710ce-7840-11ea-a130-df573469f094_story.html. Accessed 9 Oct. 2020.

Spindel, Barbara. "'Pelosi' Tracks the Career of a Powerful, Driven Politician." Review of *Pelosi*, by Molly Ball. *The Christian Science Monitor*, 11 May 2020, www.csmonitor.com/Books/Book-Reviews/2020/0511/Pelosi-tracks-the-career-of-a-powerful-driven-politician. Accessed 9 Oct. 2020.

Williams, Raymond. Review of *Pelosi*, by Molly Ball. *Ballasts for the Mind*, 23 May 2020, medium.com/ballasts-for-the-mind/review-pelosi-by-molly-ball-f6eb-4c8a3c62. Accessed 9 Oct. 2020.

Piranesi

Author: Susanna Clarke (b. 1959)
Publisher: Bloomsbury (New York). 272 pp.
Type of work: Novel
Time: Present day, with flashbacks
Locale: A mysterious, seemingly endless structure known as the House

In Piranesi, *Susanna Clarke's long-awaited second novel, the titular narrator inhabits a strange world of endless halls, seemingly empty of almost all other people. As he studies his surroundings he realizes that he has forgotten about his own past, and he begins to unravel the mystery of the place and himself.*

Principal characters

PIRANESI, the narrator, a middle-aged man who has no recollection of his past but exhibits scientific curiosity and records his observations in numbered journals

THE OTHER, seemingly the only other living person in the House, also a man; reclusive and convinced there is secret knowledge to be had

THE SIXTEENTH PERSON, a.k.a. *16*, an unseen figure mentioned by the Other as dangerous

In her debut novel, *Jonathan Strange & Mr. Norrell* (2004), Susanna Clarke created a world grounded in both real history (England during the Napoleonic Wars) and fantasy (involving both magic and dreams). While the historical world of that book is described in detail worthy of the novelists of the era, notably Jane Austen and Charles Dickens, Clarke weaves in mystical and surreal elements, including fantastical buildings that test the credulity of those who enter. The novel was a smash hit with readers and critics alike, and fans eagerly awaited further work from Clarke. Yet while she subsequently published a number of short stories, some set in the same alternate history as *Jonathan Strange*, her next novel would not appear for over a decade and a half. That follow-up, *Piranesi* (2020), is a stand-alone work and in some ways quite different from Clarke's debut effort, but it shares a deep interest in magic—and architecture—that makes for a wonderful, if strange, read.

Some readers may recognize *Piranesi*'s title from the Italian architect, artist, and engraver Giovanni Battista (or Giambattista) Piranesi (1720–78). He is most famous for idealized etchings of Rome and a series of prints known as the Imaginary Prisons (*Carceri d'invenzione*). The latter, images of massive, fantastical structures filled with mysterious staircases and machinery, captured the Gothic imagination of early

Romanticism and influenced later artists like M. C. Escher (1898–1972). Though never mentioned in the novel, the historical Piranesi is a clear influence. Not only does the narrator, a man with no knowledge of his own identity, take on the same name, but he also finds himself living in a vast, reality-warping, Classical structure reminiscent of the *Carceri*.

This setting, which the Piranesi character calls both "the House" and "the World," is an immensely large building that reaches from ocean on the lowest level to clouds on the highest. Vestibules, halls, and doorways extend to the north, west, and south farther than the narrator is able to explore; indeed, they seem to keep getting longer. Meanwhile, sections to the east have crumbled with the daily tides and rising sea levels. Statues throughout the House, ranging from nearly life-sized to colossal, attest to a human presence, though the narrator can only count thirteen skeletons of those who have gone before him. He fancies that the last of these, the skeleton of a young woman, was intended by the building's architect to be his wife and the mother of a new generation. Since the only other living person he has seen in the house, the well-groomed Other, is also a man, the narrator assumes that his species will soon die out.

Susanna Clarke

The House is a labyrinth that recalls those in stories by the Argentinian writer Jorge Luis Borges (1899–1986), whose work feels like another influence throughout *Piranesi*. But whereas the labyrinths of Borges are circular, those of Clarke are more like twists in a grid. The narrator also describes locations in the northwest, and readers may assume there were similar ones in the other quadrants before the encroaching ocean took over those in the east. Adding to the labyrinth symbolism, the House features large statues of minotaurs, like the hybrid human bull of Greek myth who inhabited a dangerous maze. These statues dominate the vestibule, which the narrator considers to lie at the building's center.

The novel unfolds through journal entries by the narrator, who is given the name Piranesi by the Other. (He later learns that the Other has assigned this name as an ironic reference that he, the narrator, is not supposed to understand). Initially, Piranesi worries little about his lack of memories or his general situation. He is curious about the House, and notes the results of his explorations, but he mostly finds the place amazing and beautiful. He considers himself and the Other to be scientists—one of many examples that show he does seem to have a frame of reference based in the normal world, despite his amnesia and isolation.

Piranesi and the Other meet twice a week, and it emerges that the narrator is a kind of assistant in the Other's search for some kind of secrets contained in the House. The two—and arguably the House itself—are the clear central characters and gain more and more depth as the narrative unfolds. However, other figures, mostly unseen, do come to play a role, casting doubt on the Other's motives and benevolence. Chief among these is the Sixteenth Person, or 16, whom the Other says is a dangerous intruder and warns Piranesi to hide from and avoid telling anything. As 16's presence becomes visible in chalk marks and words that help Piranesi find his way out of the labyrinth and back to the central room, however, the narrator begins to question the Other and wonder if this new person will become his friend. Meanwhile, Piranesi also begins looking back through his earlier journals. To his surprise, he learns that there were still more volumes, now missing. He also finds names that have no meaning in the world as he knows it, names like London and Manchester. Other names become attached to the skeletons the narrator named, and indeed to the narrator himself, as the idea of another world outside the House takes shape. The various mysteries continue to grow, effectively building tension as Piranesi and the reader learn more and more.

Though the plot ultimately does reach an engaging climax, Clarke avoids simple explanations. Magic is very much in play, but there is also room for more realistic interpretations, such as mental breakdown, or philosophical meanings. The larger forces that eventually come to light may be seen as good or evil. Much of this ambiguity, which is generally effective rather than frustrating, is due to Piranesi's status as an unreliable narrator. His limited perspective is clear from the outset in the observations he makes; for example, he notices that the Other is always impeccably dressed at their scheduled meetings while his own clothes have become rags, but he does not question the Other's ability to obtain things. Only gradually does he question the assumptions he once held so firmly, and readers will likely be several steps ahead of him. Yet this unreliability does not make Piranesi any less interesting, and, indeed, it is Clarke's humanizing depiction of this unusual character that is one of the novel's great strengths.

Clarke skillfully uses structural elements to reinforce themes and references. The central narrative takes place over a matter of months, though the journals cover a period of about seven years—a length of time that may correspond to the seven years that the mythological hero Odysseus spends on the island of the witch Calypso before resuming his journey back to Ithaca in Homer's epic poem *Odyssey* (ca. 8th century BCE). Just as Odysseus tells of his former life and experiences as he travels homeward, the narrator learns and records more about his own journey as he prepares to leave the only world he knows. Not all the references are to mythology, however, or even literature in general. For example, Clarke noted in interviews how the isolation of the House reflects her real-world experience of being housebound with a debilitating but mysterious illness. *Piranesi*'s blend of such vivid personal emotion with myth, allegory, mystery, and philosophy makes for a novel that breaks genre boundaries and will appeal to fans of both fantasy and more traditional literary fiction.

Critical reception to *Piranesi* was overwhelmingly positive. Many reviewers considered it a refreshingly unique spin on the popular trope of a postapocalyptic world featuring very few remaining survivors. Many also found the novel's release in 2020 unnervingly appropriate, coming amid the lockdowns and widespread social isolation brought on by the coronavirus disease 2019 (COVID-19) pandemic. Indeed, in a review for the *Washington Post*, Ron Charles suggested the book would make readers "appreciate life in quarantine," as Clarke is able to turn a potential horror story into a poignant narrative. Writing for the *Wall Street Journal*, Sam Sacks similarly approved of how the book subverts long-standing conventions of mystery thrillers, horror novels, and other genre fiction while maintaining a gripping, page-turner feel. Other critics praised *Piranesi* as a worthy successor to Clarke's acclaimed debut sixteen years earlier. In a review for the *Guardian*, Paraic O'Donnell pointed out the differences between the two works and called *Piranesi* "elegant and singular," a "remarkable feat, not just of craft but of reinvention." While Clarke's style and the opaque mystery of the House may not be for everyone, the anonymous reviewer for *Kirkus* succinctly captured the overall appeal of *Piranesi* for many readers: "Weird and haunting and excellent."

Author Biography
Susanna Clarke earned many honors for her best-selling first novel, *Jonathan Strange & Mr. Norrell* (2004), including the British Book Award for best new author and the Hugo Award for best fantasy or science fiction novel. Her short-story collection *The Ladies of Grace Adieu* was published in 2006.

Thomas Willard

Review Sources
Charles, Ron. "Susanna Clarke's Infinitely Clever 'Piranesi' Is Enough to Make You Appreciate Life in Quarantine." Review of *Piranesi*, by Susanna Clarke. *The Washington Post*, 8 Sept. 2020, www.washingtonpost.com/entertainment/books/susanna-clarkes-infinitely-clever-piranesi-is-enough-to-make-you-appreciate-life-in-quarantine/2020/09/08/09836026-f123-11ea-999c-67ff7bf6a9d2_story.html. Accessed 16 Oct. 2020.
O'Donnell, Paraic. "Piranesi by Susanna Clarke Review—An Elegant Study in Solitude." Review of *Piranesi*, by Susanna Clarke. *The Guardian*, 17 Sept. 2020, www.theguardian.com/books/2020/sep/17/piranesi-by-susanna-clarke-review-an-elegant-study-in-solitude. Accessed 4 Nov. 2020.
Review of *Piranesi*, by Susanna Clarke. *Kirkus*, 17 June 2020, www.kirkusreviews.com/book-reviews/susanna-clarke/piranesi/. Accessed 4 Nov. 2020.
Sacks, Sam. "A Fantastic Puzzle from Susanna Clarke." Review of *Piranesi*, by Susanna Clarke. *The Wall Street Journal*, 11 Sept. 2020, www.wsj.com/articles/piranesi-review-a-fantastic-puzzle-from-susanna-clarke-11599836134. Accessed 16 Oct. 2020.
Teitelbaum, Ilana. "The Beauty of the House: On Susanna Clarke's 'Piranesi.'" Review of *Piranesi*, by Susanna Clark. *Los Angeles Review of Books*, 18 Oct. 2020, lareviewofbooks.org/article/the-beauty-of-the-house-on-susanna-clarkes-piranesi/. Accessed 22 Oct. 2020.
Valentine, Vikki. "Susanna Clarke Divines Magic in Long-Awaited 'Piranesi.'" Review of *Piranesi*, by Susanna Clarke. *NPR*, 20 Sept. 2020, www.npr.org/2020/09/20/914369450/susanna-clarke-divines-magic-in-long-awaited-novel-piranesi. Accessed 20 Oct. 2020.

Postcolonial Love Poem

Author: Natalie Diaz (b. 1978)
Publisher: Graywolf Press (Minneapolis, MN). 120 pp.
Type of work: Poetry

Natalie Diaz's collection Postcolonial Love Poem *joins prose poetry with verse, blurring the lines between genre and form. The collection explores violence, desire, and the connections between body and land.*

Postcolonial Love Poem arrives as Natalie Diaz's second poetry collection. Fans of her work, including the American Book Award–winning *When My Brother Was an Aztec* (2012), will find her inquisitive, stirring voice alive and well in the second collection. Diaz, a Mojave, Akimel O'odham, and Latinx poet and an enrolled member of the Gila River Indian Community, draws upon her life to build her latest collection, much like her last. The former point guard for Old Dominion University and professional basketball player in Europe and Asia regularly brings basketball imagery into her writing, alongside pieces exploring the depths and limits of both familial and romantic love. A linguist and language activist, Diaz once worked on language revitalization at the Fort Mojave Indian Reservation with the last of the fluent elders. Her work reflects this dedication to preserving both the language and origin stories of her people, often blending languages and memoir with mythical imagery.

Postcolonial Love Poem is separated into five sections, each introduced by an epigraph. The first epigraph, by poet Joy Harjo, reads, "I am singing a song that can only be born after losing a country," and sets the tone for not only the title piece, "Postcolonial Love Poem," but the entirety of the collection. The poem evokes images of the natural world as Diaz grapples with loss of a home, a country, and the pain that comes from living in a place where Indigenous and other people of color are regularly the targets of violence. As Diaz writes about her own body, she turns back to the land and the stories she knows about it, writing:

> I've been taught bloodstones can cure a snakebite,
> can stop the bleeding—most people forgot this
> when the war ended. The war ended
> depending on which war you mean: those we started,
> before those, millennia ago and onward

The poem also turns erotic, with lyric images such as "wildflowers in my desert / which take up to twenty years to bloom" and the lover-opponent's "quartz-light and dangerous" hips. The land and Diaz's body are tied to each other, shaped, wounded, and remade by the violence—wars, both literal and metaphorical, and acts of nature—they are subject to. The inseparability of body and land, an aspect of the Mojave worldview, runs like a current throughout the volume.

Family is another frequent subject of Diaz's work, and *Postcolonial Love Poem* is no exception. Her first collection explores a man's struggles with mental illness and drug addiction and its impact on his family in poems like "My Brother at 3 A.M." and "How to Go to Dinner with a Brother on Drugs," laying bare the fear and uncertainty that accompany his condition and the violence that often erupts from it. Two poems in *Postcolonial Love Poem* tread on similar familial territory early on in the collection. "Blood-Light" elevates a story about a brother threatening first his father and then his sister, the speaker, with a knife to the level of mythology. She establishes a mythic connection early, saying, "This could be a story from the Bible, / if it wasn't already a story about stars." Diaz then depicts her tears as scorpions struggling on the ground that do battle with the brother. The brother's desire to stab both the speaker and their father grows more mythic as she alludes to Greco-Roman constellations and describes a body being opened by a knife as a way to "open [it] to the stars" and his intentions toward her as "One way to love a sister, help her bleed light." The poem displays another of Diaz's strengths: the seamless movement from the narrator's viewpoint into another's perspective, like that of the agitated brother.

Within the same section, the poem "Catching Copper" explores the ease with which violence comes in and out of life and how that violence is connected to the life men around Diaz lead. In the poem, brothers are connected to a single metaphorical bullet that they keep "on a leash shiny / as a whip of blood." They treat it like a pet, calling for it; speak to it about appearing too glamorous; and "kiss" it in storefronts and club dancefloors. Like so much of Diaz's poetry, "Catching Copper" speaks to the ways in which the cultures of those people around her, and those who belong to so many other groups, are mined for American culture, hollowed out, and appropriated. In this view American culture has attempted to turn those same groups into apostles to its violence. The speaker's hostile position toward the bullet is met with a deep tenderness for her brothers, whom she watches put themselves in harm's way to connect with the magical bullet. A helplessness is felt by the reader, as the speaker seems to fail to reach her kin, realizing all along that the problem is bigger than anything she can conquer, and that it is ultimately deadly.

Some of the most interesting pieces in the collection act as much like essays as they do poems, including the thematically linked prose poems "The First Water Is the Body" and "exhibits from The American Water Museum." "The First Water Is the Body," reprinted from an issue of *Orion Magazine* discussing the Dakota Access Pipeline protests, is written in fragments that lyrically explore how one's body is connected to the earth—and most importantly, water—and the lives of Indigenous peoples. Blending facts and Western theory with Mojave creation stories and meditations on water, Diaz weaves a wide-ranging view of how one's body and the land that surrounds it are one. The piece opens with the line, "The Colorado River is the most endangered river in the United States—also, it is a part of my body." The threat of violence and endangerment to Diaz and others that moves in and out of the other pieces of the collection is once again invoked here. The Colorado River is not endangered by chance, but by human activity. Moving through the piece, Diaz's speaker counters an ancient stereotype, stating, "I have never met a red Native," and wryly observing, "I lived in the desert along a dammed blue river. The only red people I've seen are white tourists sunburned after staying out on the water too long." The piece creates a container for considering the limitations of translation, how different groups of people relate to the world in different ways and how this leads to violence and oppression, and ultimately how denying one's self the very thing it needs to survive means certain death, both physically and spiritually.

"exhibits from The American Water Museum" imagines an institution dedicated to water and the memory of water. In notes included at the end of the book, Diaz says she was inspired by Luis Alberto Urrea's book *The Water Museum*, a monument that became a real place in her mind. The poem-essay imagines numbered exhibits from the museum. Each number is a new section, sometimes consisting of verse, other times imagined performance pieces, and at others, artifacts like "a dilapidated diorama of the mythical city of Flint, Michigan." The piece speaks to "The First Water Is the Body" as it considers past parts of American civilization that have died or seem so unlikely as to never have existed from the narrator's new vantage point. It is at these moments in the collection—when Diaz considers the ledge upon which she sees the land and its people perched so precariously—that bring into sharp focus her intent through the collection. She seems to ask, how can any of these smaller moments matter in the face of such destruction? Yet, they all do.

The collection brings a reminder of how important human connection continues to be with many pieces devoted to love, or specifically, the relationship between Diaz and her lover. For example, the piece "Ode to the Beloved's Hips" celebrates a woman's body and the joy it brings, opening with the lines:

> Bells are they—shaped on the 8th day, silvered
> percussion in the morning—*are* the morning.
> Swing switch sway. Hold the day away a little
> longer, a little slower, a little *easy*.

The poem also exemplifies the free flow of language in the volume, cascading from English to Spanish to words of various other origins, as it rushes from image to image, creating a kaleidoscopic effect that readers may find mesmerizing or disjointed, depending on their perspective.

The collection closes with a series of poems centered around grief, loss, and resilience. Diaz circles her themes one last time in the poems "My Brother, My Wound" and "Grief Work." In each, Diaz's narrator internalizes the pain she has accumulated, turning it into a source of renewal and strength, as the collection asks, what else can a person do?

Upon its release, *Postcolonial Love Poem* was hailed by critics as a monumental work. In a review for *The Rumpus*, Gillian Neimark called the book "stunning . . . painful, embodied, and glorious." She continued, "This is a creation myth which won't be denied or drowned out. This is a body we will never turn away from—awestruck-beloved-eaten-shot-killed-stampeded by animals-made of rivers and stars." The collection was similarly celebrated in reviews at the *New York Times*, *Times Literary Supplement*, and the *Guardian*. In the latter Emily Pérez concluded that *Postcolonial Love Poem* constituted "another breathtaking, groundbreaking book, an intellectually rigorous exploration of the postcolonial toll on land, love and people, as well as a call to fight back." Diaz's "soaring poems," she wrote, demonstrate "not only that love persists in the aftermath of colonialism, but that it provides a means of transcendence, too." Like its predecessor, this remarkable volume was named a finalist for the National Book Award for Poetry.

Author Biography

Natalie Diaz's debut collection, *When My Brother Was an Aztec* (2012), won an American Book Award, and her work has appeared in such publications as *Narrative* and *Prairie Schooner*. A MacArthur Fellow, she received a 2012 Lannan Literary Fellowship for Poetry and 2015 PEN/Civitella Ranieri Foundation Fellowship, among other awards. She teaches at Arizona State University.

Melynda Fuller

Review Sources

Janae, Dani. "Natalie Diaz Writes the Love Poem for Our Lives in 'Postcolonial Love Poem.'" Review of *Postcolonial Love Poem*, by Natalie Diaz. *AutoStraddle*, 28 Apr. 2020, www.autostraddle.com/natalie-diaz-writes-the-love-poem-for-our-lives-in-postcolonial-love-poem. Accessed 19 Oct. 2020.

Leonard, Dominic. "In Brief: Postcolonial Love Poem by Natalie Diaz Review." Review of *Postcolonial Love Poem*, by Natalie Diaz. *The Times Literary Supplement*, 7 Aug. 2020, www.the-tls.co.uk/articles/postcolonial-love-poem-natalie-diaz-review-dominic-leonard. Accessed 19 Oct. 2020.

Neimark, Gillian. "Intimate and Vast: Postcolonial Love Poem by Natalie Diaz." Review of *Postcolonial Love Poem*, by Natalie Diaz. *The Rumpus*, 20 Mar. 2020, therumpus.net/2020/03/postcolonial-love-poem-by-natalie-diaz. Accessed 19 Oct. 2020.

Pérez, Emily. "Postcolonial Love Poem by Natalie Diaz Review – Intimate, Electric and Defiant." Review of *Postcolonial Love Poem*, by Natalie Diaz. *The Guardian*, 18 Aug. 2020, www.theguardian.com/books/2020/aug/18/postcolonial-love-poem-by-natalie-diaz-review-intimate-electric-and-defiant. Accessed 19 Oct. 2020.

Phillips, Emilia. "Poems of Love and Desire That Push Back against Oppression." Review of *Postcolonial Love Poem*, by Natalie Diaz. *The New York Times*, 4 Mar. 2020, www.nytimes.com/2020/03/03/books/review/natalie-diaz-postcolonial-love-poem.html. Accessed 19 Oct. 2020.

Wabuke, Hope. "Within a Legacy of Colonization, 'Postcolonial Love Poem' Empowers Native Voice." Review of *Postcolonial Love Poem*, by Natalie Diaz. *NPR*, 6 Mar. 2020, www.npr.org/2020/03/06/812488532/within-a-legacy-of-colonization-postcolonial-love-poem-empowers-native-voice. Accessed 19 Oct. 2020.

The Price of Peace
Money, Democracy, and the Life of John Maynard Keynes

Author: Zachary D. Carter
Publisher: Random House (New York). Illustrated. 656 pp.
Type of work: Biography, history
Time: 1883–present
Locales: Great Britain and the United States

In The Price of Peace, *journalist Zachary D. Carter presents a highly readable introduction to the life and ideas of the influential economist John Maynard Keynes. Carter does not limit himself to succinctly summarizing Keynes's contributions as a statesman, philosopher, and economic theorist; he also traces the impact of Keynesian economics from Keynes's death shortly after the conclusion of World War II to contemporary times.*

Principal personages

JOHN MAYNARD KEYNES, a British philosopher and government official who became one of the most important economists of the twentieth century
LYTTON STRACHEY, his lover and longtime friend who became a famous biographer and a leader of the Bloomsbury set
VIRGINIA WOOLF, another longtime friend, a distinguished novelist and member of the Bloomsbury set
DAVID LLOYD GEORGE, the British prime minister from 1916 to 1922, with whom he worked in government
WOODROW WILSON, the president of the United States from 1913 to 1921, whom he criticized heavily in a book about the Treaty of Versailles
LYDIA LOPOKOVA, his greatest love, an internationally famous Russian ballerina whom he married in 1925
FRANKLIN D. ROOSEVELT, the president of the United States from 1933 to 1945, who experimented with Keynesian economics while battling the Great Depression
JOAN ROBINSON, a British economist at Cambridge University who helped him develop some of his ideas
JOHN KENNETH GALBRAITH, an American economist and political thinker who adapted Keynesian economics to the circumstances of the postwar United States
PAUL SAMUELSON, the influential American author of a best-selling economics textbook that popularized some aspects of Keynesianism
FRIEDRICH VON HAYEK, a leader of the Austrian School of Economics who opposed Keynesianism and government planning in favor of classical market economics

MILTON FRIEDMAN, an American economist who opposed Keynesianism and helped lead the Chicago School of Economics, emphasizing a monetarist approach to economic policy

Zachary D. Carter covers economic policy and federal politics for the left-leaning *HuffPost*. In his first book, *The Price of Peace* (2020), Carter has written an engaging homage to the liberal icon John Maynard Keynes, whose economic theories justified the expansive growth of government and government spending in the twentieth century. Not only does Carter describe the main contours of Keynes's life and expertly explicate his major works, but he carries his story beyond Keynes's death and explores the use and misuse of his ideas by political leaders from the beginnings of the Cold War to the present day. This book is not intended as a contribution to academic libraries; it is meant to illuminate and influence the important economic challenges facing the world at the beginning of the 2020s. Carter clearly believes that Keynes's heterodox approach to economics offers a pathway to a more equitable and humane society. The problem, as he explains in the last third of the book, is that Keynesianism has been hijacked by intellectual, business, and political forces antithetical to its original goals.

Carter's leftist perspective pervades his book, sometimes to its detriment. An offhand reference to President Donald Trump as a far-right demagogue, for instance, and his characterization of President Richard Nixon as being "in love with war" may undermine his argument in the eyes of some readers. The implication that President Woodrow Wilson's support for national self-determination in Europe following World War I should have led him to create a separate African American nation in the United States comes across more as historically anachronistic virtue-signaling in 2020 than a logically pertinent commentary on the problems involved with the dissolution of the German, Austrian, Russian, and Turkish empires a century ago. An observation that wealthy warmongers benefited from President John F. Kennedy's tax cuts is as rhetorically empty as it is evidentially opaque. Much more defensible are Carter's convictions that the New Deal and Great Society worked, though there are weighty arguments that they failed to meet their fundamental objectives.

There are a few errors, perhaps inevitable in a book of this scope. Most are minor. One such involves Edmund Burke. Carter repeatedly claims that the great eighteenth-century statesman and political philosopher was a major influence on Keynes because of his emphasis on the practical effects of governmental policy and antipathy to radical social experimentation. He also describes Burke as Scottish. While Burke may have shared some of the intellectual perspective of Adam Smith and other luminaries of the Scottish Enlightenment, he was not Scottish; he was Irish, a distinction that was anything but negligible in the era of the Hanoverian kings. Burke's Irishness at a time when the great majority of Irish people were oppressed and looked down upon was important to him and those around him. Keynes, who grew to political maturity amid agitation for Irish Home Rule, likely would have been aware of this crucial biographical fact about Burke. Given the importance that Carter attributes to Burke in Keynes's intellectual development, it is odd that he seems oblivious to this detail.

Fortunately, these are minor blemishes in a work that achieves the impressive feat of making economic theory comprehensible to ordinary readers. Carter's journalistic skills serve him well in explaining complicated fiscal policies in a world wracked by war and depression. His book can be read as a lucid macroeconomic history of the past century. John Maynard Keynes played a pivotal role in this story. He was a man of action as well as an original and consequential thinker. He played an important role in government during two world wars. Out of office, he was consulted by politicians and central bankers. His books and prolific journalistic writings reached millions. He would live to see his ideas shaping economic policy in the most powerful nation on the globe. In short, Keynes lived a life in full. Carter is enthralled with his subject. He clearly sees himself as an apostle of a Keynesianism purified of mostly American misinterpretations and accretions.

Carter spends little time on Keynes's childhood, instead devoting attention to his adult life from college onward. He notes that Keynes came from a middle-class background and was admitted on scholarships to Eton and the University of Cambridge, nurseries of the British elite. At Cambridge, Keynes fell in with the Apostles, a secret student society that in the early twentieth century was devoted to celebrating an artistic vision of life and questioning the moral code inherited from their Victorian forebears. At the time, homosexuality was widespread among the Apostles, and Keynes embraced this aspect of the society with his lover and longtime friend Lytton Strachey. For his first four decades, Keynes enthusiastically pursued same-sex liaisons. Keynes, Strachey, and other graduates of the Apostles would form the core of the Bloomsbury circle of writers and artists, which also included the novelist Virginia Woolf. In Carter's account, in Keynes's personal predilections and inmost convictions, he was a bohemian who was happiest talking about beauty and countercultural ethics with his artistic friends. Despite this, he was unique in the Bloomsbury circle by pursuing a very conventionally establishment career as a civil servant, spending several years in the India Office. Throughout his life he would alternate periods of government service with academic pursuits at Cambridge. Originally interested in philosophy and mathematics, Keynes's first book would be on Indian finance, establishing him as an economic theorist.

Keynes was at Cambridge at the beginning of World War I. The government recalled him to service to help quell a financial crisis concerning the gold standard. Bankers were demanding an end of the convertibility of foreign currency to gold, fearing that the gold supply would be exhausted. Keynes persuaded the government to resist this, calming the markets and preserving the British reputation for financial solidity. He went on to perform brilliantly for the Treasury during the war, handling the crucial issue of inter-Allied finances. In 1919 Keynes was part of the British delegation to the peacemaking in Paris. What he saw appalled him, especially the economic treatment of Germany. He was convinced that the onerous reparations imposed on Germany, as well as the American insistence that all wartime loans by the Allies be repaid in full, would prevent the economic recovery of Europe and lead to more war. His book *The Economic Consequences of the Peace* (1919) became an international sensation and inspired opponents of the Treaty of Versailles.

Out of government, Keynes thrived. He became wealthy on the income of his writings and the profits of judicious speculations in the currency markets. Astounding his friends, he fell in love with and happily married the glamorous ballerina Lydia Lopokova. Through the 1920s Keynes refined his heterodox economic ideas. The Great Depression brought urgency to this process, culminating with his masterpiece *The General Theory of Employment, Interest and Money* (1936). Keynes's experiences in World War I had disabused him of his earlier respect for the rationality of markets, bankers, and business executives. He believed that economies were fundamentally political phenomena. He called on governments to spend freely in bad times, using public works and other means to spur consumer spending, which in turn would revive a depressed economy. His goal was a more egalitarian society that would enable all people to enjoy the good things in life, which, for him, were leisure and art. Keynes wanted reform rather than revolution, revealing the Burkean in him. He had seen the Soviet Union and emphatically rejected totalitarianism. Ironically, his ideas received a friendlier reception in the United States than his homeland, and President Franklin Roosevelt employed Keynesian techniques in ameliorating the effects of the Depression.

Aging and ailing, Keynes served the British government as an adviser and negotiator during World War II. He took part in the 1944 Bretton Woods Conference that laid the foundations for the postwar international economic system. Keynes died in 1946, but Keynesianism lived on. Unfortunately, according to Carter, it was increasingly an Americanized system, a Keynesianism without its soul. Popular and influential scholars like Paul Samuelson merged mechanical aspects of Keynes's theories with more traditional and mathematically oriented approaches to economics. The American government often practiced a Keynesian approach to budgeting, but it was spending money on weapons and highways, not the social programs Keynes had envisaged. Economists John Kenneth Galbraith and Joan Robinson attempted to preserve a more authentic Keynesianism but were increasingly marginalized. At the same time, Friedrich Hayek's critique of governmental intervention in the economy and Milton Friedman's market-oriented monetarism became increasingly influential in the postwar years. For Carter, the postwar gutting of Keynesianism detailed in the book's final section was a tragedy.

Carter's *The Price of Peace* is a clarion call for the humanistic economics championed by John Maynard Keynes. Readers may not all share his enthusiasm and may ponder whether governments have proved any more rational or wiser than the markets Keynes dismissed. Nevertheless, this is an illuminating and useful book. Allowing for Carter's ideological bent, even followers of Hayek and Friedman will find *The Price of Peace* well worth close and respectful attention.

Author Biography

Zachary D. Carter is a senior business/environment reporter for *HuffPost*, an online news site. His journalism has also appeared in the *American Prospect*, the *Nation*, and the *New Republic*. *The Price of Peace* is his best-selling debut.

Daniel P. Murphy

Review Sources

Phillips-Fein, Kim. "The Lost Rebellious Spirit of Keynes." Review of *The Price of Peace: Money, Democracy, and the Life of John Maynard Keynes*, by Zachary D. Carter. *The New Republic*, 9 June 2020, newrepublic.com/article/158070/john-maynard-keynes-biography-review-lost-rebellious-spirit. Accessed 11 Jan. 2021.

Review of *The Price of Peace: Money, Democracy, and the Life of John Maynard Keynes*, by Zachary D. Carter. *Kirkus Reviews*, vol. 88, no. 6, Mar. 2020. *Literary Reference Center Plus*, search.ebscohost.com/login.aspx?direct=true&db=lkh&AN=142188228&site=lrc-plus. Accessed 11 Jan. 2021.

Sachs, Jeffrey. "Keynes and the Good Life: Economics as Practical Wisdom." Review of *The Price of Peace: Money, Democracy, and the Life of John Maynard Keynes*, by Zachary D. Carter, and *Keynes against Capitalism: His Economic Case for Liberal Socialism*, by James Crotty. *The American Prospect*, May–June 2020, pp. 56–59.

Steil, Benn. "The Economic Engineer." Review of *The Price of Peace: Money, Democracy, and the Life of John Maynard Keynes*, by Zachary D. Carter. *The Wall Street Journal*, 8 May 2020, www.wsj.com/articles/the-price-of-peace-review-the-economic-engineer-11588947478. Accessed 11 Jan. 2020.

Szalai, Jennifer. "John Maynard Keynes Died in 1946. An Outstanding New Biography Shows Him Relevant Still." Review of *The Price of Peace: Money, Democracy, and the Life of John Maynard Keynes*, by Zachary D. Carter. *The New York Times*, 20 May 2020, www.nytimes.com/2020/05/20/books/review-price-of-peace-john-maynard-keynes-zachary-carter.html. Accessed 15 Dec. 2020.

A Promised Land

Author: Barack Obama (b. 1961)
Publisher: Crown (New York). 768 pp.
Type of work: Memoir, history
Time: 1961–2011
Locales: Hawaii; Illinois; Washington, DC

Barack Obama's A Promised Land *is the first of a two-part account of and reflection on the Obama administration, covering his rise to political power and most of his first term in the office of the US presidency.*

Principal personages
BARACK HUSSEIN OBAMA, the forty-fourth president of the United States
MICHELLE OBAMA, his wife, the First Lady of the United States
JOE BIDEN, then the forty-seventh vice president of the United States

A Promised Land (2020) is not an in-depth biography of the life of Barack Obama, who served as president of the United States between 2009 and 2017. The former president's two previous books provide more biographical detail. He wrote his first, *Dreams from My Father* (1995), before he had begun his rise to the political apogee of the American government, and in it, he shares intimate portraits of his family and childhood as well as what drew him to public service. His second, *The Audacity of Hope* (2006), covers his political career, but from a distinctly ideological perspective, allowing Obama to make big-picture arguments for a form of political transcendence. Where his first two books delivered unique views on his life in politics, *A Promised Land* is an account of and reflection on his political career through most of his first term in the White House.

Though Americans are divided, as is the case with most politicians, on Obama's legacy, few question his considerable skill as a communicator. The internet archives are filled with examples of Obama's speeches and writings, on topics ranging from the pedestrian to high-minded political philosophy, and the eloquence with which he expresses himself helps explain his success in politics perhaps more than any other factor. *A Promised Land* is nonetheless a hefty book, clocking in at over seven hundred pages, and one that some critics found is perhaps overwritten and overly detailed. In the preface to the book, Obama explains that he had thought he could cover the relevant details of his presidential experience in a single book, of about five hundred pages. He found, as he got into the task, however, that he had much more to say. Rather than curtailing his thoughts, he decided to give himself the freedom to explore the

Barack Obama

subject as he wanted to, resulting in his decision to split the book into two parts, with *A Promised Land* consisting of the first relative half of this story.

Though the core action of the book centers around Obama's historic and unprecedented 2008 campaign and approximately his first three years in office, a considerable number of pages are dedicated to his early life and political career, including his time in the US Senate. This covers, to an extent, his work as a community organizer, his time in local Illinois government, and the decisions that brought him to the national stage. While his early life was examined more closely in his other books, here Obama chooses details that he saw as important to his rise to the presidency, or perhaps in shaping his drive for achievement. Moments with his family, in Hawaii, then later as he attended university, are framed with a retrospective view, noting how these moments and encounters may have molded the man who would later become a historic president.

Readers who follow Barack and Michelle Obama as one might follow a nonpolitical celebrity couple might enjoy the insights into his married life that Obama provides throughout the book. He reveals his wife's concern about his political ambitions and where he might take their family. Many reviewers noted that sections discussing Michelle provide a humanizing element in a book that focuses on such specific policy issues that readers might sometimes feel they are attending a lecture on American politics. There is something casual and realistic about Obama's depiction of his married life and of Michelle's frustrations with him, echoing the same kind of bickering and supportive ribbing that many married people might find relatable.

There is a sense that Obama sought to normalize himself, even to poke fun at his flaws, and these little glimpses of the very regular couple and family that the Obamas are contrast somewhat to the enormity of their celebrity and importance to so many. This was a juxtaposition that Obama seems keenly aware of, and passages of the book can alternate between banal and profound. For instance, he begins one section by saying, "As a general rule, I'm a slow walker—a Hawaiian walk, Michelle likes to say, sometimes with a hint of impatience," while the rest of the paragraph strikes a different tone, describing how his pace quickened as president, and how he was "conscious of the history that had been made there and those who had preceded me."

Sections revealing Michelle's ambivalence about Obama's political career also frame Obama's own questions and reflections about his place in American history. *A Promised Land* reveals Obama to be more than willing to question his own decisions, and some critics felt he perhaps gives himself too little credit in the end. Writing for the *New York Times*, Chimamanda Ngozi Adichie called this tendency the "modesty of the Brilliant American Liberal," and wished that he had found more room to take credit for what he accomplished, rather than spending so much time explaining more of what he did not . Each time Obama discusses a pivotal moment in his political career, such his now-famous speeches at the Democratic National Convention, his negotiations with China, his first hundred days in office, or the fight over his proposal for health-care reform, he qualifies his achievements with an explanation of why he did not achieve more or why he abandoned other alternatives.

Another of the more interesting things about *A Promised Land* is the detail with which Obama depicts the process of being in the Senate, of the presidential election campaign trail, and of being president. The hundreds of pages of the book allow him space to introduce supporting players in all of these periods, from campaign advisers to his opponents. He carefully describes the expertise and accomplishments of those he worked with and walks readers through their perspectives. Sections like these provide an interesting insight into the life of a president and into the specific kind of political balancing that Obama felt he needed to engage in.

At the same time, Obama also dedicates little time to some of the areas in which he has been most ardently criticized within his base, such as his administration's aggressive use of drone strikes and his decision to keep American forces deeply involved in the Middle East. The war on terror was something that Obama inherited, but some feel that he did far less than many of his supporters might have liked to reduce American involvement. His administration engaged in the most aggressive drone campaign in the Middle East, despite such use of drones being repeatedly criticized by human rights organizations. Others have argued that the Obama administration also did very little to address the privacy concerns shared by many Democratic voters who called for curtailing National Security Administration (NSA) and Central Intelligence Agency (CIA) use of surveillance.

On other issues, like the fight for health-care reform that produced the influential Affordable Care Act (ACA), Obama provides a wealth of information. He details discussions with aides, advisers, and political opponents about the way to explain how they arrived at the compromise of the final bill. He describes the arguments of critics on both sides, from the progressives who wanted him to take the bill much further, to those who wanted to curtail his efforts. Proudly noting the number of people who gained insurance thanks to the ACA, he also expresses regrets that the bill did not go as far as he had hoped or that he had not been more tenacious in fighting for the public option and in urging states to expand Medicare coverage. This aspect of the Obama legacy provides a good example of his unusual position in history. Obama believes in the same ideals as more progressive reformers like Senator Bernie Sanders, but he also has an enduring belief in incrementalism. Again and again, Obama explains why he felt he had to take the more moderate pace toward where he feels the country has the potential to go, but there is a clear expression of regret in his depictions of his achievements as well.

Other scholars have written in some detail about the way that Obama's campaign and presidency galvanized American politics. Obama does not directly argue the degree to which racism and prejudice played a role in the way his critics chose to attack him or to question his efforts, but it is clear nonetheless that he was very aware of the racial perceptions of his presidency, both to those wishing to hang on to the illusion that Americans of color are less capable and to the many people of color for whom Obama's achievements provided a powerful symbol. One of the more interesting aspects of Obama's reflections on his presidency is the degree to which he was keenly conscious of how his actions, words, and legacy would be scrutinized differently than that of other presidents and how his failures and successes would be both more celebrated and more criticized than any other leader in the nation's history.

Critics had a mixed reaction to *A Promised Land*. While most reviewers lauded his passion and writing skill, some found the book's length and depth frustrating or unnecessary. Nevertheless, most critics found more than enough to enjoy, and despite the book's depth and Obama's verbosity, several indicated that they never lost interest and that even overly explanatory sections were still gripping enough to keep a reader engaged. Whether or not the reviews had been positive, which they were overall, Obama and his family have generated a strong and passionate following among the public, a following strengthened by the way that Obama's legacy and accomplishments have been attacked by his immediate successor, Donald Trump, and his allies. In a period defined by political divisiveness, books about social justice and politics reached a peak in public popularity, and Obama's *A Promised Land* was the best seller of 2020, beating out a host of other political treatises from well-known public figures.

Some critics, and readers, expressed disappointment that Obama did not spend more time commenting on Trump. Many felt that any critique Obama wished to issue would have been justified, given how Trump advanced many false, often-racist claims about Obama, his background, and his presidency. Trump became a symbol for racist depictions of Obama and for the prejudicial animosity that developed among his critics. Though he says very little about Trump at least in this first book, Obama does formulate an argument that political leaders and parties that function by denying truth and facts pose a danger to any democracy. One of the messages highlighted in the book's preface is that America, as the bold political experiment, can succeed, but that fact and truth must be defended for the nation to reach its full potential.

Author Biography

Barack Obama was president of the United States from 2009 to 2017 after serving as a US senator representing Illinois from 2005 to 2008. He is also the author of *Dreams from My Father* (1995) and *The Audacity of Hope* (2006).

Micah L. Issitt

Review Sources

Adichie, Chimamanda Ngozi. "Chimamanda Ngozi Adichie on Barack Obama's 'A Promised Land.'" Review of *A Promised Land*, by Barack Obama. *The New York Times*, 23 Nov. 2020, www.nytimes.com/2020/11/12/books/review/barack-obama-a-promised-land.html. Accessed 28 Jan. 2021.

Grady, Constance. "In His New Memoir, Obama Defends—and Critiques—His Legacy." Review of *A Promised Land*, by Barack Obama. *Vox*, 19 Nov. 2020, www.vox.com/culture/21573728/barack-obama-memoir-promised-land-review. Accessed 28 Jan. 2021.

Lozada, Carlos. "The Examined Life of Barack Obama." Review of *A Promised Land*, by Barack Obama. *The Washington Post*, 17 Nov. 2020, www.washingtonpost.com/outlook/2020/11/17/obama-promised-land-memoir-autobiography. Accessed 28 Jan. 2021.

Szalai, Jennifer. "In 'A Promised Land,' Barack Obama Thinks—and Thinks Some More—over His First Term." Review of *A Promised Land*, by Barack Obama. *The New York Times*, 20 Nov. 2020, www.nytimes.com/2020/11/15/books/review-barack-obama-promised-land-memoir.html. Accessed 28 Jan. 2021.

Taylor, Charles. "An America That Could Explain: On Barack Obama's 'A Promised Land.'" Review of *A Promised Land*, by Barack Obama. *Los Angeles Review of Books*, 1 Jan. 2021, lareviewofbooks.org/article/an-america-that-could-explain-on-barack-obamas-a-promised-land. Accessed 29 Jan. 2021.

Younge, Gary. "A Promised Land by Barack Obama Review—an Impressive but Incomplete Memoir." Review of *A Promised Land*, by Barack Obama. *The Guardian*, 26 Nov. 2020, www.theguardian.com/books/2020/nov/26/a-promised-land-by-barack-obama-review-an-impressive-but-incomplete-memoir. Accessed 28 Jan. 2021.

Punching the Air

Authors: Ibi Zoboi and Yusef Salaam (b. ca. 1974–75)
Illustrator: Omar T. Pasha
Publisher: Balzer and Bray (New York). 400 pp.
Type of work: Verse novel
Time: Present day
Locale: United States

National Book Award finalist Ibi Zoboi and Yusef Salaam of the Exonerated Five team up to write a novel-in-verse for young adults. Punching the Air *tells the story of Amal and his experience of being locked up as a Black Muslim teenager, exploring institutional racism and offering a deeply personal look at the dehumanization of incarceration.*

Principal characters

AMAL DAWUD SHAHID, a sixteen-year-old artist and poet who is Black and Muslim
UMI, his mother
KADON, his friend in juvenile detention
JEREMY MATHIS, a White teen

Punching the Air (2020) is a novel-in-verse for young adults that explores the horrors of incarceration through poems written in the voice of Amal Dawud Shahid, a sixteen-year-old poet and artist who is Black and Muslim. Amal is a fictional character, but some of his experiences are based on those of coauthor Yusef Salaam. Salaam's name might be familiar to some readers as a member of the Central Park Five—today known as the Exonerated Five. There are echoes of the famous case in *Punching the Air*, though Amal's circumstances are quite different. Salaam was ensnared in the system in 1989, when a White woman named Trisha Meili was brutally assaulted and left for dead in New York's Central Park. Meili, who suffered a traumatic brain injury, spent nearly two weeks in a coma, and upon waking had no memory of what had happened to her. With scant evidence, New York police arrested five Black teenagers in connection with the attack: Korey Wise, Kevin Richardson, Raymond Santana Jr., Antron McCray, and Salaam, who was then fifteen, and notably, the second-oldest of the accused. The young men were convicted based on coerced, false confessions in 1990. The excruciating details of this march toward wrongful imprisonment are chronicled in Ava DuVernay's 2019 Netflix miniseries *When They See Us*, and also in the Ken and Sarah Burns documentary *The Central Park Five* (2012). The case of the Central Park Five garnered national attention that, as the wealth of contemporary stories about

Ibi Zoboi

it suggest, continues to captivate and enrage. It was an emblematic tale of racism in America, featuring the scapegoating of Black men for the harm of a White woman. People like former US president Donald Trump stoked racial resentment for publicity; in 1989 Trump used the case to lobby New York state to adopt the death penalty, presumably so that Salaam and his friends would receive capital punishment. Despite DNA evidence exonerating the five, as president, Trump refused to apologize or acknowledge the five's innocence.

It is important to acknowledge the gulf between the way the Central Park Five were presented to the world and the truth of their individual humanity. This is the theme at the heart of *Punching the Air*: how the justice system oversees the flattening of a human being into a criminal. Amal's story begins in court. The details of his case, and the crime he is eventually imprisoned for, are parsed out over the course of the book. The barebones facts: Amal was at the basketball court the night that a White teen named Jeremy Mathis was badly beaten. Mathis is in a coma, and unable to name his attacker. But all the reader knows in the first pages is that Amal is in trouble, and the outlook is bad. In the poem "Courtroom," he describes what it feels like to watch the jury "seeing every lie, reading every made-up word." In this version of his story, Amal says, "a black hoodie counts as a mask," or "a few fights counts as uncontrollable rage . . . like everything that I am, that I've ever been / counts as being // guilty."

In juvenile detention, Amal's entire identity is "guilty." Inside the walls of this cage, it does not matter that Amal is a gifted artist who was poised to enter a prestigious arts program, or that his mother says he was "born with an old soul." Once he is "processed," he is just another number. Amal evocatively describes juvenile detention as a "mix of kindergarten and high school." There are childish cartoons on the walls, and high-minded lectures about keeping in line. There are classes, but the teachers hardly treat Amal like a student receiving an education. To them, he is a criminal biding his time until he graduates to an adult prison. There is no assessment or support. When they meet, his social worker assumes he cannot read.

The detention facility adheres to a rigid schedule, but it is a chaotic environment. Amal must navigate the whims of the various guards, known as Tattoo, for the tattoo of a Black baby in a noose on his forearm. Another, a Black man named Officer Stanford, tries to teach Amal a lesson about showing off by letting him trip over his own shackles onto the concrete, smashing his face. Nearly every encounter is made to make Amal feel defensive, suspicious, and afraid. After he sees a fellow student dragged from his chair and beaten by a guard for cracking a joke, Amal refuses to attend class.

They threaten him with solitary confinement. When he expresses interest in a poetry workshop, his social worker dismissively tells him he has to earn the privilege of attending. Amal learns to flow with the abruptly shifting currents of his new environment, which does not rehabilitate, educate, or foster justice, but instead crushes the spirit.

There are moments of light. Amal makes a friend named Kadon, who calls him Young Basquiat after the famous artist, and he receives a letter from his school crush, Zenobia. He eventually finds his way into the poetry class, taught by a woman named Imani. She inspires Amal and her other students to think about their mistakes and regrets in regenerative terms. Her class is the only place where he is treated as a human being with thoughts and feelings worth being acknowledged. "Even as his body is imprisoned," Jennifer Harlan wrote in her *New York Times* review, "his mind ranges free." Illustrations by Omar T. Pasha recall drawings in notebook margins, evocative of Amal's attempts to infuse the ugliness of his surroundings with beauty. Through Imani's class, he also learns about prison abolition, a movement that seeks to abolish all forms of incarceration. The movement is a contemporary iteration of the movement to abolish slavery. Incarceration is inextricable from America's history of chattel slavery—the Thirteenth Amendment abolished enslavement "except as punishment for a crime"—and Amal thinks of it in those terms. Being led out of the courtroom after he is sentenced, he recalls the Door of No Return on Gorée Island off the coast of Senegal. For most enslaved people, this passageway was their last glimpse of Africa. Of being shackled, Amal thinks: "Maybe these are the / same chains that bind me // to my ancestors." He describes the bus trip from the county jail to the juvenile detention center as his Middle Passage, conveying the anxiety and fear that comes with being rendered immobile by chains. Processing, the point at which Amal is stripped of his belt, shoelaces, and personal possessions, is described in a poem titled "Auction Block."

Coauthor Ibi Zoboi met Salaam at Hunter College after his release in 1997. In the book's afterword, she writes that when they agreed to collaborate on a book their first decision was Amal's name, which means "hope" in Arabic. Zoboi is a young-adult author best known for her 2017 novel *American Street*, which was a finalist for the National Book Award for Young People's Literature in 2017. That book, about a young Haitian immigrant in Detroit, was praised for its craft; *Punching the Air* is an equal achievement in this regard. Zoboi and Salaam's verse is precise. Lines are like arrows hitting their mark, rendering the enormity of incarceration in powerfully personal terms. As Delfina V. Barbiero wrote for *USA Today*, "You could feel the fear, anguish and depression as if they were your own." In the afterword, the authors note

Yusef Salaam

Courtesy HarperCollins Publishers

similarities between Salaam and Amal. Both developed a love of poetry through hip-hop, and, at the time of their incarceration, were familiar with the writings of Black activists like Malcolm X. When Salaam was sentenced he read a poem he had written titled "I Stand Accused." Hopefully, *Punching the Air* will serve as a balm to teenagers ensnared in the system. It is also a powerful call to action. As a reviewer for *Kirkus* wrote, the book provides "a necessary calling-in to issues central to the national discourse in reimagining our relationship to police and prisons. Readers will ask: Where do we go from here?"

Author Biography
Ibi Zoboi is a young-adult writer best known for her 2017 novel *American Street*, which was a finalist for the National Book Award for Young People's Literature. She is also the author of *Pride* (2018) and *My Life as an Ice Cream Sandwich* (2019) as well as the editor of *Black Enough: Stories of Being Young and Black in America* (2019).

Yusef Salaam is a poet, prison reform activist, and motivational speaker. As one of the Exonerated Five, he served nearly seven years in juvenile detention for a crime he did not commit, the 1989 attack on Trisha Meili in New York's Central Park. Salaam was awarded a Lifetime Achievement Award by President Barack Obama in 2016.

Omar T. Pasha is an illustrator, senior user experience designer, creative and product design consultant, and a fine artist.

Molly Hagan

Review Sources
Barbiero, Delfina V. "'Punching the Air' Review: Yusef Salaam of Central Park Five Pens Moving Racial Justice Story." Review of *Punching the Air*, by Ibi Zoboi and Yusef Salaam. *USA Today*, 2 Sept. 2020, www.usatoday.com/story/entertainment/books/2020/09/02/review-punching-air-yusef-salaam-helps-young-readers-grasp-racial-justice/5685430002/. Accessed 15 Feb. 2021.
Harlan, Jennifer. "Teenagers in Turmoil." Review of *Punching the Air*, by Ibi Zoboi and Yusef Salaam. *The New York Times*, 10 Oct. 2020, www.nytimes.com/2020/10/10/books/review/young-adult-crossover-fiction.html. Accessed 15 Feb. 2021.
Njoku, Eboni. Review of *Punching the Air*, by Ibi Zoboi and Yusef Salaam. *The Horn Book*, 22 Sept. 2020, www.hbook.com/?detailStory=review-of-punching-the-air. Accessed 15 Feb. 2021.
Review of *Punching the Air*, by Ibi Zoboi and Yusef Salaam. *Kirkus*, 3 July 2020, www.kirkusreviews.com/book-reviews/ibi-zoboi/punching-the-air/. Accessed 15 Feb. 2021.
Review of *Punching the Air*, by Ibi Zoboi and Yusef Salaam. *Publishers Weekly*, 30 July 2020, www.publishersweekly.com/978-0-06-299648-0. Accessed 15 Feb. 2021.

Race against Time
A Reporter Reopens the Unsolved Murder Cases of the Civil Rights Era

Author: Jerry Mitchell (b. ca. 1959)
Publisher: Simon & Schuster (New York). 432 pp.
Type of work: Memoir, history, current affairs
Time: 1989–late 2010s
Locale: The American South

Race against Time is journalist Jerry Mitchell's account of investigating four unsolved, racially motivated murder cases in a New South grappling with the sins of the past. It is his first memoir.

Principal personages
JERRY MITCHELL, a White journalist who has helped close several major cold cases from the civil rights era
MEDGAR EVERS, a National Association for the Advancement of Colored People (NAACP) leader, a Black civil rights activist who was murdered by the Ku Klux Klan in June 1963
BYRON DE LA BECKWITH, a Klan member who murdered Evers
VERNON DAHMER SR., a Black voting rights activist who died after Klan members firebombed his home
DEAVOURS NIX, a Klan member who was complicit in Dahmer's murder
EDGAR RAY KILLEN, the Klan member who orchestrated the murders of civil rights workers James Chaney, Andrew Goodman, and Michael Schwerner

One of the most ubiquitous plot points of any superhero narrative is that of the origin story. Typically, a superhero's origin story is the formative event in their life—the moment when that person goes from being someone ordinary to someone extraordinary. For many of these characters, this transformation is the direct result of witnessing a tragedy. For journalist Jerry Mitchell, who can be described as a real-world hero, it was attending a screening of the 1988 film *Mississippi Burning* and learning that those responsible for the 1964 murders of the civil rights activists portrayed in the docudrama had gone largely unpunished. Shocked and outraged, he decided to use his investigative skills to uncover enough evidence to reopen the case. Over the next few decades, Mitchell became a seeker of justice in anti-Black hate crimes. *Race against Time* (2020) depicts his work in the *Mississippi Burning* case as well as other civil rights–era murders. The memoir is an honest look at the racist underbelly of

Jerry Mitchell

the American judicial system as well as an inspiring tale of how doing the right thing is always worthwhile—even if it seems forty years too late.

A large part of what makes a *Race against Time* such a great read is that it has the engrossing qualities of a true-crime book. Unlike other books from this genre, the memoir is written from the perspective of the journalist who was actually on the ground doing the work. Readers essentially get to ride along with Mitchell on his beat as he uncovers exactly what happened in each case and how the culprits were able to escape punishment. It is a firsthand investigator narrative that proves very exciting. His accounts of interviewing the cases' remaining witnesses and other relevant sources are fascinating, but the most enlightening of these encounters are the ones that Mitchell lands with some of the murderers. Although these individuals committed violent crimes some thirty to forty years earlier and are therefore elderly by the time that he interviews them, Mitchell successfully captures the way that they still pose a threat to society. On more than one occasion, he shares his family's fears that these men, or their family members, will discern that his true motivation is to put them in prison and will hurt Mitchell. The risk Mitchell takes interviewing them, however, proves extremely valuable as they provide an unfettered look into minds that have been warped with hatred. With insight into the twisted logic of White supremacists, it becomes possible to imagine how to identify, castigate, and even prevent such racists from developing in the future.

When reading *Race against Time*, it is easy to be awed at how Mitchell made a significant impact on multiple high-profile cases, for example, by investigating and writing an article on Edgar Ray Killen, one of the Klansmen responsible for the murders depicted in *Mississippi Burning*. Mitchell was also able to facilitate justice in the murders of NAACP leader Medgar Evers, Vernon Dahmer Sr., and the four girls who died in the Sixteenth Street Baptist Church bombing in Birmingham. These were cases that, despite attracting national attention, had gone cold over time. By bringing the right information to the public, however, Mitchell was able to force the state's hand in ordering retrials. His modus operandi of making the guilt of the White supremacists undeniable was especially evident in the case of Byron De La Beckwith. The man who murdered Evers, Beckwith was allowed to walk free in the 1960s thanks to two all-White, all-male hung juries. Through his investigation, Mitchell discovered that the segregationist agency Mississippi Sovereignty Commission had secretly helped with Beckwith's defense. After he published an article with evidence that illustrated this fact, Beckwith was retried and sentenced to life in prison by a mixed jury in 1994.

Although Mitchell's investigations required him to engage in hundreds of hours of tedious work, his storytelling never feels that way. Ultimately, Mitchell has a knack for ensuring that each step of the investigative process jumps off the page. Readers will be impressed at just how challenging it was for him to put all the pieces of each case together to find the truth. Throughout the decades that Mitchell worked on these cases, he had to develop sources to gain access to sealed state documents, track down long-lost witnesses, and get perpetrators to slip up and inadvertently confess to their crimes during interviews. He persisted despite the countless obstacles and threats of violence, determined that the defendants endure the maximum punishment for their crimes, even if it seemed as though they were too weak or old. When Klansman Deavours Nix was granted permission to remain out of prison without bond before his trial for the murder of Vernon Dahmer Sr. because of poor health, Mitchell kept pushing. During a subsequent phone interview with Mitchell, Nix let it slip that he was going to golf the following day. Mitchell sent a photographer to snap a picture of Nix in perfectly fine health on the green, which led to Nix's incarceration and undermined his credibility.

At the end of the day, *Race against Time* is extremely informative in the way that it showcases just how insidious racism is in America. The fact that so many of the murderers that Mitchell investigated went unpunished or received extremely light sentences because their victims were Black is disturbing. By putting it all on display, Mitchell illustrates just how much power and impact White supremacists have had on the nation's judicial system and how much it needs to be fixed. Beyond this, however, *Race against Time* demonstrates that it is never too late to seek justice. Mitchell pursued cases that were decades cold and subsequently aided in the conviction of many murderers who had been allowed to walk free the entire time. Indeed, a great deal of the book's satisfaction lies in knowing that Mitchell provided the families of some victims with some sort of peace and sent a message to other White supremacists that their violent actions would have consequences.

Unsurprisingly, reception of *Race against Time* has been overwhelmingly positive. *Newsweek* described it as one of the year's most-anticipated books, while National Public Radio (NPR) deemed it among the best historical books of the year. In a review for the *New York Times*, Randall Kennedy called Mitchell's memoir "brave, bracing and instructive." Similarly, David J. Garrow described it for the *Washington Post* as "valuable." Such critical commentary touches on how relevant and necessary *Race against Time* is in 2020—a year that saw widespread protests against racism and anti-Black violence. White readers have increasingly sought out books to help them better understand and dismantle racism. *Race against Time* is an excellent addition to this canon as it can help people better understand the apparatus that upholds systemic racism while inspiring them to act. Mitchell's success is a testament to how much of a difference people can make on these issues without being a lawyer, politician, or law enforcement officer. It therefore can be seen as a kind of how-to guide. The anonymous critic for *Publishers Weekly* stated in their starred review, "The fight for the truth continues with the recent rise of hate crimes in this country. This thrilling true crime account deserves a wide audience."

While excellently written, *Race against Time* is not flawless. As Kennedy noted, there are a few places where Mitchell could have provided greater substantiation for the claims he makes. Another of the memoir's shortcomings is that Mitchell examines his work through a mostly professional perspective. Although the four cases that he depicts in the memoir were both extremely dangerous and emotionally taxing, he decides to not explore how it impacted him as a person. Joseph Crespino commented on this fact in his *Wall Street Journal* review, in which he wrote, "One wishes at times that [Mitchell] had put more of himself into the story. We catch only glimpses, for example, of the toll that his single-minded devotion to this dangerous work took on his marriage and family." Indeed, diving into the other side of his tireless work would have provided readers with both a better idea of what investigative journalism can entail and possibly a more resonant story. Perhaps Mitchell did not want to share these kinds of personal details, however, because he feared he would deter others from following in his footsteps.

Nonetheless, *Race against Time* is an extremely compelling and necessary book. *Kirkus* fairly concluded with this sentiment when it declared Mitchell's memoir a "fine work of investigative journalism and an essential addition to the history of the civil rights movement." Anyone looking to educate themselves on anti-Black racism in America will that find reading *Race against Time* provides them with a better understanding of how it functions on a systemic level and how they can contribute to the fight against it.

Author Biography
Jerry Mitchell was an investigative journalist for the Jackson, Mississippi, *Clarion Ledger*. His work in uncovering the truth about several racially motivated murders in the South helped put several Klansmen in prison. He was a runner-up for the 2006 Pulitzer Prize in Beat Reporting and a 2009 recipient of the MacArthur genius grant.

Emily E. Turner

Review Sources
Crespino, Joseph. "A Reporter for Justice." Review of *Race against Time*, by Jerry Mitchell. *The Wall Street Journal*, 19 Feb. 2020, www.wsj.com/articles/race-against-time-review-a-reporter-for-justice-11582156889. Accessed 21 Dec. 2020.
Garrow, David J. "A Journalist's Quest to Bring Murderous Klansmen to Justice." Review of *Race against Time*, by Jerry Mitchell. *The Washington Post*, 14 Feb. 2020, www.washingtonpost.com/outlook/a-journalists-quest-to-bring-murderous-klansmen-to-justice/2020/02/13/b380d922-36d0-11ea-9541-9107303481a4_story.html. Accessed 21 Dec. 2020.
Kennedy, Randall. "The Journalist and the Murderers." Review of *Race against Time*, by Jerry Mitchell. *The New York Times*, 10 Mar. 2020, www.nytimes.com/2020/02/04/books/review/race-against-time-jerry-mitchell.html. Accessed 21 Dec. 2020.

Review of *Race against Time*, by Jerry Mitchell. *Kirkus*, 19 Nov. 2019, www.kirkus-reviews.com/book-reviews/jerry-mitchell/race-against-time-mitchell. Accessed 21 Dec. 2020.

Review of *Race against Time*, by Jerry Mitchell. *Publishers Weekly*, 9 Dec. 2019, www.publishersweekly.com/978-1-45164513-2. Accessed 21 Dec. 2020.

Weinberg, Steve. Review of *Race against Time*, by Jerry Mitchell. *Star Tribune*, 24 Jan. 2020, www.startribune.com/review-race-against-time-by-jerry-mitchell/567267362. Accessed 21 Dec. 2020.

Reaganland
America's Right Turn 1976–1980

Author: Rick Perlstein (b. 1969)
Publisher: Simon and Schuster (New York).
    Illustrated. 1120 pp.
Type of work: History
Time: Primarily 1976–80
Locale: The United States

In Reaganland, *the journalist and popular historian Rick Perlstein concludes his series of books about the development of modern American conservatism. Here he provides a highly detailed narrative of the years 1976 to 1980, which saw an increasingly effective grassroots movement among conservatives challenging a liberal establishment divided and demoralized by domestic problems and foreign embarrassments. The culmination of this conservative resurgence was Ronald Reagan's landslide victory in the presidential election of 1980.*

Principal personages
JIMMY CARTER, the president of the United States from 1977 to 1981
RONALD REAGAN, the former governor of California, the Republican presidential nominee in the 1980 election
RICHARD VIGUERIE, a New Right organizer and master of direct-mailing campaigns
PAUL WEYRICH, a New Right leader who cofounded the Heritage Foundation, a conservative think tank
PHYLLIS SCHLAFLY, a conservative activist who led the effort to defeat the Equal Rights Amendment
JERRY FALWELL, a minister and televangelist who became the president of the Moral Majority
RALPH NADER, a well-known consumer activist, best known for his criticism of the auto industry
PAUL VOLCKER, chair of the Federal Reserve under Carter
GERALD FORD, the president of the United States from 1974 to 1977, a contender for vice president in 1980
EDWARD "TED" KENNEDY, a US senator from Massachusetts and liberal rival of Carter
GEORGE H. W. BUSH, a candidate for the 1980 Republican presidential nomination, Reagan's eventual running mate

JOHN CONNALLY, a former governor of Texas and cabinet member, a contender for the 1980 Republican presidential nomination

JOHN ANDERSON, an influential, longtime Republican congressman, an independent presidential candidate in 1980

Rick Perlstein's *Before the Storm: Barry Goldwater and the Unmaking of the American Consensus* (2001) was a study of the rise of a militant conservatism in the Republican Party that rejected Dwight Eisenhower's accommodation of elements of the New Deal welfare state. Though Senator Barry Goldwater, the standard bearer of this uprising in the GOP, suffered a crushing defeat in the presidential election of 1964, his conservative movement did not die. One of Goldwater's most eloquent spokesmen, the actor Ronald Reagan, attracted such favorable attention in right-wing circles that he was encouraged to run for office. Because 1964 was a beginning, and not the end, for modern conservatism, Perlstein did not stop there. In the books *Nixonland: The Rise of a President and the Fracturing of America* (2008) and *The Invisible Bridge: The Fall of Nixon and the Rise of Reagan* (2014), he carried the story through the reaction against the Great Society and the unrest of the late 1960s and then the years dominated by Richard Nixon. *Reaganland* (2020) is the fourth and final installment in a two-decade-long project. The title of the book might at first seem odd to some readers, because it covers the years when Democrat Jimmy Carter dominated the headlines, first as an insurgent candidate and then as president of the United States. Perlstein's theme is that appearances proved deceptive. While Democrats controlled Congress, the presidency, and most statehouses in the late 1970s, a political revolution was brewing. As Perlstein's subtitle indicates, Americans were about to take a "right turn." Ronald Reagan, the affable and telegenic former governor of California, came to personify this resurgent conservatism, but Perlstein takes great pains to demonstrate that the New Right of the 1970s and 1980s was a populist movement that had many fathers and mothers, some intellectual and others not.

Rick Perlstein
Courtesy Simon & Schuster

Though Perlstein has devoted at least twenty years of his life to tracing the surprising resurrection of conservatism after the political debacle of 1964, he is no conservative himself. A contributing editor to the resolutely progressive *In These Times* magazine, he is a man of the Left, and he makes no effort to mask this in his historical writing. *Reaganland* is neither an academic tome nor a dispassionate and balanced historical account of the rise of the New Right. It is an extended indictment, both of the conservative activists who clawed their way to victory by means Perlstein often considers foul and of the complacent and confused liberals who inadvertently facilitated that triumph. A journalist by trade, Perlstein's book is written in a reportorial style. There is little formal analysis. Instead, *Reaganland* is an exhaustive chronicle of events. It is even organized by year, emulating the annalistic structure of the ancient Roman historians. Readers are immersed in a cascade of detail. Perlstein has masterfully exhumed the headlines of the period, occasionally taking time to discuss such cultural phenomena as the popularity of *Star Wars* or the fear engendered by the Son of Sam serial killings. Anyone who lived through the period will be reminded of people and episodes half-forgotten, such as the Libyan entanglements of Jimmy Carter's bumptious brother Billy, the travails of his budget director Bert Lance, the antigay crusade of singer and pitchwoman Anita Bryant, and the accident at the Three Mile Island nuclear plant. Others may be overwhelmed by the detail crammed into more than nine hundred pages of text or find such apparent digressions annoying. But there is method to Perlstein's textual logorrhea. His careful accretion of action and incident convincingly captures both the cumulative effects of New Right leaders gradually coordinating their efforts, and the ensuing tectonic movement of American public opinion. The result is a sweeping political panorama that persuasively demonstrates how the efforts of many unsung laborers prepared the ground for a charismatic leader like Ronald Reagan, who captured the attention of contemporaries and the imagination of posterity. Reading a book like *Reaganland* requires commitment. Anyone interested in getting beyond the headlines of a period will find that effort rewarded.

Despite Perlstein's own ideological bent, he does not shy from depicting the foibles of figures on the Left, particularly Jimmy Carter. Carter won the presidency as a populist candidate who capitalized on anti-Washington sentiment at a time when Watergate and other government scandals were fresh memories. While an effective campaign strategy, Carter's stance as an outsider won him few friends on Capitol Hill. Washington insiders loathed the inner circle of advisers that the president brought with him from Georgia. Carter himself often came across as an aloof technocrat. Despite his Democratic Party enjoying large majorities in Congress, Carter experienced great difficulty enacting legislation, and some of his highest priorities, such as bills promoting energy conservation, were stymied and watered down. Carter faced challenges that transcended his relations with congressional grandees. The 1970s were an economically anomalous time when the United States was simultaneously afflicted with low growth and inflation, known as *stagflation*. Unemployment rose at the same time as inflation eroded purchasing power and ate away at the value of savings. A solution to this economic conundrum eluded Carter as it had his predecessors.

While the Carter administration and Congress were unintentionally demonstrating some of the limits of government, grassroots activists began to harness antigovernment sentiment that had been galvanized by the Goldwater campaign and had continued to grow ever since. Doubts about big government merged with concerns about social issues, ranging from abortion to gay rights, that established power seemed to favor. This led to the birth of the New Right, an increasingly integrated grouping of organizations that more and more vocally, and more and more successfully, advocated for their causes. Playing a crucial operational role in building alliances and focusing energies on the Right were activists such as Richard Viguerie and Paul Weyrich.

Viguerie became a pioneer of modern mass-mailing campaigns, and his mailing list a formidable tool for conservative organizers. Weyrich helped launch some of the most influential institutions of the New Right, having a hand in the establishment of the Heritage Foundation and the Moral Majority. Disparate groups coalesced into the New Right. Phyllis Schlafly and the conservative women she mobilized successfully derailed the passage of the Equal Rights Amendment that had once seemed assured. Shared concerns about abortion and other perceived threats to the family broke down traditional antipathies between religious denominations and fueled the rise of the Christian Right. An eloquent televangelist named Jerry Falwell became the head of the Moral Majority, the most visible religiously based organization that ventured into the unfamiliar realm of politics.

Hard economic times intensified conservative criticisms of what they deemed government waste on ineffective social programs and growing bureaucracies. For instance, in 1978 a tax revolt in California led to the passage of Proposition 13, which amended the state constitution to limit property taxes. Big business had grown comfortable with big government since the New Deal. But, according to Perlstein, the threat posed by consumer activists like Ralph Nader bestirred what Perlstein calls "boardroom Jacobins" to ally with conservative free marketers in resisting government oversight.

Even foreign policy stirred popular passions. Many citizens opposed Carter's treaties promising to turn the Panama Canal over to Panama as a humiliating "giveaway." A conviction that Carter was weak on foreign policy united traditional conservatives with neoconservatives, former liberals who took a hawkish approach to the Cold War. The hostage crisis that followed the 1979 breach of the American embassy in Tehran, Iran, confirmed their dim view of Carter's approach to world affairs.

Ironically, as Perlstein describes, Carter and many congressional Democrats moved rightward over the course of his presidency. Carter encouraged the deregulation of transportation industries. As inflation intensified, he attempted to limit government spending, even at the expense of social programs. Paul Volcker, Carter's choice to head the Federal Reserve in 1979, so aggressively raised interest rates to combat inflation that he engineered a recession just in time for the election year of 1980. Alarmed by the Soviet Union's invasion of Afghanistan, Carter abandoned efforts at détente with Moscow and launched a major arms buildup toward the end of his presidency. None of this did him any good; he was associated with the national malaise that he accurately but unfortunately diagnosed in a badly received speech.

Reagan benefited from Carter's troubles and the ferment of the New Right. An able political team helped him pursue a winding path to the presidency. Through newspaper opinion pieces and speeches, Reagan helped publicize the New Right. Perlstein portrays Reagan as often confused in his facts and undisciplined in his messaging, but he grudgingly concedes that the former governor performed brilliantly when it counted, such as in his debates with Republican rivals and with Carter. Reagan led the conservative movement to a period of political dominance just sixteen years after it had appeared to be extinguished in 1964.

Although *Reaganland* is not a definitive account of the triumph of the New Right, it will be a starting point for many hoping to understand an important political turning point. Surprisingly from a publisher of Simon and Schuster's stature, the book is littered with typos, and Perlstein's stylistic affinity for sentence fragments will likely frustrate grammatical purists. These, however, are minor blemishes in a work that impressively concludes Perlstein's tetralogy on twentieth-century conservatism.

Author Biography

Rick Perlstein is a contributing editor and board member of *In These Times* magazine. He is the author of a quartet of books tracing the history of modern American conservatism, of which *Reaganland: America's Right Turn, 1976–1980* (2020) is the last installment.

Daniel P. Murphy

Review Sources

Bobelian, Michael. "How Reagan Captured the Presidency, and the Right Captured Politics." Review of *Reaganland: America's Right Turn, 1976–1980*, by Rick Perlstein. *The Washington Post*, 28 Aug. 2020, www.washingtonpost.com/outlook/how-reagan-captured-the-presidency-and-the-right-captured-politics/2020/08/27/7a515a9c-cab3-11ea-91f1-28aca4d833a0_story.html. Accessed 9 Feb. 2021.

Iber, Patrick. "All about the Base." Review of *Reaganland: America's Right Turn, 1976–1980*, by Rick Perlstein. *The New Republic*, vol. 251, no. 9, Sept. 2020, pp. 46–51. *EBSCOhost*, search.ebscohost.com/login.aspx?direct=true&db=aph&AN=144913306&site=eds-live. Accessed 10 Feb. 2021.

Mills, Curt. "Power to the People?" Review of *Reaganland: America's Right Turn, 1976–1980*, by Rick Perlstein, et al. *The American Conservative*, Nov.–Dec. 2020, pp. 41–42.

Smith, Jordan Michael. "When Conservatism Triumphed." Review of *Reaganland: America's Right Turn, 1976–1980*, by Rick Perlstein. *Progressive*, vol. 84, no. 4, Aug.–Sept. 2020, p. 65. *Academic Search Premier*, search.ebscohost.com/login.aspx?direct=true&db=aph&AN=144838962&site=eds-live. Accessed 10 Feb. 2021.

Thomas, Evan. "How Ronald Reagan Rose—and Rose." Review of *Reaganland: America's Right Turn, 1976–1980*, by Rick Perlstein. *The New York Times Book Review*, 27 Sept. 2020, p. 9.

Walker, Jesse. "Was the Reagan Revolution Really Reagan's?" Review of *Reaganland: America's Right Turn, 1976–1980*, by Rick Perlstein, and *Getting Right with Reagan*, by Marcus Witcher. *Reason*, vol. 52, no. 10, Mar. 2021, pp. 62–65. *EBSCOhost*, search.ebscohost.com/login.aspx?direct=true&db=aph&AN=148175497&site=eds-live. Accessed 10 Feb. 2021.

Real Life

Author: Brandon Taylor (b. ca. 1989)
Publisher: Riverhead (New York). 336 pp.
Type of work: Novel
Time: The present
Locale: An unnamed city in the midwestern United States

In Real Life, *graduate student Wallace grapples with interpersonal relationships, the trauma of his past, and racism over the course of a late-summer weekend.*

Principal characters
WALLACE, the protagonist, a graduate student in biochemistry at a university in the Midwest
MILLER, his friend and fellow graduate student
YNGVE, his friend and fellow graduate student
LUKAS, his friend and fellow graduate student
COLE, his friend and fellow graduate student
EMMA, his friend and fellow graduate student
SIMONE, his graduate adviser
DANA, an adversarial fellow student who works in Simone's laboratory
BRIGIT, a friendly fellow student who works in Simone's laboratory
VINCENT, Cole's boyfriend, a worker in the finance industry
ROMAN, a French student who is friends with Cole and Vincent

The debut novel by writer and editor Brandon Taylor, *Real Life* (2020) presents a compelling portrait of three days in the life of Wallace, a young man pursuing graduate studies in biochemistry at an unnamed university in the midwestern United States. Wallace is an outsider at the university for several reasons, including his low-income upbringing and the fact that he is gay, but several years into his graduate education, race remains the primary factor setting him apart. While he has succeeded in forming a group of friends made up of gay men and allies, both his social circle and the university's population as a whole are predominantly White. Indeed, Wallace is the first Black student to enroll in his program in more than thirty years.

The events of the novel begin on a Friday evening in late summer, shortly after Wallace has discovered that the nematode worms he had been carefully breeding all summer have been contaminated with mold. As his experiment is the sole one in the laboratory's incubator to be contaminated, he and others come to suspect that someone deliberately sabotaged his work, with suspicion falling primarily on one particularly

Brandon Taylor

adversarial and racist colleague. Not yet ready to begin to begin the taxing process of salvaging his experiment, Wallace decides to meet up with a group of White friends at the lake near campus, having not done so for some time. At one point during the meetup, he tells his friend Emma about another significant recent event in his life: the death of his father, an event that has filled Wallace not with grief but with more ambiguous emotions. Emma, however, does not understand or truly respect Wallace's feelings about that loss, instead expecting him to grieve in a more outward way. Against his wishes, she goes on to tell the rest of the group about his father, which in turn prompts a new round of overbearing sympathy.

In addition to setting the events of the novel in motion, the incidents at the beginning of *Real Life* are in some ways emblematic of recurring challenges that Wallace experiences within his social and academic environments. While his friends' responses to the news of his father's death may arise out of genuine sympathy and care for Wallace's well-being, Emma and the others disregard his true feelings and do not inquire about his relationship with his father, instead projecting their own expectations and experiences with grief onto him. Even after Wallace declares himself to be "okay" with the event, those around him continue to insist that he is not. Their interactions with him are thus highly self-centered ones, and Wallace often finds himself compelled to prioritize his friends' emotions and needs over his own, even though he does not receive the same consideration.

The apparent sabotage of his nematode-breeding experiment, likewise, is only the latest incident in a long history of mistreatment within his laboratory, which is headed by a researcher named Simone, Wallace's adviser. Simone and the more senior White students working in the laboratory have historically treated him poorly, questioning his capabilities and blaming him for the mistakes of others. The most egregious treatment has come from Dana, a younger White graduate student who has been antagonistic toward Wallace for some time and has demonstrated racist and homophobic attitudes while doing so, all the while accusing Wallace himself of being misogynistic for daring to correct her. Following a confrontation between the two students later in the novel, Dana lies about Wallace to Simone, further endangering his reputation in the laboratory as well as his future in the biochemistry program.

Alongside such issues, the early portion of *Real Life* begins to establish the complicated relationship between Wallace and his friend Miller, whose interactions and growing closeness take on great importance over the course of the novel. Although Wallace has more in common with Miller—including similar economic backgrounds—than with others in their social circle, their friendship has been strained since the previous academic year, when each made an insensitive joke about the other. After an unexpectedly intimate moment during the Friday evening at the lake that begins the novel, however, that starts to change. Miller accompanies Wallace to his home and, despite identifying himself as straight, reveals that he wants to kiss Wallace, who allows him to do so. Their relationship rapidly becomes sexual but retains a significant degree of ambiguity, a result of both Miller's stated orientation and Wallace's emotional detachment. Although they do not yet reveal their deepening relationship to their friends, the two continue to grow closer over the course of the weekend.

Wallace also becomes immersed in the relationship problems of other members of the group during that weekend. These include strains between his friend Cole, a fellow graduate student, and Cole's boyfriend, Vincent, a finance professional who resents the long hours and strict schedule represented by the graduate program. After Cole reveals Vincent's suspected infidelity to Wallace but proves reluctant to discuss the issue with Vincent, Wallace confronts Vincent at a dinner party attended by the group of friends, forcing the conflict into the open.

Wallace's willingness to speak up for Cole, though motivated in part by a petty "desire to see someone brought low," strikes an uncomfortable contrast with a moment earlier during the dinner party, when party guest Roman—whose unfriendliness Wallace has long attributed to racial bias—makes bigoted comments about Wallace's career prospects and background. Despite witnessing Roman's behavior, none of the guests speak out in Wallace's defense, and Wallace himself is obligated to moderate his own verbal and physical responses to avoid appearing aggressive. Though his friends' unwillingness to call out Roman's bigotry is disappointing, Wallace by no means finds it surprising. Much like their self-centeredness in regard to his feelings, that reluctance to speak out is a recurring facet of their interactions with Wallace and is one of a multitude of microaggressions that wear away at him day by day.

Yet despite the pain it causes him, his friends' failure to defend him is not the most egregious lapse in protection that he has faced, as Wallace hints throughout the novel and eventually reveals to Miller. In a brief chapter that trades the detached third-person narration of the bulk of the novel for an intense first-person recollection, he tells Miller about the traumatic events of his childhood, including his experience of being sexually abused by an adult friend of his parents and his parents' failure to protect him from that abuse. That information, as well as Wallace's recollections of the years following the abuse, not only provide additional insight into Wallace's personality and relationships but also recontextualize his response to his father's death, rendering his friends' insistence that he must display grief for his father even more blatantly inappropriate. Following that conversation, Miller opens up about his own history of trauma as well, revealing past events that complicate his adult life and his developing relationship with Wallace.

A compelling and thought-provoking novel, *Real Life* fits a great deal of action and character development into the brief period it depicts. It benefits heavily from Taylor's personal experience with the academic and extracurricular minutia of graduate-student life. In interviews and essays published following the release of the novel in 2020, Taylor revealed that multiple aspects of the novel were inspired by real-world experiences with racism and abuse, both his own and others', and such real-world inspiration may contribute to the novel's emotional verisimilitude. Wallace's balancing act between asserting himself and catering to the needs of those around him is palpably exhausting, and his friends' apparent unwillingness to respect his boundaries and emotions is both realistic and infuriating. Indeed, some readers might at times find themselves wondering why Wallace is friends with such people at all. At other times, however, they have legitimate moments of camaraderie that appear to make maintaining the friendships worthwhile. Wallace's relationship with Miller is particularly complicated and fascinating, wrapped up as it is in their troublesome history, the experiences they have in common, and the violence that pervades their pasts and has shaped their shared present. Though much remains ambiguous at the close of the novel, much has also changed, and the beginning of a new academic year brings with it new possibilities.

Real Life received largely positive reviews from critics, with *Guardian* reviewer Anthony Cummins describing the novel as a whole as "brilliant." Writing for the *Washington Post*, Charles Arrowsmith described the work as a strong example of campus novel, one that both fits within that literary subgenre and expands upon it. Many reviewers focused heavily on the portions of *Real Life* dealing with trauma, and the anonymous critic for *Kirkus* wrote that the novel "deserves accolades for its insights into the ways trauma hollows out a person's soul." In a review for *Vox*, Constance Grady called particular attention to the section of the novel in which Wallace tells Miller about the events of his past, noting that the change in perspective is accompanied by stylistic changes that render the prose in that section especially "rich and lush." Many critics also highlighted Wallace's relationship with Miller, the ambiguity of which *Time* reviewer Michael Arceneaux described as "devastatingly effective."

While reviews were primarily positive, some reviewers did critique elements of the work that they considered detrimental to the novel's overall effectiveness. Writing for the *New Yorker*, Eren Orbey praised Taylor's depiction of Wallace's isolation but wrote that at the same time, "Wallace's remove . . . can blunt the rendition of his surroundings." Nevertheless, Orbey appreciated the novel as a whole and noted that Taylor "endows his narrative with the precision of science and the intimacy of memoir." In addition to earning acclaim from critics, *Real Life* was included on the shortlist for the 2020 Booker Prize for Fiction, longlisted for the Center for Fiction First Novel Prize, and designated a New York Times Book Review Editors' Choice.

Author Biography
A former doctoral student in biochemistry, Brandon Taylor is a senior editor for the publication *Recommended Reading* and a staff writer for the website *Literary Hub*. *Real Life* is his first published novel.

Joy Crelin

Review Sources

Arceneaux, Michael. "Black Gay Writers Deserve to Tell Our Stories. Brandon Taylor's *Real Life* Achieves That and More." Review of *Real Life*, by Brandon Taylor. *Time*, 18 Feb. 2020, time.com/5786026/brandon-taylor-real-life-review/. Accessed 25 Jan. 2021.

Arrowsmith, Charles. "With 'Real Life,' Brandon Taylor Twists the Traditional Campus Novel." Review of *Real Life*, by Brandon Taylor. *The Washington Post*, 24 Feb. 2020, www.washingtonpost.com/entertainment/books/with-real-life-brandon-taylor-twists-the-traditional-campus-novel/2020/02/24/8d18ae52-5720-11ea-9b35-def5a027d470_story.html. Accessed 25 Jan. 2021.

Cummins, Anthony. "*Real Life* by Brandon Taylor Review—A Brilliant Debut." Review of *Real Life*, by Brandon Taylor. *The Guardian*, 17 Aug. 2020, www.theguardian.com/books/2020/aug/17/real-life-by-brandon-taylor-review-a-brilliant-debut. Accessed 25 Jan. 2021.

Grady, Constance. "In *Real Life*, a Queer Black Scientist Tries to Survive Grad School." Review of *Real Life*, by Brandon Taylor. *Vox*, 24 Feb. 2020, www.vox.com/culture/2020/2/24/21147513/real-life-review-brandon-taylor. Accessed 25 Jan. 2021.

Orbey, Eren. "'Real Life' Is a New Kind of Campus Novel." Review of *Real Life*, by Brandon Taylor. *New Yorker*, 19 Feb. 2020, www.newyorker.com/books/page-turner/real-life-is-a-new-kind-of-campus-novel. Accessed 25 Jan. 2021.

Review of *Real Life*, by Brandon Taylor. *Kirkus*, 9 Dec. 2019, www.kirkusreviews.com/book-reviews/brandon-taylor/real-life-taylor/. Accessed 25 Jan. 2021.

Recollections of My Nonexistence

Author: Rebecca Solnit (b. 1961)
Publisher: Viking (New York). 256 pp.
Type of work: Memoir
Time: 1980s–2020
Locale: San Francisco

Recollections of My Nonexistence focuses on two intertwined themes: a personal retelling of Rebecca Solnit's professional arc and the internalized reality of gender-based violence and discrimination against women. Solnit weaves a powerful narrative of her own growth as a public intellectual and leading feminist thinker, while laying bare the personal toll of the constant weight of aggression and discrimination.

Principal personages
REBECCA SOLNIT, author and principal subject
TINA, her close friend and correspondent
MARINA, her friend and sometimes roommate
CATHERINE HARRIS, her longtime friend, and an assistant to artist Meridel Rubenstein
DAVID CANNON DASHIELL, her friend, an artist, who died from AIDS
JOHN COPLANS, an author, artist, and cofounder of *Artforum*, who engaged in legal action against Solnit
VIRGINIA SANCHEZ, organizer, activist, environmentalist for the Western Shoshone

Rebecca Solnit, an activist and writer who came to be considered one of the foremost political and cultural commentators in the United States in the early twenty-first century, has been compared to essayists such as Susan Sontag and Joan Didion. Their shared ability to combine personal experience with cultural history has resonated with readers for decades. Solnit has written on a wide range of topics, from a rumination on the habit of walking to essays about the Iraq War and climate change. In her memoir *Recollections of My Nonexistence* (2020) she further delves into her personal history. The book follows Solnit from the age of nineteen, when she rents her first apartment, through the present.

Solnit's childhood with an abusive father haunts the narrative but is only brusquely mentioned. Having escaped from a dangerous and unhappy childhood home in the suburbs and lived, for a period of time, in a rented room, Solnit describes her first apartment in San Francisco as a haven and a space within which she could begin to grow into her adult and professional selves. But she is not actually qualified for the rental and her application is only accepted when she gets her mother to apply in her place. Though she lives in the apartment for more than two decades, most of those years her mother is the official tenant, leaving Solnit to feel like a ghost.

The narrative serves as a backdrop against which Solnit can begin to weave an exploration of the "nonexistence" that gives the book its title and presents the feminist core of the memoir. Solnit describes femininity as a cultural and systematic "perpetual disappearing act," in which for women "your existence is considered an aggression and your nonexistence a form of gracious compliance," ensuring that men continue to dominate in society. As in some of her previous writings, Solnit presents a serious exploration of gender-based violence, discrimination, and oppression across the pages of this book. Significantly, though, the feminist intellectual framework is here always situated within the structure of a memoir. The nonexistence that Solnit explores is her own, a fact that ultimately allows her to conclude on a positive note of resilience.

Gender-based violence—or the constant lingering threat of it—hangs over the first half of the book, which engages with Solnit's teenage and young adult years, alongside discussion at a larger level about the pervasive nature of violence against women. Solnit writes: "To be a young woman is to face your own annihilation in innumerable ways or to flee it or the knowledge of it." In introducing this concept, she cites Edgar Allen Poe's Romantic characterization of the death of a beautiful woman, but this allusion is just one of many cultural and philosophical instances she cites in which female death and violence against women are fetishized. Whether in newspaper headlines, on television, or in music, Solnit observes women are presented with a constant barrage of reminders of the potential of violence against them. She historicizes this information as well, discussing the 1980s as an environment of such pervasive violence against women that it could feel like a war zone and young women might experience posttraumatic stress disorder as a result of these encounters. Although she avoids many detailed narratives about her own experiences with abuse and harassment, she includes a vivid and terrifying account of a walk at night toward her childhood home, in which a man followed her for blocks with clear bad intent. All of these instances contribute to the "erasure" of women and, importantly, Solnit also identifies that they contribute to the silencing of women. Avoiding eye contact, staying quiet, and being physically unobtrusive are all techniques she discusses as common mechanisms by which young women seek to navigate the world without drawing attention. Further, she identifies that for her young self, silence was the default mode because "it didn't occur to me that I had the authority to assert myself."

For Solnit, the process of finding a voice, then, was linked both to these gendered experiences and to her aspirations of becoming a professional writer. The second half of the book transitions to a selective overview of her growing career as a researcher and writer. The transition feels natural. Even though the early chapters describe a period of Solnit's life before writing became a full-time career, she lays the foundations for her first books clearly in the concerns of those years. For example, she discusses her frequent long walks around San Francisco, despite the danger that they might have placed her in as a young woman, and eventually this passion develops into one of her highly successful publications, *Wanderlust: A History of Walking* (2000). Her graduate school opportunity to work in a museum unfolded into a book on Bay area beat artists and was the origin point of many important contacts and experiences discussed throughout the book.

Yet the realities of gender discrimination do not disappear from the second half of the book. Across these chapters, Solnit transitions to a consideration of the ways that professional women are silenced and sidelined. She identifies and calls out an array of different moments in her career when men sought to undercut her possibility for success—a lawsuit that could have found all copies of her first book destroyed before circulation and a publicist who failed to set up any of the stops on her book tour are two stand-out examples. Although some critics have complained that Solnit does not expose herself to deeply personal accounts in her memoir, those specific mentions from her early career are deeply telling. They pertain to her professional career, but they are clearly also defining moments of her "self." Indeed, Solnit makes clear that any one of these acts of silencing could easily have ended her writing career. As a woman who began her career in the 1980s, Solnit notes that she did not have a vocabulary to call out these types of experiences; rather they were just the pervasive, oppressive grind of gender bias against women with a professional voice.

Many readers will turn to this book because of Solnit's feminist writings, seeking greater insight into this aspect of her career. These are introduced only in the final section of the book ("Audibility, Credibility, Consequence"), and Solnit notes that "Everything else I ever wrote was on a subject I chose and approached intentionally, but feminism chose me or was something I couldn't stay away from." Indeed, the structure of the memoir is shaped to make clear why this was the case. The book opens with a photograph of Solnit's writing desk, which turns out to play an important role in her feminism. The desk, as we learn, was gifted to her (while she was still living in her first apartment) by an unnamed friend who had been brutally stabbed by an ex-boyfriend and nearly died. For Solnit, the desk became the constant physical support of her writing, but also a metaphorical foundation of her career. She reflects: "I wonder if everything I have ever written is a counterweight to that attempt to reduce a young woman to nothing." Solnit's transition into a feminist icon was the result of her essay "Men Explain Things to Me" (2008), described here (as elsewhere) as a spontaneously written essay in response to conversations with her friends. Online commentary on the essay resulted in the development of the term "mansplaining," an illustration of the work's pervasive influence and success. Here, Solnit reflects that the essay has been one of her most gratifying experiences as a writer because she has received so much feedback and direct accounts of its influence on women's lives; the piece has helped women "locate their power and their value and reject their subjugation."

The various strains of the memoir resolve themselves in the final chapters. Critics have noted that Solnit chafes against the memoir genre, especially with her reticence to expose personal accounts too deeply. Writing for the *Washington Post*, reviewer Lauren Sarazen lamented Solnit's "sense of reserve that feels deliberate even as it is unsatisfying." However, some critics also suggested that the book seems to open up the genre of memoir in some new directions. In particular, Solnit's avoidance of personal anecdote has wisely been noted as central to the feminism behind the book. She does not shy away from personal accounts when they can open up the reader's mind to the deeper issues at hand, but she does not introduce them when such accounts would distract the reader fundamentally into the individual, rather than the systemic, narrative. In *Recollections of My Nonexistence*, the female author's experience of erasure is central, and the strategic sidelining of deeply personal anecdotes helps highlight the experience of women and the ongoing necessary work of feminism.

Solnit's closing chapter, "Afterword: Lifelines," is her parting gift to readers, particularly young females, offering some retrospective reflection on her journey and brief thoughts on healing and resilience. While her memoir offers the account of her objective success in obtaining a career as a writer, she concludes the book with the reminder, "People aren't really meant to be anything, because we're not made; we're born, with some innate tendencies, and thereafter molded, thwarted, scalded, encouraged by events and encounters." Rather than suggesting she has fulfilled a destiny, Solnit asks her readers to understand her professional journey as a series of causes and effects, questions and answers. The scars experienced along the way have contributed to that journey and, if erased, would not result in the same voice. Lest readers misunderstand this point as a perverse celebration of gender violence, it is necessary to clarify that Solnit's point here is maintaining strength and finding one's voice in the face of adversity. She concludes, one survivor to another: "Damage begets a different destiny than one you might have had otherwise, but it does not preclude having a life or making things that matter. Sometimes it's not despite but because of something terrible that you . . . set to the work you're meant to do."

Author Biography
Rebecca Solnit is a renowned essayist and cultural critic. She gained wide popular renown for her essay "Men Explain Things to Me" (2008). She has published more than twenty books and is the recipient of numerous literary awards, including a Guggenheim Fellowship, National Book Critics Circle Award, and the Lannan Literary Award.

Julia A. Sienkewicz, PhD

Review Sources
Berry, Lorraine. "Review: Rebecca Solnit's Anti-Confessional Memoir." Review of *Recollections of My Nonexistence*, by Rebecca Solnit. *The Los Angeles Times*, 17 Mar. 2020, www.latimes.com/entertainment-arts/books/story/2020-03-17/review-rebecca-solnit-recollections-review. Accessed 18 Oct. 2020.

Merritt, Stephanie. "Recollections of My Non-Existence by Rebecca Solnit Review—Figuring Out What Stories to Tell." Review of *Recollections of My Nonexistence*, by Rebecca Solnit. *The Guardian*, 9 Mar. 2020, www.theguardian.com/books/2020/mar/09/recollections-of-my-non-existence-rebecca-solnit-review. Accessed 18 Oct. 2020.

Odell, Jenny. "How Rebecca Solnit Found Her Voice." Review of *Recollections of My Nonexistence,* by Rebecca Solnit. *The New York Times*, 6 Mar. 2020, www.nytimes.com/2020/03/06/books/review/recollections-of-my-nonexistence-rebecca-solnit.html. Accessed 18 Oct. 2020.

Sarazen, Lauren. "Rebecca Solnit, Who Inspired the Term 'Mansplaining,' Explains Herself (Sort of)." Review of *Recollections of My Nonexistence,* by Rebecca Solnit. *The Washington Post*, 7 May 2020, www.washingtonpost.com/entertainment/books/rebecca-solnit-who-inspired-the-term-mansplaining-explains-herself-sort-of/2020/05/05/9ff78032-888c-11ea-9dfd-990f9dcc71fc_story.html. Accessed 18 Oct. 2020.

Scholes, Lucy. "Recollections of My Non-Existence by Rebecca Solnit, Review: Life Before 'Mansplaining.'" Review of *Recollections of My Nonexistence,* by Rebecca Solnit. *The Telegraph*, 7 Mar. 2020, www.telegraph.co.uk/books/what-to-read/recollections-non-existence-rebecca-solnit-review-life-mansplaining/. Accessed 18 Oct. 2020.

Waldman, Katy. "Rebecca Solnit's Memoir is Much More Than a Feminist Manifesto." *The New Yorker*, 11 Mar. 2020, www.newyorker.com/books/page-turner/rebecca-solnits-memoir-is-much-more-than-a-feminist-manifesto. Accessed 18 Oct. 2020.

Ring Shout

Author: P. Djèlí Clark (pseudonym of Dexter Gabriel)
Publisher: Tor.com (New York). 192 pp.
Type of work: Novella
Time: 1922
Locale: Georgia

This novella, set in an alternate 1920s Georgia, imagines a world in which the White supremacist terrorist group the Ku Klux Klan is backed by otherworldly monsters. A team of monster hunters assembles to fight them, leading to a rollicking tale of resistance that combines fantasy, adventure, horror, African and African American folklore, and incisive social commentary.

Principal characters

MARYSE BOUDREAUX, the narrator, a young Black woman who wields a magical sword
SADIE, one of her sidekicks, a sharpshooter
CORDELIA LAWRENCE, a.k.a. *Chef*, her other sidekick, a World War I veteran
NANA JEAN, a Gullah woman who can commune with spirits
BUTCHER CLYDE, a monster who feeds on hatred

P. Djèlí Clark's swashbuckling novella *Ring Shout* (2020) opens in Macon, Georgia, in 1922, four years removed from World War I and seven years removed from the release of D. W. Griffith's film *The Birth of a Nation* (1915), a notorious paean to White supremacy. Yet while the historical references and especially the atmosphere of racial tension throughout the book are highly realistic, paranormal elements also quickly become apparent. This is a world where magic and alternate dimensions are very much real—and responsible for both threats to humanity and means of defense. By skillfully interweaving Lovecraftian horror, Black folk traditions, and raw historical truths, Clark builds a gripping narrative that twists and rises above genre tropes.

The novella's opening scene finds its protagonist and narrator, Maryse Boudreaux, crouched atop an old cotton warehouse, watching members of the Ku Klux Klan (KKK) parade through Macon on the Fourth of July. With her are two friends and trusted sidekicks: Sadie, an expert shooter who fiddles with her Winchester rifle, and Chef, a veteran who fought with all-Black US Army regiment known as the Black Rattlers. The women are lying in wait. They have placed their bait, the carcass of a stray dog, in an alley below, and it soon attracts three white-robed figures who feed gruesomely on the raw meat. What Maryse and her friends call Ku Kluxes—as opposed to

P. Djèlí Clark

ordinary KKK members, known as Klans—are interdimensional beings, capable of possessing and blending in with normal humans but with monstrous natural forms. Only some people, including Maryse, Sadie, and Chef, can see these demonic creatures for what they are.

The trio are dedicated to hunting down these monsters, who thrive off the hatred espoused by the KKK. But Ku Kluxes cannot be killed easily. This is where Maryse comes to the forefront, as she wields a magical sword fueled by the rage and grief of millions of enslaved people and their descendants. Their stories, projected behind her eyelids when her sword appears from the ether, are entwined with her own complex background, the full details of which are revealed over the course of the book. Suffice it to say that Maryse has good reason to relish killing Ku Kluxes, a vocation that she feels is both a responsibility to her ancestors and a penance.

Clark's knack for blending history and fantasy is exemplified by the important role of *The Birth of a Nation* in the plot. As the book describes, newspapers of the day wrote that White audiences experienced a visceral reaction to the melodrama, acting "like a people possessed." One viewer pulled out his pistol and began shooting at the screen to "rescue" the White woman in the film from the arms of a Black character. Yet while the film really did spur a surge in KKK membership, Clark imagines its effect even more literally: in the world of *Ring Shout*, Griffith's film casts an actual spell that turns human Klans into Ku Kluxes. The climax of the book involves a plot to screen the film on the side of Georgia's Stone Mountain, generating demonic monsters en masse. (Stone Mountain is no arbitrary setting; the second iteration of the KKK is said to have been "born" there. It became the site of an annual cross-burning and a designated Confederate memorial that stands to this day.)

It is up to Maryse and her fellow monster hunters, guided by a Gullah woman named Nana Jean, to foil Ku Kluxes and Klans alike. They are used to the task, if not the scale of this mission. Nana Jean's successful bootlegging business—she and her acolytes peddle an elixir called Mama's Water, part liquor and part root magic—funds their ongoing efforts to defeat evil. In this world, spasms of White supremacist terrorism, as in East St. Louis, Missouri, in 1917 and Tulsa, Oklahoma, in 1919 were actually battles in a larger spiritual war, fought among humans but also entities from other realms.

The story's central villain, Butcher Clyde, is one such entity. He looks human, but on command, his skin sprouts tiny holes that become yawning mouths with jagged teeth. (Here and elsewhere, Clark's vivid, gruesome descriptions push the novella clearly into horror territory.) After he appears to Maryse in a dream, she seeks advice from the Aunties, a trio of women who appear in a kind of liminal space between reality and imagination. The Aunties are modeled after the Fates of ancient Greek mythology. They are warm to Maryse, like real aunties, but they cannot entirely be trusted. Maryse, who loves the Br'er Rabbit tales based on African folklore, compares them to the trickster Br'er Fox. The Aunties confirm what Maryse already can sense; a "storm" is coming, and Butcher Clyde is its catalyst. They also reveal that Butcher Clyde will try to enlist Maryse, and his offer proves more tempting than might be expected.

One of the great strengths of *Ring Shout* is how it successfully balances between two major strains of fantasy and horror: the gleeful kitsch of classic pulp fiction and a more somber, socially conscious approach tackling deep themes. On one level, the book is an enjoyable adventure romp with a good amount of tongue-in-cheek awareness and homages to genre tropes. Yet, on another, it is an incisive work of social commentary, with insight into racial issues in both the 1920s and the present. Importantly, too, Clark's deeper messages are not simplistic or didactic. The complex characterizations, particularly of Maryse, are crucial in this regard. As Danny Lore wrote in a review for NPR, "Clark acknowledges hate on all sides of this battle for survival . . . we learn about different kinds of hate, with different roots." Lore and other critics also highlighted how Clark carefully avoids the insinuation that racism and violence are solely a product of supernatural forces; the inclusion of human Klans alongside the monster Ku Kluxes shows that ordinary people are certainly capable of evil on their own.

Another strength of the book is the inclusion of numerous captivating historical details, some of which may be unfamiliar to many readers. These insightful tidbits illuminate a lengthy history of racism and resistance. For instance, there is mention of Amanirenas, the eyepatch-wearing warrior queen of Meroe in East Africa who fought off the Roman army. More integral to the narrative is the titular ring shout, a communal ritual that was first performed by enslaved Africans. Its history has been preserved in part by the work of writers such as Zora Neale Hurston, who recorded the stories of formerly enslaved people for the Works Progress Administration (WPA) in the 1930s. Clark prefaces each chapter with a quote from these oral histories, in which people describe various shouts and what they mean. One in particular—a shout called "In This Field We Must Die?"—offers a glimpse of the rage and sorrow bound up in Maryse's sword. The shout has many meanings, a woman named Ms. Henrietta Davis explains. "The field where the slaves was forced to toil away they whole lives. Or it's this world everybody got to leave one day. What else there was to do in that drudgery, working from can't see morning to can't see night, but to get to thinking on life, death, and God's purpose? All them grand thinkers lost to the whip. Gone and took they secrets with 'em to the grave."

While the wealth of historical information in *Ring Shout* is always interesting, it does at times risk distracting from the central plot. This is especially true as the novella is quite brief, despite its many layers, which will disappoint readers who get engrossed in the worldbuilding. The story can even occasionally seem muddled, as there is simply not enough space to digest all the information Clark presents. In their review, Lore noted another potential stumbling block for some readers: "*Ring Shout* doesn't cater to a non-Black audience, let alone a white one," with African American Vernacular English and specific cultural references. Yet, like the historical asides, this can be seen as a strength as well, as it allows for a richness that would not be possible with so-called Standard American English or with more explanation.

Overall, critical reception of *Ring Shout* was highly positive. Both *Kirkus* and *Publishers Weekly* awarded the novella starred reviews. The critic for *Kirkus* concluded, "Thrills, chills, macabre humor, and engaging heroines to root for: What more could a reader want?" Therein lies *Ring Shout*'s unique appeal. The early twentieth century, particularly in the years following World War I, was an era of unspeakable anti-Black violence: terrorism and lynching, and oppression codified in the form of Jim Crow laws. Amid the horror, it is all too easy to forget the ways in which people resisted, found joy, and fought back. Clark chronicles an age-old war against hatred and oppression that parallels the one that continues in our world, reminding us that struggle for liberation is long but filled with heroes.

Author Biography

P. Djèlí Clark—the pseudonym of historian Dexter Gabriel—is an award-winning writer of speculative fiction. His published works include numerous short stories, such as the Nebula Award–winning "The Secret Lives of the Nine Negro Teeth of George Washington"(2018), and the novellas *The Black God's Drums* (2018) and *The Haunting of Tram Car 015* (2019).

Molly Hagan

Review Sources

Brown, Alex. "An Entirely New Take on Cosmic Horror: *Ring Shout* by P. Djèlí Clark." Review of *Ring Shout,* by P. Djèlí Clark. *Tor.com*, 13 Oct. 2020, www.tor.com/2020/10/13/an-entirely-new-take-on-cosmic-horror-ring-shout-by-p-djeli-clark/. Accessed 27 Jan. 2021.

Lore, Danny. "History and Hatred Drive the Horror in 'Ring Shout.'" Review of *Ring Shout,* by P. Djèlí Clark. *NPR*, 21 Oct. 2020, www.npr.org/2020/10/21/924604118/history-and-hatred-drive-the-horror-in-ring-shout. Accessed 27 Jan. 2021.

Review of *Ring Shout,* by P. Djèlí Clark. *Kirkus*, 29 Jul. 2020, www.kirkusreviews.com/book-reviews/p-djeli-clark/ring-shout/. Accessed 27 Jan. 2021.

Review of *Ring Shout,* by P. Djèlí Clark. *Publishers Weekly*, 17 Aug. 2020, www.publishersweekly.com/978-1-25076-702-8. Accessed 27 Jan. 2021.

Wolfe, Gary K. Review of *Ring Shout,* by P. Djèlí Clark. *Locus*, 29 Nov. 2020, locusmag.com/2020/11/gary-k-wolfe-reviews-ring-shout-by-p-djeli-clark/. Accessed 27 Jan. 2021.

The Rise and Fall of Charles Lindbergh

Author: Candace Fleming (b. 1962)
Publisher: Schwartz & Wade (New York). 384 pp.
Type of work: Biography
Time: Largely the twentieth century
Locales: The United States and Western Europe

In this biography for young adults, Candace Fleming focuses on Charles Lindbergh, a flight hero who was also seen as a Nazi sympathizer. She highlights the enigmatic qualities of a person admired and respected by many but who was also deeply flawed.

Principal personages
CHARLES AUGUSTUS LINDBERGH, an aviation hero of the twentieth century who was also deemed to be a Nazi sympathizer
ANNE MORROW LINDBERGH, his wife, a noted writer
EVANGELINE LAND LINDBERGH, his mother, a teacher
CHARLES AUGUST LINDBERGH, his father, a lawyer and US congressman representing Minnesota
DR. ALEXIS CARREL, a scientific collaborator of his, a French surgeon

The two most widely known facts about Charles Lindbergh are that he was the first person to fly alone on a nonstop transatlantic flight from New York to Paris in 1927 and that his toddler son, Charles Augustus Lindbergh Jr., was kidnapped and murdered. One event was heroic and the other tragic. While author Candace Fleming examines those two impactful events with detailed attention in *The Rise and Fall of Charles Lindbergh* (2020), she also delves much deeper into Lindbergh's life, providing a full account of a complicated and flawed man. To know Lindbergh as an aviation hero and the bereft father of a missing and murdered child is to know a small part of who he was—a man who did not seem to value friendship, who compartmentalized his life and kept many of those compartments a secret from those closest to him, and who fervently believed and supported the theory of eugenics. (Eugenics was the practice of creating a superior race of humans by encouraging people with certain desired genetic traits to procreate while often seeking to keep others perceived as less fit from reproducing, through methods such as sterilization.) Fleming deftly organizes the many puzzle pieces of Lindbergh's life in a comprehensive and honest biography that juxtaposes his heroism with his flaws, portraying Lindbergh in all his enigmatic complexity. Fleming achieves this multifaceted and nuanced portrayal in several significant

Candace Fleming

ways: she connects Lindbergh's personal philosophy to a pivotal family event, quotes extensively from primary sources, including his journals, and finds common threads among the disparate story lines of his life.

As with most biographies, Fleming covers Lindbergh's life in its entirety, from his birth as the only child from his father's second marriage to his last years in Hawaii. In chapter 1, however, Fleming explains a defining event from the Lindbergh family's past. She begins the biography with "On a sticky summer day in 1861, Charles Lindbergh's grandfather, August, accidentally cut off his left arm." Fleming, in her concise and gripping writing style, titles the first section of the chapter "The Origin Story" and keeps readers engrossed as she continues to relay the details of August Lindbergh's sawmill accident, in which he lost not only an arm but also part of his back, exposing his heart and a portion of his lungs. Though no one believed August would survive, he exhibited such strength and determination to live that it became a family legend that became a philosophy of life his grandson would follow and embody. As Fleming notes, Lindbergh came to believe that even the most serious and difficult of obstacles could be overcome with effort and determination. He also interpreted from his grandfather's survival the importance of genetics—that it was his grandfather's superior genetic makeup that allowed him to endure and recover. Lindbergh lived his life believing he was strong, capable, and descended of such "exceptional stock" that it was his duty to ensure it continued. Thus, Fleming's introduction of "the origin story" is powerfully critical to understanding Lindbergh since he took that philosophy into every project he began and decision he made, from his meticulous and unconventional preparation for his solo transatlantic flight in the *Spirit of St. Louis*; to his invention of a perfusion pump and scientific experiments with Dr. Alexis Carrel, the concepts of which would eventually contribute to more successful heart surgeries; to his choice of a wife in Anne Morrow; and to his later involvement with the eugenics movement and his apparent sympathy with the Nazis during World War II (1939–45). Lindbergh was someone who believed in himself and his abilities, and because Fleming so effectively explains the origin of his thinking, readers can come away from the book understanding him more deeply than they would otherwise.

Another important and intriguing decision Fleming made to help readers comprehend Lindbergh, especially his views on eugenics and his sympathy for the Nazi regime and its leader, Adolf Hitler, was to include Lindbergh's own words rather than solely summarize or editorialize to explain his thinking. To allow readers to develop their own interpretation of Lindbergh's ideas and reasoning, Fleming frequently supplements the text with relevant quotes from his journals. Both Lindbergh and his wife,

Anne, kept detailed diaries throughout their lives. Lindbergh wrote his entries in the present tense, as if he were recounting events as they were happening rather than reflecting on the past. Fleming sometimes italicizes passages from his writings, including an autobiographical book published in the 1950s, to portray them as his internal thinking. In the following excerpt, for example, Lindbergh reflects on Hitler while in Germany for the 1936 Olympics at the behest of Major Truman Smith, an attaché to the American embassy in Berlin. Smith hoped Lindbergh would visit German aircraft factories and report back on Germany's technical progress and capabilities. Yet despite his directive, Lindbergh was impressed with what he saw of Hitler and the German regime:

> Charles was rethinking his opinion of dictatorships, too. Despite how newspapers in England and America depicted Hitler, he knew what he saw. "The organized vitality of Germany was what impressed me," he wrote. "The unceasing activity of the people, and the convinced dictatorial direction to create the new factories, airfields, and research laboratories." To him, the country concretized his values: "science and technology harnessed for the preservation of a superior race."

Lindbergh left his visit to Germany with an admiration for the productivity and ingenuity of the German people and their leader, reinforcing his views on eugenics. Because Fleming quotes Lindbergh directly, she encourages readers to develop their own view of Lindbergh and decide for themselves where, if at all, he falls on the spectrum between "hero" and "deeply flawed." Ultimately, Fleming's use of quotes is much more engaging and thought-provoking than summarization, especially for younger readers who are learning to grapple with complicated historical figures.

Fleming also deftly juggles the many disparate story lines in Lindbergh's life and finds common threads to connect them. In addition to the already noted "origin story," which Fleming links to numerous aspects of Lindbergh's life, the author also relates events through Lindbergh's treatment of the press and their treatment of him. Once Lindbergh made his transatlantic flight, he became a fixture in the press, largely due to the rise of tabloid journalism, which usually focuses on celebrities, scandal, and sensational stories. Lindbergh was unprepared for the invasion into his personal life. He was a loner and very private, yet after this solo flight, the press hounded him to such a degree that he developed elaborate schemes to outwit them, attempting to exclude them from his wedding and honeymoon. Later, after the murder of Lindbergh's son, the press broke into the funeral parlor where the autopsy occurred to photograph and then sell pictures of the deceased child. This horrific event and its aftermath prompted Lindbergh and his family to move to Europe, where the press was far less invasive and generally left them alone. Eventually, Lindbergh found ways to use the press to his advantage, such as in publicizing his speeches on isolationism and eugenics and, more positively, publicizing his support of the World Wildlife Federation and animal conservation after a trip to Kenya in the 1960s. Fleming highlights these many incidents with the press to convey the contradictions of a man who wanted his accomplishments known and widely appreciated but not at the expense of his privacy, which he prized intently. By connecting many of Lindbergh's life events to his interactions with the press, Fleming unifies the biography and makes it more coherent while offering insight into Lindbergh's complex personality.

For these and numerous other reasons, critics overwhelmingly praised Fleming's biography. Jonathan Hunt, writing a review for the *Horn Book*, noted that Fleming "creates a cohesive and comprehensive biography of a charismatic, flawed figure," while the anonymous reviewer for *Publishers Weekly* stated that Fleming "skillfully crafts a layered portrait of a controversial figure." Although this biography is targeted toward a young-adult audience, *Kirkus* observed that it "measures up to the best Lindbergh biographies for any audience" thanks to Fleming's writing style, attention to detail, use of extensive sources, and approach to revealing all aspects of Lindbergh's life that make him "hateable, pitiable, and admirable all at the same time." Additionally, several critics applauded Fleming's decision to present the events in Lindbergh's life without editorializing about them. She accomplishes this not only in her use of quotes from Lindbergh's diary but also in her restraint in not commenting on them. Rather than being told what to think about Lindbergh's decisions and actions, critics appreciated that readers are subtly encouraged to decide for themselves. This makes for a much more interactive reading experience and one that will engage readers of all ages. Fleming not only succeeded in writing a full and well-researched account of Lindbergh's life, but one that is thought-provoking and lends itself to discussion and comparison to contemporary politics and figures.

The Rise and Fall of Charles Lindbergh opens with Lindbergh about to speak at an America First rally and ends with the revelation of a long-held personal secret. The speech highlighted Lindbergh's views on isolationism (he opposed US involvement in World War II) and was perceived as pro-Nazi and anti-Semitic. The long-held family secret, revealed years after the deaths of Lindbergh and his wife, showed his secretive, sometimes duplicitous, nature. These events, like numerous others in the biography, are far from depicting the straightforward aviation hero or tragic father many thought Lindbergh to be. As *New York Times* critic Steve Sheinkin noted, Fleming's biography is "rich and unflinching," providing a nuanced portrait of a very complex person.

Author Biography

Candace Fleming is a prolific author of children's picture books, fiction, and young-adult historical nonfiction, including *The Family Romanov: Murder, Rebellion, and the Fall of Imperial Russia* (2014), winner of the Los Angeles Times Book Prize for Young Adult Literature and the Boston Globe-Horn Book Award for Nonfiction.

Marybeth Rua-Larsen

Review Sources

DeCampli, Cathy. Review of *The Rise and Fall of Charles Lindbergh*, by Candace Fleming. *School Library Journal*, 1 Jan. 2020, www.slj.com/?reviewDetail=the-rise-and-fall-of-charles-lindbergh. Accessed 2 Dec. 2020.

Hunt, Jonathan. Review of *The Rise and Fall of Charles Lindbergh*, by Candace Fleming. *The Horn Book*, 29 Jan. 2020, www.hbook.com/?detailStory=review-of-the-rise-and-fall-of-charles-lindbergh. Accessed 2 Dec. 2020.

Review of *The Rise and Fall of Charles Lindbergh*, by Candace Fleming. *Kirkus*, 10 Nov. 2019, www.kirkusreviews.com/book-reviews/candace-fleming/the-rise-and-fall-of-charles-lindbergh/. Accessed 2 Dec. 2020.

Review of *The Rise and Fall of Charles Lindbergh*, by Candace Fleming. *Publishers Weekly*, 19 Dec. 2019, www.publishersweekly.com/978-0-525-64654-9. Accessed 2 Dec. 2020.

Sheinkin, Steve. "Uncovering Charles Lindbergh's Secret Lives." Review of *The Rise and Fall of Charles Lindbergh*, by Candace Fleming. *The New York Times*, 20 Feb. 2020, www.nytimes.com/2020/02/20/books/review/the-rise-and-fall-of-charles-lindbergh-candace-fleming.html. Accessed 2 Dec. 2020.

The Searcher

Author: Tana French (b. 1973)
Publisher: Viking (New York). 464 pp.
Type of work: Novel
Time: Present day
Locale: Ardnakelty, Ireland

Cal Hooper, a retired Chicago police officer, moves to a small town in Ireland, looking for peace and quiet. After befriending a local child, Hooper becomes involved in a missing persons case that will change his view of his new community and his own life.

Principal characters
CAL HOOPER, a retired Chicago police officer
TREY REDDY, a struggling teen who asks him for help
BRENDAN REDDY, Trey's missing older brother
MART, Cal's elderly neighbor
LENA, a local woman who befriends Cal
SHEILA REDDY, Trey's mother
NOREEN, the town busybody and shopkeeper

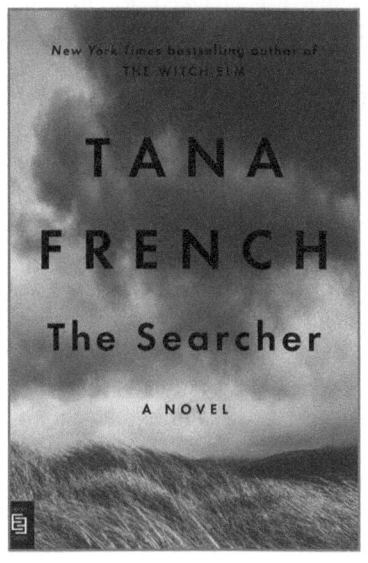

Tana French has become well known for her mystery novels and has been called one of the best mystery writers of her time. In French's eighth novel, *The Searcher* (2020), the author continues to explore the mystery genre but also ventures into some new territory—the Western genre. French admitted she was influenced by classic Westerns, such as Larry McMurtry's *Lonesome Dove* (1985), when writing *The Searcher*. The novel explores the dark secrets behind both individual and community choices as it follows Cal Hooper, a retired Chicago police officer, while he searches for a new sense of purpose. The story's strengths include strong characterization as well as a variety of surprising twists as the mystery reveals hidden depths behind the decisions that will protect a community even when they could destroy individual lives.

The characterization focuses on Cal Hooper and the relationships he builds after moving across the world to live in a small Irish village where a dilapidated house offers him an escape from the trials of life as a police officer in Chicago. After his divorce and a series of disappointments in his job, Cal decides he wants a complete change in his life. He enjoys the quiet and begins to reconnect with nature. However, he feels a sense of restlessness that he cannot explain. As the story progresses, readers learn a number of things that have changed his view of life. First, his wife has left him for another man. He is not sure how to deal with this, often thinking about her as if she were right beside him. Second, his daughter was attacked, leaving him feeling helpless in the face of her suffering. Finally, he left the police force because of his dissatisfaction with the job. As Cal investigates the disappearance of Brendan Reddy, he begins to understand himself in a deeper way, which allows him to relate better to others and find a peace in his own life that he had only hoped to achieve.

Trey Reddy is the second significant character in the novel. This young person seeks out Cal after discovering his background as a police officer. At first, Trey is hesitant to engage with Cal, but as Cal quietly accepts the youth's presence, Trey opens up to him. A revelation between the characters later in the novel puts Cal in an awkward place, but when the child needs him most, he steps up. Another major character is Mart, the elderly man who lives next to Cal. Mart provides comic relief, shares human insight, and challenges Cal in uncomfortable ways. Though Mart's actions are questionable, Cal finds himself twisted about how to feel in regard to the older man, revealing a depth of characterization that will draw readers further into the story.

Tana French

Next to the characterization, the mystery will keep readers interested in the tale. The case starts with Trey's plea to Cal to find an older brother who had disappeared several months earlier. Though Cal says he does not want to take on a case, he finds himself drawn into the search to help Trey find a sense of closure more than anything. As he takes simple steps to find out what Trey's impulsive brother did to lead to his disappearance, Cal is confronted with an active drug trade, a group of young men who were not the friends Brendan might have thought, and a dangerous set of people who will take extreme measures to protect their secret. The drug activity suggests an easy solution to Brendan's disappearance since the young man had been trying to set up a meth lab. His bragging about an easy income and his later fear of police implicate this as a motive for his disappearance. Injected into the mystery are seemingly random attacks on sheep in several local farms. These complicate Cal's attempts to understand what happened as they distract from the direct case. After both Trey and Cal are severely injured, he has to decide whether to continue the case or let it go.

Throughout the novel, the author presents a number of serious issues prevalent in today's news that interject thoughtful critique and help to tie the story together. One of the issues French introduces into the story is that of police violence and systemic racism. Cal has retired after an incident involving his partner shooting an eighteen-year-old Black man named Jeremiah whom he thought was reaching for a gun. It turned out that the teen was armed with a switchblade, not a gun. Cal struggles with the knowledge that this kind of situation should not happen. He thinks, "He was sure, absolutely, that O'Leary had believed Jeremiah was going for a gun in his pocket, which for a lot of guys would have been enough. But for Cal, that fact seemed to be overlaid and underlaid by so many layers that he couldn't tell whether or not it was important. What was important was that he and O'Leary were supposed to be out there keeping people safe." He particularly struggles with the teen's fear that he would die, a situation that was, in Cal's heart and mind, "unspeakably wrong." French's treatment of the incident is sensitive to both the boy and the police officers, revealing the complexity of these situations. She also touches on the issue of police prejudice in small towns. The local police in Ireland deal only with simple cases like speeding, drunk driving, and theft. When Cal tries to get information about Brendan being missing, he is told, "Sure, no surprise there, then. And, being honest with you, no loss." Brendan's life is not worth investigating because his family is poor, his siblings do not attend school, and his mother is "a bit . . . you know. Not mental or anything, like. Just not up to much."

French also explores the topic of family. Cal's family is an obvious focus for this theme, and his relationships with his parents as well as his own wife and child are highlighted. Though he had a good relationship with his mother and was partially raised by a loving grandfather, his father was an absentee parent. The man did not take responsibility by caring for Cal or his mother, instead wandering in some search for his own fulfillment without much concern about his son. Cal's desire to be different in his own marriage led him to putting more time into the job and into solving problems than in handling the emotional needs of his wife and daughter. As the novel progresses and Cal works with Trey, he begins to understand where he failed and where he can continue to improve his relationship with and understand his daughter. Trey's family is another focus in the story. The Reddy family matriarch, Sheila, is overwhelmed by the poverty she is thrust into after her husband leaves her to raise their children alone. Trey's relationship with Brendan is strong, however, and the teen worries about the older boy's disappearance. Everyone in the community sees the problems Sheila has, but few people step in to help, and too often both teachers and the local police just make empty threats when the children miss school. As Cal and Trey grow close, he offers the teen a more stable example of what a parent should be like, especially after Sheila beats Trey after being threatened by the people responsible for Brendan's disappearance.

Another theme French explores is that of betrayal. Cal has been betrayed by his job, by his wife, and by his new friends. Trey has been betrayed by Brendan, by their mother, and by the world in general. Sheila has been betrayed by her husband and her community. Mart and the other older men in Ardnakelty feel betrayed by the young people in the area. These betrayals serve to build up to the climax of the novel.

Though the novel's tone is often dark, French does include some humor and hope. For instance, Noreen, the town's grocer, is constantly trying to get Cal to ask her sister, Lena, on a date. Cal's friendship with Mart is often built around humor as well. One memorable scene finds Cal in the local pub with Mart and his cronies. One of the men has brought moonshine, and the others find it hilarious to test Cal's ability to hold his liquor. Their taunts to each other as well as of the newcomer make Cal feel accepted in the community. Hope is found as the novel moves toward closure.

The critical reviews of French's eighth novel presented a mostly positive overview of the book. The *Publishers Weekly* reviewer noted that "insightful characterizations, even of minor figures, and a devastating reveal help make this a standout." Stephanie Klose, the *Library Journal*'s reviewer, called it "a slow-burn stunner that will keep readers turning the pages late into the night." Meanwhile, the reviewer for *Kirkus* faulted the novel's sometimes slow pace and potentially unsatisfying "morally ambiguous ending." Reviewing for the *New York Times*, Janet Maslin likewise pointed out that the reader is "nearly 100 pages into the novel before its hook comes along." Nevertheless, Maslin praised the novel for its many delights, including "French's way of building Cal and Trey's bond" and scenes which are often "keenly observed, with a strong sense of place, and unfailingly entertaining."

Author Biography
Tana French has written eight novels, including the Dublin Murder Squad series. Her novels have won awards such as the Anthony, Edgar, and Macavity awards, the Los Angeles Times Book Prize for Best Mystery/Thriller, and the Irish Book Award for Crime Fiction. French is also known for her theatrical acting career.

Theresa L. Stowell, PhD

Review Sources
Klose, Stephanie. Review of *The Searcher*, by Tana French. *Library Journal*, 1 Sept. 2020, www.libraryjournal.com/?reviewDetail=the-searcher. Accessed 11 Dec. 2020.
Maslin, Janet. "Tana French's Irish Western Features a Retired Lawman and a Missing Boy." Review of *The Searcher*, by Tana French. *The New York Times*, 5 Oct. 2020, www.nytimes.com/2020/10/05/books/review/tana-french-the-searcher.html. Accessed 11 Jan. 2020.
Review of *The Searcher*, by Tana French. *Kirkus*, 14 July 2020, www.kirkusreviews.com/book-reviews/tana-french/the-searcher-french/. Accessed 11 Dec. 2020.
Review of *The Searcher*, by Tana French. *Publishers Weekly*, 17 Aug. 2020, www.publishersweekly.com/978-0-7352-2465-0. Accessed 11 Dec. 2020.

The Second Chance Club
Hardship and Hope after Prison

Author: Jason Hardy
Publisher: Simon & Schuster (New York). 288 pp.
Type of work: Memoir, current affairs, sociology
Time: 2013–16
Locale: New Orleans, Louisiana

This memoir of four years working as a probation and parole officer in New Orleans, Louisiana, takes a critical view of one of the most overlooked parts of the US criminal justice system. Focusing on seven representative cases, it details the challenges and frustrations endured by both parole officers and offenders.

Principal personages

JASON HARDY, the author, a probation and parole officer in New Orleans
SHEILA, an offender he works with, a young woman dealing with drug use and mental health issues
HARD HEAD, another offender, a homeless Vietnam veteran in his sixties
KENDRICK, an offender dealing with mental illness and outbreaks of violent behavior
DAMIEN, an offender suspected of being a drug-dealing "don"
JAVARON LANDRY, an offender who breeds dogs
RONALD LANDRY, an offender, Javaron's brother, who has epilepsy
TRAVIS, an offender who struggles with addiction
CHARLES LEWIS, his coworker and mentor
BETH, his coworker and mentor
DAN, the supervisor of the New Orleans District of the Louisiana Division of Probation and Parole
LAMAR, his coworker, a newer member of the New Orleans office

The US criminal justice system has been subject to frequent and intense criticism. The issue of mass incarceration in particular has often made headlines, as the United States leads the world in keeping people behind bars, including a disproportionate percentage of Black Americans. Yet less attention has been paid to probation and parole, two closely related systems that include far more people than prisons. In *The Second Chance Club*, first-time author Jason Hardy provides a compelling view into this realm, revealing the struggles of both probation and parole officers and the individuals with whom they work.

Hardy brings an insider's perspective to the world of probation and parole. A former high school English teacher, he returned to school to earn a master's degree in creative writing but was discouraged in his first attempt to write a novel. After working low-end service and retail jobs, he eventually ended up spending four years as an officer (PO) in the New Orleans District of the Louisiana Division of Probation and Parole, or P&P. *The Second Chance Club* is chiefly a memoir of his time in that position. The title comes from the nickname parolees and probationers give to the system they contend with as they try to avoid returning to prison—one that proves rather ironic, highlighting the inherent deficiencies of the system. As one parolee says in the book, "They wouldn't call it the second chance club if they didn't expect you to f— up." The book's subtitle speaks of "Hardship and Hope after Prison," but the hardships of both the offenders and the officers seem to outnumber the hopes by a wide margin.

Jason Hardy

As he explains, Hardy's indirect path to this field was not unusual. Though he applied for the job with vague notions of trying to do some good in public service, even working directly against mass incarceration, it was mostly a last resort after failing at other careers. Almost all his coworkers had similar stories. It also proved quite easy to get into the profession, as there are few applicants for jobs that demand hard work and intense emotional strain but pay modest wages. Hardy's college degree and clean criminal record were credentials enough, and the understaffed P&P also appreciated the fact he could leave his previous job quickly. Even the officer training camp was not designed to filter anyone out.

Anyone with experience of government bureaucracies of any kind will likely find much of what Hardy encounters as he begins work to be sadly familiar. He and his fellow POs are given wildly unrealistic caseloads. While best practices suggest a load of around 50 cases per officer, Hardy and his officemates have 220 each. It is clear to everyone in P&P that more could be accomplished with more funding, but budgetary restraints seem to be an unmovable obstacle. At the time, Louisiana spent far less than federal guidelines suggest on supervising parolees; Hardy identifies this as a false economy because when an offender returns to prison, the cost to the state is much greater. Red tape proves to be especially frustrating. Many parolees and probationers, especially those with physical or mental disabilities, lack the ability to navigate all the steps necessary to get them the help they need. On the other hand, drug dealers with money to hire a private attorney are often successful in claiming a disability that qualifies them for state or federal assistance.

While the typical struggles of bureaucracy are a challenge, Hardy also identifies a basic disconnect in the two main goals of the parole and probation system. On one hand, POs try to help keep people out of prison, but on the other hand, they must see that those who break the terms of their parole or probation are incarcerated. And officers ultimately have few tools other than the threat of prison to help them accomplish their work. On more than one occasion, Hardy and his colleagues found themselves sending a parolee back to prison because that is the only way to get the person the detox or other life-saving treatment they need.

Hardy's mentors teach him not to expect great successes; the best one could hope to do was to prevent disasters or reduce the threat of harm. He is taught by the more experienced POs to put his time and energy into the cases needing the most attention. He would never meet some of the parolees assigned to him, as they had failed to keep in contact with the system and eventually warrants had been issued for their arrest. Few of them are found, however; it is assumed many have moved out of the jurisdiction, and the state shows little interest in tracking them down. Parolees are placed into three categories: minimum risk, medium risk, and high risk. Offenders who seem to pose the greatest risk of harming themselves or others need the most attention. Hardy estimates that he spent 90 percent of his time dealing with only 50 of his 220 cases.

Hardy also learns that there is a significant amount of discretion in dealing with minor offenses. Parolees and probationers are supposed to stay away from alcohol and drugs, but officers mostly overlook drinking and smoking marijuana. This allows them to focus on more serious problems and potentially build more trust and rapport with the people they supervise. Indeed, the POs at times have a surprisingly good rapport with offenders, making jokes and chatting. The details of their interactions humanize both sides. One parolee, an older, homeless Vietnam veteran identified as Hard Head (nicknames and pseudonyms are used for many of the subjects in the book), tells Hardy he likes having somebody "to be accountable to."

Yet the vivid characterization of the offenders—Hardy focuses on seven individuals throughout the book—also often hints at the structural inequality undergirding the criminal justice system. For example, when Hardy and fellow PO Beth make a home visit, they find parolee brothers Javaron and Ronald Landry watching a police procedural show, and Beth asks them which side they root for. The brothers reveal that they typically identify with the police on TV shows, who seem fairer than the police they have encountered in their own lives. TV criminals, meanwhile, seem to be real dangers to society—greedy and evil—whereas many offenders feel they have broken the law only as a way to get by in a system that seems stacked against them.

Throughout *The Second Chance Club*, Hardy does present some signs of the hope that is spoken of in the book's subtitle. He joined the P&P at a time when Louisiana seemed to want to shed its image as the top US state in terms of incarceration rate, and some money was directed toward programs that seemed to be doing some good. Two of those are drug court and mental health court, where offenders have regular meetings with judges and counselors as well as access to professional help with drug addiction or mental health issues. Another program, NOLA for Life, was rolled by the city government in New Orleans. This provided additional funds for more intensive supervision of those thought to be at risk of suffering or perpetuating violence—including gang members and drug dealers. Besides the higher level of supervision, there was also access to social service programs, such as job training, mental health services, and housing assistance.

Thanks in part to such programs, some of the offenders Hardy discusses throughout the book find a degree of success in turning their lives around while under his supervision (he gives them the ultimate credit for their improvement, however). Sheila, a teenager when Hardy first meets her and later a twenty-something single parent, stays away from drugs, gets treatment for depression through the mental health court, and works a steady job. Hard Head, who had been battling drug addiction, found steady work at decent wages as a construction laborer and qualified for housing assistance. Yet Hardy is clear that many more cases are not so successful, due to many complex factors but not least the structure of the probation and parole system itself. It is heartwrenching to read the stories of people who seem to have everything working against them and frustrating to see how the public servants meant to help them can do little.

In an epilogue, Hardy suggests some needed reforms. One is to shorten the time of parole from five years to two years, as he and other POs found the most fruitful interactions with offenders happen early on. Money saved by these shorter periods could then be put into programs to address specific needs, such as the promising mental health and drug courts. He also suggests granting parole six months earlier for those eligible, which in many states would save thousands of dollars in prison costs, money that could be used for things like preventing parolees from becoming homeless. While those steps are fairly small and face significant obstacles, it is refreshing to see concrete ideas rather than just grand ideology.

Hardy's writing style is engaging, and amid the tragedies of so many damaged lives and the failed expectations of the parole officers, he crafts a compelling narrative. He also strives for a relatively balanced perspective, especially seeing how the issue of criminal justice reform can be politicized and otherwise polarizing. He is empathetic toward the offenders he describes, but he pulls no punches as he points out their failures. He recognizes structural inequality, with the deep disadvantages facing those who grow up in poverty with an inadequate social safety net, let alone additional layers such as racism and mental health problems. But, as some of Hardy's colleagues often pointed out—many people grew up in similar situations and did not turn to crime or drugs. Similarly, Hardy does not make heroes out of his fellow workers in P&P. Many come across as people who truly hope to make a difference, but they have their own flaws and struggles.

The Second Chance Club was generally well received by reviewers, with many noting that it provides welcome insight into a little-known field. Police, lawyers, and judges are staples in everything from news to fiction, but POs are rarely in the spotlight. Laurie L. Levenson, writing for the *Los Angeles Review of Books*, praised how Hardy "gives us a glimpse of how bad the criminal justice system is while offering a peek at how good some of the people are who still try to work within that system." A reviewer for *Publishers Weekly* described the book as "a revelatory account that threads the needle between exasperation and optimism." Some critics were less impressed, however. Notably, Reginald Dwayne Betts, a poet and former incarcerated person, argued in a *New York Times* review that Hardy stigmatizes people on probation and parole, overemphasizing drug use and personal responsibility over the problem of mass incarceration. Yet for most readers, *The Second Chance Club* will be eye-opening, even if only as an introduction to a vast and complex subject. And bringing the challenges of probation and parole to the attention of the general reading public could ultimately help the push for reform.

Author Biography
Jason Hardy has worked as a high school English teacher, a probation and parole officer, and an FBI agent. *The Second Chance Club* is his first release as an author.

Mark S. Joy, PhD

Review Sources
Betts, Reginald Dwayne. "Out of Prison but Still Not Free." Review of *The Second Chance Club: Hardship and Hope after Prison*, by Jason Hardy. *The New York Times*, 11 Feb. 2020, nytimes.com/2020/02/11/books/review/the-second-chance-club-jason-hardy.html. Accessed 11 Dec. 2020.
Humphreys, Keith. "Inside the Chaotic, Underfunded World of Probation and Parole." Review of *The Second Chance Club: Hardship and Hope after Prison*, by Jason Hardy. *Washington Monthly*, April/May/June 2020, washingtonmonthly.com/magazine/april-may-june-2020/inside-the-chaotic-underfunded-world-of-probation-and-parole. Accessed 10 Dec. 2020.
Levenson, Laurie L. "How Bad Is the Criminal Justice System?" Review of *The Second Chance Club: Hardship and Hope after Prison*, by Jason Hardy. *Los Angeles Review of Books*, 19 July 2020, lareviewofbooks.org/article/how-bad-is-the-criminal-justice-system. Accessed 13 Dec. 2020.
Review of *The Second Chance Club: Hardship and Hope after Prison*, by Jason Hardy. *Kirkus*, 21 Oct. 2019, www.kirkusreviews.com/book-reviews/jason-hardy/the-second-chance-club. Accessed 22 Dec. 2020.
Review of *The Second Chance Club: Hardship and Hope after Prison*, by Jason Hardy. *Publishers Weekly*, 5 Dec. 2019, www.publishersweekly.com/978-1-982128-59-3. Accessed 10 Dec. 2020.

The Secret Lives of Church Ladies

Author: Deesha Philyaw (b. 1971)
Publisher: West Virginia University Press (Morgantown, WV). 192 pp.
Type of work: Short fiction
Time: Twentieth and twenty-first centuries
Locale: Southern United States

Deesha Philyaw's debut collection of short stories, The Secret Lives of Church Ladies, *explores the unseen lives of Southern, Black, church-going women whose stories discuss subjects such as the role of religion, marriage, infidelity, and individuality.*

The Secret Lives of Church Ladies (2020), Deesha Philyaw's debut short-story collection, explores the hidden lives of Black women for whom Christianity and the church play a major role, but whose experiences often subvert stereotypes. The book contains nine different stories, each focusing on a different woman, or women, and how their personal experiences clash with the religious norm. Reviewers noted that the church itself also serves as a character in many of Philyaw's stories, which explore how a person's relationship with faith and the church can shape a person's life. The underlying themes are complex, often involving love, sex, longing, and identity as shaped and constrained by religion and conservatism. Deeper still, Philyaw utilizes these nine stories to explore undercurrents of isolation, sadness, and lives that are unfulfilled.

Prior to the release of her fist fiction collection, Philyaw had published several of the stories individually in other magazines. In addition, she had written essays and articles with similar themes for a large number of publications, including the *New York Times*, the *Washington Post*, *McSweeney's*, *Harvard Review*, and *Ebony*. Racial and gender issues often feature prominently in her writing and she frequently turns her lens to the conflicts and comforts of the family and different manifestations of family life in Black communities.

Though the entire collection received warm praise from reviewers, the standout story cited by many literary critics as the best of the collection is the fourth short story, "Peach Cobbler," which serves as an encapsulation of many of the broader themes found in the collection. The story is narrated by Olivia, whose mother—an accomplished baker and caretaker—is having an affair with the family's married pastor. Once each week, Olivia's mother makes a peach cobbler for the pastor, who comes to their home to eat a massive portion of the dessert before retreating to the bedroom for their weekly tryst. Later in the story, a now teenage Olivia develops personal relationships

Deesha Philyaw

with both the pastor's son and wife. Conflicted in her feelings and doubting her religion due to the actions of the man who is supposed to embody it most, Olivia makes her own version of the mother's cobbler and delivers it to the pastor's wife and son, who praise the quality of the dessert.

Philyaw's "Peach Cobbler" depicts a decades-long affair, as seen through the eyes of Olivia at various stages in her life. The short story brings two of the primary themes of the book, the Black church and heterosexual marriage, into focus. Writing for the *Los Angeles Review of Books*, reviewer Renee Simms noted, "Philyaw's fiction stands within a tradition of writing that's about the beauty and burden of Black life within oppressive social systems." With "Peach Cobbler," the notion of marriage and fidelity forms one backbone of the story, set against the power dynamics of church community. The story also explores something deeper: the way that Black women's gifts are exploited. Oliva's mother, whose peach cobbler is described as something unusual and quite special, finds her gifts exploited by the pastor for his own ends. This story also reflects on the way that religious patriarchy affects young minds. Olivia has been taught to worship and honor men, and to believe that the pastor—as a representative of this patriarchic structure and direct stand-in for God—was supposed to represent virtue in her life. Instead, the pastor becomes a flawed and self-interested force in the decades-long exploitation of his own family and Olivia's mother.

While there are multiple ways to express and to internalize the role of religion in one's family life or in the broader context of Black communities or other subsets of American culture, Philyaw is most interested in exploring themes of religious patriarchy and oppression. "Peach Cobbler" depicts the abuse of trust, authority, and status on the part of the pastor and Olivia's effort to reconcile this with her religious upbringing. Another story, "Dear Sister," features sisters arguing about the relevance of the Bible's order to "Honor thy father" after the death of their deadbeat father from whom the sisters have largely been estranged. Their argument focuses on the conflict of being told to respect a person because religion tells them to even though the person has not given them a reason to be respected.

Several of the stories included in *The Secret Lives of Church Ladies* explore how religious inculcation can limit a woman's ability to explore her sexuality and how it can shape the views of others. In the first story in the collection, "Eula," two forty-something single women, who have been best friends since they were children, meet on the eve of 2000. Since their thirties, the narrator, Caroletta, and Eula meet every year on New Year's Eve for a secret sexual rendezvous. Caroletta is in love with Eula and this year, she wants to acknowledge that they could be more than secret lovers. Eula, however, cannot get past how admitting her sexual desires would impact her view of herself and others' views of her as a Christian woman. She cannot let go of her unsatisfying yet outwardly goal of finding a religious husband. In "Jael," a woman raising her orphaned great-granddaughter finds the fourteen-year-old's diary and realizes that the child she has been raising has sexual feelings for the wife of their preacher. Because of the grandmother's faith, she struggles with the idea that the young girl she loves like a daughter is, in the eyes of her faith, a wayward creature given to evil.

Both "Eula" and "Jael" ask interesting questions about sexuality and religion. The characters in both stories face a conflict between their identities and how they are perceived in the realm of conservative Christian culture. For Eula, the need to conform to the morals of the Christian church prevent her from living a life that might be more fulfilling and honest, while in Jael, a loving grandmother struggles against her own religious prejudices in the face of learning that her granddaughter might be a lesbian. Both stories cast a light on the unique struggles that LGBTQ people experience in Black religious communities and how homophobia both limits actualization and can threaten the bonds between family members.

Philyaw also turns her attention to other ways that religion and sex intersect. For instance, in the story titled "Instructions for Married Christian Husbands," the narrator is a woman who unapologetically engages in adulterous transgressions with men from the church. The story's primary focus is the hypocrisy of Christian men who profess religious ideals and yet who all too easily cave to the narrator's efforts at seduction. Philyaw writes this particular story as an instructional guide on engaging in infidelity, specifically with married Christian men.

Another of the stories in Philyaw's collection that received significant critical attention was "How to Make Love to a Physicist," a humorous story that focuses on another area of conflict in the lives of followers of the church. Here, Philyaw's narrator is a middle-aged woman who struggles with body-image issues and finds her own needs in conflict with the view of her mother, a dedicated church woman who believes that faith should be able to solve any problems that her daughter has. Through the narrator's reflections, Philyaw deconstructs the way that the judgments of religious communities can impact body image and self-confidence, but the story also documents the narrator's journey toward psychotherapy, an active effort at self-improvement that is often discounted or actively discouraged within some subsets of the American Black community. This overlaps with the Black church, in which believers often eschew the value of psychotherapy or other types of personal well-being management in favor of relying on faith and the church.

Philyaw's *The Secret Lives of Church Ladies* was a major success with critics. The collection was a finalist for the 2020 National Book Award. Simms said that *Secret Lives* is a "strong and certain" collection and praised Philyaw for her sensitive and probing look at the lives of Black church women. An anonymous reviewer for *Kirkus* noted, "No saints exist in these pages, just full-throated, flesh-and-blood women who embrace and redefine love, and their own selves, in powerfully imperfect renditions." The review concluded, "Tender, fierce, proudly Black and beautiful, these stories will sneak inside you and take root." Writing for *Publishers Weekly*, the anonymous reviewer lauded Philyaw's success in "turning her characters' private struggles into a beautiful chorus" through the combination of stories she tells in the volume.

While the stories in *The Secret Lives of Church Ladies* might not capture every church-going person's experience with their family, faith, or church, the nine stories contain a variety of perspectives that cover an unusual and broad cross section of hidden church experience. In interviews, Philyaw said that the stories in the book were directly inspired by her own religious upbringing, her relationship with her mother, and women she had known in her past. Her characters find, as many do, comfort in their church, faith, and religious communities, as well as in the way that their membership in these facets of their culture help them to construct their identities. But, the stories are also about the restrictiveness of religious thought, stereotypes, and traditions. Philyaw's characters, more often than not, are women who refuse to be bound by traditions in exploring their own lives.

Author Biography

Deesha Philyaw is a Pushcart Prize–nominated writer whose work has appeared in a number of prominent publications, including the *New York Times*, *McSweeney's*, and the *Washington Post*. Her first nonfiction book, *Co-Parenting 101: Helping Your Kids Thrive in Two Households after Divorce* (2013), was cowritten with her ex-husband Mike Thomas.

Micah L. Issitt

Review Sources

Review of *The Secret Lives of Church Ladies*, by Deesha Philyaw. *Kirkus Reviews*, 1 Aug. 2020. *Literary Reference Center Plus*, search.ebscohost.com/login.aspx?direct=true&db=lkh&AN=144285924&site=lrc-plus. Accessed 16 Nov. 2020.

Review of *The Secret Lives of Church Ladies*, by Deesha Philyaw. *Publishers Weekly*, 8 June 2020, www.publishersweekly.com/978-1-949199-73-4. Accessed 19 Jan. 2021.

Simms, Renee. "Strong and Certain: On Deesha Philyaw's 'The Secret Lives of Church Ladies.'" Review of *The Secret Lives of Church Ladies*, by Deesha Philyaw. *Los Angeles Review of Books*, 12 Nov. 2020, lareviewofbooks.org/article/strong-and-certain-on-deesha-philyaws-the-secret-lives-of-church-ladies. Accessed 16 Nov. 2020.

Wright, Wendeline O. "Deesha Philyaw's Debut Short Story Collection Explores Faith and Fidelity." Review of *The Secret Lives of Church Ladies*, by Deesha Philyaw. *Pittsburgh Post-Gazette*, 9 Sept. 2020, www.post-gazette.com/ae/books/2020/09/10/Deesha-Philyaw-Secret-Lives-Church-Ladies-review/stories/202009100026. Accessed 16 Nov. 2020.

Shuggie Bain

Author: Douglas Stuart (b. 1976)
Publisher: Grove Press (New York). 448 pp.
Type of work: Novel
Time: 1981–92
Locale: Glasgow, Scotland

In Douglas Stuart's debut novel, a young boy deals with his mother's alcoholism in the bleak public housing projects of 1980s Glasgow.

Principal characters
SHUGGIE BAIN, a young boy who cares for his alcoholic mother
AGNES BAIN, his mother
HUGH "SHUG" BAIN, his father, an abusive taxi driver
ALEXANDER "LEEK" BAIN, his older half-brother, a talented artist
CATHERINE BAIN, his older half-sister
LIZZIE CAMPBELL, Agnes's mother

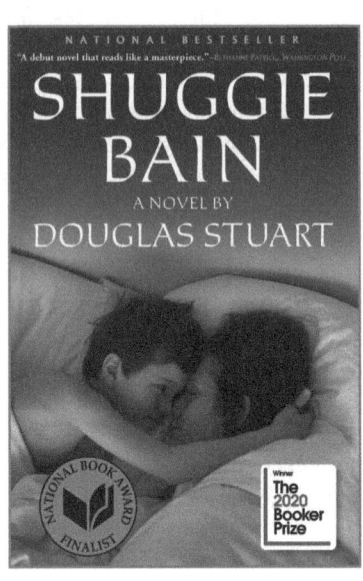

In the novel *Shuggie Bain* (2020), the reader is introduced to the title character in the year 1992. He is sixteen, living alone in a squalid room in a boarding house in Glasgow's South Side and working at a supermarket deli counter where he is simultaneously proud of the neatness of the display cases and willing to pick a dirty chicken up off the floor. It is the key contradiction of Shuggie—this tension between his pride and fussiness and his familiarity with the dirty and low. He is terribly poor, making barely enough to pay for his room and feed himself. His schooling is "patchy," and he dreams of attending hairdressing college, while he is not above offering his body in exchange for a little cash. He is gay, as the ladies from the grocery store discover when they try to make passes at him, and he is alone, looking through the dented cans for salmon. These cans appear again at the end of the book, when Shuggie is returned to 1992, but the bulk of this beautiful, gritty, painful story takes place in the 1980s—during the decade that explains why Shuggie is alone at age sixteen.

The novel's second section flashbacks to 1981, and Agnes Bain, formerly Agnes Campbell, is bored with life in her parents' high-rise flat where she lives with her three children and her second husband, Shug Bain. Her mother and friends are playing cards and picking out items they cannot afford but will buy on credit, while complaining about their children and their men as they drink and swear and try on new brassieres. The hardness of these women's lives is softened by a kind of irritable solidarity, an easy banter that is captured in its Glaswegian dialect by author Douglas Stuart, who

Douglas Stuart

grew up surrounded by women like these. (Many of the characters in *Shuggie Bain* are based on people from Stuart's own life, including the title character who shares many traits with Stuart himself.)

As the women dance and gamble and get slowly drunk, Agnes's husband, Shug, a taxi driver, comes back to the flat to bring the ladies home. It is a telling scene, with Agnes trying to sober up and look attractive to her faithless brute of a husband, hoping he will come back home, though she knows that he is having multiple affairs with other women. Their relationship, in fact, began as one of Shug's affairs, and she knows her hold on him is tentative at best. She also knows that she is beautiful, modeling herself after Elizabeth Taylor, and she has learned the value of her beauty in the hard world she inhabits. When Shug leaves, she is crushed. As many parents do, in her sorrow and disappointment she looks to her children for comfort, considering waking young Shuggie up so she does not have to sleep alone. Their relationship is already one of dysfunction: Shuggie bends to the needs of his beautiful, volatile mother, who turns to a bottle of vodka instead. These two comforts—her devoted youngest child and the pleasure and obliteration of alcohol—are impossibly intertwined for Agnes.

As Agnes drinks, she recalls a holiday night out in Blackpool with Shug. It was an evening that began promisingly, with Agnes fascinated by the lights that transformed what she saw in daylight as a grubby town. The night disintegrates as Shug becomes aggressive and she continues drinking, finally unable to stand and making a spectacle of herself. Shug, enraged and embarrassed, drags her up the stairs of their hotel by her hair, beats and rapes her. Then, to justify his actions, he tells her he will take her out dancing. Agnes is left to ruminate on how she has left a steady husband—a man who she did not love but who took care of her and was a good father to her first two children—for an unintelligent, vain, philandering brute. After fathering Shuggie, Shug abandons Agnes, but not before he is sure he has irretrievably broken her.

So enamored of Shug is Agnes, so desperate to keep her husband, she moves from the high-rise where her parents live to a housing project on the outskirts of Glasgow called Pithead, a poverty-stricken former mining town whose residents barely survive on government support. Shug has scored the apartment in Pithead as some sort of scheme, but he admits that his actual goal was to see if he had enough control over Agnes that she would be willing to live in such a degraded place. Having proven his point, he leaves her for the last time with her three children, surrounded by bogs and slag heaps and families that hate her instinctively for her pride in her appearance. Isolated and spurned, Agnes sinks deeper into her alcoholism, vulnerable to predatory men and women, even as she picks fights and sleeps with other women's husbands. In the bleak landscape of Pithead, where unemployment and poverty—the results of Thatcher-era economic policies in Britain—stalk the streets, Agnes dulls the pain in any way she can.

Meanwhile, Shuggie tries to be "normal," to walk like a regular boy and fit the expectation of brutal manliness he sees all around him. He is repeatedly reminded that he is not like other children and is abused and bullied throughout his childhood. Shuggie's two older half-siblings try to help, but in the end, they must pull away and save themselves. Catherine, the oldest, marries young and moves away. Alexander, known as Leek, loses a university placement because he tries to stay and help Shuggie and Agnes, but later he also abandons them.

A break from the unremitting smoking, screaming, vomiting, and violence comes partway through the novel. Agnes manages to get clean following one of many deranged, suicidal scenes, and she forms a community of Alcoholics Anonymous (AA) members. She meets a widower named Eugene—a man who treats her well and who is ready to make a life with her. However, at an elegant dinner, he encourages Agnes to have a little bit of wine now that she is "cured"—with predictably cataclysmic results. After a short period of Eugene's guilt-fueled caregiving, Agnes is left alone, with only Shuggie to manage the fallout. The last quarter of the book is a long slog down to a somewhat predictable end. There is a lovely final scene, back in 1992, that shows Shuggie continuing his habit of caring for those who have ceased to care for themselves.

Shuggie Bain received a resoundingly positive critical response and was tapped for several major honors, including a nomination for the National Book Award. It won the UK's top literary award, the Booker Prize, and appeared on numerous best-book lists of 2020. The Booker Prize announcement called the book, "a blistering and heartbreaking debut," a sentiment that was shared by most critics. "Reading *Shuggie Bain* cannot but be a grim experience," said Sarah Moss in her *Guardian* review, describing the prevalent "bruised thighs and gouged breasts . . . vomit and bile." Leah Hager Cohen, in her *New York Times* review, was equally taken with the graphic descriptions of brutality in the book. She wrote: "Hair is ripped from heads, people are dragged up the stairs and down the street, faces and groins are bloodied and bruised, and all with a nearly quotidian inevitability." Writing for the *Scotsman*, Allan Massie described a "harsh, bleak novel, for that decade was a harsh and bleak time in Glasgow . . . Stuart paints the grimmest of pictures."

While critics agreed on the grim picture painted by Stuart, most equally agreed upon the beauty and vividness of the book. The Glaswegian dialect, phonetically rendered, was noted by many reviewers as adding depth and richness to the novel; Cohen commented, "Douglas Stuart writes in a sense-drenched Glaswegian prose so studded with slang ("papped," "boak," "laldy," "smirr") and phonetically rendered dialogue ("Wit are the pair of ye stauning there all glaikit fur?") that the language itself adds up to another layer of physicality." Reviewers also commented on the novel's characterization. Moss praised the book's "deep understanding of the relationship between a child and a substance-abusing parent, showing a world rarely portrayed in literary fiction." Overall, however, Moss was less laudatory about the rich language that Stuart employs, noting that "sometimes impatience with the heavy-handed prose interrupted my interest." Moss also found particular fault with the overall negative depiction of women.

Several critics faulted the length of the book; Massie complained "it's about a quarter too long" and also noted some editing oversight, though Cohen praised its over four hundred pages as "crucial to its overall effect." Massie also felt it was too early yet to be calling the book a masterpiece, but he conceded, "it isn't that, but it is a very good and often moving novel." Cohen was less qualified in her enthusiasm for the book and its author: "He's lovely, Douglas Stuart, fierce and loving and lovely."

Author Biography
Douglas Stuart is a Scottish American writer and fashion designer. *Shuggie Bain*, his debut novel, won the 2020 Booker Prize.

Bethany Groff Dorau

Review Sources
Cohen, Leah Hager. "In 1980s Glasgow, a World of Pain Made Bearable by Love." Review of *Shuggie Bain*, by Douglas Stuart. *The New York Times*, 11 Feb. 2020, www.nytimes.com/2020/02/11/books/review/shuggie-bain-douglas-stuart.html. Accessed 13 Jan. 2021.

Lichtig, Toby. "Glasgow Kiss." Review of *Shuggie Bain*, by Douglas Stuart. *TLS*, 11 Sept. 2020, www.the-tls.co.uk/articles/shuggie-bain-douglas-stuart-review-toby-lichtig/. Accessed 13 Jan. 2021.

Massie, Allan. "Book Review: Shuggie Bain, by Douglas Stuart." Review of *Shuggie Bain*, by Douglas Stuart. *The Scotsman*, 21 Aug. 2020, www.scotsman.com/arts-and-culture/books/book-review-shuggie-bain-douglas-stuart-2950033. Accessed 13 Jan. 2021.

Moss, Sarah. "Shuggie Bain by Douglas Stuart Review—a Rare and Gritty Debut." Review of *Shuggie Bain*, by Douglas Stuart. *The Guardian*, 31 July 2020, www.theguardian.com/books/2020/jul/31/shuggie-bain-by-douglas-stuart-review-a-rare-and-gritty-debut. Accessed 13 Jan. 2021.

Review of *Shuggie Bain*, by Douglas Stuart. *Kirkus*, 14 Oct. 2020, www.kirkusreviews.com/book-reviews/douglas-stuart/shuggie-bain/. Accessed 21 Jan. 2021.

Sigh, Gone
A Misfit's Memoir of Great Books, Punk Rock, and the Fight to Fit In

Author: Phuc Tran (b. 1974)
Publisher: Flatiron Books (New York). 320 pp.
Type of work: Memoir
Time: 1975–91
Locale: Carlisle, Pennsylvania

Sigh, Gone: A Misfit's Memoir of Great Books, Punk Rock, and the Fight to Fit In, published in 2020, is a coming-of-age memoir of a young Vietnamese American who finds his way in small-town Pennsylvania with the help of great literature and punk rock music.

Principal personages
PHUC TRAN, the narrator, a young Vietnamese immigrant, student, skateboarder, and fan of punk rock and its associated subculture
CHANH, his father
CHI, his mother
LOU, his younger brother and sidekick
LIAM, his first punk friend, a skateboarder and fellow student
MOLLY, his high school girlfriend

In his first book, 2020's *Sigh, Gone: A Misfit's Memoir of Great Books, Punk Rock, and the Fight to Fit In*, Phuc Tran describes how he was four years old when he and his father decided how to say his name outside of the family. There were three choices: stay true to the Vietnamese pronunciation, which is not phonetic in English; decide on a name that matches the English spelling; or pick an Anglicized name. This decision, and the conversation around it, is a microcosm of the multiple identities Tran would try out as he came of age in Carlisle, Pennsylvania. As with many things, Tran and his family chose the middle path—keep the Vietnamese name (for the most part, as he was called Peter very briefly) but make it palatable to English speakers. For the Tran family, like for many immigrants, negotiating a complex identity amid the idea and societal pressures of assimilation was a constant process. This, along with many years spent as a teacher of Latin and Greek, helped make Tran deeply interested in the nuances of language and identity over the years. Inspired to write by his exploration of these concepts in relation to his experiences growing up as a young immigrant, he brings a unique, multilayered, and engaging perspective to his memoir.

Phuc Tran

When he was merely a toddler, Tran and his extended family fled Saigon, Vietnam, in 1975. After being separated and reuniting after some time in a refugee camp on Wake Island, the family landed in Carlisle, Pennsylvania, sponsored by two Lutheran families. Tran's father, a lawyer in Vietnam, found work driving a cement mixer before taking a job in a tire factory, where he was mocked by some fellow factory workers for his accent. Tran points out that the cruelty of these few was "offset by the kindness that our sponsors showed our family, week after week." Not a simple tale of cruelty experienced in a foreign country, everything in Tran's story is complicated and negotiated—how could his family tell who were the "good" Americans? Tran's younger brother, Lou, was born in 1976, and the name he was given, as the author highlights, served as another mark of the family's ongoing assimilation; Vietnamese Lu became Louis.

Several members of Tran's extended family came with them to Carlisle, or joined them soon after, adding to the depth and complexity of their family narrative. When Tran leaves home later in the book, he seeks refuge with an uncle, and he visits cousins in New York City, learning from their experiences as well. In one of the most poignant parts of the book, Tran tells the story of Ba Co, his great-grandmother, who would pretend to be a witch, unloosing her hair and removing her teeth. He saw an apparition of her as her apartment burned blocks away, causing her death. Like with so many other events in his life, Tran finds connections to literature as he later ponders this experience. As he reads Dickens's *A Christmas Carol* (1843), he thinks of how he and his family, like the reformed Ebenezer Scrooge, must live in the past, present, and future, "each of us an element of that continuum, yet constantly shifting."

The Tran family was quite aware of their status as outsiders, reminded again and again by schoolyard bullying and racist epithets. Tran explains the subtle but sinister reminders that they were seen as representatives of the Vietnam War, which had obsessed and traumatized Americans for over a decade before the Tran family even arrived in the US. "That was my inheritance," Tran writes. "The anxiety of being stared at." They learned early on that it was better to go through the drive-through at fast food restaurants rather than expose themselves to the embarrassment of mispronounced words in a crowded lobby.

Still, the Tran family discovered ways to engage with life in their adopted country. Tran's mother initially found work at an apple orchard, and his parents threw themselves into their work while also joining a church. His father found a comfortable place to learn about his adopted home as well—as a wealth of information about how to fix cars and household items—at the local library. It was there, as a teenager, that Tran purchased Clifton Fadiman's curated and summarized list of must-read texts titled *The Lifetime Reading Plan* (1960). For Tran, this was an invitation "to be part of an intellectual conversation that was hundreds of years old," one that promised the acceptance and level of positive estimation that he sought in his strategic path toward assimilation. In an effective homage to his subsequent love for and frequent escape into books, *Sigh, Gone* is structured around some of the works that resonated with him and with his experience. At that point, he began to understand that his feelings of alienation and desire for connection were shared across time and space and described by the likes of Nathaniel Hawthorne, Franz Kafka, and Oscar Wilde.

Before Tran found a way to grapple with the Western literary canon, his family moved across town, just prior to the start of his eighth-grade school year. He wondered whether, like Eliza Doolittle in George Bernard Shaw's *Pygmalion* (1913), he could change his status in his new school. He bought a used skateboard from a neighbor and accidentally did just that, finding himself invited into a tribe of punk skateboarders whose acceptance of each other's outlier status offered him a new kind of identity. Tran could be proud of being different, and perhaps most importantly, there was a soundtrack to this new way of being, a wardrobe, and a crew of people who would back him up in any kind of conflict. He notes—characteristic of the sense of humor that affectingly runs throughout the book—the irony of running to his beloved library to look up punk rock, and the understanding that he still wanted to fit in, even with misfits.

Meanwhile, Tran's recounting of his relationship with his father creates a key tension in this book. He details times when his father was often angry, and at points violent, hinting at some of the trauma and stress he suffered in Vietnam. He routinely disciplined Tran with a metal rod, and during the punk years, when Tran did not make honor roll because of a failing gym grade, his father rushed at him with a pair of scissors and then destroyed the cherished symbols of his punk identity—his leather jacket, his vinyl records, and his posters and concert flyers. Tran escaped and was briefly homeless, staying with relatives and sleeping in a friend's closet. The reader is also reminded of several times when his parents abandoned him, or pretended to, once dropping him off by the side of the road and once pretending to pack suitcases and leave him and his brother in the house to fend for themselves. These things were done in place of corporal punishment, after a teacher intervened to put a stop to beatings so severe that Tran was unable to sit at his desk. His place in his family could feel precarious at best, which made the support and acceptance of his punk friends that much more precious.

Despite the camaraderie and acceptance of his punk friends, Tran eventually struggled to reconcile their varying aspirations, or lack thereof, with his love of language and literature. He realized that his identity was even more complex than he had imagined. He successfully navigated this difficult time, which could have spelled the end of his cherished friendships, through the example of another punk kid in town who had gone off to college and unabashedly loved it, and through his emersion in Fadiman's book. He was also encouraged by the efforts of stand-out teachers, one of whom introduced him to *The Autobiography of Malcolm X* (1965), challenging his simplistic view of racism. Another took him to see a production of Wilde's play *The Importance of Being Earnest*, which he connected to strongly. Still, his deep relationship with the arts and literature also created distance between Tran and his parents. In one impactful passage, he notes, "Ironically, the arts were connecting me to strangers, and yet they widened the already yawning gulf between me and my family."

Tran's trajectory is clear as the book nears its end. He describes a scene in which, planning to leave Carlisle and his childhood and head to college on a scholarship, he made common cause with the truck drivers at his local diner. He recalls his father's joy in gunning the engine of their car and flying down the back roads of rural Pennsylvania, offering a rarer moment of fun and connection between parents and children to poignantly conclude a book that most vividly describes their frequent conflict and alienation.

Sigh, Gone was met with generally positive reviews, with many critics pointing out the significance of the universal questions and themes that the book explores. In a review for NPR Maureen Corrigan called it "a congenial read for our chaotic time," though E. Alex Jung, writing for the *New York Times*, struck a more critical note as he bemoaned that Tran's story is "preoccupied with the project of assimilation." Some reviewers noted the honesty of Tran's writing as a highlight, an attribute that led *Marie Claire* to include the book in its list of the Best Memoirs of 2020. The anonymous *Publishers Weekly* reviewer, focusing on the power of Tran's connection to reading demonstrated in his memoir, called it a "complex and rewarding story of a book-enriched life" that "vividly illustrates how literature can serve as a window to a new life." . The New England Independent Booksellers Association awarded *Sigh, Gone* a 2020 New England Book Award in the nonfiction category.

Author Biography

Phuc Tran has spent many years as a Latin teacher and tattoo artist. *Sigh, Gone* is his first book, for which he won a 2020 New England Book Award.

Bethany Groff Dorau

Review Sources

Corrigan, Maureen. "'Sigh, Gone' Is a Refugee's Chaotic Memoir of Displacement and Belonging." Review of *Sigh, Gone: A Misfit's Memoir of Great Books, Punk Rock, and the Fight to Fit In*, by Phuc Tran. *NPR*, 23 Apr. 2020, www.npr.org/2020/04/23/842360478/sigh-gone-is-a-refugee-s-chaotic-memoir-of-displacement-and-belonging. Accessed 14 Oct. 2020.

Jung, E. Alex. "From Saigon to the Suburbs, a Vietnamese-American's Struggle to Assimilate." *Sigh, Gone: A Misfit's Memoir of Great Books, Punk Rock, and the Fight to Fit In*, by Phuc Tran. *The New York Times*, 21 Apr. 2020, www.nytimes.com/2020/04/21/books/review/sigh-gone-phuc-tran.html. Accessed 14 Oct. 2020.

Review of *Sigh, Gone: A Misfit's Memoir of Great Books, Punk Rock, and the Fight to Fit In*, by Phuc Tran. *Kirkus*, 2 Jan. 2020, www.kirkusreviews.com/book-reviews/phuc-tran/sigh-gone/. Accessed 14 Oct. 2020.

Review of *Sigh, Gone: A Misfit's Memoir of Great Books, Punk Rock, and the Fight to Fit In*, by Phuc Tran. *Publishers Weekly*, 22 Oct. 2019, www.publishersweekly.com/978-1-250-19471-8. Accessed 14 Oct. 2020.

The Silent Wife

Author: Karin Slaughter (b. 1971)
Publisher: Morrow (New York). 496 pp.
Type of work: Novel
Time: Present day; eight years before the present
Locales: Atlanta, Georgia; Grant County, Georgia

In The Silent Wife, *Georgia Bureau of Investigations agent Will Trent, medical examiner Sara Linton, and their colleagues investigate a series of disturbing murders that may be the work of a serial killer that they missed eight years earlier.*

Principal characters
WILL TRENT, agent with the Georgia Bureau of Investigations (GBI)
SARA LINTON, medical examiner with the GBI, his girlfriend
FAITH MITCHELL, agent with the GBI, his partner
AMANDA WAGNER, deputy director of the GBI, his supervisor
JEFFREY TOLLIVER, chief of police for Grant County; Sara's late husband
LENA ADAMS, detective with the Grant County Police Department
DAN BROCK, county coroner for Grant County
DARYL NESBITT, inmate at Phillips State Prison
REBECCA "BECKEY" CATERINO, college student
GERALD CATERINO, Beckey's father
LESLIE TRUONG, college student

Having established herself as a bestselling author of crime fiction with the 2001 publication of her debut novel *Blindsighted*, Karin Slaughter further built her reputation as a writer over the next two decades, publishing compelling thrillers dealing with disturbing crimes and the dedicated individuals tasked with preventing them. While she published a number of standalone novels during the first two decades of her career, she became best known for the novels that fall within her Grant County series, about several members of law enforcement and their associates in the titular fictional Georgia county, as well as her Will Trent series, which follows the eponymous Georgia Bureau of Investigations (GBI) agent as he conducts investigations in and around the city of Atlanta. Slaughter merged her two series in 2009 with the novel *Undone*, bringing together characters from both and introducing a developing romantic relationship between Will and GBI medical examiner Sara Linton, a former Grant County coroner. Her 2020 novel *The Silent Wife* expands upon that merger, bringing together characters

Karin Slaughter (Courtesy HarperCollins Publishers)

from both series as well as past and present timelines to explore a deeply disturbing but compelling mystery.

The Silent Wife begins with a prologue that follows Beckey Caterino, a college student in Grant County. After fighting with her roommates, who have been eating her food and may have stolen a hair clip of great sentimental importance to her, Beckey decides to go for an early morning run, which initially proceeds without incident. As she runs through a wooded area, however, an unknown man attacks her, knocking her unconscious with a hammer, and the prologue ends. The action then moves eight years into the future and to the Atlanta area, as Will Trent and his partner, Faith Mitchell, travel to a state prison outside of the city. Upon arriving at the prison, the GBI agents and their colleagues, including medical examiner Sara Linton, are tasked with investigating the murder of an inmate during a recent prison riot. Their investigation takes a turn, however, when an inmate named Daryl Nesbitt requests to speak with the agents, claiming to have knowledge about the deceased inmate and a smuggling operation taking place within the prison. Daryl was convicted and sent to prison on charges of possessing child pornography but was also suspected of having attacked Beckey eight years before. However, he insists that he was not guilty, that the former Grant County chief of police framed him for the attack, and that the police had illegally accessed his computer when they found the pornography for which he was imprisoned.

Presenting the agents with a selection of newspaper clippings focused on unexplained deaths of women that had occurred over the previous eight years, Daryl insists that Beckey's attack was the work of a serial killer who is still at large. He refuses to provide information about the smuggling operation at the prison until the agents begin to investigate his claims. The idea of listening to Daryl is an unpleasant one for the agents for several reasons. First of all, they are reluctant to consider the claims of a convicted pedophile, and second, they acknowledge that any investigation into potential misconduct by the Grant County police will quickly become complicated due to the desire of police officers to protect one another.

For Will, however, the situation is particularly troubling on a personal level: the police chief who may have framed Daryl was Jeffrey Tolliver, Sara's late husband, who was murdered five years before the events of the present, and the officer who may have illegally accessed Daryl's computer was Lena Adams, the corner-cutting—or possibly thoroughly corrupt—detective whom Sara blames for Jeffrey's death. Though reluctant to tell Sara about Daryl's claims, Will eventually does so, as he knows that the investigation will need Sara's medical expertise. Further, he and his colleagues will

The Silent Wife / SLAUGHTER 561

need crucial information Sara possesses, as she was the first medical professional to encounter Beckey all those years before.

Over the course of the novel, the narrative alternates between the events taking place in the present and the events of the past, weaving together those two timelines to great effect. Eight years prior to Will's meeting with Daryl, Jeffrey Tolliver arrives at the wooded area where Beckey was attacked and meets with Lena Adams, who responded to the area after a college student named Leslie Truong discovered Beckey's body and called the police. Lena informs Jeffrey that she had verified that Beckey was dead and that she allowed Leslie to walk back to campus without an escort. The police at the scene are soon joined by Sara, who had served as county coroner but had resigned from her position amid her divorce from Jeffrey, who had repeatedly been unfaithful. As the later events in the Atlanta area make clear, the couple remarried at some point in the three-year span between the attack on Beckey and Jeffrey's death. While *The Silent Wife* does not deal extensively with the circumstances surrounding that reunion, Slaughter makes the complicated relationship between the characters and their complex backstories easy to understand, even for readers who are unfamiliar with her earlier novels.

Although Sara is no longer employed as a coroner, she arrives at the crime scene to support current coroner Dan Brock, who is struggling due to the recent death of his father and welcomes her assistance. She quickly realizes that contrary to Lena's findings, Beckey is actually still alive but is struggling to breathe and unable to move. Unable to clear a blockage in the young woman's throat, Sara performs an emergency tracheostomy and, after that fails, performs a more extensive operation while still in the woods, hoping to save Beckey's life. In keeping with Sara's medical training and experience, the scene is both detailed and plausible, though undoubtedly extreme. Indeed, the novel as a whole takes a frank approach to the medical side of the investigation, which also comes to encompass examinations of living rape survivors and autopsies of the attacker's deceased victims. The details about the horrifying ways in which some of the attacker's victims were subdued and mutilated are at times difficult to read, and the novel as a whole is decidedly not for the squeamish. At the same time, though, Slaughter's emphasis on the medical side of the investigation greatly emphasizes Sara's competence and qualifications, and the scene in which Sara performs a field tracheostomy, in particular, highlights the lengths to which she is willing to go to save a life. While Sara is able to help Beckey, who survives the attack but remains partially paralyzed and suffers from severe brain damage, the Grant County police department, and Lena in particular, fail Leslie, who is brutally murdered by the same attacker soon after leaving the crime scene.

Over the next days, Jeffrey works to identify a suspect in the attacks and comes to focus on Daryl, a local drug dealer whose telephone number had been saved in Beckey's phone. The portions of the novel set in Grant County also explore Jeffrey's troubled relationship with Sara as well as his misgivings about Lena, whose willingness to bend the truth and conceal her own mistakes both concern Jeffrey and render Lena a useful tool when laws about searching suspects' homes get in the way of making progress in the investigation. The eventual arrest of Daryl brings Jeffrey's investigation to a close. However, it does not bring the true perpetrator to justice.

Eight years after the attack on Beckey and the murder of Leslie, Will and his colleagues recruit Sara to examine the body of a woman who has recently died under unknown, but apparently accidental, circumstances. Upon examining the woman—one of the individuals Daryl believed to have been murdered by a serial killer—Sara finds that the woman's body displays a small puncture injury just below the C5 vertebrae, which would have damaged her spine and paralyzed her. As Beckey was paralyzed in the same way, the investigators begin to suspect that the same individual committed both crimes. Daryl was in prison at the time of the later murder, and the investigators thus determine that he could not have been the perpetrator, and the true killer must thus still be at large. Throughout the remainder of the narrative, the Atlanta-based investigators work to support the serial-killer theory, examining autopsy photographs and exhumed remains to determine that several other women had been paralyzed in the same way, raped, and killed over the previous eight years. They further identify several additional individuals who were assaulted by the perpetrator in question but managed to escape before being killed, a discovery that sheds light on the attacker's methodology as well as his motivations. Will, Sara, and their colleagues continue to investigate the crimes until the novel's conclusion, when they uncover the true identity of the killer—a truth that shocks everyone involved.

A best seller following its release, *The Silent Wife* received praise from critics, many of whom identified the novel as a strong and fitting addition to Slaughter's Will Trent and Grant County series. The reviewer for *Publishers Weekly* called attention to the novel's complex narrative and multiple timelines and described Slaughter's depiction of the trauma experienced by the characters in the novel as "unflinching" and "deeply empathetic." The critic for *Kirkus* likewise described Slaughter's work as "unflinching" and further wrote that while the novel was more slowly paced than other works by the author, it would nevertheless "rattle [its readers] down to [their] bones." In a thriller-focused review roundup published in the *Guardian*, critic Alison Flood also responded positively to *The Silent Wife*, describing the novel as "sharp and absorbing." She went on to call attention to the book's status as an installment in a long-running series but wrote that Slaughter's skill as a writer made it "perfectly possible" for readers unfamiliar with the author to introduce themselves through *The Silent Wife*.

Author Biography
Karin Slaughter is the author of numerous crime novels, including the works in her Grant County and Will Trent series and the standalone novel *Pieces of Her* (2018).

Joy Crelin

Review Sources

Flood, Alison. "The Best Recent Thrillers—Review Roundup." Review of *The Silent Wife*, by Karin Slaughter. *The Guardian*, 16 June 2020, www.theguardian.com/books/2020/jun/16/the-best-recent-thrillers-review-girl-widow-hills-miranda-other-passenger-candlish-last-wife-hamilton-silent-wife-slaughter. Accessed 15 Feb. 2021.

Review of *The Silent Wife*, by Karin Slaughter. *Kirkus*, 14 July 2020, www.kirkusreviews.com/book-reviews/karin-slaughter/the-silent-wife/. Accessed 15 Feb. 2021.

Review of *The Silent Wife*, by Karin Slaughter. *Publishers Weekly*, 28 Apr. 2020, www.publishersweekly.com/978-0-06-285810-8. Accessed 15 Feb. 2021.

Sisters

Author: Daisy Johnson (b. 1990)
Publisher: Riverhead Books (New York). 224 pp.
Type of work: Novel
Time: Present day
Locale: North York Moors, United Kingdom

Daisy Johnson's sophomore novel, Sisters, *is a gothic thriller set in a crumbling seaside cottage called Settle House. July, September, and their mother, Sheela, have fled their home in Oxford after a mysterious and devastating event. As Sheela, deep in the throes of a depressive episode, nurses her grief and rage, the two teenage sisters with an eerie bond explore the old house and test the boundaries of adulthood.*

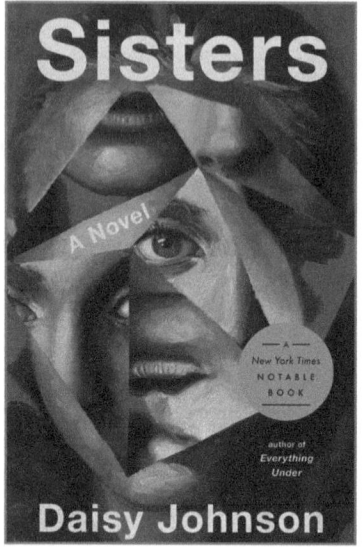

Principal characters
JULY, a teenage girl
SEPTEMBER, her older sister
SHEELA, their mother; a children's book author

It is difficult to categorize *Sisters*, a 2020 book by British novelist and short-story writer Daisy Johnson. Johnson's first novel, *Everything Under* (2018), made her, at twenty-seven, the youngest person to ever be short-listed for the Man Booker Prize. That book is a retelling of Sophocles's *Oedipus Rex*, with a focus on the character of Jocasta—Oedipus's mother and wife—and depicts a mother-daughter story plagued with childhood trauma and fantastical monsters. *Sisters* is wholly different, but just as captivating and strange. It is a psychological thriller with gothic tropes such as an isolated, crumbling old house; an unreliable narrator; and mental deterioration. Several reviewers compared Johnson's sensibility to the writer Shirley Jackson, best known for her haunting 1948 short story about human sacrifice, "The Lottery." Ian Mond, who reviewed *Sisters* for *Locus*, saw parallels to Jackson's 1962 masterpiece *We Have Always Lived in the Castle*, about two exiled sisters living with their uncle in an isolated old house in rural Vermont. Meanwhile, Alex Preston, writing for the *Guardian*, memorably described Johnson as the "demon offspring of Shirley Jackson and Stephen King." Though Johnson has cited King as an influence, that comparison feels less apt. The horror in *Sisters* is more oblique, than, say, King's *The Shining* (1977), which is referenced in *Sisters*. A cloud of unease suffuses *Sisters* from its first line: "My sister is a black hole." The cloud gathers, building toward a climax that reveals not a monster, but a new way of seeing everything that came before.

Much like a black hole, September, the elder sister by ten months, exerts a powerful pull on July, the teenage narrator of *Sisters*. She is the ringleader and the overseer of a bond more common in twins. The girls move as one unit, and even claim to communicate telepathically. "They always seemed to be telling some great secret, some truth only they could know," Johnson writes from the perspective of their mother, Sheela. Their intimacy can be alienating. "The look in their eyes when she came across them, the sudden silence that fell and that she could not quite break into." Sheela frets that her daughters are becoming elusive. In one scene, a memory, Sheela secretly follows the girls after being forbidden from accompanying them trick-or-treating. (They are costumed as the identically dressed sisters from *The Shining*.) An author and illustrator, Sheela sets about writing adventure stories about them to some success. "There they were," Johnson writes of Sheela's stories, "somehow more understandable with pen and paper, made holdable." Perhaps Sheela's frustrated relationship with her daughters springs from her rocky and, later, abusive relationship with their father, Peter. Raising the girls on her own, she falls into long periods of serious depression, unable to leave her bed. She enters such a period as the book begins, though it can be attributed to a specific, yet unnamed event. Something has gone wrong, and July is to blame.

July's indiscretion is presented in fragmented images: a flood, a knife, and a group of July's bullies in a dilapidated shed behind the school. Whatever it was, it has forced the family to flee their home in Oxford and take up residence at Settle House in the North York Moors. The seaside setting is wild; the grass and thornbushes are overgrown and the house's foundation is warped by salt and sand. Johnson imbues Settle House with human-like qualities, suggesting that it is a character with stories and secrets of its own. As it pulls into view in the book's first pages, Johnson describes it as "squatting like a child by the small slate wall." Upon closer inspection: "The white walls of the house are streaked with mud handprints and sag from their wrinkled middles, the top floor sunk down onto the bottom like a hand curved over a fist." Settle House is owned by Peter's sister, Ursa. It has been in his family for generations. Peter was born there, as was September. This information comes as a surprise after the way mother and daughters interact with the house, testing its doors and feeling their way along its walls. After breaking in through a window—the key was not, as Ursa had promised, "under the frog"—July observes the house feels just plain "wrong." In fairness, Settle House has fallen into disrepair. The tiled floor is chipped, and dead insects collect in corners. The yard and interior are strewn with the detritus of previous tenants. The sink is scummy and filled with dishes. It is clear that Ursa, who lives elsewhere, booted the last tenants out in a hurry, one small kindness to Sheela and her girls even though the families are mostly estranged.

Settle House is a mirror of July's cluttered mind. (Both July and Sheela, at different points in the book, describe themselves as a house.) Johnson explores this idea through various images, including closed doors and secret labyrinths. Upon arrival, July accidentally knocks over an ant farm in the living room. Johnson pays particular attention to the tunnels collapsing in on themselves. In another arresting passage, July conjures a miniature version of Settle House, imagining the rooms as the organs of one living being. A tiny version of September inhabits nearly every room. The reader will quickly discern that July is not well. The event at the school has upset her, and her anxiety is only exacerbated by her sister. In many ways, September is July's caretaker; she is her "sleep shadow," tasked with waking her from her frequent night terrors, in which she imagines someone sitting on her chest. September also feeds July. Even if, ever the impatient teenager, she only stabs open a dusty can of peaches, it is a gesture of love. When July suffers from a particularly painful menstrual period, September tends to her body with maternal gentleness. But September is also July's tormentor. Her care for July can be suffocating, and the demands of her love, eclipsing, as when she insists that they merge their birthdays so that they both share her own. Despite their age, they continue to play a game called September Says, a version of Simon Says in which September forces her sister to perform increasingly alarming tasks: "September says cut off your fingernails and put them in milk," "September says eat all the mayonnaise," and "September says put all your clothes in the bin and stand in front of the window." July claims to love the game, but an interaction with a handyman offers a glimpse of her inner turmoil. September steals a cord from the man's bag. When he questions them, July feels forced to play along. From July's perspective, Johnson writes, "He blinks at me, pleadingly. I say nothing. He doesn't understand. What does he want me to say?"

Age is slippery in *Sisters*. July and September act young for their age, their behavior more fitting for children than teenagers. Their relative innocence emphasizes Johnson's interest in their coming of age. July is particularly vulnerable in an adult world. Shy and reclusive, she is unpopular in school. When she is tricked into sharing naked photos of herself, the fallout is devastating. The incident is one of many that focuses on the girls' bodies. Johnson writes about September and July's bodies in incredible detail, capturing the distinctly teenage sensation of feeling alienated from one's physical self. July wishes she felt as comfortable in her skin as her sister. "I will always think that September's body makes more sense than my own," July thinks. The two share a kind of intimacy particular to young women, not quite sexual but intense and curious. They frequently bathe together, and July fixates on a long black hair sprouting from September's collarbone "that I want badly to pluck out but that she says she is growing forever." They are also possessive of each other's bodies. When September has sex for the first time—at a party on the beach, that July is also at—July cannot help but feel betrayed. As the same time, however, July is convinced that she feels the sensations in her own body.

For all that they share, the girls do not look alike. September, with her fair skin and hair, takes after their Danish father, Peter. July takes after Sheela. July and September did not really know their father—he died when the girls were still children after he and Sheela had separated. In the book, he exists in Sheela's memory, and in a pair of binoculars September finds in their bedroom. He also exists in September. (The cover of the book is the shattered image of a girl's face, rearranged over what appears to be the face of an adult man.) Sheela notes unsettling similarities between the two, going as far as to say, "The way September was with July sometimes reminded her of how Peter had been with her: his withholding of love for tactical advantage, the control concealed within silky folds of care." *Sisters* is a careful exploration of abuse, but Johnson's reasoning here is a little too pat. Abusive behavior is not genetic; more often abusers are victims of abuse themselves. September is a fully formed character, but the suggestion that she simply inherited her father's sadism makes her seem alien, a rote "bad guy." Though irksome, this is a small complaint in terms of the novel as a whole.

Sisters combines genre tropes and haunting poetry. Despite small complaints, most critics commended Johnson for her eerie story. As Harriet Lane explained for the *New York Times*, "*Sisters* is a gripping ordeal, a relentlessly macabre account of grief and guilt, identity and codependency, teenage girls and their mothers." Some critics gave special attention to her imaginative prose. *Publishers Weekly* called it "achingly lyrical prose," while Mond stated, "Johnson's impressionistic style leans heavily on imagery rather than detail, often twisting the ordinary and mundane out of shape." Overall, critics agreed that *Sisters* is shattering, surprising, and surreal.

Author Biography

Daisy Johnson's debut novel, *Everything Under*, was short-listed for the Man Booker Prize in 2018. She is also the author of *Fen*, a 2017 collection of short stories.

Molly Hagan

Review Sources

Lane, Harriet. "'Sisters' Builds a Gothic Plot to an Artful and Shocking Climax." Review of *Sisters*, by Daisy Johnson. *The New York Times*, 25 Aug. 2020, www.nytimes.com/2020/08/25/books/review/sisters-daisy-johnson.html. Accessed 29 Jan. 2021.

Mond, Ian. "Ian Mond Reviews *Sisters* by Daisy Johnson." Review of *Sisters*, by Daisy Johnson. *Locus*, 27 Aug. 2020, locusmag.com/2020/08/ian-mond-reviews-sisters-by-daisy-johnson. Accessed 29 Jan. 2021.

Preston, Alex. "*Sisters* by Daisy Johnson Review—Complex and Chilling." Review of *Sisters*, by Daisy Johnson. *The Guardian*, 24 Aug. 2020, www.theguardian.com/books/2020/aug/24/sisters-by-daisy-johnson-review-complex-and-chilling. Accessed 29 Jan. 2021.

Review of *Sisters*, by Daisy Johnson. *Kirkus*, 3 June 2020, www.kirkusreviews.com/book-reviews/daisy-johnson/sisters-johnson. Accessed 29 Jan. 2021.

Review of *Sisters*, by Daisy Johnson. *Publishers Weekly*, 18 May 2020, www.publishersweekly.com/978-0-59-318895-8. Accessed 29 Jan. 2021.

The Smallest Lights in the Universe

Author: Sara Seager (b. 1971)
Publisher: Crown (New York). 320 pp.
Type of work: Memoir
Time: 1980s–the present
Locales: Toronto; Boston; Cambridge, Massachusetts; Concord, Massachusetts

The Smallest Lights in the Universe is a memoir by astrophysicist Sara Seager that reflects on her search for habitable exoplanets as well as her journey through grief.

Principal personages

SARA SEAGER, the author, a Canadian-born astrophysicist and Massachusetts Institute of Technology (MIT) professor whose research focuses on the search for and study of exoplanets

MIKE WEVRICK, her first husband; an avid outdoorsman who dies of cancer

MELISSA, a woman who introduces Sara to a local group for widows and becomes her best friend

CHARLES DARROW, an amateur astronomer who makes Sara believe that she can love again

MAX, Sara's eldest son who has blue eyes like his father and likes tennis

ALEX, Sara's youngest son who becomes a hiking enthusiast at a young age

Most memoirs only look backward. They are, after all, intended to be collections of carefully curated memories that, when put together, provide readers with a better understanding of who the author is. While Sara Seager's memoir *The Smallest Lights in the Universe* (2020) does satisfy that definition, it is also quite unusual in how much its content seems to look to the future. This is largely because Seager is an astrophysicist and planetary scientist whose work focuses on finding habitable planets at the farthest corners of the known galaxy. Throughout the memoir, she reflects on her groundbreaking discoveries and the new technologies she helped develop that ultimately pushed humankind closer to a reality that includes alien life. As such, reading its pages often feels like getting a front row seat to what the field of astronomy will offer the world in the years to come.

And yet *The Smallest Lights in the Universe* is far from a dry work of nonfiction. In part this is because Seager, a tenured professor at MIT, is adept at not only breaking down complex ideas but also explaining them in an accessible, fascinating way. Beyond this, however, it can be argued that the memoir never feels overtly esoteric because Seager balances descriptions of her professional accomplishments with something extremely personal: the story of losing her first husband, Mike. It is thanks to this extremely honest narrative about loss that *The Smallest Lights in the Universe* has a compelling emotional pulse. The end result is a book that not only gives readers a better understanding of what it means to work in astronomy today, but also a firsthand look at the complexities of grief.

Although *The Smallest Lights in the Universe* consists of several familiar autobiographical beats, Seager does not overwhelm the memoir's earliest chapters with a deluge of childhood nostalgia. Instead, she offers the broad strokes of her origin story—just enough context for her audience to understand how she came to be who she is as an adult. Perhaps one of the most fascinating pieces of personal information that she introduces to readers at this time is her feeling of "otherness." From the time she was a child, Seager felt that she was somehow different as a result of the fact that she struggled to connect with other people. She simply saw the world through a different lens—advanced math and science came easy to her, but making friends did not. While having such a mind enabled her to become a gifted astronomer, it also often made her feel alienated. Seager never dwells on any specific moments of social alienation for too long but does make note of them. In turn, the individuals she encounters who do really understand her come across as small miracles.

Sara Seager

It is these miraculous people that anchor the memoir and give it a kind of chronological framework as Seager moves through the major chapters of her life. The most formative figure of her early years is her father, a physician who proves to be one of the only bright lights in her childhood. Later, it is her husband, Mike, who succeeds in making her feel special and loved as she earns her doctorate, launches her career, and becomes a mother. After she loses both her father and Mike to cancer in quick succession, Seager becomes overwhelmed with grief and struggles to function in her everyday life. It is only when she meets an amazing woman named Melissa, who welcomes her into a local group for widows in Concord, Massachusetts, that she is slowly able to move forward. Despite much of the book being focused on the hunt for life on other planets, *The Smallest Lights in the Universe* is ultimately about the importance of connecting with other people on Earth.

A large part of what makes Seager's memoir so powerful is the way in which she explores the pain of losing a loved one. Much of the book is spent on the first few years following Mike's death, when Seager was first navigating the rocky terrain of grief. Here, she is unwavering in the way that she details young widowhood. Some of the most rewarding passages are those in which she reflects on her darkest days, the ones where she felt self-pity or anger toward anyone who seemed to have a "perfect" life.

Her documentation of all the unexpected emotions and experiences that she endured after losing Mike reads almost like a captain's log. In turn, it becomes a map for those who might be going through something similar and are in need of guidance. In this way, *The Smallest Lights in the Universe* is a welcome addition to the somewhat limited canon of grief literature. While there are many practical guides to surviving the loss of loved ones written by psychiatrists, there is a surprising dearth of well-written firsthand accounts. One of the few truly noteworthy books that feels comparable to Seager's is Joan Didion's *The Year of Magical Thinking* (2005).

In interviews, Seager has stated that the primary theme of *The Smallest Lights in the Universe* is exploration. Ostensibly, this theme is most evident in the story line of her career, which follows her contributions to peoples' understanding of exoplanets and to the technologies that have enabled astronomers to determine whether or not life could exist on those planets. The way in which she describes her work is clear and exciting; indeed, readers are provided with the satisfying feeling that they are along for a ride with an intrepid pioneer who is pursuing answers to the universe's biggest questions. While this type of exploration is important to the narrative, the personal exploration that Seager undergoes plays an even larger role in the book. It can be argued that at its core, this is a story about someone having to probe into an untapped part of themselves as they rediscover who they are in the wake of a tragedy. Without Mike, Seager is forced to push herself into new aspects of life like domestic duties and friendships. In the process, she experiences unprecedented emotional growth.

One of the greatest pleasures of reading *The Smallest Lights in the Universe* is being able to spend time examining the world through its author's unique perspective. There are too few books written by female scientists about their experiences. Seager's memoir is important not just because it is another step toward filling this gap but because she is willing to provide readers with a complete picture of what it means to be a woman in science. Furthermore, Seager demonstrates that being a scientific genius and emotionally vulnerable are not mutually exclusive. It should also be noted that she provides her audience with a firsthand look of what it is like to be an autistic woman in the world today. Like many autistic women, Seager was not diagnosed until much later in life. Learning about this part of herself helped her finally understand the "otherness" that she had felt since she was a child.

While somewhat limited, critical reception of *The Smallest Lights in the Universe* was positive. *Kirkus* concluded that it was a "singular" story written by a "singular scientist." Other critics focused on the quality of the book's writing. In his review for the *New York Times*, Anthony Doerr commended Seager for her prose, which he described as being "full of blues and blacks, written in the ink of grief, suffering, healing and—ultimately—clarity." It is true that one of the most enjoyable aspects of *The Smallest Lights in the Universe* is the quality of the writing, which *Publishers Weekly*, in a starred review, called "openhearted" as well as "clean and exact." Seager is not just an analytical mind capable of advanced computation and abstract thought—she is also an exceptional storyteller with a poetic talent for capturing what it means to be human. Readers do not need an understanding of astrophysics or to have lost a loved one to connect to the memoir. One of its biggest strengths is how accessible Seager makes the unusual events of her life feel.

While *The Smallest Lights in the Universe* has very few flaws to make note of, there is a chance that some readers who are enduring their own personal grief might feel frustrated rather than comforted by Seager's experiences. Seager is a world-renowned scientist working at one of the top universities in the world. As such, she has had opportunities that many other people in different socioeconomic groups do not. When she is struggling to balance taking care of her sons, Max and Alex, and work, for example, she considers quitting her job at MIT. Once her boss hears this, he offers to pay her as much as she needs to hire a housekeeper. Additionally, she has the ability to hire babysitters and have graduate students stay in her spare bedrooms in exchange for helping with domestic duties. In these ways, Seager is extraordinarily fortunate. Some readers who are struggling after loss and not as lucky may subsequently find her story to be alienating.

It is likely, however, that an even greater number of readers will find *The Smallest Lights in the Universe* to be hopeful. In many ways, Seager's memoir is a celebration of kindness and how, in the darkest moments of life, other people can come through in extraordinary ways. Through her story, Seager demonstrates that grief does get easier over time and that life can still bring joy even after the death of a loved one. Ultimately, it is a beautifully written and gripping memoir that will provide people with a new understanding of what constitutes life—both here on Earth and on planets that are lightyears away.

Author Biography

Sara Seager, an astrophysicist and planetary scientist, became a member of the faculty at MIT in 2007. For her groundbreaking research on exoplanets, she was the recipient of, among other honors, a 2012 Sackler Prize and a 2013 MacArthur Fellowship.

Emily E. Turner

Review Sources

Doerr, Anthony. "These Books Transport You to a Galaxy Far, Far Away." Review of *The Smallest Lights in the Universe*, by Sara Seager, and *The Sirens of Mars*, by Sarah Stewart Johnson. *The New York Times*, 18 Aug. 2020, www.nytimes.com/2020/08/18/books/review/smallest-lights-in-universe-sara-seager.html. Accessed 8 Dec. 2020.

Review of *The Smallest Lights in the Universe*, by Sara Seager. *Kirkus*, 30 Apr. 2020, www.kirkusreviews.com/book-reviews/sara-seager/the-smallest-lights-in-the-universe. Accessed 8 Dec. 2020.

Review of *The Smallest Lights in the Universe*, by Sara Seager. *Publishers Weekly*, 10 Feb. 2020, www.publishersweekly.com/978-0-525-57625-9. Accessed 8 Dec. 2020.

Some Assembly Required
Decoding Four Billion Years of Life, from Ancient Fossils to DNA

Author: Neil Shubin (b. 1960)
Publisher: Pantheon (New York). 288 pp.
Type of work: Science, history of science
Time: Four billion years ago to the present day
Locale: Earth

In Some Assembly Required: Decoding Four Billion Years of Life, from Ancient Fossils to DNA, *paleontologist and evolutionary biologist Neil Shubin describes the development of scientific understanding of evolution, genetics, DNA, and the genomes of various forms of life, including human life.*

Principal personages

CHARLES DARWIN, a British naturalist who was a pioneer in developing the theory of evolution

RAY LANKESTER, a British zoologist and evolutionary theorist

CALVIN BRIDGES, an American geneticist known for his work on fruit flies and heredity

FRANÇOIS JACOB, a French scientist known for his work on enzyme level control in cells

LYNN MARGULIS, an American biologist noted for her interest in the role of symbiosis in evolution

BARBARA MCCLINTOCK, a Nobel Prize–winning American cytogeneticist

ST. GEORGE JACKSON MIVART, a British biologist and critic of the theory of natural selection

SUSUMU OHNO, a geneticist of Japanese descent noted for his work on molecular evolution

DAVID BURTON WAKE, an American scientist known for his contributions to integrative biology

Paleontologist and evolutionary biologist Neil Shubin was eminently qualified to write his 2020 book *Some Assembly Required: Decoding Four Billion Years of Life, from Ancient Fossils to DNA*. While studying and training at Columbia University, Harvard University, and the University of California, Berkeley, he quickly distinguished himself as an up-and-coming scientist with an especially strong interest in paleontology and evolutionary biology. His career has since involved important discoveries, such as unearthing fossils of a long-extinct creature resembling both a fish and a crocodile.

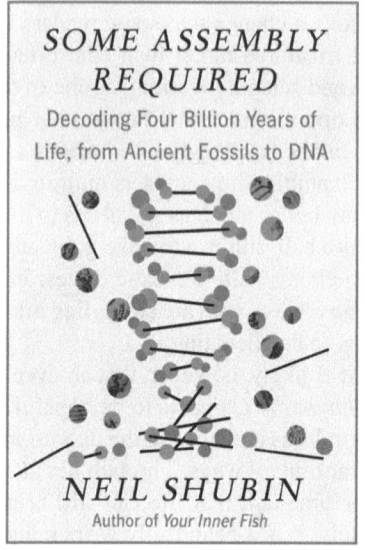

At the same time, Shubin has also revealed talent for other kinds of significant research, particularly in the lab. His career has additionally exemplified his growing gift for explaining science to nonscientists in well-received books such as *Your Inner Fish: A Journey into the 3.5-Billion-Year History of the Human Body* (2008) and *The Universe Within: Discovering the Common History of Rocks, Planets, and People* (2013). A popular lecturer and television interviewee, Shubin was teaching and conducting research at the University of Chicago and serving as a major administrator of that city's famed Field Museum of Natural History by the time of the book's publication. He has been elected to various important scientific societies and has received assorted prizes for his skills as a writer who tries to make scientific concepts accessible to a general readership.

Neil Shubin

Early in *Some Assembly Required*, Shubin writes that he has been running a kind of "split-brain laboratory, spending summers in the field looking for fossils and working the rest of the year with embryos and DNA." Both approaches, he says, can help scientists answer a significant question about how major changes in the history of life occur. *Some Assembly Required* is especially interesting because of this double focus: it would be intriguing enough if it dealt merely with the fossil record, but it is particularly compelling when it recounts the development of cutting-edge techniques for studying the inner workings of living cells. Shubin notes that the kind of genome sequencing that once took years of time and billions of dollars to perform can "now be completed in an afternoon for under one thousand dollars." When the famous Human Genome Project initially achieved its goals, the results were understandably seen as astonishingly important news. Now, genomes of various creatures are mapped all the time and attract hardly any attention. Yet each new sequence adds to a better comprehension of the history and evolution of life on Earth.

Shubin has had the good fortune not only to live during one of the most exciting periods in the history of science but also to have made his own important contributions to a true revolution in human understanding. Two more reasons, then, that his book is so well worth reading. He takes readers not only out into the fossil fields but deep inside the inner workings of cells, molecules, and other tiny bits of life, and it is in his discussion of these latter aspects that his writing becomes especially fascinating. Besides focusing on science itself, Shubin combines equally strong interests in history and biography, even adding some touches of autobiography as he recounts his own movement from one stage to another of his career and reports his personal encounters with various major figures.

Of all the many influential figures Shubin describes, Charles Darwin, of course, looms largest. But Shubin also depicts many other significant, but often lesser-known, people from the nineteenth century to the present day. These scientists, either intentionally or by sheer happenstance and luck, made important discoveries about biology, chemistry, and the intersections between the two. Shubin never lets readers forget the human dimensions of the people he describes (such as the philandering major researcher with an impressive head of hair whom, he notes, died tragically early from syphilis), and he also strongly emphasizes the important contributions of women, who often had to deal with incredible prejudice and unjust restrictions, in the field of science. Shubin's book is dotted with photographs of key figures, but the photos themselves are often less interesting than the word pictures he creates in readers' minds when discussing the ways scientists work both as individuals and as groups—sometimes cooperating, sometimes competing, but often, in both ways, advancing the larger cause of discovering truth.

The people he depicts often spent decades working on topics that can at first sound arcane and trivial to nonspecialists—such as the minute biology of obscure worms or specific kinds of salamanders—but that ultimately resulted in breakthroughs with major implications for the foundational understanding of life. One comes away from Shubin's book feeling great gratitude for scientists and for the institutions and societies that encourage and fund their work. One need only view the photo of the men who nearly died in the Antarctic while collecting penguin eggs to inspire an even greater appreciation of how fortunate humanity is to have people willing to take such huge risks for such seemingly insignificant reasons—reasons that eventually prove very significant indeed.

As Shubin moves through the history of evolution and biological science from the times of Darwin to the present day, he also moves through a series of improved understandings of how and why life on this planet developed as it did. He notes, for instance, that evolution often involved not the development of new organs but changes in the functions of organs that already existed. Thus, in fish, swim bladders became repurposed as lungs. As Shubin writes, "Air sacs shifted from being used for life in water to later enabling creatures to live and breathe on land." In explaining this concept, as in explaining so many others, he provides many useful drawings that make it much easier for readers to visualize the matters he explores. These drawings, in turn, are often juxtaposed with photographs; the drawings facilitate the interpretation of the photos, as when a drawing helps illuminate the details of the photographed fossil of a feathered dinosaur. Additionally, the photo and drawing are accompanied by two of Shubin's own characteristically affecting and elucidating sentences: "The more we look, the more we see that the anatomical inventions that birds use to fly, such as feathers, are not unique to them. Carnivorous dinosaurs get successively more birdlike over time." Usually, Shubin argues, evolution does not involve some relatively sudden innovation in an organism. Instead, evolution usually results from the transformation of some anatomical feature that already existed but begins to serve a new function.

This book, like many books about science written for lay readers, inevitably describes various false starts or blind alleys in the development of scientific understanding.

But Shubin does not, as some authors do, take readers all the way through a chapter only to reveal, at the very end, that all the claims the chapter presented were proved wrong. The pace of the book is relatively quick, and its length is thus reasonable: readers need not wade through an eight-hundred-page tome to get, finally, to some brief explanations of the current scientific consensus. Nor does Shubin waste readers' time with forced cleverness, as some writers do. Nor, thirdly, does he devote an excessive amount of time and space to writing about himself. The autobiographical portions are pertinent touches merely, not indulged in for their own sakes.

By the time readers put down *Some Assembly Required*, which critics also largely praised as both informative and intriguing, they will have learned about a variety of fascinating facts and theories. These include the finding that cells can migrate between different layers of an embryo; enormous consequences can result from even one tiny difference in a bit of DNA; and there are incredibly close genetic similarities between humans and chimpanzees. He also incorporates the interesting story of the discovery of the so-called molecular clock. Other intriguing revelations found in Shubin's book concern the greater genetic complexity of certain plants as compared to most animals, the relative scarcity of genes themselves in genomes, the crucial importance of the various "switches" that control how genes and proteins function, and the importance of various kinds of timing in embryonic development in particular. All these factors help explain not only why some individuals can differ so much from one another, but also how and why evolution can occur over the long, long term. One gene, for instance, played an outsized role in the relatively rapid expansion of the human brain over the last three million years. In one of the most interesting of his discussions, Shubin explains how an infectious virus from the vastly distant past was "tamed" by the body and came to play a key role in the healthy development of embryos. Again and again, Shubin reveals details of the sheer complexity of life on this planet that will leave most readers not only astonished by these facts but also enormously grateful for the science —and scientists—responsible for the facts' discovery.

Author Biography

Neil Shubin is a paleontologist, evolutionary biologist, and writer affiliated with the University of Chicago and with Chicago's Field Museum. He has won several awards in recognition of his work.

Robert C. Evans, PhD

Review Sources

Goldman, Michael A. "Engaging Anecdotes Add Intimacy to Tales of Earth's 4 Billion Years of Evolution." Review of *Some Assembly Required: Decoding Four Billion Years of Life, from Ancient Fossils to DNA*, by Neil Shubin. *Science*, 23 Mar. 2020, blogs.sciencemag.org/books/2020/03/23/some-assembly-required. Accessed 13 Oct. 2020.

Levitin, Daniel J. "'Some Assembly Required' Review: How Nature Finds a Way." Review of *Some Assembly Required: Decoding Four Billion Years of Life, from Ancient Fossils to DNA*, by Neil Shubin. *The Wall Street Journal*, 27 Mar. 2020, www.wsj.com/articles/some-assembly-required-review-how-nature-finds-a-way-11585346924. Accessed 13 Oct. 2020.

Nichter, Caren. Review of *Some Assembly Required: Decoding Four Billion Years of Life, from Ancient Fossils to DNA*, by Neil Shubin. *Library Journal*, 1 Jan. 2020, www.libraryjournal.com/?reviewDetail=some-assembly-required-decoding-four-billion-years-of-life-from-ancient-fossils-to-dna. Accessed 13 Oct. 2020.

Review of *Some Assembly Required: Decoding Four Billion Years of Life, from Ancient Fossils to DNA*, by Neil Shubin. *Kirkus*, 11 Nov. 2019, www.kirkusreviews.com/book-reviews/neil-shubin/some-assembly-required-shubin. Accessed 13 Oct. 2020.

Review of *Some Assembly Required: Decoding Four Billion Years of Life, from Ancient Fossils to DNA*, by Neil Shubin. *Publishers Weekly*, 11 Oct. 2019, www.publishersweekly.com/978-1-101-87133-1. Accessed 13 Oct. 2020.

The Southern Book Club's Guide to Slaying Vampires

Author: Grady Hendrix (b. ca. 1972)
Publisher: Quirk Books (Philadelphia). 408 pp.
Type of work: Novel
Time: November 1988–December 1999
Locales: Mt. Pleasant and Charleston, South Carolina

The Southern Book Club's Guide to Slaying Vampires *follows Patricia Campbell, who, in the midst of a changing life, where she feels unneeded by her husband and growing children, is accused of building a fiction around a new neighbor. Nonetheless, with the help of her closest friends, she sets out to defend family and community and takes on the dangers of an unknown entity that attempts to destroy everything she has built.*

Principal characters
PATRICIA CAMPBELL, a homemaker and former nurse
SLICK PALEY, her religious and conservative friend
KITTY SCRUGGS, her irreverent and witty friend
GRACE CAVANAUGH, her socially uptight and organized friend
MARYELLEN, another of her book-club friends
MISS MARY, her mother-in-law, who is developing dementia
MRS. GREENE, a caregiver for her mother-in-law
JAMES HARRIS, a handsome and mysterious new neighbor whom she believes is a vampire

Grady Hendrix opens *The Southern Book Club's Guide to Slaying Vampires* with an author's note telling readers that he wanted to write a book about the strength of parents, mothers specifically. He says, "I wanted to pit a man freed from all responsibilities but his appetites against women whose lives are shaped by their endless responsibilities. I wanted to pit Dracula against my mom. As you'll see, it's not a fair fight." Thus begins the tale of a woman who refuses to ignore a situation that would put her family and her friends in mortal peril, even when she is threatened physically, emotionally, mentally, and socially.

The novel is loosely based around the idea of a book club, but Hendrix mocks the traditional expectations that a book club should focus on the literary canon or on contemporary books that people say they have read even when they have not. The idea of that kind of club is illustrated in Marjorie Fretwell's Literary Guild of Mt. Pleasant, which Patricia had joined with the idea that it would give her socially acceptable time outside of the house. As the novel begins, Patricia is panicking over leading the discussion over *Cry, the Beloved Country* (1948) by Alan Paton. While Marjorie has found Paton's novel to be stimulating, she is shocked to find that none of the members of her club, including Patricia, has read it. Because they hate the pieces Marjorie picks, two other women, Kitty and Maryellen, decide to start their own book club. Though Patricia is hesitant, already overwhelmed with the busyness of her life, Kitty's friendliness entices her, and the new book is tempting. Kitty tells her their choice, *Evidence of Love: A True Story of Passion and Death in the Suburbs* (1983), "has passion, love, hate, romance, violence, excitement. It's just like Thomas Hardy, only in paperback and with eight pages of photos in the middle." The book, like Kitty, pulls Patricia into a group of women who will fight to protect each other no matter what happens.

Grady Hendrix

Hendrix continues to play with the idea of books throughout the novel, naming many sections after real-life books that Patricia's new group is reading. Often, those books parallel something happening in the text as well. For instance, the third section of the novel, titled "The Bridges of Madison County," takes place in June 1993—the year after the forbidden-romance novel of that name was published in real life—and introduces James Harris, the grandnephew of a recently deceased neighbor, to the group of women. The women's discussion of the novel takes a hilarious turn when Kitty claims the main male character is "clearly a serial killer" who "doesn't have any family ties, no roots, no past . . . He doesn't even belong to a church." Unsurprisingly, this description also fits James Harris. The women's penchant for choosing true crime books, like Vincent Bugliosi and Curt Gentry's *Helter Skelter: The True Story of the Manson Murders* (1974) and Ann Rule's *The Stranger beside Me: The Shocking Inside Story of Serial Killer Ted Bundy* (1980), or mystery novels like Tom Clancy's *Clear and Present Danger* (1989), leads them to conclusions that cause problems in their marriages and almost destroy their friendship.

The problems begin when Patricia meets James Harris. The first time James comes to Patricia's home, Miss Mary, Patricia's mother-in-law, calls him Hoyt Pickens and has a startling reaction. Her conviction that Harris is Hoyt Pickens, a man she knew as a child, sends the novel more strongly into a supernatural direction. (This supernatural element began earlier when Patricia was attacked in her own backyard by Harris's great aunt, who was gobbling the carcass of a raccoon.) As disturbing as this event is, Patricia tries to put it behind her. However, Harris's odd behavior sets her off on a search for answers, which, amusingly, she searches for in novels about vampires, including classics of the genre such as Anne Rice's *Interview with the Vampire* (1976). When Miss Mary later, in a moment of lucidity, tells Patricia about her childhood connection to this Hoyt Pickens, Patricia's suspicions grow. Miss Mary's rediscovery of an old picture of Pickens and her mysterious and disturbing death further solidify Patricia's desire to identify the man as a predator, which becomes the unifying element throughout the rest of the novel.

Although the supernatural becomes a constant background motif, common themes of so-called women's literature, such as friendships between women and familial relations, become major factors in the novel as well. Patricia's life is overwhelmingly busy with raising her children, catering to her husband, and caring for her ailing mother-in-law, although those on the outside often see women like her as "lightweights." Sharing burdens and everyday duties with each other illuminates the inside view of the women's lives, building their personalities in often humorous but sometimes depressing ways. Kitty is often the center of the humor, and her light-hearted sarcasm gives the other women a chance to laugh at themselves and each other. Slick, on the other hand, is usually more serious, but the need to belong leads her to lie to her deeply religious husband about the book club, telling him that she is attending a Bible study. Grace is the organizer; her life seems to have everything in place but belies the power her husband wields over her. Patricia's marriage is, on the surface, the most stable, but her psychiatrist husband works all the time and analyzes his family when he is home. Being together gives the women an escape from their relationships with men, allowing them to laugh, to scheme, and to share in each other's lives. Their loyalty to each other is showcased several times, particularly when members of the group become the victims of bizarre and violent encounters.

The reality is that friendships are not perfect and often run into bumps. While Patricia realizes almost immediately that the strange disappearances of Black children are connected to the new neighbor and builds her case against Harris, he ingratiates himself with the other women and their families, investing in the housing development the husbands began. They begin to rake in money, but Patricia remains suspicious of Harris and convinces her friends that he is dangerous. When their husbands find out that they believe Harris is a monster, the men threaten their wives and tear the book club apart. The women struggle with the repercussions and withdraw from their friend to protect their own interests.

True to his opening, Hendrix also explores the challenges of motherhood, primarily through Patricia and her growing children, Korey and Blue. Korey's teenage angst challenges Patricia's patience, while Blue, her son, is fascinated with World War II and the Nazis, which Harris uses to connect with the boy but which worries his mother. Maryellen provides a touch of honest humor, telling Patricia, "No one likes their children . . . We love them to death, but we don't like them." Slick unwittingly adds to the humor by telling her friends that she makes sixty sandwiches "on the first Monday of the month, freeze them, and every morning I pull one out of the freezer and pop it in their bag." Ultimately, though, Hendrix demonstrates the women love their children and are willing to do anything for them. On the surface these women might seem weak, controlled by the men in their lives and the social expectations they attempt to fulfill in the choices they make, but they prove their mettle with a scheme to remove the threat of a monster not only from their community but from the world.

Several racial issues are also introduced, though these are less fully developed than the book's feminist strands. After Miss Mary's death, Patricia pursues a social obligation to visit Mrs. Greene, which allows Hendrix to contrast Patricia's White upper-class suburb and the rundown area where Mrs. Greene and the local Black community live, with its pothole-pocked roads. Later in the novel, Harris and the women's husbands drive out much of the Black community as they claim the land for their housing development. More relevant, however, is the inadequate police protection for the members of the area. Mrs. Greene tells Patricia that children have been disappearing and dying, but no one believes the parents or cares enough to find out. Though Patricia, devastated by the stories Mrs. Greene shares, tries to convince her friends that all children are worth their attention, it is the threat against Patricia's own White children and friends that motivates them to take a stand at last.

Reviews of the novel were primarily positive, with multiple venues awarding it starred reviews. One from *Publishers Weekly* noted, for example, "This powerful, eclectic novel both pays homage to the literary vampire canon and stands singularly within it." Becky Spratford, in her starred *Booklist* review, also commented on the novel's place in literature, calling it "the perfect mix of *American Housewife*, by Helen Ellis (2016); Ann Rule's true crime classic, *The Stranger beside Me* (1980); and Dacre Stoker and J. D. Barker's *Dracul* (2018)—and a cheeky, spot-on pick for book clubs." The reviewer for *Kirkus* deemed it Hendrix's "best book yet." Several reviewers cited Hendrix's unique blend of humor and horror as a particular draw.

Author Biography
Grady Hendrix is a speculative-fiction novelist, short-story writer, entertainment critic, and screenwriter. His book *Paperbacks from Hell: The Twisted History of '70s and '80s Horror Fiction* won the 2017 Bram Stoker Award for Non-Fiction. His earlier novels include *Horrorstör* (2014), *My Best Friend's Exorcism* (2016), and *We Sold Our Souls* (2018).

Theresa L. Stowell, PhD

Review Sources
Leache, Kathryn Justice. Review of *The Southern Book Club's Guide to Slaying Vampires*, by Grady Hendrix. *BookPage*, Apr. 2020, pp. 19–20. *Complementary Index*, search.ebscohost.com/login.aspx?direct=true&db=edb&AN=142079790&site=eds-live. Accessed 16 Oct. 2020.

Planchard, Durin. Review of *The Southern Book Club's Guide to Slaying Vampires*, by Grady Hendrix. *Deep South Magazine*, Oct. 2020, deepsouthmag.com/2020/10/02/review-of-the-southern-book-clubs-guide-to-slaying-vampires. Accessed 16 Oct. 2020.

Spratford, Becky. Review of *The Southern Book Club's Guide to Slaying Vampires*, by Grady Hendrix. *Booklist*, vol. 116, no. 12, Feb. 2020, p. 43. *Literary Reference Center Plus*, search.ebscohost.com/login.aspx?direct=true&db=lkh&AN=141839083&site=eds-live. Accessed 16 Oct. 2020.

Review of *The Southern Book Club's Guide to Slaying Vampires*, by Grady Hendrix. *Kirkus Reviews*, vol. 88, no. 3, Feb. 2020. *Literary Reference Center Plus*, search.ebscohost.com/login.aspx?direct=true&db=lkh&AN=141439311&site=eds-live. Accessed 16 Oct. 2020.

Review of *The Southern Book Club's Guide to Slaying Vampires*, by Grady Hendrix. *Publishers Weekly*, vol. 267, no. 1, Jan. 2020, p. 27. *Literary Reference Center Plus*, search.ebscohost.com/login.aspx?direct=true&db=lkh&AN=141038620&site=eds-live. Accessed 16 Oct. 2020.

Thorlakson, Linda. Review of *The Southern Book Club's Guide to Slaying Vampires*, by Grady Hendrix. *ForeWord Reviews*, vol. 23, no. 2, Mar.–Apr. 2020, p. 50. *Literary Reference Center Plus*, search.ebscohost.com/login.aspx?direct=true&db=lkh&AN=141707958&site=eds-live. Accessed 16 Oct. 2020.

The Splendid and the Vile
A Saga of Churchill, Family, and Defiance during the Blitz

Author: Erik Larson (b. 1954)
Publisher: Crown (New York). 608 pp.
Type of work: History, biography
Time: May 1940 to May 1941
Locale: Great Britain

The Splendid and the Vile *presents a gripping profile of British prime minister Winston Churchill and members of his intimate circle during the intense World War II bombing known as the Blitz.*

Principal personages
WINSTON CHURCHILL, prime minister of the United Kingdom
CLEMENTINE CHURCHILL, his wife
MARY CHURCHILL, his adolescent daughter
RANDOLPH CHURCHILL, his son
PAMELA CHURCHILL, his daughter-in-law
W. AVERELL HARRIMAN, an American special envoy, his daughter-in-law's lover
JOHN "JOCK" COLVILLE, his private secretary, who kept a detailed diary
FREDERICK LINDEMANN, his chief science adviser
LORD BEAVERBROOK, his friend, minister of aircraft production
HASTINGS "PUG" ISMAY, his military assistant
FRANKLIN DELANO ROOSEVELT, his eventual ally, the US president
HARRY HOPKINS, an American emissary from Roosevelt to him

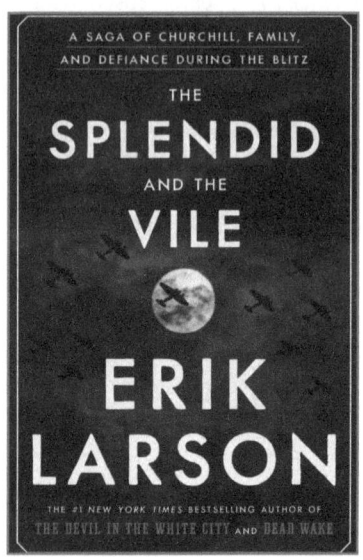

In chapter 93 of *The Splendid and the Vile: A Saga of Churchill, Family, and Defiance During the Blitz*, entitled "Of Panzers and Pansies," author Eric Larson alternates between two unlikely narratives. While British prime minister Winston Churchill is subjected on May 6, 1941, to Parliament's withering criticism of his handling of World War II, his eighteen-year-old daughter, Mary, dithers about a suitor in her diary. It could be an almost comic contrast: the bombastic politician facing down his detractors at a monumental point in his nation's history while a young woman earlier described as "so naïve that it hurts" wonders if she is in love. By this point in this masterful work, however, it is clear that this kind of duality is central to Larson's fascinating take on an already well-covered slice of history. Not only does his story hang on the splendid and the vile (embodied Churchill and Adolf Hitler, respectively), but on the grand and the ordinary. Mary's struggle to make a choice that she will not regret highlights the broad range of voices and stories that made up the British experience during the Blitz, perhaps the most trying time in the nation's history. Though Mary was not an ordinary person by any stretch, Larson's inclusion of her voice and those of a cross-section of other Britons adds depth and nuance to what could otherwise have been a standard political biography of a great man in a dangerous time.

Larson is well known for his ability to weave nonfiction narratives that are accurate, well-researched, readable, and accessible while following several characters and story lines simultaneously. Subjects of his previous best-selling and award-winning works have included the serial killer H. H. Holmes and the 1893 World's Fair, the sinking of the ocean liner *Lusitania*, and the first US ambassador to Nazi Germany. Though there is no doubt that Winston Churchill is the subject of *The Splendid and the Vile*, Larson approaches him both directly, as a standard biographer would, and through the perspective of his family, colleagues, friends, and enemies. The scope of this book is limited to Churchill's first year as prime minister, and so it allows for a nearly day-to-day examination of the man and his actions. The tight focus also allows the other figures in the narrative to blossom as vivid people in their own right, not simply sources of information about Churchill.

Erik Larson

The book begins with Churchill's appointment by King George VI to the position of prime minister following the resignation of Neville Chamberlain. With the benefit of hindsight, this may appear an obvious selection, but at a time when the United Kingdom's very survival weighed in the balance, Churchill—heavy-drinking, eccentric, deeply in debt—seemed a risky choice. Many still blamed him for one of the greatest military disasters in history, the 1915 Gallipoli Campaign. With the Nazis rampaging through mainland Europe, the United Kingdom was unprepared for an invasion and lagged far behind Germany in war production. Parliament was divided and the public deeply apprehensive, and the situation was about to get much worse. Civil servant Jock Colville reflected general British sentiment when he confided to his diary, "I cannot help fearing that this country may be maneuvered into the most dangerous position it has ever been in." The stage was set for Churchill to prove his worth, and he ultimately did so in a spectacular fashion.

A social project called Mass-Observation had been launched before World War II to study the experience of ordinary British citizens through diaries and questionnaires. The voices of the people who contributed to that project are sprinkled throughout Larson's narrative, offering insight into how Churchill was perceived by the public. One Nella Last noted, "I would sooner have Churchill if there was a storm," echoing the feeling that at least he was a man of action as compared to Chamberlain, whose efforts to avoid war with Germany had begun to seem cowardly. Churchill did not disappoint, taking the post of minister of defense and filling government positions with people whom he liked and trusted and who could keep up with his boundless energy. He understood his shortcomings and was a keen judge of character, as evidenced by his appointment of the tactful and popular Major General Hastings "Pug" Ismay as military chief of staff and of the powerful and not-so-popular Lord Beaverbrook as the minister of aircraft production. Churchill was upfront about the challenges ahead, promising only "blood, toil, tears and sweat" in his first speech before the House of Commons, but also confident and charismatic.

As May 1940 turned into June, Nazi forces swept into France, pushing the British Expeditionary Force to the sea and almost certain annihilation at Dunkirk. Catastrophe was narrowly averted by the heroic efforts of private citizens and an unaccountable delay by the Nazis, but it was now clear that Germany would turn its full force on the United Kingdom. An invasion was imminent. Churchill responded with a speech in the House of Commons combining a frank assessment of dire peril, a glimmer of hope, and an expression of steely resolve, a combination that he would employ deftly throughout the war. On June 4, 1940, the final day of the Dunkirk evacuation, he famously proclaimed, "We shall fight on the beaches, we shall fight on the landing grounds, we shall fight in the fields and in the streets, we shall fight in the hills; we shall never surrender." Tellingly, Churchill, who understood just how vulnerable his island nation was, added privately, "And . . . we will fight them with the butt end of broken bottles, because that's bloody well all we've got."

There in the stands, listening to his speech, was Churchill's seventeen-year-old daughter, Mary. Her experience during this crucial period is a key thread of Larson's narrative. Jock Colville, who warmed to Churchill and became one of his trusted companions, provides another important thread thanks to his detailed diary. Both Mary Churchill and Colville, along with other figures close to the prime minister, are allowed to live separately from Winston Churchill in this book, their loves, hopes, and disappointments creating distinct people whose observations of the man at the center of the story are all the more interesting as a result.

As the bombs began to rain down on London and other industrial cities, British people famous and ordinary alike shared in the peril. Larson skillfully reveals both the intimate details of that experience and the broader political forces in play. Churchill understood that the involvement of the United States, then still nominally neutral and deeply ambivalent about becoming entangled in another foreign war, was key to the survival of the United Kingdom. Though President Franklin Delano Roosevelt was sympathetic, he and his representatives were cagey about potential aid, hamstrung by an isolationist Congress. To encourage their help, Roosevelt and his representatives were courted and cajoled by Churchill. Roosevelt adviser and emissary Harry Hopkins, described as forgetful, disheveled, and sickly, becomes another vivid figure in Larson's telling. Hopkins was at Churchill's side in early 1941 and saw firsthand the devastation wrought by Nazi bombs. He and Churchill understood each other, and the latter's ability to convey both the gravity of the situation and his nation's determination to continue to fight convinced Hopkins that the United States must intervene. He returned to the United States after declaring that their interests would be united "even to the end." When the Lend-Lease Act was finally signed into law in March 1941, Churchill became equally close to Roosevelt envoy and Lend-Lease coordinator William Averell Harriman. The description of Harriman's affair with Pamela Churchill, the young wife of the prime minister's ne'er-do-well son, Randolph, is an example of Larson's ability to give his nonfiction writing the intrigue and readability of a page-turning novel.

Churchill's personal and political life were so completely intertwined during that time that there is no need to focus on one to the detriment of the other. Larson paints a vivid picture of Churchill at his vibrant, eccentric, complicated best, conducting business in the bath, marching around in his blue romper, chomping on cigars, and keeping houseguests from their beds until morning. He is a distracted but loving father to Mary, an exasperated but indulgent parent to Randolph, a moody but generous boss, and a powerhouse strategist with a persnickety eye for detail. With the exception of his foes in Germany, he was nearly universally loved by those who knew him.

Churchill's personal courage and ability to connect with people served him well during the Blitz. It would be simple enough to follow his actions through the bombings, but that story has been told in other biographies. Larson wisely expands the personal connections to tell a much wider story of the British experience during that time, relying on the personal writings of Churchill's friends and family as well as reports from Mass-Observation diarists and newspapers. He paints a rich sensory picture as well, with details like the stench of the latrine buckets in shelters, the smell of smoke and cordite, and the feel of the dust of centuries of London buildings settling onto everything. Most of all, he captures the impenetrable darkness of a city in a blackout, where people wandered into lampposts and off curbs and drove into fish-and-chip wagons that burst into flames. Yet amid the horror, people fell in love, worried about what to wear, danced and worked and lived their ordinary lives in an extraordinary time. In her *New York Times* review, Candice Millard noted, "These small, forgotten stories, which Larson uses to such moving effect, make it possible for us to understand, even 80 years later, what made hearts race and break, and are best told by the people who experienced them."

Millard was not alone in her high praise for *The Splendid and the Vile*, which reached the top spot on multiple best-seller lists. Reviewers almost unanimously remarked on the quality of the writing, which makes for a gripping read much like Larson's previous books. Many critics also agreed that the attention to the largely unpublished personal writings of people around Churchill presents a fresh and intimate view of a man and a time about which much has already been written. As Michael Shaub put it in his review for NPR, "It's a more than worthy addition to the long list of books about World War II and a bravura performance by one of America's greatest storytellers."

Author Biography
Erik Larson is known for his best-selling, award-winning narrative nonfiction works, including *Dead Wake: The Last Crossing of the* Lusitania (2015) and *The Devil in the White City* (2002). He has also written for various publications and taught writing at several institutions.

Bethany Groff Dorau

Review Sources
DeGroot, Gerard. "Winston Churchill and the Power of English Myth." Review of *The Splendid and the Vile*, by Erik Larson. *The Washington Post*, 28 Feb. 2020, www.washingtonpost.com/outlook/winston-churchill-and-the-power-of-english-myth/2020/02/27/edcabe26-42e3-11ea-b503-2b077c436617_story.html. Accessed 19 Oct. 2020.
Millard, Candice. "How Churchill Brought Britain Back from the Brink." Review of *The Splendid and the Vile*, by Erik Larson. *The New York Times*, 25 Feb. 2020, www.nytimes.com/2020/02/25/books/review/the-splendid-and-the-vile-erik-larson.html. Accessed 19 Oct. 2020.
Schaub, Michael. "Churchill's 1st Year as Prime Minister Is Electric in 'The Splendid and the Vile.'" Review of *The Splendid and the Vile*, by Erik Larson. *NPR*, 20 Feb. 2020, www.npr.org/2020/02/20/807027681/churchills-first-year-as-prime-minister-is-electric-in-the-splendid-and-the-vile. Accessed 19 Oct. 2020.
Review of *The Splendid and the Vile*, by Erik Larson. *Kirkus*, 25 Feb. 2020, www.kirkusreviews.com/book-reviews/erik-larson/the-splendid-and-the-vile. Accessed 19 Oct. 2020.
Review of *The Splendid and the Vile*, by Erik Larson. *Publishers Weekly*, 31 Jan. 2020, www.publishersweekly.com/978-0-385-34871-3. Accessed 19 Oct. 2020.

Squeeze Me

Author: Carl Hiaasen (b. 1953)
Publisher: Alfred A. Knopf (New York). 352 pp.
Type of work: Novel
Time: Present day
Locale: Palm Beach, Florida

In his fifteenth novel about life in Florida, Carl Hiaasen uses the formula of the classic crime story as the framework for a devastating satire on contemporary society.

Principal characters
KATHERINE "KIKI" PEW FITZSIMMONS, a seventy-two-year-old socialite
ANGELA "ANGIE" ANDERSON, a wildlife wrangler, the owner of a pest removal company
FAY ALEX RIPTOAD, an outspoken member of Kiki's social group
SPALDING, an assistant restaurant manager and love interest of Angie
JERRY CROSBY, the police chief of Palm Beach
TRIPP TEABULL, the grounds manager of Lipid House, the estate where Kiki disappeared
MASTODON, the Secret Service codename for the president of the United States
MOCKINGBIRD, the codename for the first lady
URIC BURNS, a dim-witted burglar for hire
KEEVER BRACCO, a.k.a. *Prince Paladin*, Uric's equally dim-witted assistant
PAUL RYSKAMP, the Secret Service agent in charge of the president's detail
KEITH JOSEPHSON, a.k.a. *Ahmet Youssef*, the Secret Service agent assigned to the first lady
DIEGO BELTRÁN, a Honduran returning illegally to seek work in Florida

Carl Hiaasen has written enough best sellers over the last three decades that he could easily afford to give up writing and live the leisured life of the affluent Floridians who populate most of his novels. Instead, and luckily for readers, the former newspaper reporter continues to write about them with his usual wit and sense of humor. Hiaasen has set his latest novel, *Squeeze Me* (2020), in the vicinity of the winter White House in Palm Beach, Florida, though he has changed the name of the property to Casa Bellicosa (literally, the warlike house). Though Hiaasen does not refer to the president by name (using only his assigned Secret Service codename, the Mastodon), the character is clearly based on Donald Trump. The novel's president takes the codename as a compliment, as recognition of his mental ferocity rather than his physical size. When he asks to be driven to the Washington Zoo, so that he can see the mastodons there, a Secret Service agent tactfully tells him that the prehistoric animals are on a long-term loan to a zoo in New Zealand.

Carl Hiaasen

Meanwhile, Hiaasen locates the novel's central mystery—the disappearance of an elderly socialite—at an older estate on the island, currently used for fundraising galas. It does not take a modern Sherlockian to guess the killer, only an experienced wildlife worker named Angie who specializes in relocating creatures that find their way into urban spaces on the island. The manager of the estate's grounds crew, Tripp Teabull, calls Angie in to dispose of a nineteen-foot-long Burmese python, found sleeping in a tree while digesting the previous night's dinner. When a sizeable award is announced for information about the location of the missing socialite, Angie sets the investigation in motion. She collects information much faster than the local police chief. The chief is not incompetent, but he is distracted from his purpose by the wealthy friends of the missing woman and by political associates of the president, all of whom think that her disappearance must be tied to the apprehension of an undocumented immigrant on the same night. In an election year, when anti-immigration tensions run high, the president himself is soon speaking about the need to find and punish the man, a Central American named Diego. Speaking from a golf course that bears his brand name, though it is owned mainly by a Swiss bank and a Russian oligarch, the president promises Secret Service protection for all the women in the victim's regular luncheon group at his hotel. When one agent asks whether Washington realizes how ridiculous this proposition is, his superior replies in the affirmative. "No one's pretending that this assignment is anything but a colossal waste," says the superior—a waste at least if it fails to garner votes in the upcoming election.

The various extras who are drawn into the investigation allow the novelist to write humorously about the diverse people who come to Palm Beach to spend their time and money, as well as those who come to take their share of the money and power that reside there. Many of them, like the police chief and the naturalist, could never afford to live in this zip code, but they have learned how to make it work for their benefit. The sketches of minor characters, from acupuncturists to drug dealers and hotel staff, help make the relatively small island town of Palm Beach, with its year-round population of around nine thousand people, into a microcosm of the United States today.

There are no heroes here, though there is a strong antihero in Angie. Although she has the traditional hero's role of serpent slayer, Angie has a colorful past. As a young veterinarian working for the state's wildlife service, she took revenge on an unprincipled and abusive boss. Convicted of felony assault, she served time in prison and lost her veterinarian's license at about the same time that she lost her former husband to a wealthy woman. By her sheer knowledge of wildlife and her personal convictions,

Angie makes an unlikely reentry into Florida society. She is the only person to defend Diego when the local police chief and the head of the president's security detail both realize that he had nothing to do with the socialite's death. The men feel their hands are tied for as long as the president has made Diego and the "Diego Border Cartel" a centerpiece of his reelection campaign. Meanwhile, the president's slogan, "No More Diegos," has inspired White nationalists in the local jail to hatch a death plot against the Honduran refugee with reward money offered by people who distinguish bad immigrants like Diego (who had earned a doctorate degree at a state university) from the good immigrants employed at Casa Bellicosa. Disgusted with the system that is threatening the asylum seeker, Angie devises a scheme to make the president free Diego.

The novel has two parts of fourteen chapters each. The first part, titled "Get a Grip," contains the whodunit (or "what did it") portion of the book. The second part, titled "Muscle of Love," prepares for and culminates in a formal ball at Casa Bellicosa—a lavish fundraiser for the president's reelection campaign. There is no mystery to work out here beyond the matter of arranging Diego's release from prison. This leaves plenty of room for Hiaasen to introduce new characters as the others go about their business. For example, the women's group that has just lost a senior member—a group that calls itself the Potussies—prepares a song with the title and refrain "Big Unimpeachable You." One new character named Skink is a former governor of Florida who has deserted his post to become an ecological warrior, raising pythons of exceptional length in the Everglades. Based on the character of Hayduke in Edward Abbey's 1975 novel, *The Monkey Wrench Gang*, he will be familiar to Hiaasen's regular readers, though he is definitely up to new tricks here. A new character known as the Knob serves as a body double for Mastodon, and his main job is to ensure that the presidential tanning bed is working properly. A drug dealer and small-time crook named Stanleigh agrees to escort the president's "nutritionist" mistress and to bring a Chinese aphrodisiac. Two stepsons of the recently deceased socialite, appropriately named Chase and Chance, provide an upper-class counterpart to the lower-class burglars, Uric and Prince, their chief aim being to collect as much of their inheritance as possible while enjoying the amenities of Casa Bellicosa without paying for their own memberships. A prisoner named Nutter organizes the White supremacist gang that proudly calls itself the Cawks (for "Caucasians"), as they sharpen bed springs to attack Diego. Somehow all of them, except Nutter, appear at the ball.

Critics described *Squeeze Me* as vintage Hiaasen. The reviewer for *Booklist* found it full of the "outrageously surrealistic" turns of phrase that have made him famous as "the Hieronymous Bosch of crime fiction." (The image of the human bulge in a python is certainly worthy of the fifteenth-century Dutch painter's famous landscapes depicting hell.) Writing for the *New York Times*, Janet Maslin recognized that the book will appeal to Hiaasen's regular readers more than to those who prefer media outlets that echo the views of Hiaasen's fictional president. The *Washington Post* reviewer, Richard Lipez, focused on the novel's "deeply mordant humor" and noted that Hiaasen fits nicely into the "American literary pastime" of lampooning the filthy rich. Lipez, himself the author of crime novels, warned that the plot wanders at times to enlarge the curious cast of characters. Meanwhile, Oline Cogdill, the regional *South Florida Sun*

Sentinel reviewer, pointed out that much of the satire is not specifically political. For people who follow the local news as well as the national, the real focus will seem to be on "Florida's foibles." Readers in other states will likewise recognize similarities as traditional barriers between wildlife and domestic life are breached by new developments to accommodate expanding populations.

Cogdill also called *Squeeze Me* Hiaasen's "most political novel." As such, the novel may prove in time to be his most ephemeral. Allusions to government agencies and the "unimpeachable" president may soon be lost to readers, but not the story of a snake large enough to consume an elderly woman or the humor associated with Skink and his dramatic escapades as he tries to bring Floridians back to their senses. Readers may well think that Hiaasen has similar aspirations.

Author Biography
A former reporter for the *Miami Herald*, Carl Hiaasen produced three novels with a friend before his first solo novel appeared in 1986. In addition to numerous comedic crime novels, Hiaasen has written a half-dozen children's books, one of which won a Newbery Award.

Thomas Willard

Review Sources
Cogdill, Oline H. "Review: 'Squeeze Me'—with a Python, a President and Palm Beach—Is Vintage Hiassen." Review of *Squeeze Me*, by Carl Hiaasen. *South Florida Sun Sentinel*, 18 Aug. 2020, www.sun-sentinel.com/entertainment/theater-and-arts/books/fl-et-squeeze-me-hiaasen-review-20200818-yjgfyj6i2fe-7hevseog65a6txy-story.html. Accessed 20 Nov. 2020.

Lipez, Richard. "'Squeeze Me' Proves That the Trump Era Is Carl Hiaasen's Moment." Review of *Squeeze Me*, by Carl Hiaasen. *The Washington Post*, 22 Aug. 2020, www.washingtonpost.com/entertainment/books/squeeze-me-proves-that-the-trump-era-is-carl-hiaasens-moment/2020/08/21/51a40838-db07-11ea-b205-ff838e15a9a6_story.html. Accessed 20 Nov. 2020.

Maslin, Janet. "A Python Ate the President's Neighbor? Only in Carl Hiaasen's Florida." Review of *Squeeze Me*, by Carl Hiaasen. *The New York Times*, 29 Aug. 2020, www.nytimes.com/2020/08/29/books/review-carl-hiaasen-squeeze-me.html. Accessed 20 Nov. 2020.

Ott, Bill. Review of *Squeeze Me*, by Carl Hiaasen. *Booklist*, July 2020, www.booklistonline.com/Squeeze-Me/pid=9737787. Accessed 20 Nov. 2020.

Stamped
Racism, Antiracism, and You

Authors: Ibram X. Kendi (b. 1982) and Jason Reynolds (b. 1983)
Publisher: Little, Brown (New York). 320 pp.
Type of work: Current affairs, history
Time: 1415–2020
Locale: The United States

Activists and authors Ibram X. Kendi and Jason Reynolds's Stamped *is an exploration of racism in US history and an examination of how race is constructed and how American society might move toward an antiracist future.*

Principal personages
GOMES EANES DE ZURARA, a Portuguese commander and writer
COTTON MATHER, an American minister
THOMAS JEFFERSON, a former president of the United States
WILLIAM LLOYD GARRISON, an abolitionist and founder of antislavery newspaper
W. E. B. DUBOIS, a founder of the NAACP
ANGELA DAVIS, a civil rights activist and author

A sly and sophisticated discussion about race, *Stamped: Racism, Antiracism, and You* (2020) is a young adult version of author and activist Ibram X. Kendi's National Book Award–winning history of racism written for adults *Stamped from the Beginning: The Definitive History of Racist Ideas in America* (2016). Jason Reynolds—who was chosen in 2020 by the Library of Congress as the new National Ambassador for Young People's Literature—is one of the book's accomplished writers, and his skill for imbuing complex subjects with a style that crosses generational boundaries is on full display in this latest addition to his oeuvre.

Ibram X. Kendi, who writes the introduction to *Stamped*, is one of the most well-known scholars of racism in America. Kendi has explored the history of America's fraught race relations from many different perspectives, but he is best known for his Stamped series, in which he examines the way that racism, and more specifically, racist ideas, have been created over time and continue to color the way that Americans view one another. While other scholars have explored the history of racism, Kendi's approach is unique in that it looks specifically at the history of race as a social construct—that is, an idea created and held by members of a society about themselves or others in their society.

Kendi has built his career on helping to bring the idea of race as a construct out of the academic realm and into the mainstream conversation about race and racism. One of his most popular works was the 2019 best seller *How to Be an Antiracist*, in which Kendi attempts to explain the experience of racism through his own experiences and offers practical advice for people wishing to adopt antiracist ideas and for policy changes that might mitigate the impact of racism in society. This book received mixed reviews from critics, with some disagreeing with Kendi's characterization of race and the depth of his historical investigation; however, it was extremely popular with audiences despite this criticism. With *Stamped: Racism, Antiracism, and You*, Kendi sought to translate the ideas he cultivated in his original book for children and young adults. To achieve this, Kendi partnered with Jason Reynolds, a best-selling novelist whose books are aimed at younger readers. In interviews, Reynolds said he was initially reluctant, feeling that he had too little expertise to write nonfiction or history, but Kendi's persistence convinced him to take on the project.

Kendi and Reynolds describe their book as a "remix" of *Stamped from the Beginning*, taking the same basic ideas and history and gearing them toward readers around ages twelve and up. Many reviewers noted that this remix is not a typical history book. In fact, Reynolds—who writes the bulk of the book following the introduction—states this up front, beginning the first chapter with the note:, "Before we begin, let's get something straight. This is not a history book. . . . At least not like the ones you're used to reading in school." Reynolds opts to speak not to a general audience as a whole but to each specific reader individually. Throughout the book, he repeatedly refers to the readers as "you," and there are many attempts to craft the narrative of the book as if speaking directly to a young student, guiding them through the subjects of the book.

Also, like in Kendi's earlier history (which was twice as long and much denser in exposition), the authors introduce several historical groups that their readers can use to classify the people they encounter both in the book and in real life—segregationists, assimilationists, and antiracists. The definitions given in the new *Stamped* are simplified versions of concepts introduced in earlier Kendi books but are still rich in significance. Boiled down, Kendi describes the groups in this way in the introduction: "The antiracists try to transform racism. The assimilationists try to transform Black people. The segregationists try to get away from Black people." As the book continues, Reynolds works to deconstruct these ideas, showing how real people do not fall easily into any of these categories, but can occupy multiple groups at once, depending on the situation. The categorization scheme is helpful for classifying attitudes about otherness, though it does not dominate the focus of the book.

Though the remix of *Stamped* is billed as not being a history book, it is a thoughtful exploration of history through interesting biographies and moments, rather than a chronological march through important dates. The book begins with a note on the origins of racism, which Kendi traces back to the fifteenth century. From a certain perspective, beginning the history of racism so late in history might seem to omit much of how racist perceptions were constructed in the ancient world—and this argument is valid—but the authors' focus is squarely on the particular lineage of racism that is most relevant to the world as it exists today—the beginnings of the Atlantic slave trade. Here, the authors focus on a Portuguese commander in Prince Henry's army, Gomes Eanes de Zurara—a man whom the authors captivatingly call the world's first racist.

Jason Reynolds

It was Zurara who first wrote a book that defended the African slave trade, and the ideas in his book spread to other places, eventually including America. Under Prince Henry, the Portuguese explored other parts of the world, including Africa, and discovered many different cultures during their travels. They sought to exploit the individuals they encountered for profit. The exploitation of Africans was justified by Zurara's depiction of these individuals as living in a primitive, savage state, without reason, logic, or higher intellectual capacities. Indigenous inhabitants in other places were described as "weak," thus passing along the message that these people could be easily pushed aside to take their territory. By contrast, Africans were described as "strong," which helped to create the perception that such people were good to utilize for labor, much like any of the other beasts of burden common in European society.

Reynolds explores the history of racism with considerable humor and employs the use of plain language in his writing. Discussing Zurara, for instance, he writes that he was "a man who made sure the team he played for was represented and heralded as great. He made sure Prince Henry was looked at as a brilliant quarterback making ingenious plays, and that every touchdown was the mark of a superior player." This simple, metaphorical way of explaining the motivation behind some of the earliest racist writing in the Western canon is one of many techniques that Reynolds uses to ensure that the book remains accessible and understandable to younger readers. He also does not shy away from opinions and doles them out liberally, such as in saying that Zurara is not just dead but "thankfully" so. The remix is not a detached, purely scholarly exploration in which the authors intend to give the various sides of this issue equal play or treatment. The understanding given, from the beginning, is that racism is an evil that has curtailed and limited the lives of millions around the world and that the ideas and presuppositions underlying racism are faulty and false.

Though the book starts with a brief exploration of racism as it occurred within the environment of early colonialism, Zurara and other Portuguese pioneers of dehumanization are not the primary historical figures introduced. As in *Stamped from the Beginning*, the lives of five historical figures are used as a framework to discuss assimilation, segregation, and antiracism in the United States. Reynolds begins with famed minister Cotton Mather, whose sermons helped to craft the uniquely American views on race that supported the import of slaves and fueled American expansion. He then discusses Thomas Jefferson, the founding father whose cherished role as the champion of small government and individual liberty has long overshadowed his complex relationship to slavery and racism. Abolitionist William Lloyd Garrison, whose antislavery newspaper the *Liberator* represented an important shift in racial concepts in America, is also explored, as is W. E. B. DuBois. DuBois was an African American academic and activist who founded the National Association for the Advancement of Colored People (NAACP) and played a pioneering role in America's ongoing battle for civil rights. Finally, the book explores writer and activist Angela Davis, whose activism in the 1960s and 1970s called many aspects of American culture into question and demonstrated how race and racial constructs had fatally poisoned the nation's education system, the women's rights movement, and the criminal justice system.

Each of the pioneers discussed by Reynolds allows the book to move forward through history, catching readers up with the state of racist ideas during different eras. The lives that are explored also enable Reynolds to paint a much more detailed picture of how the three basic categories—segregationism, assimiliationism, and antiracism—exist in plurality in different people at different times. Along the way, Reynolds encourages readers to see these qualities in themselves, asking how their own prejudices might shape the idea that individuals within a society need to conform to certain norms.

Kendi and Reynolds' "remix" was nearly as well received as Kendi's original book. Writing for the *Michigan Daily*, Lilly Pearce pointed out that Kendi and Reynolds do a formidable job explaining that a young person's daily life is not isolated from history but is, rather, "a product of history." She went on to explain that the book's importance lies in its ability to show that "our lives are all affected by the past. To be true activists, to be antiracists, we must understand the entire history that brought us here." Other reviewers praised the authors' style—writing in loose, conversational prose with humor and wit but without shying away from difficult topics and ideas. As Kaitlyn Greenidge wrote for the *New York Times*, complicated terms "are defined in direct, accessible language, becoming real tools for a reader" and the book's "radical changes in font and text size force the reader to stop and really consider what is being deconstructed." Throughout the book, Reynolds tells many stories, and one of the overarching themes is that stories can shape reality because they provide people with a feeling about their world and what might be true. Reynolds and Kendi, each drawing on their respective strengths, have created a new story with *Stamped*—one in which a young person can learn about history and come to understand how their identity is shaped and imposed upon, both from within and without.

Author Biography
Ibram X. Kendi is an author, professor, and antiracism activist. He is the author of four New York Times Best Sellers, including *How to Be an Antiracist* (2019). In July 2020, Kendi was appointed director of the new Center for Antiracist Research at Boston University.

Jason Reynolds is a best-selling author most famous for his Track series of young adult novels. In January 2020, Reynolds was appointed the Library of Congress's National Ambassador for Young People's Literature.

Micah L. Issitt

Review Sources
Greenidge, Kaitlyn. "Can You Dismantle White Supremacy with Words?" Review of *Stamped: Racism, Antiracism, and You*, by Ibram X. Kendi and Jason Reynolds. *The New York Times*, 6 Mar. 2020, www.nytimes.com/2020/03/06/books/review/stamped-ibram-x-kendi-jason-reynolds.html. Accessed 29 Mar. 2021.

Lewis, Janaka B. Review of *Stamped: Racism, Antiracism, and You*, by Ibram X. Kendi and Jason Reynolds. *Children's Literature Association Quarterly*, vol. 45, no. 4, Winter 2020, muse.jhu.edu/article/780949. Accessed 30 Mar. 2021.

Nadworny, Elissa. "A History Book That Isn't: Finding a Way to Teach Racism to a New Generation." Review of *Stamped: Racism, Antiracism, and You*, by Ibram X. Kendi and Jason Reynolds. *NPR*, 14 Mar. 2020, www.npr.org/2020/03/14/814630039/a-history-book-that-isnt-finding-a-way-to-teach-racism-to-a-new-generation. Accessed 30 Mar. 2021.

Pearce, Lilly. "'Stamped: Racism, Antiracism and You' Is Not Your Regular History Book." Review of *Stamped: Racism, Antiracism, and You*, by Ibram X. Kendi and Jason Reynolds. *The Michigan Daily*, 13 May 2020, www.michigandaily.com/books/stamped-racism-antiracism-and-you-not-your-regular-history-book/. Accessed 30 Mar. 2021.

Review of *Stamped: Racism, Antiracism, and You*, by Ibram X. Kendi and Jason Reynolds. *Kirkus*, 10 Nov. 2019, www.kirkusreviews.com/book-reviews/jason-reynolds/stamped/. Accessed 31 Mar. 2021.

Summer

Author: Ali Smith (b. 1962)
Publisher: Pantheon Books (New York). 400 pp.
Type of work: Novel
Time: 2020
Locale: Primarily the United Kingdom

Summer is the final installment of Scottish author Ali Smith's seasonal quartet of novels exploring the present moment through a kaleidoscopic lens. Smith revisits characters from the previous volumes, interweaving stories across time and space to craft a work that provides both searing sociopolitical commentary and literary reflection on issues such as memory and family.

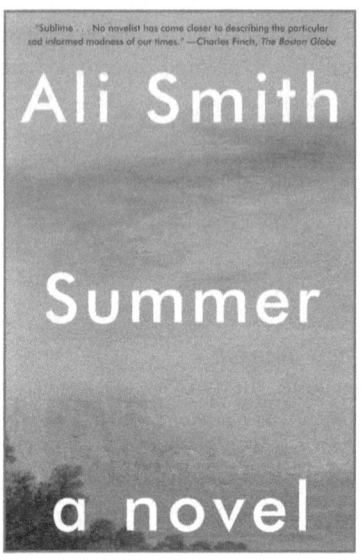

Principal characters
SACHA GREENLAW, a sixteen-year-old climate activist
ROBERT GREENLAW, her thirteen-year-old brother, a troublemaker
GRACE GREENLAW, their mother
DANIEL GLUCK, a centenarian former songwriter
HANNAH GLUCK, Daniel's sister; an underground activist during World War II
ART, a writer
CHARLOTTE, a writer
HERO, a detained political refugee

Ali Smith's *Summer* (2020) has been hailed as one of the first major novels to be set, at least partially, during the globally disruptive coronavirus disease 2019 (COVID-19) pandemic. When the Scottish novelist began her seasonal quartet in 2016, she could not have predicted the world of 2020: on lockdown, beset by both natural disasters such as wildfires and widespread social unrest. Yet Smith set out to capture current events in fiction, with the intention of being directly in conversation with the present moment by writing and publishing each volume in just a few months. Each novel in the series is also a meditation on the season of its title. *Autumn* (2016) tackles Brexit, the United Kingdom's stunning decision to leave the European Union in 2016; it features a dying man as its protagonist and explores autumnal themes of transformation and change. *Winter* (2017) is about the refugee crisis and existential fears of environmental catastrophe; it explores themes of balance—stillness and deadness, but with the promise of rebirth. *Spring* (2019) directly engages the horrors of immigrant detention; it explores rage, relationships torn apart as if ripped from the earth.

Summer, the final book in the acclaimed quartet, is actually rooted in February 2020, just as the COVID-19 pandemic is sweeping across the globe. It is also partially set decades before, during World War II. Warping time and space is a major theme of the book. The beauty of summer, in Smith's telling, is its evanescence. For example, one character, Grace, fondly recalls performing summer stock theater years before. She describes this formative season of her life as her "immortal summer," long past but alive in memory. This is the paradox of summer and *Summer*: how can time be both fleeting and constant? Smith writes that summer is the "briefest and slipperiest of the seasons." It is a metaphor for the author's seasons project as a whole and a fitting conclusion. She writes, in the voice of Grace, "Look at me walking down a road in summer thinking about the transience of summer. Even while I'm right at the heart of it I just can't get to the heart of it."

Ali Smith

One does not have to have read the previous novels in Smith's seasonal quartet to enjoy *Summer*, but if one has, there will be the added pleasure of revisiting familiar characters. There is Daniel Gluck, the elderly songwriter from *Autumn*, and his young caretaker and friend, Elisabeth. There is also Art, the protagonist of *Winter*, and his ex-girlfriend, Charlotte. Art's aunt, the aging firebrand Iris, also makes an appearance. There are also satisfying moments of dramatic irony thanks to the preestablished narratives that intersect here. Readers of the full series will be able to see a web of relationships, spanning generations, that goes far deeper than some of the characters ever realize.

Fans of Smith, who is best known for exuberant stand-alone novels like *There but for The* (2012) and *How to Be Both* (2015), will also notice that the author returns to favorite themes and images. Shakespeare, puns and wordplay, precocious children, and obscure female artists crop up frequently in *Summer*, as in the previous volumes of the seasonal quartet. There are strangers meeting and embarking on symbolic journeys, echoing the characters Brit and Florence in *Spring*. There are moments of incredible tenderness between characters who are far apart in age. These include the bond between Elisabeth and Daniel, first established in *Autumn*, and thirteen-year-old Robert's ardent and ultimately transformative love for Charlotte, an adult woman. There are also thematic riffs on the multiplicity of the self. Like her beloved Shakespeare, Smith loves gender-swapping and characters who inhabit multiple identities. An overt example comes when the elderly Daniel believes that the young Robert, a stranger, is his long-dead little sister, Hannah. This detail, a small plot point, is in keeping with another favorite theme of Smith's: memory as time travel. "He was just full of happiness," Charlotte says of Daniel's misidentification. "His sister, there in front of him. Even though she wasn't."

Much like its predecessors, *Summer* weaves a complex narrative, often jumping from subject to subject and requiring close attention from the reader. The plot structure is fairly loose, but in some ways is centered on a new set of characters: the Greenlaw family living in Brighton, England. Early on, the perspective is that of Sacha, a sixteen-year-old girl who is passionate about environmentalism and various social causes. Her mother, Grace, a former actor and Brexiteer, teases her for her refusal to travel by car. In the book's first scene (following a short, prose-poem-like introduction, as in the other entries in the seasonal quartet), Grace becomes obsessed with remembering the origin of a particular phrase: "Whether I shall turn out to be the heroine of my own life." (It is in fact a line from Charles Dickens's *David Copperfield* (1849–50)—another Smith favorite—with the word "hero" swapped for the feminine "heroine.") Grace refuses to consult the internet, infuriating Sacha, who shows little concern over the source of any quote, and making clear the tensions between generations.

Sacha's little brother, Robert, has a substantial mean streak, exacerbated by a video game that simulates gruesome torture techniques, and an appreciation for the conservative politics of Prime Minister Boris Johnson. Largely absent from the novel's action is Sacha and Robert's father, who lives next door with his young girlfriend, Ashley. Ashley is writing a book about language and politics, but she has stopped speaking. (Robert, who for nefarious reasons is the only person who knows about Ashley's book, shares one startling passage, in which pages of information about the word "letterbox" turn to Johnson's flippant use of the word to describe the appearance of Muslim women wearing burkas; the episode offers commentary on the way in which politicians use "jokes" to stir social resentments.) Robert is the catalyst of the story. After he superglues a glass egg timer to his sister's palm—a "joke" about needing time on her hands—Sacha meets Art and Charlotte, who take her to the hospital. They return her to Grace, striking up a lively and wide-ranging conversation. Art and Charlotte explain that they are returning an object—an important one, from *Autumn*—to another stranger, an elderly man named Daniel Gluck. For a multitude of reasons, Grace, Sacha, and Robert decide to tag along.

The other key narrative thread is Daniel's early life, as told through his disjointed memories. These sneak up on him, often triggered by real-life stimuli, and when they arrive they are all-encompassing. He compares them to a snowflake melting on his skin and absorbing itself into his pores. A German emigre, Daniel and his father were detained by the British government at the Hutchinson Internment Camp on the Isle of Man during World War II. His experience mirrors that of other immigrant detainees and other political prisoners in *Spring*, and also *Summer*. For example, the character Hero emerges as a contemporary refugee stuck in a detainment center, and Smith's sociopolitical commentary is incisive.

Daniel's story also provides some of the book's almost philosophical digressions into art, language, and other issues. While interned, he encounters real-life artists Fred Uhlman and Kurt Schwitters. As Daniel recalls, in an impromptu performance Schwitters spoke the word "*liese*"—German for "quiet," though it sounds like the English word "lies"—over and over again, his voice becoming progressively louder until he smashed his coffee cup. To Daniel, the performance made him feel alive for the first time since being arrested. The interlude provides a concrete example of an observation Smith makes later in the book in the voice of Charlotte. Asked to define art, she says that it "is a shock that brings us back to ourselves."

Meanwhile, in the novel's historical moments, Daniel's sister Hannah works underground as a member of the French resistance. The rise of fascism has been another frequent theme in Smith's books. Today, Hannah might be called "antifa." She helps shepherd people out of occupied France and into Switzerland. Her job is dangerous, and she assumes various names and identities to protect herself. She plucks the names from gravestones and imagines being reborn as each new person. "It's not subterfuge. It's much more complex," Smith writes. "Something real happens, something as metamorphic as caterpillar and butterfly." Hannah describes it as a profound act of connection.

Some readers may be frustrated by Smith's rollicking, fragmented style, which moves quickly from one idea to the next. Others will delight in it. To wit: there is an entire passage in Smith's own voice in which she relates the biography of the filmmaker Lorenza Mazzetti. The sometimes-confusing effect of this style is, of course, intentional. It reflects all at once the frequently chaotic landscape of 2020, the overload of the information age in general, and the feeling of a quick-moving summer.

Reviewers were mostly effusive in their praise for *Summer*, especially its poetic prose and its engagement with of-the-moment issues. Many called it a triumphant conclusion to the seasonal quartet, a likely classic as a whole. Writing for the *New York Times*, Dwight Garner acknowledged that "Smith's seasonal novels can be pretty on-the-nose, politically. Sometimes they veer into the saccharine," but tempered this critique with the observation that "as with a strong river, their motion is fundamentally self-purifying." In a review for the *Guardian*, Alex Preston aptly described the entire series as "a four-dimensional collage." Indeed, though often challenging, the series is ultimately rewarding in its accumulation of images and ideas, as well as its valiant attempt to capture time as it flows. Tellingly, Preston wrote that he had eagerly anticipated *Summer*, as the prior installments had become a "central part of my cultural life, one of the tools with which I attempt to read the moment." This comment illuminates the point of Smith's project. There will be other works of art made about topics such as Brexit and COVID-19, perhaps enhanced by the benefit of hindsight, but Smith's books serve a particular need to give voice to the disorienting feeling of being alive right now.

Author Biography
Acclaimed writer Ali Smith has earned many honors for her fiction, including the Baileys Women's Prize for Fiction, the Costa Novel of the Year Award, and the Goldsmiths Award for the novel *How to Be Both* (2014). She was also short-listed for the Man Booker Prize four times.

Molly Hagan

Review Sources

Akins, Ellen. "Ali Smith's 'Summer' Concludes Her Seasonal Quartet on a High Note." Review of *Summer*, by Ali Smith. *The Washington Post*, 14 Aug. 2020, www.washingtonpost.com/entertainment/books/ali-smiths-summer-concludes-her-seasonal-quartet-on-a-high-note/2020/08/14/e4755d88-de40-11ea-8051-d5f887d73381_story.html. Accessed 6 Feb. 2021.

Garner, Dwight. "Ali Smith's 'Summer' Ends a Funny, Political, Very Up-to-Date Quartet." Review of *Summer*, by Ali Smith. *The New York Times*, 17 Aug. 2020, www.nytimes.com/2020/08/17/books/review-summer-ali-smith.html. Accessed 6 Feb. 2021.

Kelly, Stuart. Review of *Summer*, by Ali Smith. *The Scotsman*, 11 Aug. 2020, www.scotsman.com/arts-and-culture/books/book-review-summer-ali-smith-2939508. Accessed 6 Feb. 2021.

Preston, Alex. "*Summer* by Ali Smith Review—A Remarkable End to an Extraordinary Quartet." *The Guardian*, 2 Aug. 2020, www.theguardian.com/books/2020/aug/02/summer-by-ali-smith-review-a-remarkable-end-to-an-extraordinary-quartet. Accessed 6 Feb. 2021.

Review of *Summer*, by Ali Smith. *Kirkus*, 1 July 2020, www.kirkusreviews.com/book-reviews/ali-smith/summer-smith/. Accessed 6 Feb. 2021.

The Sun Down Motel

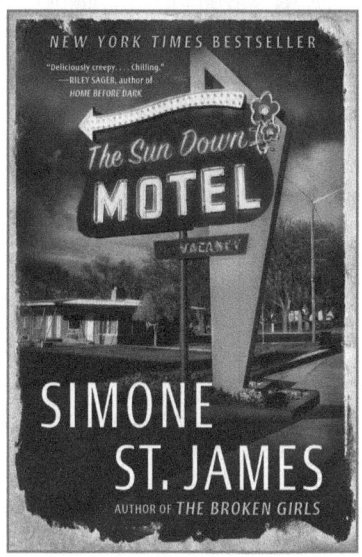

Author: Simone St. James
Publisher: Berkley (New York). 336 pp.
Type of work: Novel
Time: Largely 1982 and 2017
Locale: Upstate New York

The Sun Down Motel follows a young woman as she investigates the mystery surrounding the disappearance of her aunt thirty-five years earlier.

Principal characters

VIVIAN "VIV" DELANEY, a twenty-year-old woman who moves from Illinois to the strange town of Fell, New York, in 1982 only to soon disappear while working nights at a local motel
ALMA TRENT, a night-duty police officer whom she befriends
MARNIE, a photographer who teaches her about the unsolved murders of Fell
CARLY KIRK, her niece, who travels to Fell in 2017 to uncover what happened to her
HEATHER, Carly's roommate in Fell, a young college student who offers assistance in Carly's investigation
NICK HARKNESS, a handsome stranger staying at the Sun Down Motel in 2017

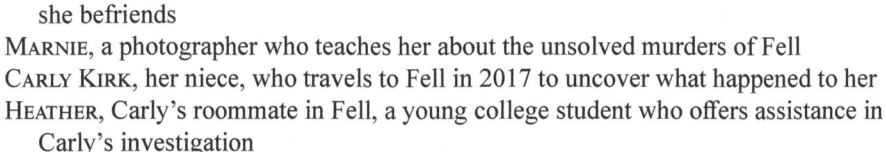

There is a scene in *The Sun Down Motel* (2020) when one of its protagonists, Vivian "Viv" Delaney, reflects on the fact that there is a killer on the loose in the town where she lives. As she gets ready for her shift as the night clerk at the local motel, she anticipates what the evening news will advise its viewers to do in light of this information: "Women should look over their shoulders, try not to be alone at night. Parents should look out for their daughters and always know where they are. Women should carry a whistle or a flashlight." Viv knows this is what they will say because from the moment she left home several months earlier, she had been surrounded by predatory men. Even the "good guys" who offer to help her always seem to want something in return. As feeling vulnerable and afraid has become her new status quo, she concludes what so many of her gender have before: the world is a dangerous place for women.

Tucked away in an otherwise uneventful scene, it is easy to read over this passage without pause. And yet, Viv's conclusion here is not a throwaway piece of internal dialogue but arguably the thesis of the entire novel. While on its surface *The Sun Down Motel* appears to be a simple supernatural murder mystery, at its thematic core, it is a story about the danger that all women face in their everyday lives simply for existing.

This is demonstrated most clearly by the fact that Viv is surrounded by actual ghosts at the motel where she works but is less afraid of the undead than she is of the living men who check in after dark. She comes by her fear honestly; in addition to being repeatedly objectified, she has been surrounded by too many murdered women. So deeply unsafe is the 1982 world that she lives in rendered that when the book's earliest pages reveal that she has disappeared without a trace, readers can confidently assume that she is dead, as her sister mournfully proclaims early in the story.

Author Simone St. James successfully infuses *The Sun Down Motel* with a suspenseful narrative by toggling between the story line of the last few weeks of Viv's life prior to her disappearance and the story line of her niece Carly. St. James effectively presents Carly as a kind of echo to Vivian. Arriving in the town of Fell in 2017 to attempt to find out what happened to her aunt there thirty-five years earlier, Carly is like Viv in that she is also twenty years old and a natural detective. Viv, as Carly eventually learns, was trying to track down the killer behind the murders of several local women when she disappeared. Carly is also like Viv in that she, too, gets hired as the night clerk at the eerie Sun Down Motel. By drawing these parallels between the two protagonists, St. James amplifies the novel's underlying sense of dread. Beyond wondering what exactly happened to Viv back in 1982, readers will keep turning the pages to make sure that Carly does not meet a similar fate.

Perhaps one of the most unique aspects of *The Sun Down Motel* is the way that St. James seamlessly weaves supernatural elements into the plot. As both Viv and Carly ultimately witness, the motel where they work is haunted with the ghosts of people who died there. At night, the specters are omnipresent, always reminding the two women of how quickly and violently life can end. St. James ensures that these figures are as terrifying to readers as they are to the characters by focusing on sensory details—the smell of cigarette smoke when no one is around, the sound of the motel room doors opening and closing on their own, and the feeling of someone else's breath in a darkened room. It is these little things that heighten the narrative's sense of horror and danger. This atmosphere is furthered by quick flashes in which Viv and Carly actually see the ghosts and hear their warnings. In a lesser author's hands, such scenes might come off as tacky. Fortunately, St. James is a seasoned master of supernatural storytelling and therefore these moments feel both believable and chilling.

One of St. James's strengths as a writer is world-building. The author sets the novel in the fictional upstate New York town of Fell. On the surface, Fell appears to be a prototypical northeast municipality in that it is home to a tiny liberal arts college and

Simone St. James

Courtesy Penguin Random House

is not especially big or small in size. What makes Fell unusual, however, is its higher-than-average homicide rate. During the late 1970s and early 1980s, the town became home to at least three unsolved murders. The ubiquity of supernatural events, which all the residents seem to accept, also makes it a strange place to live. To bring the town to life, St. James populates it with a cast of colorful characters. While working nights at the Sun Down motel, Viv befriends everyone from a handsome drug dealer, to a spying photographer named Marnie, to local police officer Alma Trent. Many of these people try to either help or deter her as she investigates the murders of local women. Three and a half decades later, Carly also befriends several misfits who live in Fell, including her roommate, Heather, a true-crime and supernatural junkie who also has mental health issues, and a mysterious motel tenant named Nick. These characters are compelling because they are multidimensional and fleshed out. In addition to their quirks, strengths, and assets, St. James also informs readers of their myriad shortcomings.

While written for a general audience, there are times that *The Sun Down Motel* feels as though it is a young-adult novel. This is due to the story's primary focus on the experiences of two twenty-year-olds, Viv and Carly, who are trying to find their way in the world after leaving home for the first time. In turn, the novel has a coming-of-age essence to it. This feeling is amplified by the chaste way that St. James presents their love interests, which often feel like schoolyard crushes rather than serious romances. Furthermore, St. James's decision to depict the novel's murders and supernatural elements in a light-handed rather than gruesome manner ultimately makes the content seem intended for a wider audience. While this does not deter from the quality of storytelling, mature readers looking for more adult horror might not be as engaged. Another aspect of the novel that some people might feel is lacking is the way that St. James at times leaves loose ends with her characters. This is to say that after creating a lot of intrigue into the mysterious backstories of certain secondary characters, St. James does not go beyond cursory explanations as to why they are who they are. As there is so much going on in the plot, however, few readers will notice or be too bothered by this.

Critical reception of *The Sun Down Motel* was somewhat limited, with very few major publications taking the time to write about it. Those that did, however, were largely positive in their reviews. Oline H. Cogdill, writing for the Associated Press, deemed the book "engrossing," remarking that "St. James keeps the tension high with myriad surprising twists as she alternates between the voices of Carly and Viv." Similarly, a review in the *Boston Herald* also called it "taut and twisty" as well as "thoroughly entertaining." Indeed, one of the strengths of *The Sun Down Motel* is just how fresh and unexpected St. James manages to make the central narrative. While murder mysteries are perhaps one of the most popular and saturated genres, the novel does not rely on tired tropes. In addition to balancing two complementary timelines, St. James integrates nuanced supernatural elements into the plot. Readers who enjoy her earlier novels, a few of which were also ghost stories, will likely find *The Sun Down Motel* to be enjoyable, as will fans of Stephen King. The anonymous reviewer for *Publishers Weekly* commented on this facet, concluding that "horror fans will also want to check this one out."

Although its critical acclaim was somewhat limited, *The Sun Down Motel* was well loved by readers. In addition to becoming a *New York Times* and *USA Today* best seller, the novel was optioned by a production company to be developed into a television series. Arguably, a part of the reason that *The Sun Down Motel* has enjoyed such a favorable response is because it fits into the broader cultural conversation that began back in 2017 with the #MeToo movement. Without being heavy-handed, St. James has successfully created a highly engaging narrative that effectively illustrates just how dangerous the world can be for women affected by the predatory culture fostered by toxic masculinity. She also demonstrates how strong women are—how they survive, look out for each other, and generally make their communities safer places to live. It is this potent combination of social commentary, dynamic characters, and a searing supernatural mystery that ultimately makes *The Sun Down Motel* a riveting and worthwhile read.

Author Biography
Canadian writer Simone St. James transitioned from working behind the scenes in television to writing novels with her award-winning debut, *The Haunting of Maddy Clare* (2012). The author of several books, she is the recipient of a 2013 Arthur Ellis Award bestowed by Crime Writers of Canada.

Emily E. Turner

Review Sources
"Check Out the Ghostly Twists in 'Sun Down Motel.'" Review of *The Sun Down Motel*, by Simone St. James. *Boston Herald*, 30 Mar. 2020, www.bostonherald.com/2020/03/30/check-out-the-ghostly-twists-in-sun-down-motel. Accessed 21 Dec. 2020.

Cogdill, Oline H. "Review: Author Keeps Tension High in 'The Sun Down Motel.'" Review of *The Sun Down Motel*, by Simone St. James. Associated Press, 18 Feb. 2020, apnews.com/article/ab2e699ca10701b5787c22c29e1c355b. Accessed 21 Dec. 2020.

Review of *The Sun Down Motel*, by Simone St. James. *Publishers Weekly*, 29 Oct. 2019, www.publishersweekly.com/978-0-440-00017-4. Accessed 21 Dec. 2020.

Supreme Inequality
The Supreme Court's Fifty-Year Battle for a More Unjust America

Author: Adam Cohen
Publisher: Penguin Press (New York). 448 pp.
Type of work: History, law
Time: 1950–present day
Locale: United States

Lawyer and journalist Adam Cohen's book Supreme Inequality: The Supreme Court's Fifty-Year Battle for a More Unjust America *traces a half-century of Supreme Court cases that have contributed to the current era of extreme economic disparity. Divided into chapters exploring democracy, poverty, criminal justice, and labor, among others, Cohen makes a powerful argument for adopting a new "blueprint" to repair the damage that the nation has incurred at the hands of the highest court over the past fifty years.*

Principal personages

JACOBUS TENBROEK, a constitutional law scholar who argued for the legal rights of the poor
EARL WARREN, chief justice of the US Supreme Court from 1953 to 1969
THURGOOD MARSHALL, associate justice of the US Supreme Court from 1967 to 1991
WARREN BURGER, chief justice from 1969 to 1986
WILLIAM REHNQUIST, chief justice from 1986 to 2005
RUTH BADER GINSBURG, associate justice from 1993 to 2020
JOHN ROBERTS, chief justice from 2005 to present

Journalist Adam Cohen's book *Supreme Inequality: The Supreme Court's Fifty-Year Battle for a More Unjust America* (2020) outlines the history of the United States Supreme Court from the liberal Warren Court of the 1950s and 1960s through the conservative era begun under President Richard Nixon in the 1970s. Cohen's argument is straightforward: while Chief Justice Earl Warren largely expanded the rights of poor and marginalized people, the conservative courts that followed have dismantled those rights in favor of corporations and the wealthy, sometimes usurping the powers of Congress to do so. Cohen, a former member of the *New York Times* editorial board, offers a startling thesis in the book's conclusion: "The Supreme Court is more than a legal tribunal, ruling on disputes between parties—it is also an architect," Cohen writes.

Adam Cohen

"The Court's interpretations of the Constitution and other laws become blueprints for the nation. . . . For the past half century, the Court has been drawing up plans for a more economically unequal nation, and that is the America that is now being built."

Cohen writes about Justice Brett Kavanaugh, President Donald Trump's controversial nominee who narrowly won a Senate vote to replace Anthony Kennedy in 2018. At the time, legal commentators warned that Kavanaugh's confirmation would herald a major ideological shift for the court. While, indeed, the Trump administration oversaw the formation of a Supreme Court more conservative than any in recent memory, Cohen argues that such a shift began decades ago.

Michael O'Donnell, writing for the *Atlantic* magazine, contrasted Cohen's book with other histories of the court, such as Jeffrey Toobin's engaging multiple biography *The Nine: Inside the Secret World of the Supreme Court* (2007), and called *Supreme Inequality* almost "pure law." It focuses on specific cases and their impact on the country—not, notably, the justices themselves. Divided into chapters exploring various areas of jurisprudence, including democracy, poverty, criminal justice, and labor, Cohen's book builds a powerful argument that over the past half-century, the Supreme Court has laid the foundations of an American autocracy.

In his review, O'Donnell found this last point, mentioned explicitly in the book, hyperbolic. But there are plenty of readers—particularly those whose constitutional rights are determined by the ideological views of nine political appointees—who might disagree. O'Donnell complains that Cohen is occasionally too "strident," but Cohen is not an activist. A graduate of Harvard Law School, he worked for the Southern Poverty Law Center and the American Civil Liberties Union (ACLU). He is also the author of several books, including *Nothing to Fear: FDR's Inner Circle and the Hundred Days That Created Modern America* (2009), a history of President Franklin Delano Roosevelt's first one hundred days in office. The later *Imbeciles: The Supreme Court, American Eugenics, and the Sterilization of Carrie Buck* (2016) explores the 1927 Supreme Court case *Buck v. Bell*, which held that the government could forcibly sterilize "undesirable" people, a gross miscarriage of justice. If that book tested the reader's faith in the courts, however fragile, *Supreme Inequality* threatens to shatter it.

Cohen begins with the progressive Warren Court. Earl Warren, then the governor of California, was appointed chief justice of the Supreme Court by Republican president Dwight D. Eisenhower, in 1953. Warren spearheaded a progressive revolution, expanding rights for African Americans, the poor, and those accused of a crime. Major rulings included the unanimous *Brown v. Board of Education of Topeka* (1954), which deemed school segregation unconstitutional, and *Gideon v. Wainwright* (1963), which held that the state must provide an attorney for defendants in criminal cases too poor to afford one themselves. Lesser known, though no less important, rulings included the unanimous *King v. Smith* in 1968. In that case, a widow named Sylvester Smith sued the state of Alabama after she was denied welfare benefits for having a boyfriend. This "man in the house" rule, as it was then called, was surprisingly common. It held that a man in the house was as a good as a "substitute father" and was thus responsible for providing for the family. The Warren Court struck down this rule, writing that poor children should not be deprived of assistance under the "transparent fiction" that someone else was providing for them. In *King v. Smith*, a gauntlet was laid: the Warren Court, with the blessing of President Lyndon B. Johnson, who dreamed of waging a "war on poverty," sought to build a legal argument for protecting the rights of the poor as a "discrete and insular minority." Thus, laws seeking to place a special burden on poor people simply for being poor would receive extra scrutiny from the courts and would likely be struck down.

This legal argument, developed as part of a larger movement led by the constitutional law scholar and disability rights activist Jacobus tenBroek, was never fully realized. Warren, eager for the court to continue expanding the rights of individual Americans, resigned near the end of Johnson's term in hopes that the president would replace him with a chief justice that shared his views. Johnson nominated liberal justice Abe Fortas, but conservatives threatened to filibuster his confirmation vote, and Johnson withdrew his name. Thus, the president charged with replacing Warren was Nixon, who nominated conservative judge Warren Burger, a critic of the Warren Court. Throughout his tenure, Nixon wielded his influence to replace two more justices, tipping the ideological balance of the once-liberal court to the right. Here, Cohen makes a point that is often overlooked: the Supreme Court has had a steady conservative majority ever since. Despite disparate liberal victories—notably, *Roe v. Wade* (1973), which ruled that restrictive regulation of abortion was unconstitutional, and *Obergefell v. Hodges* (2015), which affirmed same-sex marriage—Cohen demonstrates how the fifty-year conservative lock on the highest court has weakened the rights of marginalized groups and bolstered the rights and privileges of wealthy individuals and corporations. Cohen occasionally makes stark comparisons, as with two rulings regarding punishment. In 2003 the Supreme Court refused to overturn the sentence of a man serving twenty-five years to life for stealing $150 worth of videotapes, under California's "three strikes" law. A few months later, the same court argued that the multibillion-dollar State Farm insurance company should not have to pay $145 million in punitive damages for defrauding customers, as this punishment, in the court's view, was "excessive."

A running theme in the book is disdain for and dismissal of the middle-class and the poor—economic classes made up of people who are often marginalized in other ways as well. Cohen is deeply concerned with the human cost of the Supreme Court's decisions, wondering what the world would look like had Johnson, not Nixon, installed a chief justice to replace Warren. He offers chilling examples of cases that might have changed the course of history, as with *Dandridge v. Williams* (1970), in which the

Burger Court ruled that states may cap welfare benefits without respect to how large a family is, a rule that punishes families with more children. In 1941, pre-Warren, the court moved to protect the poor, striking down a so-called anti-Okie law. Drawing a line in the sand, it wrote: "Poverty and immorality are not synonymous." With *Dandridge v. Williams*, the Burger Court drew a new line; as Justice Potter Stewart wrote: "The intractable economic, social, and even philosophical problems presented by public welfare assistance programs are not the business of this Court."

The result of *Dandridge*, unfamiliar as it will be to many readers, is quantifiable. Such caps have directly led to more children living in deep poverty, Cohen writes. Other cases have fueled the mass incarceration crisis, ruining the countless lives of those in prison as well as the lives of their families. Cohen cites data revealing that the children of incarcerated individuals are more likely to do poorly in school and face other, significant obstacles in their lifetime. The Supreme Court has also made it harder for workers to organize for better working conditions and higher pay, and it has made it more difficult to prove racial, gender, and age discrimination, or sexual harassment, by one's employer. It has made it easier for corporations to influence politicians—a direct contributor to the stagnant federal minimum—and harder for ordinary citizens to vote. It has also rendered impotent what was once considered the crowning achievement of the Warren Court, *Brown v. Board of Education*, allowing school segregation to flourish across the country unchecked. *Supreme Inequality* is a history and a rallying cry for a better future. Aptly described by *Kirkus* as "maddening," the text is also a tough but necessary pill to swallow, knowing that, as Cohen writes, a "different set of blueprints would have built a different society."

Author Biography

Adam Cohen is a journalist and former member of the editorial board of the *New York Times*. His other books include *Nothing to Fear: FDR's Inner Circle and the Hundred Days That Created Modern America* (2009) and *Imbeciles: The Supreme Court, American Eugenics, and the Sterilization of Carrie Buck* (2016), which was long-listed for the National Book Award for Nonfiction.

Molly Hagan

Review Sources

Emmert, Steve. Review of *Supreme Inequality: The Supreme Court's Fifty-Year Battle for a More Unjust America*, by Adam Cohen. *American Bar Association*, 13 Jan. 2021, www.americanbar.org/groups/judicial/publications/appellate_issues/2021/winter/supreme-inequality. Accessed 17 Feb. 2021.

Fishkin, Joseph. "Conservatives Have Controlled the Supreme Court for 50 Years. These Are the Results." Review of *Supreme Inequality: The Supreme Court's Fifty-Year Battle for a More Unjust America*, by Adam Cohen. *The Washington Post*, 27 Mar. 2020, www.washingtonpost.com/outlook/conservatives-have-controlled-the-supreme-court-for-50-years-these-are-the-results/2020/03/27/6a6d95f0-526d-11ea-b119-4faabac6674f_story.html. Accessed 17 Feb. 2021.

O'Donnell, Michael. "The Supreme Court's Enduring Bias." Review of *Supreme Inequality: The Supreme Court's Fifty-Year Battle for a More Unjust America*, by Adam Cohen. *The Atlantic*, 1 Mar. 2020, www.theatlantic.com/magazine/archive/2020/03/the-supreme-courts-enduring-bias/605545. Accessed 17 Feb. 2021.

Review of *Supreme Inequality: The Supreme Court's Fifty-Year Battle for a More Unjust America*, by Adam Cohen. *Kirkus*, 18 Nov. 2019, www.kirkusreviews.com/book-reviews/adam-cohen/supreme-inequality. Accessed 17 Feb. 2021.

Yoshino, Kenji. "A Supreme Court for the Rich." Review of *Supreme Inequality: The Supreme Court's Fifty-Year Battle for a More Unjust America*, by Adam Cohen. *The New York Times*, 21 Feb. 2020, www.nytimes.com/2020/02/21/books/review/supreme-inequality-adam-cohen.html. Accessed 17 Feb. 2021.

Swimming in the Dark

Author: Tomasz Jedrowski (b. 1985)
Publisher: William Morrow (New York). 208 pp.
Type of work: Novel
Time: 1980s
Locale: Poland

Tomasz Jedrowski's debut novel, Swimming in the Dark, *is set in Communist Poland in the early 1980s. Addressing his former lover, a young man named Ludwik recounts his coming-of-age in a country where citizens are constricted by authoritarianism and conservative mores; where sex between men is illegal and one must participate in the economy of graft to survive.*

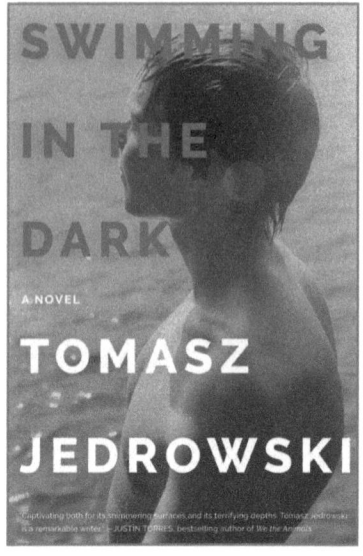

Principal characters

LUDWIK GLOWACKI, a young man grappling with his sexuality; critical of the Polish government
JANUSZ, his lover; supportive of the Polish government
PANI KOLECKA, his landlady
HANIA, a young woman, daughter of an apparatchik

Tomasz Jedrowski, born in Germany to Polish parents, was working as a corporate lawyer and grappling with the shame he had felt coming out as gay when he decided to become a writer. *Swimming in the Dark* (2020), a lush, melancholy coming-of-age tale set in Communist Poland in the early 1980s, is his first novel. Its tone could be compared to André Aciman's 2007 novel-turned-Academy Award-winning film, *Call Me By Your Name*, but its content has more in common with James Baldwin's classic *Giovanni's Room* (1956), to which *Swimming in the Dark* is an homage. Baldwin's novel, about an American in Paris who embarks on a love affair with an Italian bartender named Giovanni, explores guilt, desire, and social repression. Though the characters in the book are white, it is also haunted by Baldwin's experiences as a Black American expatriate, who fled an oppressive country is search of freedom. Jedrowski tackles similar issues of identity and displacement.

Ludwik, the narrator of *Swimming in the Dark*, addresses his story to his former lover, Janusz, from his new home in Greenpoint, Brooklyn, a haven for Poles who have fled the Communist regime. He watches the news, helpless as martial law is declared in an effort to squash the emerging resistance movement. Ludwik, like Baldwin, is a political refugee, forced from his home for reasons revealed at the book's end. His formative experiences are shaped by the dawning realization that he is gay, but also by his political subterfuge. Raised by his mother and grandmother, Ludwik recalls the two women disappearing each evening into his mother's bedroom. Later, he learns that they are listening to the broadcasts of Radio Free Europe, forbidden in Poland. This early glimpse of the world beyond the Iron Curtain lights a fire in Ludwik, informing his actions in life and love.

There are recurring images in *Swimming in the Dark*, invoked in the book's title: darkness and light; suspension in a void; weightlessness. The book begins with an anecdote about Ludwik's childhood friend, a young boy named Beniek. Together, the two children would sneak away after Bible study and visit Warsaw's city center, illicit in its foreignness. Ludwik's attraction to Beniek emerges slowly. One afternoon, after a heavy rain, the two strip naked to bathe. "I was aware of wanting to see Beniek naked, surprised by the swiftness of this wish, and my heart leapt when he undressed," Ludwik writes. This attraction culminates at a church camp. There is a dance, and the lights go out. In the darkness, Ludwik acts on his desire; he and Beniek kiss just as the lights switch on. This moment, torn from the safety of the dark by the exposure of the light, is an awakening to love but also shame; it will color the rest of Ludwik's youth. Pulling away from Beniek, he writes: "I was transported into a vision of my life that made me so dizzy my head began to spin. Shame, heavy and alive, had materialized, built from buried fears and desires."

Tomasz Jedrowski

This experience, personal as it was, is inseparable from political events. After the kiss, Beniek and his family, who are Jewish, flee to Israel. Their abrupt departure is a result of a larger anti-Semitic campaign in which Jewish people in Poland were fired from their jobs and harassed into exile. "Beniek's departure spelled the end of my childhood, and of the childhood of my mind: it was as if everything I'd assumed before had turned out to be false, as if behind every innocuous thing in the world lay something much darker and uglier," Ludwik writes. Jedrowski situates this event, some twenty years after the war, amidst the history of Jewish people in Poland, most notably the thousands who lived and died in the Warsaw ghetto. This brutal history is invoked later when the adult Ludwik lives in the neighborhood that is built where the ghetto once stood. His lover, Janusz, an eager adherent of the regime, lives across town in Praga, "one of the few neighborhoods that had made it unscathed through the war," Ludwik notes. At the end of the war, Russians in Praga placidly watched the Germans destroy the oldest parts of the city. Their indifference becomes a metaphor for Janusz's willful blindness to the regime's impending collapse. In this passage and throughout the book, Jedrowski draws a firm line between those who see injustice and cruelty, and those who ignore it.

A few years after his brief relationship with Beniek, teenage Ludwik enjoys his first sexual encounter with an older man in a desolate park. The man is kind and the darkness soothes Ludwik's nerves, but tales of the man's thwarted life instill terror. At the age of twenty-two, Ludwik arrives at work camp—a mandatory sojourn for Poles his age—determined to repress his attraction to men and pursue a traditional path. His determination crumbles when he meets Janusz, the son of rural peasants who exudes the confidence Ludwik lacks. Janusz spends his evenings swimming in the river; Ludwik prefers to read, and has brought with him an illegal copy of *Giovanni's Room*, its pages neatly cut and pasted into the binding of another book. (The book is censored by the Polish government because it depicts gay sex.) The young men develop a tentative bond. Ludwik entrusts Janusz with the book and Janusz, finally, coaxes Ludwik into the water. Ludwik knows how to swim but resists the sensation of surrender that comes with being submerged. The moment comes when camp is over, and he and Janusz embark on an idyllic backpacking trip. The scenes of their budding romance are cinematic: a sudden rainstorm in the forest; a hitched ride on the back of a truck laden with cherries that they feast on. On the advice of a kindly farmer's wife, who lets them spend the night in her barn, the two make camp on the banks of a secluded lake. In the water, Ludwik writes, "I felt myself anew, as if something in me had been switched on after a long time. It was a sensation of lightness and power and total inconsequence." But like all idylls, it cannot last.

Back in the city, Ludwik and Janusz begin their adult lives. As a literature student, Ludwik aims to complete a doctorate, and proposes to write a dissertation about James Baldwin and racism in America—the closest he is allowed to get to his beloved *Giovanni's Room*. Janusz takes a job with a government-sponsored book publisher as a censor. Described in this way, their paths seem a little too obvious, but Jedrowski's world is compellingly real, and the juxtaposition of their careers is painfully believable. Ludwik and Janusz continue their romance in secret, but the economic downturn puts a strain on their relationship. No one—or almost no one—has enough to eat. Ludwik lives with an elderly widow named *Pani* Kolecka, who spends her days waiting in lines for bread and other necessities. "Waiting for nothing, queuing for a possibility," she says, ruefully. As the food shortage worsens, there are many days that she returns to the apartment empty-handed. Still, there are echoes of her perverse hope in possibility everywhere, as in: one day, there will be meat; one day, Ludwik will benefit from the system that seeks to destroy him.

When *Pani* Kolecka falls ill, a favor from a well-connected stranger saves her life. Ludwik is grateful but also livid: he questions why only those with coveted "connections" get to survive. This question becomes more pressing as Ludwik and Janusz are absorbed into a circle of wealthy new friends. At the center are siblings Hania and Maksio, children of a party leader. They drive foreign cars, drink foreign liquor, and wear foreign clothes—all astounding in their casual breach of the closed Soviet economy. While Ludwik's existence with *Pani* Kolecka is characterized by want, the lives of Hania, Maksio, and their friends are brimming with excess. In one scene, Ludwik joins them at a restaurant. Vodka flows and a decadent meal is capped with an ice cream sundae, the image of which clashes absurdly with the meager potatoes in *Pani*

Kolecka's kitchen. From the moment Hania is introduced, it is clear that she is in love with Janusz. At first, he rebuffs her advances, but the promise of her wealth—and the dazzling possibilities it represents—proves too strong a temptation. Ludwik endures Janusz's flirtation with Hania, while Janusz insists that in this cutthroat world, "Everyone is leading someone on."

Ludwik and Janusz's relationship is put to the test on a trip to Hania's family estate in the country, culminating in a climactic moment that mirrors Ludwik's illicit kiss with Beniek. By this point, the story's scope has grown much larger than the two lovers. Ludwik has had a taste of what it really looks like to resist the regime, and with his proximity to power through Hania, the stakes of his choices have become quite high. *Swimming in the Dark* is a love story, but it is also the story of a young man grappling with his place in the world. Ludwik confronts the question of what is the role of an individual trapped in an oppressive regime. In Communist Poland, where criticism of the party can only be whispered, universal questions of the self take on a new and dangerous significance. Is it more selfish to lie or to tell the truth? How do we square what we owe each other with what we owe ourselves? These questions set the book apart from similar works.

As Marcus Field wrote in a review for the London *Evening Standard*, Jedrowski's political lens yields a story that is "elegant" and "compelling." Other critics agreed, with an anonymous reviewer for *Publishers Weekly* noting, "Jedrowski's portrayal of Poland's tumultuous political transformation over several decades makes this a provocative, eye-opening exploration of the costs of defying as well as complying with social and political conventions." Several critics took particular note of Jedrowski's mastery writing in the English language despite it not being his first language. However, some reviewers did level critiques; the critic for *Kirkus* noted that Jedrowski's "prose can turn overripe and his characters feel undernourished." Still, overall critics agreed that *Swimming in the Dark* contains a masterfully crafted story. As Field concluded, the novel "has all the ingredients of the best coming-of-age gay love stories, but with its 1980s Eastern Bloc setting providing enough edginess to make it feel entirely original."

Author Biography
Swimming in the Dark is Tomasz Jedrowski's first novel. He was formerly corporate lawyer.

Molly Hagan

Review Sources
Field, Marcus. Review of *Swimming in the Dark*, by Tomasz Jedrowski. *Evening Standard*, 13 Feb. 2020, www.standard.co.uk/culture/books/swimming-in-the-dark-by-tomasz-jedrowski-review-a4361566.html. Accessed 21 Feb. 2021.

Larson, Richard Scott. "Love is Political in Tomasz Jedrowski's Debut *Swimming in the Dark*." Review of *Swimming in the Dark*, by Tomasz Jedrowski. *Slant*, 23 Apr. 2020, www.slantmagazine.com/books/review-love-is-political-in-tomasz-jedrowski-debut-swimming-in-the-dark. Accessed 21 Feb. 2021.

Review of *Swimming in the Dark*, by Tomasz Jedrowski. *Kirkus Reviews*, 13 Jan. 2020. *Literary Reference Center Plus*, search.ebscohost.com/login.aspx?direct=true&db=lkh&AN=141439345&site=lrc-plus. Accessed 21 Feb. 2021.

Review of *Swimming in the Dark*, by Tomasz Jedrowski. *Publishers Weekly*, 3 Feb. 2020, p. 44. *Literary Reference Center Plus*, search.ebscohost.com/login.aspx?direct=true&db=lkh&AN=141500866&site=lrc-plus. Accessed 21 Feb. 2021.

They Went Left

Author: Monica Hesse
Publisher: Little, Brown (New York). 384 pp.
Type of work: Novel
Time: 1945
Locales: Sosnowiec, Poland; Munich, Germany

They Went Left shares the postwar experiences of Zofia Lederman, a Jewish girl from Poland. After recovering from the concentration camps and being released from the hospital, Zofia returns to the apartment where she grew up, searching for her younger brother. When he is not there, she journeys across Europe in search of him.

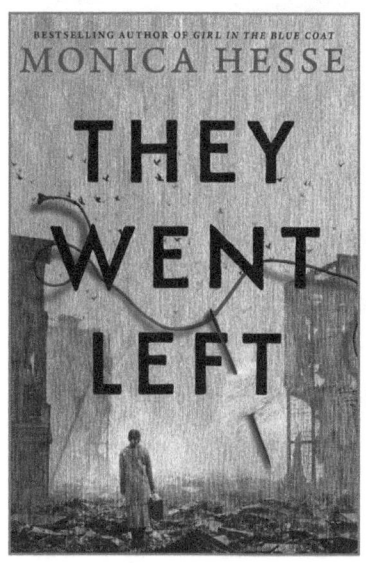

Principal characters

ZOFIA LEDERMAN, a young Jewish woman liberated from the Gross-Rosen concentration camp
ABEK LEDERMAN, her twelve-year-old brother
JOSEF, a romantic interest for Zofia
BREINE, a young woman from the refugee camp who befriends Zofia
MIRIAM, a refugee who is searching for her twin sister
DIMA, a Russian soldier who helps Zofia

Monica Hesse's *They Went Left* (2020) follows the journey of Zofia Lederman, an eighteen-year-old Jewish girl who is searching for her twelve-year-old brother, Abek, after the end of World War II. Beginning as Zofia is released from a hospital three months after her liberation from Gross-Rosen, Zofia travels first to her hometown, Sosnowiec, Poland, before crossing the border into Germany alone in search of her brother. Along her journey, she faces residual anti-Semitism from her old neighbors and kindness from strangers, witnesses the pain of other survivors, and finds happiness among the refugees at the Foehrenwald refugee camp near Munich, Germany. She also struggles with memory loss and fake memories; her mind is blocking out trauma from her time in the camps, and she struggles to piece together her past in order to find a hint to where her brother could be now. Connecting her to her life before the war is an alphabetical story Zofia had written for a then nine-year-old Abek before they were taken from their home. To help him remember the story, Zofia had written it on a piece of cloth and sewn it into the collar of his jacket. Each letter represents some part of their lives: *A* is for Abek; *B* is for Baba Rose; *C* is for Chomicki and Lederman, the family's tailoring company; *D* is for the name of the prince in Abek's favorite

Monica Hesse

fairy tale; and *Z* is for Zofia. The alphabet provides a tie to Zofia's life before the concentration camps, as she struggles with the losses forced upon her by the war. The novel is separated into three parts with chapters labeled alphabetically. Interspersed between the lettered chapters, Zofia's memories of the war are written as flashbacks in italics. These passages include snippets of times she caught a glimpse of Abek after they were separated, as well as memories of her other family members' deaths.

In writing the novel, Hesse did extensive research on the experiences of Holocaust survivors after the war; she provides some of that history in a closing section titled "A Note on History and Research." Here, she relates her desire to expose readers to the reality of the trauma faced by a whole continent in addition to the continuing devastation of the lives of those who had been incarcerated in concentration camps. To do this, she created a series of characters whose lives closely resemble the lives of Holocaust survivors. Zofia's experiences during the war are based on true events. Specific historical connections for Zofia are found in her skill as a seamstress and her transfers to different camps. Hesse relates, "In the middle of the war, a small group of young women with sewing skills were taken from Birkenau, forced into slave labor at a textile factory called Neustadt, and then later forced to march, in the winter, to the concentration camp Gross-Rosen to evade the approaching Allies. I patterned Zofia's imprisonment off that journey."

In addition to Zofia's imprisonment, other factual historical elements pervade the novel. For instance, the refugee camp that Zofia stays at— Foehrenwald—did exist "on the repurposed grounds of the I. G. Farben pharmaceutical factory, famous for making Zyklon B." The children's refugee center where Zofia searches for Abek was also a real place. Though these places are based in fact, Hesse admits to fictionalizing some aspects or intermixing features from other camps. Some of the other characters are also based on figures from the war. Miriam's separation from and later search for her twin sister, for example, is based on the story of Alice Cahana and her sister Edith, twins who were experimented on during the war and only separated after they were liberated.

These historical connections give gravity to Zofia's journey through layers of her trauma during the story. Her physical trauma is clearly stated as she tells about the loss of toes to frostbite and then later thinks, "My breasts are gone. . . . My cycle is dried up. I am shriveled." Other characters also reveal the depth of the physical horror. Miriam, one of the women who shares Zofia's cottage in Foehrenwald, has lost a twin sister after the war as a result of experiments that had been run on both of them. The twins survived the war only to be separated when Miriam's sister was sent to a hospital, where she later died. Zofia also remembers the physical scars of other women, including one who had "gashed, angry holes in her legs." While these injuries were survivable, they had lasting effects on Zofia and the others.

In addition to the physical horrors, the emotional and mental trauma Zofia experienced from the very beginning of the war illustrates the devastation the Jewish people underwent at the hands of the Nazis. At the beginning of the novel, Zofia describes herself and the women in the hospital as nothing girls "who had trouble keeping track of the days, who sometimes needed gentle reminders not to wander in the hallways with our blouses half-buttoned, who laughed and cried at inappropriate times." The emotional trauma affected everyone differently; Zofia struggles with her memory and experiences vivid flashbacks, while another woman in the hospital that the other girls called Bissel took her own life after laughing hysterically.

Zofia's psychological trauma is effectively seen in flashbacks to the years in the camps. As soon as she arrives in Sosnowiec, she meets her aunt's friend Gosia at a local grocer. As they talk about who was lost when the Jews were shipped out of town, Zofia is taken "back to that day, and that day is something I try to never think about." She falls into a memory, "slipping back . . . yelling in my ears, the smell of decay in my nostrils, feeling so thirsty and so weak and barely able to breathe." Gosia pulls her back to the present, but the depth of the trauma is revealed in her knowledge of that trigger: "The train station in Birkenau is my black ice, a sleeping black monster guarding the door of my memory. Nudge it too hard and it will wake. If it wakes, it will consume me." The depth of that pain is revealed slowly as the novel progresses. Zofia admits throughout that her memory has holes in it, and she feels like she is fantasizing her last meeting with her brother. Over time, she strips away her fake memories to confront the truth about her past.

Zofia's journey takes her through the physical and mental scarring to find a way to live the rest of her life. Though she spends the first half of the novel searching for her younger brother, she recognizes her sanity may be based on the answer to the question of whether her brother is dead. Hesse provides an answer to this when Abek arrives at the refugee camp looking for Zofia. This early search as well as the later reunion further emphasizes the importance of family to those who were left behind. Zofia knew that her father, her grandmother, her mother, and her aunt had died at the beginning of the war, but her mind would not accept that Abek may also have been killed. Miriam's search for and loss of her sister Rose provide another example of the desperation for family. Breine, who is engaged to a man she met only weeks before, teaches Zofia the importance of grabbing onto the happiness and family available rather than holding onto the grief of a past that cannot be changed. The significance of this theme is further revealed as the novel draws to a close with Zofia and Abek leaving for Ottawa, Canada, to start a new life.

Though the emotional and physical trauma experienced by the Jewish people during the war is clearly the focus of the story, Hesse does challenge readers to consider the Germans who were forced to participate in the Nazi atrocities, those who defied the Nazis by hiding Jews, and those who helped survivors start new lives. In the final historical notes appended to the novel, Hesse comments, "I don't know which is more unfathomable to me: the base evil and cruelty of the Holocaust, or the undying hope that survivors managed to take out of it." In an effort to illustrate that hope, the author has inserted several uplifting stories throughout. Zofia's search for Abek becomes an all-consuming obsession, seeming to limit her own ability to accept kindness or find happiness, but there are many people who encourage and help her in her search. For instance, Dima, the Russian soldier who was there when she was liberated, searches on his own for her brother and attempts to shield her from the lack of news he has been able to gather. Nurse Urbaniak, Mrs. Yost, Mr. Ohrmann, and Sister Therese are other characters who offer aid at various points in the novel. Zofia also sees kindness in the people in the refugee camp. Breine and Esther, her roommates, take her into their hearts, offering friendship, laughter, and hope for the future. A group of friends who plan to go to Israel offers a hope for a new kind of life as well.

There is a strong body of positive commentary on the novel. In a review for *School Library Journal*, Maryjean Riou called the book "heartbreaking and heartwarming." Elissa Gershowitz's review for the *Horn Book Magazine* pointed to the characters as "believable and sympathetic." *Booklist*'s reviewer, Michael Cart, lauded Hesse for her "verisimilitude, bringing the realities of existence in the immediate postwar period to visceral life through painstaking detail," as well as for her characterization, and for the "tone and sensibility" of the novel. Other reviews reinforced each of these qualities, recommending it as a choice piece of young adult literature for schools, libraries, and individuals interested in realistic historical fiction.

Author Biography
Monica Hesse is an award-winning journalist and novelist. She is a columnist for the *Washington Post*, where her writing focuses on gender issues and has garnered attention from the Society for Feature Journalism, the Livingston Award, and the James Beard Award. *They Went Left* is her fifth novel.

Theresa L. Stowell, PhD

Review Sources
Cart, Michael. Review of *They Went Left*, by Monica Hesse. *Booklist*, vol. 116, no. 9/10, Jan. 2020, pp. 89–90. *Literary Reference Center Plus*, search.ebscohost.com/login.aspx?direct=true&db=lkh&AN=141181596&site=lrc-plus. Accessed 13 Oct. 2020.
Gershowitz, Elissa. "Review of *They Went Left*, by Monica Hesse. *The Horn Book Magazine*, vol. 96, no. 4, July/Aug. 2020, pp. 138–39. *Literary Reference Center Plus*, search.ebscohost.com/login.aspx?direct=true&db=lkh&AN=144416021&site=lrc-plus. Accessed 13 Oct. 2020.
Riou, Maryjean. Review of *They Went Left*, by Monica Hesse. *School Library Journal*, vol. 66, no. 3, Mar. 2020, pp. 116–17. *Literary Reference Center Plus*, search.ebscohost.com/login.aspx?direct=true&db=lkh&AN=141910994&site=lrc-plus. Accessed 13 Oct. 2020.

Review of *They Went Left*, by Monica Hesse. *Kirkus Reviews*, 1 Feb. 2020, p. 1. *Literary Reference Center*, search.ebscohost.com/login.aspx?direct=true&db=lkh&AN=141438986&site=lrc-plus. Accessed 13 Oct. 2020.

Review of *They Went Left*, by Monica Hesse. *Publishers Weekly*, 17 Feb. 2020, p. 201. *Literary Reference Center Plus*, search.ebscohost.com/login.aspx?direct=true&db=lkh&AN=141765722&site=lrc-plus. Accessed 13 Oct. 2020.

Those Who Forget
My Family's Story in Nazi Europe—A Memoir, a History, a Warning

Author: Géraldine Schwarz (b. 1974)
First published: *Les Amnésiques*, 2017, in France
Translated from the French by Laura Marris
Publisher: Scribner (New York). 320 pp.
Type of work: Memoir, history, current affairs
Time: 1910s–2010s
Locales: Germany, France, Europe

Géraldine Schwarz's book combines personal, national, and social history in a complex exploration of her family's—and her nations'—involvement in the rise and remembrance of fascism and nationalism in Europe.

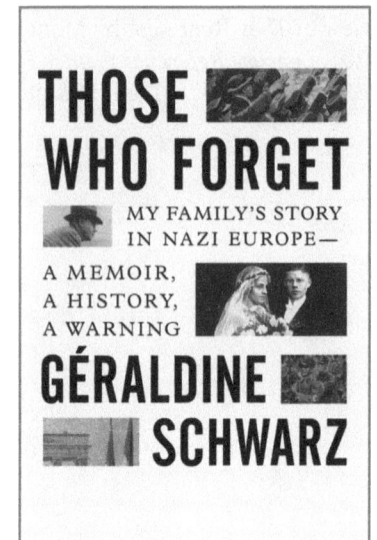

Principal personages
GÉRALDINE SCHWARZ, the author, whose complicated familial past the book explores
KARL SCHWARZ, her German grandfather
LYDIA SCHWARZ, her German grandmother
VOLKER SCHWARZ, her German father
JOSIANE SCHWARZ, her French mother
INGRID SCHWARZ, her father's sister, her aunt

Géraldine Schwarz has written an intriguingly complex but highly readable book—a book that some readers, in fact, may find difficult to put down. A surprisingly effective combination of each of the approaches mentioned in its subtitle, it manages to be, at once, autobiographical, historical, and political without being simplistic in any of these categories. When discussing her family, Schwarz finds much that is troublesome but also much to admire in all the various personalities she mentions. When discussing the history of Europe in the previous one hundred years, she manages to find several examples—not just the obvious villains—of people and behavior that fell short of the ideal. And, when discussing the political implications of the stories she tells, she once again goes beyond transparent assessments to explore subtler shadings of responsibility.

The broad outlines of the book are clear: Schwarz descended, on one side of her family, from German grandparents who lived under the twentieth-century Nazi regime and openly admired Adolf Hitler (her grandmother) and/or voiced few complaints (her grandfather, who joined the Nazi Party). Her grandparents actually profited from Hitler's campaign against German Jews when her grandfather purchased, at a bargain price, the business owned by a family of Jewish people who feared they would have to flee Germany as anti-Semitic persecution increased. Later, after the end of the war, her grandfather was sued by the Jewish family for allegedly having taken advantage of their plight, although her grandfather insisted that he had done nothing legally or even morally wrong. Schwarz's father, on the other hand, was always deeply disturbed by Germany's Nazi legacy in general and by his own father's behavior in particular. Unlike many Germans who lived in the aftermath of the war, Schwarz's father, who had sought to understand the whole truth of Nazi Germany, taught his children to despise the Nazis and to question authority in general.

Géraldine Schwarz

In the 1960s—a decade, along with the 1970s, that Schwarz explores in valuable detail—Schwarz's father met a young woman from France whom he would marry in 1971. This fact helps explain Schwarz's interestingly hybrid name. She is, in a sense, a literal embodiment of the new, postwar Europe. Raised in France, she lives and works in Germany, obviously loves both her father and other members of her father's family, and even has many positive memories of her German grandparents. Her grandfather, who comes across as tough minded both as a parent and as a businessman, had some genuinely admirable traits. Her German grandmother, who admired Hitler even after the war, nonetheless comes across as a genuinely loving person, especially in her treatment of her Hitler-hating son. Schwarz makes absolutely no apologies for her grandparents' conduct or attitudes, and in fact she seems persistently skeptical about some of her grandfather's explanations of his behavior. But her purpose, it would seem, is less to judge her grandparents than to try to understand just how and why they thought, felt, and behaved as they did. She wants to show how ordinary people could wind up supporting Hitler.

The Nazi leaders, of course, are the clear and unequivocal villains in Schwarz's book. But, once again, Schwarz seems less interested in restating the obvious than in trying to explore just how and why so many ordinary Germans found themselves supporting Hitler and his regime not only before the war but also once the war had obviously become a lost cause. Schwarz operates less as a judge than as a psychologist, and when she *does* criticize or assign blame, she finds more than enough figures and movements, among practically every part of the political spectrum and in practically every European nation, to hold accountable to various degrees. For example, her hatred of Hitler and the Nazis, and her contempt for their plan to exterminate Europe's Jews, are beyond dispute. But she also asserts that one of the failures of the postwar Nuremberg trials was to neglect various "Allied war crimes: the Vichy collaboration; the massive American and British bombardments against German civilians; the atrocities committed by the Red Army in the Reich's eastern territories; the atomic bombs dropped by the United States on Japan." She also declares that "one of the greatest failures of the trials was to neglect the genocide of the Jews, as this offense did not yet exist."

Of great interest is Schwarz's treatment of the widespread anti-Semitism that existed in France, both before and during the war. She is especially tough on the Vichy government, which technically governed the parts of occupied France not directly ruled by the Nazis. Many citizens of France, both during and after the war, tended to ignore or justify the conduct of the Vichy regime, which often collaborated with the Germans in their persecution of Jews and others. Discussing a French concentration camp that existed not far from the childhood home of her own mother, Schwarz writes, "'I had no idea what Drancy was,' my mother says, with a slightly guilty air. 'Not in the fifties, and not in the sixties either.'" Continuing, Schwarz considers "how she managed to be unaware that one of the biggest Vichy dramas had taken place right next to where she was living, just a few years before her family moved to the area." This quotation is representative of Schwarz's method to leave no one off the hook, a commendable example of her determination to explore the complexities of any situation, no matter where such exploration leads. Yet while such instances authentically indicate the limits of the author's knowledge, the frequency of times in which Schwarz assumes, or imagines, or speculates that people "must have" thought or behaved in one way or another is, perhaps, the most unsettling aspect of an otherwise very fine book.

Schwarz *does* frequently pass judgment on the many individual people, and peoples, she describes. But her assessments of responsibility are even-handed. Even when she does find fault, she tries to suggest why the fault occurred, or at least how those at fault justified their actions. For example, her book highlights that millions of Germans supported Nazism at least in part due to their struggles in the aftermath of World War I. And after World War II, numbers of Nazis who might have been prosecuted were not partly because the lack of prison space—and the rise of the Cold War—made mass prosecutions impractical. The Allies were horrified by Hitler's anti-Semitism, but they did little to prevent it before the war, and during the war they argued that they had more pressing efforts to deal with than conducting any direct intervention on behalf of the Jews.

Ironically, by the end of the book, Germany as a twenty-first century nation comes off pretty well. One main argument of Schwarz's book is that the West Germans (not governed by communism) eventually, by the 1960s, 1970s, and 1980s, began to make real efforts to come to terms with Germany's guilt for the crimes committed under Hitler's reign. By the end of the 1980s, the West Germans had done the hard work of learning about, and accepting responsibility for their own (or their parents' and grandparents') culpability in the reach and damage of Nazism. In other nations in Europe—such as France, Italy, and Austria—this attempt to come to an honest reckoning with an embarrassing past was actually much less advanced than it was in West Germany. Schwarz gives most modern Germans credit for having done what she calls the necessary "memory work" to come to terms, honestly, with the nation's past. She writes, "One of the great achievements of this work in Germany is that it has not only involved large groups but has also managed to place an emphasis on how an individual might transform into an offender, or at least a *Mitläufer* ["follower"]." Germany, she says, "has fully exploited memory work to anchor democracy in its society and its institutions. Other countries have missed that chance." In this way, a book that begins as an indictment of the Germany of the 1930s and 1940s ends as a tribute to the Germany of the twenty-first century. (Although even here Schwarz sees complications, as when she notes some of the negative effects, mainly an increased influence of populism and nationalism, of German chancellor Angela Merkel's acceptance of refugees fleeing the Middle East).

Those Who Forget, in short, is an immensely complex and thought-provoking work. It was critically acclaimed both in France, where it was first published, and many other countries. It also received numerous prizes, with reviewers praising it as a remarkable debut book. Schwarz's focus on the importance of nations facing up to their own responsibilities for and coming to terms with any problems that exist, past or present, and not taking the easy way out by merely blaming others or practicing selective remembrance, is universally relevant. Hitler is the true villain of the book, but most other figures emerge as something more complicated than simple victims or collaborators, and this is a substantial message for readers of any time or country.

Author Biography

Géraldine Schwarz is a European journalist and filmmaker. *Those Who Forget: My Family's Story in Nazi Europe—A Memoir, a History, a Warning*, is her first book.

Translator Laura Marris has written her own prose and poetry published in such outlets as the *New York Times* and *North American Review*. She has translated works by authors that have included Christophe Boltanski and Louis Guilloux.

Robert C. Evans, PhD

Review Sources

Cole, Diane. "'Those Who Forget' Review: Accounting for Evil." Review of *Those Who Forget: My Family's Story in Nazi Europe—A Memoir, a History, a Warning*, by Géraldine Schwarz. *The Wall Street Journal*, www.wsj.com/articles/those-who-forget-review-accounting-for-evil-11599836504. Accessed 14 Jan. 2021.

Goldman, Crystal. Review of *Those Who Forget: My Family's Story in Nazi Europe—A Memoir, a History, a Warning*, by Géraldine Schwarz. *Library Journal*, 1 Mar. 2020, www.libraryjournal.com/?reviewDetail=those-who-forget-my-familys-story-in-nazi-europe-a-memoir-a-history-a-warning. Accessed 10 Jan. 2021.

Power, Samantha. "A Memoir of a Family's Holocaust Complicity, with Lessons for Today." Review of *Those Who Forget: My Family's Story in Nazi Europe—A Memoir, a History, a Warning*, by Géraldine Schwarz. *The Washington Post*, 16 Oct. 2020, www.washingtonpost.com/outlook/a-memoir-of-a-familys-holocaust-complicity-with-lessons-for-today/2020/10/15/cec30112-e308-11ea-8181-606e603bb1c4_story.html. Accessed 10 Jan. 2021.

Review of *Those Who Forget: My Family's Story in Nazi Europe—A Memoir, a History, a Warning*, by Géraldine Schwarz. *Kirkus*, 5 Feb. 2020, www.kirkusreviews.com/book-reviews/geraldine-schwarz/those-who-forget/. Accessed 10 Jan. 2021.

Review of *Those Who Forget: My Family's Story in Nazi Europe—A Memoir, a History, a Warning*, by Géraldine Schwarz. *Publishers Weekly*, 13 Mar. 2020, www.publishersweekly.com/978-1-5011-9908-0. Accessed 14 Jan. 2021.

The Thursday Murder Club

Author: Richard Osman (b. 1970)
Publisher: Pamela Dorman Books (New York). 368 pp.
Type of work: Novel
Time: Present day
Locale: Kent, England

Four retirees work together to solve cold cases in The Thursday Murder Club, *but when a local contractor is killed, they become involved in two present-day cases that are closely connected to the retirement village where they live.*

Principal characters
JOYCE, a retired nurse, the newest member of the Thursday Murder Club
ELIZABETH, a leader of the Thursday Murder Club
RON RITCHIE, a retired political leader, a member of the Thursday Murder Club
IBRAHIM ARIF, a retired psychiatrist, a member of the Thursday Murder Club
PENNY GRAY, a cofounder of the Thursday Murder Club, a retired police inspector
DONNA DE FREITAS, a police inspector befriended by the club members
CHRIS HUDSON, the police detective in charge of murder cases
IAN VENTHAM, a wealthy businessman
TONY CURRAN, a shady contractor

In the acknowledgements of *The Thursday Murder Club* (2020), television personality and comedian Richard Osman writes, "I first had the idea for this book a few years ago, when I was fortunate enough to visit a retirement community full of extraordinary people with extraordinary stories." This book, Osman's first novel, follows fictionalized versions of four of those residents and the friendship they develop as they join the Thursday Murder Club, a social group with a shared interest in trying to solve cold-case murders. The group was founded by Elizabeth, an enigmatic woman whose murky background hints at governmental or police work, and her friend Penny Gray, a retired police officer. After Penny becomes comatose, Elizabeth asks retired nurse Joyce to join the group, adding her to the ranks of former psychologist Ibrahim Arif and former union leader Ron Ritchie. As the group works together to solve one of Penny's first cases, lives are changed when contemporary events force secrets from the past into the open.

The novel is structured in a collection of short chapters told from varied points of view. There are a number of first-person journal entries written by Joyce, who records the actions and events as witnessed by the Thursday Murder Club. Interspersed between Joyce's thoughts are third-person narrated chapters that move the action of the story along, as well as a few limited omniscient chapters focusing on several other characters. Some chapters showcase the other members of the Thursday Murder Club, while others provide additional insight into Donna De Freitas and Chris Hudson, two police officers whom the group befriends. Ian Ventham, Tony Curran, and Bogdan Jankowski, the three men involved with the development and building of the retirement community Coopers Chase, are given time as well. Even Father Mackie—a local priest whose interest in the community is based on its proximity to a Catholic cemetery dedicated to the nuns who once ran the convent now at the center of the complex—is the focus of a few chapters. This quick alternation between narrative chapters gives a lively pace to the action and helps build the suspense as murders occur and theories abound about who should be a suspect and who should not.

Richard Osman

The Thursday Murder Club begins as Elizabeth, Ibrahim, Ron, and the newly joined Joyce are working on the cold case of a young woman's murder in the 1970s, one of Penny Gray's first cases. The young woman's boyfriend had been the primary suspect, and Penny had overseen transporting him. Unfortunately for the young officer, the man attacked her on their way to the jail, escaping, never to be seen again. This case is pushed to the background as Tony Curran, a developer and a minor partner in Coopers Chase, is killed in his own kitchen right after being kicked off the project by Ian Ventham, the charismatic lead investor in the project. Later, Ian himself is murdered on the same day that Bogdan Jankowski, another person involved in the construction, finds the bones of a yet another murder victim buried in a grave in the convent's cemetery. The four protagonists seek out clues to identify the murderer or murderers, partly in an effort to lift suspicion from Ron's son, Jason, and partly out of sheer curiosity. Though their search for clues interferes with the police investigation, Elizabeth gets Donna De Freitas—a young, inexperienced inspector whom the Thursday Murder Club has befriended—assigned to the case. The four octogenarians provide invaluable insight that helps Donna and her superior officer, Chris Hudson, discover the truth behind the deaths of Tony and Ian, as well as a few deaths from years before. Osman creates an intricately intertwined series of murders that include a variety of twists before the real killers are revealed.

The mystery itself would not be nearly as engaging without a cast of characters who give the story an emotional and humorous depth. Ibrahim is a dignified retired psychologist who sees under the masks people wear. Ron is a former political leader and is comfortable protesting anything he feels might be unfair. Joyce is seen as a go-getter and is the newest member of the community and of the club, having moved to Coopers Chase after the death of her husband. Elizabeth's background is less concrete. She possesses the ability to manipulate people, but her maneuvers are so appealing that everyone is disarmed by her behavior, even Donna and Chris. Donna and Chris become almost as important as the four elderly murder investigators, as their official connection to the cases intertwines with the friends' inquiries. Donna has left her post in the big city after a nasty breakup. Though her career in her former post was going well, she has been relegated to the bottom of the roster in her new position, so when she befriends Elizabeth, Joyce, Ron, and Ibrahim, and they help her become part of the murder team under Chris, she is thrilled. Chris is a middle-aged man whose body, attitude, and career are in a slump. Though he is good at his job, he is lonely. As the Curran murder case progresses, his interactions with the group and Donna give him a new sense of purpose.

Another important aspect of the novel is the setting: the fictional Coopers Chase Retirement Village. Built around a Catholic convent and bordering the cemetery for the nuns, Coopers Chase is "billed as 'Britain's First Luxury Retirement Village.'" Ironically, Ibrahim points out that "it was actually the seventh," but that does not take away from the luxury accommodations, including a pool, a jacuzzi, a bowling green, and "twelve acres of woodland and beautiful open hillside." It holds almost three hundred residents in its apartments and in the Willows, the nursing home annex to which people relocate at the end of their lives. Though the complex is financially successful, Ian Ventham strives to expand, working to purchase neighboring land and sweet-talking officials into allowing him to move the nun's graveyard. Despite Ventham's problematic dealings, the residents are content with the peaceful setting, social outlets, and comfortable accommodations.

Osman's comedic background is seen at several points in the book, offering humorous commentary to lighten the mood. For instance, early in the novel, when talking about Coopers Chase, the description notes, "The Parking Committee is the single most powerful cabal within Coopers Chase." Ron's son, Jason, is often the subject of humor as well. Jason is a retired boxer who is not ready to leave the limelight of fame, so he clings to national attention through participation in televised contests such as *MasterChef* and *Celebrity Ice Dancing*. This leaves him open to mockery, especially as Chris and Donna observe him failing at learning to ice skate. Joyce's rambling journal entries add to the humor as well. Her naivete and gentle soul inspire a chuckle throughout. She bluntly comments, "People without a sense of humor will never forgive you for being funny." Her confession that she pretends to be out when flowers arrive from her daughter, so someone else will sign for them and notice the attention she is getting is "Terrible of me, really" but makes her even more likable.

Though there are touches of humor throughout the novel, Osman also highlights a few serious end-of-life topics. The loss of a loved one is one of the most inclusive. Joyce is trying to move on after the death of her husband; her friend Bernard Cottle grieves the loss of his wife; and Elizabeth struggles with Penny's move to the Willows nursing home unit as well as her own husband's declining mental state. While Penny lies comatose in the Willows, her husband, John, sits patiently at her bedside. Elizabeth and Ibrahim visit regularly, but Ron is uncomfortable seeing his friend in this state. Osman is not afraid to confront euthanasia, end-of-life choices, regret, secrets and confessions, or dementia. Relationships with adult children are also mentioned. Joyce's pride in her daughter, Joanna, abounds, but Joanna does not visit as often as Joyce would like. Jason, in contrast, is often at the facility visiting with Ron and his friends. In addition, the novel touches on the importance of love in the lives of the main characters. Joyce, ready to love again, flirts with Bernard. Elizabeth's relationship with her husband, Stephen, is bittersweet. She loves him more than herself, but she grieves him as he loses touch with the reality of present-day life. Father Mackie's youthful love life, which ended with tragedy, is even brought into the story. Chris, on the other hand, is young enough to have the hope of a new relationship with an unexpected introduction that could tie him even more closely with his young protégé.

The critical attention for the novel is largely positive. The *Library Journal* dubbed it a debut of the month. In their review for the magazine, Lesa Holstine called the book "suspenseful, funny, and poignant." Osman was repeatedly praised for his characters. Candace Smith's review of the audio version of the novel, written for *Booklist*, stated, "The four seniors have colorful backstories, of course, and their behind-the-scenes plotting make this even more fun," while Henrietta Verma's review of the print novel for *Booklist* commented, "A thicket of characters demands some concentration, but it's worth it to soak up Osman's wry character building and dialogue." In addition, many critics acknowledged Osman's ability to fuse his comedic personality with an interesting story in a well-written way. The *Publishers Weekly* review noted, "Osman's witty prose . . . is a highlight." An anonymous reviewer for *Kirkus Reviews* concluded that the novel was "a top-class cozy [mystery] infused with dry wit and charming characters who draw you in and leave you wanting more."

Author Biography
Richard Osman is best known as an English television personality, comedian, and producer who has appeared on a variety of programs, most notably as the presenter on the quiz show *Pointless*. *The Thursday Murder Club* is his first novel.

Theresa L. Stowell, PhD

Review Sources
Holstine, Lesa. Review of *The Thursday Murder Club*, by Richard Osman. *Library Journal*, vol. 145, no. 8, Aug. 2020, p. 43. *Literary Reference Center Plus*, search.ebscohost.com/login.aspx?direct=true&db=lkh&AN=144664732&site=lrc-plus. Accessed 11 Dec. 2020.

Smith, Candace. Review of *The Thursday Murder Club*, by Richard Osman. *Booklist*, 1 Nov. 2020, p. 79. *Literary Reference Center Plus*, search.ebscohost.com/login.aspx?direct=true&db=lkh&AN=147007689&site=lrc-plus. Accessed 11 Dec. 2020.

Review of *The Thursday Murder Club*, by Richard Osman. *Kirkus Reviews*, 15 July 2020. *Literary Reference Center Plus*, search.ebscohost.com/login.aspx?direct=true&db=lkh&AN=144522657&site=lrc-plus. Accessed 11 Dec. 2020.

Review of *The Thursday Murder Club*, by Richard Osman. *Publishers Weekly*, 6 Aug. 2020, p. 48–52. *Literary Reference Center Plus*, search.ebscohost.com/login.aspx?direct=true&db=lkh&AN=144381750&site=lrc-plus. Accessed 11 Dec. 2020.

Verma, Henrietta. Review of *The Thursday Murder Club*, by Richard Osman. *Booklist*, 1 Aug. 2020, p. 31. *Literary Reference Center Plus*, search.ebscohost.com/login.aspx?direct=true&db=lkh&AN=145062828&site=lrc-plus. Accessed 11 Dec. 2020.

Tigers, Not Daughters

Author: Samantha Mabry (b. 1980)
Publisher: Algonquin Young Readers (Chapel Hill, NC). 288 pp.
Type of work: Novel
Time: Present day
Locale: Southtown neighborhood, San Antonio, Texas

In Samantha Mabry's third young adult novel, three sisters try to cope with the death of their fourth sister, whose ghostly presence haunts their home, as well as with the overbearing men in their lives.

Principal characters
JESSICA TORRES, the second youngest of the Torres sisters, sixteen, who works at a pharmacy
ROSA TORRES, the youngest sister, twelve, who is kind and has an affinity with animals
IRIDIAN TORRES, the third youngest sister, fifteen, who is an avid reader and writer
ANA TORRES, the oldest sister, seventeen, who dies and reappears as a ghost
RAFE TORRES, the girls' father
JOHN CHAVEZ, Jessica's boyfriend
PETER ROJAS, Jessica's coworker at the pharmacy

Samantha Mabry's haunting young adult novel *Tigers, Not Daughters* (2020) is a meditation on grief with a feminist twist. Mabry delves into the inner lives of the three surviving Torres sisters, Jessica, Iridian, and Rosa, who grieve for their oldest sister, Ana, after she falls from a window trying to make a late-night escape to see her boyfriend. The sisters are also frustrated and sometimes abused by the men in their lives, including a father who enforces rigid rules and is lost in his own grief, and a controlling boyfriend. Further complicating the plot is Ana's ghost, who makes her presence known and forces the sisters to face their grief and make decisions about their future. Thus, Mabry weaves together a complex tale of the ways these young Latina women experience the grief, ghosts, and overbearing men in their lives, ultimately finding their voices and their paths forward.

Tigers, Not Daughters is set mainly in the present day a year after Ana's death, in the Southtown neighborhood of San Antonio, Texas, where the Torres family lives. Each of the surviving sisters copes with her grief differently, and Mabry highlights these differences with a multinarrator format. Chapters alternate between each sister's point of view, though with close third-person narration rather than their direct words.

Samantha Mabry

Other chapters do present first-person perspective, that of the neighborhood boys who observe the sisters (in particular, they would gather to watch Ana undress by her window). This narrative difference subtly emphasizes the fact that girls and women are often defined and controlled by the male gaze rather than their own agency. Yet the story shows how the Torres sisters ultimately transcend this kind of objectification, proving very capable of taking care of themselves and each other even as they grieve and struggle.

Mabry's characterization is strong and realistic, especially for the three central protagonists. Their different responses to Ana's death are important aspects of both their personalities and the plot that develops. Jessica's grief sometimes manifests itself as anger, such as when she lashes out at a priest who criticized Ana at her funeral. More often, however, her grief is expressed by her trying to become her older sister. Jessica moves into Ana's room, secures most of Ana's possessions, including lipstick and old cigarettes, and takes Ana's boyfriend, John Chavez, as her own. Iridian, on the other hand, turns her grief inward. She gathers Ana's collection of fantasy romance novels, especially Anne Rice's *The Witching Hour* (1990), her favorite, which she reads over and over. She also becomes an obsessive writer, filling notebook after notebook with passages of her own fantasy novel, one she hopes to publish. Iridian is so obsessed with her writing she rarely leaves the house. Rosa, meanwhile, is the most spiritual of the sisters and is known for her kindness. She expresses her grief by being the only member of her family to attend church weekly after Ana's death. She also has an affinity with animals, believing she has the potential to communicate with them, especially the fireflies in her yard and the hyena who escapes from the zoo on the anniversary of Ana's death. Overall, the sisters' very different reactions affirm that there are many ways to grieve, while also establishing each character as a distinct, nuanced individual.

While the sisters are the clear heroes of the story and provide the bulk of the novel's perspective, the narration by the boys across the street also plays an important part. Their chapters focus mostly on the past, before Ana died, and offer insight into the background of the Torres family and the dynamics of the Southtown neighborhood. They introduce the reader to pivotal events from the past year, such as explaining why Iridian spends all her time at home, on the couch reading and writing, rather than in school. (Their chapters are very aptly titled after these events, for example "The Day Iridian Torres Walked Away from the Tenth Grade.") The boys are also the first to see Ana as a ghost. They function as a kind of Greek chorus, commenting on the behavior of the main characters in a collective voice. This is one of the reasons Mabry's novel is often compared to *The Virgin Suicides* (1993) by Jeffrey Eugenides, which also used neighborhood boys for commentary on the main characters and important events.

The neighborhood boys also serve another role in addition to providing backstory. Because they are "watchers," they do not often engage with the sisters, and they notably fail to help the girls in several situations. The boys watch Ana fall out of the window but do nothing to help her, and when Iridian encounters the hyena and runs to them for help, they fail to assist or even believe her. Though they collectively regret their actions later and wish they had done more, they are useless when it matters. In this way they represent the weakness of the male gaze.

Furthermore, as Emma Carbone noted for the *Washington Independent Review of Books*, the incidents the boys relate "chronicle all the ways the sisters have been objectified—and failed—by the men in their lives." This extends beyond the pathetic, peeping boys themselves and to adult figures who should know better. Most notably, this includes the Torres sisters' father, Rafe, who is equally unresponsive and controlling. He is lost in his own grief over Ana, but channels this into drunkenness and other irresponsible behavior. Therefore, he is almost completely incapable of supporting his other daughters in dealing with their own loss or their everyday lives. Instead he leans on them, even asking them for money, while strictly enforcing the house rules and criticizing the girls to the point of cruelty. For example, he berates Iridian about her writing and compares her unfavorably to her sisters.

The other major example of negative male presence in the sisters' lives is John, Jessica's boyfriend who used to date Ana. He is controlling and physically abusive. He wants to know where Jessica is at all times and constantly texts her for her whereabouts. After he suspects that Jessica is getting closer to her coworker Peter Rojas, John's obsessive jealousy turns violent. All too realistically, it is difficult for Jessica to break free of his control. The overarching feminist message is clear as the Torres sisters come to understand that they are on their own and must rely on each other.

Another important element of *Tigers, Not Daughters* is Mabry's use of magical realism, the literary style that blurs the lines between reality and fantasy. (Significantly, magical realism is heavily associated with Latino authors, complementing the Latino focus of Mabry's story.) The presence of a ghost in an otherwise highly realistic world is of course the main expression of this. Mabry does not present the ghost story element like typical supernatural or horror fiction, but rather takes a more literary approach in which the fantastical elements provide deeper meaning. For example, one or more of the sisters often smell oranges as a sign that Ana's ghost is about to make an appearance. Oranges signal a happier time, when the Torres sisters were all together and happy at their Aunt Francine's. She lived near orange groves, and they spent a peaceful week with her after Ana died. The literary nature of the supernatural elements is reinforced when Iridian sees evidence of a ghostly visit: "Scattered down the staircase were the books—Iridian's books, Ana's books—that had once been stacked neatly in Iridian's closet with the spines facing the wall. They were now spread out, some with their pages yawned open."

Ana's ghostly presence increases and intensifies throughout the novel. She appears to Jessica as a hand on her shower curtain, and again to Iridian in writing on the wall.

All the surviving sisters hear Ana's laughter. Though they are scared, they are also eager to figure out the message Ana is trying to convey. At first, Jessica thinks Ana wants them all to escape and leave their home and controlling father, since Ana had initiated a similar plan when she was alive. However, by the end of the novel, they all realize Ana's message is much different and a more positive one. In this way, Mabry uses magical realism as a vehicle to help the sisters better understand each other and their future path.

Critical reception to *Tigers, Not Daughters* was highly positive, with starred reviews in many trade publications. Some reviews did point out a few minor issues or concerns. The critic for *Publishers Weekly* pointed out that the "multiple narratives read more like a series of vignettes than a cohesive whole," while Chris Rhodes, in a review for the website *Latinxs in Kid Lit*, felt the story was at times "muddled" and "might prove alienating to readers who want a straightforward narrative." But both those reviewers praised the novel overall, and other critics also found much to admire, especially in the strong portrayal of young women and the skillful prose. For example, the reviewer for *Kirkus* noted that "the evocative language and deft characterization will haunt—and empower—readers." Writing for the *Washington Independent Review of Books*, Emma Carbone called the novel a "timely ode to sisterhood and feminism." Mabry's novel gives voice to those who have suffered palpable grief, and though *Tigers, Not Daughters* is a novel filled with difficult moments of death, grief, hauntings and abuse, the sisters ultimately move beyond their grief and learn to appreciate the bonds they have with each other.

Author Biography

Writer and teacher Samantha Mabry made her literary debut with the young adult novel *A Fierce and Subtle Poison* (2016). She earned a National Book Award for Young Peoples' Literature nomination for her second novel, the Western *All the Wind in the World* (2017).

Marybeth Rua-Larsen

Review Sources

Carbone, Emma. Review of *Tigers, Not Daughters*, by Samantha Mabry. *Washington Independent Review of Books*, 20 Mar. 2020, www.washingtonindependentreviewofbooks.com/index.php/bookreview/tigers-not-daughters. Accessed 17 Mar. 2021.

Foster, Ann. Review of *Tigers, Not Daughters*, by Samantha Mabry. *School Library Journal*, 1 Apr. 2020, www.slj.com/?reviewDetail=tigers-not-daughters. Accessed 17 Mar. 2021.

Paxson, Caitlyn. "'Tigers, Not Daughters' Is Haunting—with or without a Ghost." Review of *Tigers, Not Daughters*, by Samantha Mabry. *NPR*, 26 Mar. 2020, www.npr.org/2020/03/26/821587156/tigers-not-daughters-is-haunting-with-or-without-a-ghost. Accessed 17 Mar. 2021.

Rhodes, Chris. Review of *Tigers, Not Daughters*, by Samantha Mabry. *Latinxs in Kid Lit*, 7 Sept. 2020, latinosinkidlit.com/2020/09/10/book-review-tigers-not-daughters-by-samantha-mabry/. Accessed 17 Mar. 2021.

Review of *Tigers, Not Daughters*, by Samantha Mabry. *Kirkus*, 21 Dec. 2019, www.kirkusreviews.com/book-reviews/samantha-mabry/tigers-not-daughters/. Accessed 17 Mar. 2021.

Review of *Tigers, Not Daughters*, by Samantha Mabry. *Publishers Weekly*, 9 Jan. 2020, www.publishersweekly.com/978-1-61620-896-7. Accessed 17 Mar. 2021.

Tokyo Ueno Station

Author: Yu Miri (b. 1968)
First published: *JR Ueno-eki Koen-guchi*, 2014, in Japan
Translated from the Japanese by Morgan Giles
Publisher: Riverhead Books (New York). 192 pp.
Type of work: Novel
Time: ca. 2014
Locales: Tokyo and Fukushima Province, Japan

In the novel Tokyo Ueno Station, *a ghostly narrator who haunts a public park tells his life story and sheds light on the economic divide in modern-day Japan.*

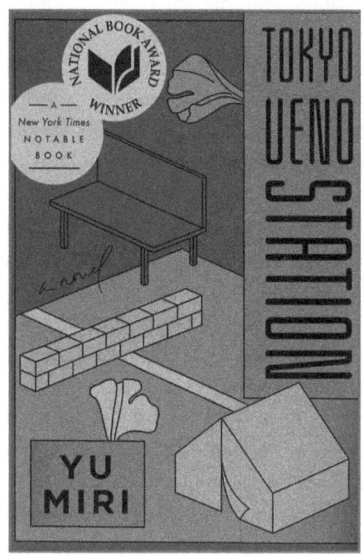

Principal characters

Kazu, the narrator, a ghost haunting Tokyo's Ueno Park, where he spent the last several years of his life in a homeless encampment
Setsuko, his wife, who remained in Fukushima to raise their children when Kazu had to leave to find work
Kōichi, his son, who died at the age of twenty-one
Yoko, his daughter
Mari, his granddaughter
Shige, his friend, a gentle and erudite homeless man who shared various historical facts

Yu Miri's *Tokyo Ueno Station* is a luminous novel that is at once the story of an individual's life and a window onto the economic divide in modern-day Japan. It focuses on a man named Kazu, who finds that after his death his consciousness continues to dwell in and around Tokyo's Ueno Park, where he had lived in a makeshift homeless encampment for the last several years of his life. In the stylistically inventive narrative, Kazu's life story is interspersed with announcements from the nearby train station, snatches of dialogue from walkers in the park, and the text of plaques posted by statues or signs put up by park officials. The overall effect is kaleidoscopic and otherworldly, as the reader is immersed in the world of this urban park and the lives of its residents. For a slim and compact novel, *Tokyo Ueno Station* offers a remarkably wide-ranging view of Japanese history and culture and sheds light on the social inequality that is the underbelly of the country's seeming prosperity.

Kazu's life is marked by disappointment and tragedy. As a young man and as the oldest of his siblings, he leaves his remote farm town in Fukushima prefecture to find work in more prosperous parts of Japan. For most of his adult life, Kazu works with his hands, whether trawling for clams or helping to dig out the foundations for athletic facilities for Tokyo's 1964 Olympic Games. He sleeps in worker dormitories, eats simple meals, and works overtime in order to send home the checks that are a lifeline for his parents, siblings, wife, and children. The great irony of Kazu's story is that these sacrifices provide a life for his family that ultimately does not include him. He travels home perhaps twice a year, and so misses seeing his children grow up. In scenes that he recalls with his children, the laconic Kazu seems almost a stranger to the family. He will later lament that he has no pictures of himself with his son, Kōichi, who dies in Tokyo as a young man. In a sense, the itinerant Kazu was a ghost even before he died.

Kazu does have a period of some years where he is able to retire to Fukushima and be reunited with his wife, Setsuko. But when first his elderly parents and then Setsuko die, Kazu finds himself alone again. While his daughter Yoko and granddaughter Mari try to care for him, Kazu feels that he is a burden to them. He leaves for Tokyo, where he lives in a makeshift shack in Ueno Park, makes a little money by scavenging for recyclable cans and magazines, and becomes part of a community of homeless people who have left their former lives and families behind them.

At the other end of the social and economic spectrum from Kazu lies the Emperor of Japan. Yet Kazu sees parallels between his life and that of the sovereign. Both men were born in the same year, and their sons were born on the same day. Kazu even chooses a name for his son that shares a character with that of the emperor's son. Ueno Park, Kazu's adopted home, was a gift from a former emperor (its official name is Ueno Imperial Gift Park). When members of the Imperial family are processing through or along the park, officials require that homeless people break down their encampment and vacate the area. On the last day of his life, Kazu wanders Tokyo, having been evicted from Ueno Park for the day, and then sees the emperor pass by in his motorcade. The parallels between the two men are powerful and haunting. While Yu does not overstate the point, the reader may find themselves asking why one man should live in luxury while another sleeps under a tarp.

The novel presents other parallels and ironies that underscore the unfairness of Kazu's situation. As a young man, he helped build the facilities for the 1964 Olympics; in old age he is displaced by officials eager to clean up Tokyo in order to impress the 2020 Olympic Committee. Kazu's years of toil and sacrifice bring not a well-deserved retirement among family members, but further hardship. By the same token, his death does not reunite him with his departed loved ones, but rather continues his lonely existence in the park. While Kazu is haunted by his mother's observation, after Kōichi's death, that he never had any luck, his life is not merely one of bad fortune. Rather, Kazu is a victim of economic forces that lie beyond his control. Though Kazu himself does not seem to harbor any animosity toward the emperor or the state, Yu makes it clear that his life was shaped not by poor choices or bad luck, but by deep structural inequalities in the country. By extension, this must be true of many of the other homeless people in the park and across Japan. Kazu compares being homeless to being invisible, and Yu, in telling Kazu's story, is determined to make visible the lives of people at the bottom of the economic and social ladder.

Despite its brevity, *Tokyo Ueno Station* is discursive in nature and touches on many aspects of Japanese history and culture. An acquaintance of Kazu's in the homeless community, Shige, has a scholarly bent and becomes one of the mouthpieces for Yu's discussion of history. Shige talks, for example, of the American firebombing of Tokyo. Not only did these raids target civilians, but they focused on the poorer neighborhoods where light industry and the labor force were concentrated. In these discussions, history becomes not an abstract set of events and dates, but an illustration of the forces that explain present-day gaps in wealth and opportunity. A statue in Ueno Park of a nineteenth-century rebel leader, Saigō Takamuri, likewise prompts the reader to think about the situations of Kazu, Shige, and other disenfranchised people. What is the point at which one should turn against one's leaders? In Fukushima, Kazu's mother discusses their family's religion, Pure Land Buddhism. The central tenant of the Pure Land sect is a hopeful one: upon death its adherents believe they will be reunited with their loved ones in a better place. Yet Kazu's afterlife in Ueno Park is nothing like what has been promised him. He has worked hard and done his duty, yet both his government and his religion have failed to recognize and reward his obedience.

Finally, the specter of natural and human-made disasters hangs over this novel. Today, the name Fukushima is as associated with nuclear catastrophe as Chernobyl or Three Mile Island. From the moment that Kazu mentions his home prefecture, the reader is braced to learn of who he might lose to the 2011 earthquake and tsunami that ravaged this area, causing a nuclear reactor meltdown and explosion. The immense power and scope of such forces is palpable in Yu's novel. The suggestion is that self-determination is an illusion; rather, each of our lives are buffeted and shaped by things that lie beyond our control.

One of the delights of *Tokyo Ueno Station* is Yu's inventive mode of narration, in which Kazu's narrative is punctuated by other voices from in and around the park. An announcement in the train station, the text of a sign on the grass, or conversation between two walkers in the park might suddenly appear in the midst of Kazu's story. It is as if his consciousness has become permeable, or as if his story is as ghostly as his body. This Joycean, multivalent technique allows Yu to expand the range of characters and voices she includes in the novel. The reader hears scraps of conversation between various visitors to the park and glimpses lives that are very different from those of Kazu, Shige, and the other homeless people. At times, these scenes come across as parodic. For example, a woman describes the meals she makes for her dogs, who eat far better than Kazu does. Yet on the whole, these are ordinary lives of people enjoying the park and each other's company. An invisible presence, Kazu is privy to conversations and confidences that he would not have heard while he was alive. In a sense, all narrators are ghosts, hovering over a past that they no longer inhabit. Yu's inventive narrative device amplifies this effect and makes Kazu a sort of conduit for the voices of the living. This technique of shifting perspectives also helps to explain why the homeless people have become invisible to their more affluent neighbors: everyone is caught up in their own lives and concerns. Part of the challenge of addressing the wealth divide is for people to see beyond their own circumstances and to empathize with those who are not prospering.

Tokyo Ueno Station received rapturous reviews and was awarded a National Book Award in 2020 for best novel in translation. Writing for NPR, Michael Schaub praised its "harsh, uncompromising look at existential despair," as well as Yu's "gorgeous, haunting writing and Morgan Giles's wonderful translation." In the *New York Times*, Abhrajyoti Chakraborty termed it "a glorious modernist novel." Many readers and reviewers noted the relevance of the novel's central theme of economic inequality. Lauren Elkin, reviewing the book for the *Guardian*, called it "an urgent reminder of the radical divide between rich and poor in postwar Japan."

Ultimately, *Tokyo Ueno Station* is a powerful novel that explores the human condition at both the individual and societal levels, with particular attention to the economic and historical forces that shape everyday lives. While Yu touches on many aspects of Japanese history and culture, the main themes and concerns are universal, making the book a compelling read for people of any background. As Schaub and other critics noted, Giles's excellent translation should also not be overlooked, as it deftly captures the interplay of disparate voices and texts that are central to the narrative structure. In an era of rising economic inequality in many parts of the world, the story of Kazu and those around him is one that deserves to be heard.

Author Biography

Yu Miri has published more than twenty books, including fiction, drama, and essays. She received the Akutagawa Prize, Japan's highest literary award, and is also known for her community work focused on the recovery from the 2011 Fukushima earthquake, tsunami, and nuclear disaster.

Morgan Giles is a reviewer and translator of Japanese literature.

Matthew J. Bolton

Review Sources

Chakraborty, Abhrajyoti. "Four Social Novels in Translation Consider the World's Ills." Review of *Tokyo Ueno Station*, by Yu Miri, et al. *The New York Times*, 23 June 2020, www.nytimes.com/2020/06/23/books/review/miri-alvarez-shibli-appanah.html. Accessed 5 Jan. 2021.

Elkin, Lauren. "*Tokyo Ueno Station* by Yu Miri Review: A Haunting Novel of Life after Death." *The Guardian*, 3 Apr. 2019, www.theguardian.com/books/2019/apr/03/tokyo-ueno-station-yu-miri-review. Accessed 5 Jan. 2021.

Schaub, Michael. "A Painful Past and Ghostly Present Converge in 'Tokyo Ueno Station.'" Review of *Tokyo Ueno Station*, by Yu Miri. *NPR*, 27 June 2020, www.npr.org/2020/06/27/883949974/a-painful-past-and-ghostly-present-converge-in-tokyo-ueno-station. Accessed 5 Jan. 2021.

Review of *Tokyo Ueno Station*, by Yu Miri. *Kirkus*, 29 Mar. 2020, www.kirkusreviews.com/book-reviews/miri-yu/tokyo-ueno-station/. Accessed 8 Jan. 2021.

Review of *Tokyo Ueno Station*, by Yu Miri. *Publishers Weekly*, 24 Mar. 2020, www.publishersweekly.com/978-0-593-08802-9. Accessed 8 Jan. 2021.

Transcendent Kingdom

Author: Yaa Gyasi
Publisher: Knopf (New York). 288 pp.
Type of work: Novel
Time: Present day; the 1990s
Locales: Stanford, California; Huntsville, Alabama

Transcendent Kingdom is the story of a Ghanaian American family and their struggles with identity, immigration, addiction, and mental health in Huntsville, Alabama, all told by youngest daughter and narrator, Gifty.

Principal characters

GIFTY, a twenty-eight-year-old Ghanaian American who is a graduate student at Stanford University
NANA, her older brother who died in his teens from an opioid overdose
GIFTY'S MOTHER, who goes unnamed in the novel, a Ghanaian woman who suffers from bouts of severe depression
CHIN CHIN MAN, her father, who returned to Ghana when she was young and never came back
HAN, her lab mate at Stanford
MR. THOMAS, the old man her mother cares for
PASTOR JOHN, the leader of the White church that her mother attends
MARY, Pastor John's daughter
KATHERINE, her friend at Stanford
ANNE, her close friend at Harvard
RAYMOND, her ex-boyfriend

Transcendent Kingdom is a story of isolation, a laser-focused portrait of a family trying to survive in America. Though dramatic, *Transcendent Kingdom* is a book of interiority and quiet places—the quiet of a bedroom or a science lab—much closer and simpler than Gyasi's first book, *Homegoing* (2016), which told the stories of a large cast of characters across time and oceans facing enslavement, racism, and inherited trauma in Ghana and the United States. *Transcendent Kingdom*, on the other hand, is a narrowing of scope for Gyasi but is ultimately a heartfelt and successful portrait of love, loss, and meaning-making.

The book opens with Gifty's mother coming to stay with her in California to weather a depressive episode. From there, Gyasi weaves together the story of Gifty's childhood, her family's struggles with racism, addiction, and depression, and her present-day research and struggle to help her mother and herself. As an adult, Gifty still lives in some of the isolation in which she and her mother and brother lived in Alabama. Single, she keeps to herself, maintaining few friends, spending a lot of her time in the lab. With her research, she is trying to understand and isolate reward-seeking behaviors in rats, with the aim of identifying how that behavior can translate to addiction and isolating where in the brain addictive behavior originates. Gifty has traded the evangelical Christianity of her youth for science, which through her work can provide more answers to her brother's death, and possibly help others like him, than Christianity could.

Yaa Gyasi

In her childhood, Gifty's family was several layers removed from everyone around them in Huntsville, Alabama. They were African, but not American; not part of the White majority, but not really a part of the Black community, either. As Africans, but not African Americans, Gifty and her family live in a liminal space where they have to endure the racism of being Black, but do not reap the benefits of a found community. They endured racism for the first time in America, but were beholden by two different kinds of oppression, as both immigrants and Black people. Nana and Gifty are caught in between, as Ghanaians being raised in an American culture that their parents won't ever fully understand.

Gifty's mother takes a job as an at-home nurse for an old White man, enduring and smiling through the racial slurs he uses and for which she doesn't have the full context to understand. When the Chin Chin Man joins his wife in the United States, he takes a job as a janitor. Gifty observes the effect America has on her father—she "saw him try to shrink to size, his long, proud back hunched as he walked with my mother through the Walmart, where he was accused of stealing three times in four months." Eventually, the Chin Chin Man feels that he cannot endure life in America any longer and returns to Ghana. Gifty's mother never dates or remarries, but finds support in religion. Not understanding enough about the culture of the American South, she joins a White church instead of a Black one, a decision that in many ways isolates her further, instead of providing the support of community she really needs.

Nana is just a boy, and never makes it out of adolescence, but in many ways holds the weight of the family's promise and American success story on his shoulders. Nana is an incredibly gifted athlete, and it is his success as a local athlete that does the most for the family's acceptance, in part because it fits the preconceived storylines for accepted immigrant and/or Black success—that is, success as a star athlete. He started with soccer; Gifty would go with her father to watch Nana play a sport the Chin Chin Man loves. After their father leaves, Nana abandons soccer and turns to basketball, slotting into another narrative of being a Black man in America. But then he suffers an injury playing basketball, and when a doctor prescribes him OxyContin for the pain, Nana falls into another predetermined narrative—that of the poor Black victim of opioid addiction. In the end, it is the void left by his absence that has the most presence in the story, but one wishes for more. As James Wood for the *New Yorker* points out, "Nana's downfall remains blurred and somewhat generic" and, in places, the prose is "cliché."

Nana's death has an irreversible impact on each family member's life. The heart of this story is the relationship Gifty and her mother have, and the ways that they continue to shape each other even when they are apart, as well as the way that Nana's death shapes who they become. They mirror each other in personality, in the ways that they shrink away from grief and each other to cope. Gifty's mother sinks into her mental illness, while Gifty buries herself in work and the pursuit of perfection. In the wake of Nana's passing, Gifty's mother sinks into the first of her prolonged depressive episodes and sends Gifty away to live with an aunt in Ghana while she rides it out. Her mother's Christianity does not provide the language to identify what she goes through, and neither does her Ghanaian culture, exactly; people outside of the West view mental health disorders in a completely different light, and Gifty's mother in particular does not believe that depression is a real affliction, just something Americans invented.

Gifty, throughout all of this family turmoil, is largely the observer, and seeks answers for why things are happening the way they are. She is the meaning maker. There is always a fierce precociousness in Gifty, but as an obedient child, this mostly comes out in her journal entries, where she rails against her mother whom she refers to as the Black Mamba. (It later comes out in her determination for success.) Her mother pitches between fierceness—she is a "matter-of-fact kind of woman, not a cruel woman, exactly, but something quite close to cruel," according to Gifty—and the vulnerability of bald-faced love and the complete withdrawal of a deep depression.

As the perpetual observer, Gifty's own emotional life is somewhat cold and analytical. She eventually sees through the cracks in the façade of her mother's evangelicalism and turns to science for her answers. She embarks on her own acceptable immigrant story of success, though she refuses to bow to this narrative. In fact, she rejects any sort of traditional narrative at all. She does not have the immigrant mother who insists on academic success. Likewise, she rejects the plaudits of being a successful Black woman, or a woman in the science, technology, engineering, and mathematics (STEM) field. She insists that she did not pursue her work because of her brother's addiction and subsequent death, but rather because "I wanted to do the hardest thing. I wanted to flay any mental weakness off my body like fascia from muscle." But as the story progresses, it becomes clear to the reader that accomplishing what is very hard is not the only thing that motivates her, and that running away from her grief is also a huge part of that. Gifty largely has to raise herself, and it is her steadfast pursuit of "goodness" that drives her and keeps her from becoming her mother.

Transcendent Kingdom stands apart from other immigrant narratives in that assimilation is never quite the objective—this is perhaps to the characters' detriment, though not in terms of loss of cultural identity but in isolation and lack of community.

And yet, while Gifty tries to deny it, and although her mother does not actively push her in one direction or another (a drive that died with Nana, it would seem), there is still an awareness, if not guilt, that her mother's hard and thankless work allowed her to attend elite universities and pursue research in neuroscience. However, while her work has the potential to earn her accolades (in addition to a PhD), it is thankless in one particular way: Gifty cannot earn the approval of her mother.

One area that feels less successful is the end of the book. While happy for Gifty, the conclusion feels tacked on in a way, a tidy bow on a gift perhaps better left unwrapped. Nell Freudenberger, the reviewer for the *New York Times* agrees, writing that the conclusion "felt unsatisfying, seeming to tie up the strands of this fascinating woman's [Gifty's mother's] life too quickly." Gifty's goal is to find answers, to make sense, but an ending containing some kind of answer feels somewhat incongruous. All the same, after so much heartache and disconnect, it is gratifying to leave Gifty with some semblance of peace.

Author Biography
Yaa Gyasi is a Ghanaian American whose first novel, *Homegoing*, won the PEN/ Hemingway Award for Best First Novel in 2017.

Meaghan O'Brien

Review Sources
Charles, Ron. "Yaa Gyasi's 'Transcendent Kingdom' Is a Book of Blazing Brilliance." Review of *Transcendent Kingdom*, by Yaa Gyasi. *The Washington Post*, 25 Aug. 2020, www.washingtonpost.com/entertainment/books/yaa-gyasis-transcendent-kingdom-is-a-book-of-blazing-brilliance/2020/08/25/718fd326-e60a-11ea-97e0-94d2e46e759b_story.html. Accessed 1 Dec. 2020.
Freudenberger, Nell. "In Yaa Gyasi's New Novel, a Young Scientist Tries to Understand Her Family's Pain." Review of *Transcendent Kingdom*, by Yaa Gyasi. *The New York Times*, 31 Aug. 2020, www.nytimes.com/2020/08/31/books/review/transcendent-kingdom-yaa-gyasi.html. Accessed 1 Dec. 2020.
Grady, Constance. "In the Ruminative New Novel Transcendent Kingdom, a Neuroscientist Searches for the Soul." Review of *Transcendent Kingdom*, by Yaa Gyasi. *Vox*, 9 Sept. 2020, www.vox.com/culture/21427878/transcendent-kingdom-review-yaa-gyasi. Accessed 1 Dec. 2020.
Wood, James. "Yaa Gyasi Explores the Science of the Soul." Review of *Transcendent Kingdom*, by Yaa Gyasi. *The New Yorker*, 7 Sept. 2020, www.newyorker.com/magazine/2020/09/14/yaa-gyasi-explores-the-science-of-the-soul. Accessed 1 Dec. 2020.

Twilight of the Gods
War in the Western Pacific, 1944–1945

Author: Ian W. Toll (b. 1967)
Publisher: W. W. Norton & Company (New York). 944 pp.
Type of work: History
Time: 1944–45
Locales: The Western Pacific, from Hawaii to Japan

In the third volume of Toll's masterful narrative history of the Pacific War, he covers the conflict between the Allies and the Empire of Japan in the final years of World War II.

Principal personages

FRANKLIN DELANO ROOSEVELT, the president of the United States
GENERAL DOUGLAS MACARTHUR, the commander of the United States Army in the Pacific
ADMIRAL CHESTER NIMITZ, the commander of the United States Pacific Fleet
ADMIRAL RAYMOND SPRUANCE, the commander of the Fifth Fleet, Fifty-Eighth Task Force
ADMIRAL WILLIAM "BULL" HALSEY, the commander of the Third Fleet, Thirty-Eighth Task Force
HIROHITO, the emperor of Japan

Twilight of the Gods: War in the Western Pacific, 1944–1945 (2020) is the third and final book in historian Ian W. Toll's Pacific War trilogy. The first book, *Pacific Crucible: War at Sea in the Pacific, 1941–1942*, was published in 2011, followed by *The Conquering Tide: War in the Pacific Islands, 1942–1944* in 2015. In the author's note that opens this final installment, Ian Toll explains why this nearly thousand-page tome covering the last eighteen months of World War II in the Pacific theater has anything new to offer. After all, beginning with Samuel Eliot Morison's comprehensive, fifteen-volume series, *History of United States Naval Operations in World War II* (1947–62), the subject has received scrutiny from nearly every angle, from close studies of the leaders of the conflict—Japan's Emperor Hirohito, General Douglas MacArthur, Admiral Chester Nimitz, and President Franklin Delano Roosevelt chief among them—to a deep look at each individual battle as the Allies crawled toward Japan. Toll, aware that he is covering well-trodden ground, argues for the value of a narrative that "colors outside the lines" of traditional military history. It is only possible to understand the complex decisions made in the last year of the war—when all players had an eye both to victory and to their own legacies and their place in the postwar world—if not only familiar sources but other voices from the periphery are considered. Toll had access to several of these, including the diary of General Robert C. Richardson Jr., commanding army general in Hawaii, who hosted General MacArthur during a July 1944 conference in Hawaii that is detailed in the first chapter.

While the prologue examines the relationships between the president of the United States, military leaders, and the press, it serves as a necessary introduction to the characters that will dominate the long year ahead and to the antagonism that loops through this story: the struggle for authority, supplies, and control of the public discourse between the United States Army and Navy.

Ian W. Toll

The opening chapter of the book sets the scene for this interplay as General MacArthur and Admiral Nimitz meet in July 1944 in Hawaii with President Roosevelt to decide how the war in the Pacific will be brought to its climactic end.

By the time of this meeting, the cataclysmic conflicts of Guadalcanal and the Battle of the Philippine Sea had given the United States the offensive in the Pacific and destroyed much of the Japanese carrier fleet. War production in the United States was booming, and supplies, though always a logistical challenge, were plentiful. The key question at hand was if the US would focus its attention on the heavily defended Philippines; the subtext of this question lay in General MacArthur's legendary promise to the people of the occupied territory that he would return. Toll gives ponderous detail of the meeting between MacArthur and Nimitz, who rather reluctantly agrees in the end that the invasion of the Philippines is a military—and not just a public relation—necessity.

MacArthur's outsize ego and love of a photo opportunity is well documented, while the naval commanders whose decisions cost or save thousands of lives, including Admirals Nimitz, Ernest J. King, Raymond Spruance, and William "Bull" Halsey, are lesser known. Their characters and proclivities, and the fateful decisions they would make over the remainder of the war are explored in detail in this volume, from what they liked to eat to how well they slept. The complexities of their relationships with each other, the troops under their command, and the press, are given close attention.

While this deep exploration of the naval commanders in the Pacific is engaging and informative, Toll is also a painstaking chronicler of the minutia of life for ordinary service members at war. For a reader without a military background, whose understanding of the unique landscape of a naval destroyer or a B-29 bomber may be limited, these details are crucial to a micro-level understanding of the experience of war. The second chapter carries a minute-by-minute description of the experience of an airman aboard a United States aircraft carrier on "strike-day," complete with a three o'clock wake-up call and trying to follow exhaust fumes to stay in formation in the pre-dawn darkness. An equally detailed description of the "D-Day ablutions" of the marines aboard ship preparing to strike the island of Peleliu follows these men closely as they wake, wash (down to the "critical" bowel movement), and dress. Topography, weapons, and vehicles are all carefully described, along with choice quotes from the boots on the ground and on deck, painting a compelling picture of the sensory experience of the fighting men in battle, as well as at rest.

The book opens with Admiral Spruance in command of the massive fast carrier the Fifty-Eighth Task Force (alternatively, the Thirty-Eighth Task Force, a strategic ruse), the main offensive arm of the United States Navy from January 1944 to the war's end. Spruance is unflappable and disciplined, sleeps soundly at night, and walks five miles a day. He is a careful tactician, sometimes criticized for being too conservative. In August 1944 he is replaced by Admiral William Halsey, who is a very different man. Halsey had not had a command at sea since 1942, but he had made a name for himself as a "charismatic, swaggering, limelight-loving warrior," whose quotable anti-Japanese tirades made him a favorite of the popular press and secured his position as a popular hero, and he once declared that he would ride Emperor Hirohito's white horse though downtown Tokyo. He is a friend and favorite of Nimitz, whose confidence in him begins to waver as Toll deftly sets the stage for the blunders that will mark his legacy. Halsey reads as sloppy, egocentric blowhard on these pages, buoyed by ill-deserved confidence in his own decision-making and eager to blame anything—weather, communications, other officers—for his mistakes. Still, he is clearly charming, with one fighter pilot commenting that although he was a "clown," "if he said, 'Let's go to hell together,' you'd go to hell with him." He was nearly relieved of command on several occasions; however, it is quoted that his groveling apologies to Nimitz, who had not only his personal affection but the reaction of the American press and people to consider, saved him.

In October 1944 Halsey fell for a Japanese trick, sending the lion's share of the task force under his command in pursuit of a group of carriers while leaving the rest of the fleet dangerously, almost catastrophically, exposed. The results of his actions, the heroic defense of the fleet by smaller escort carriers, known as Taffy Groups 1–3, and the fallout from this terrible decision are given a great deal of coverage. Halsey was not relieved of command, even after a sharp demand from Nimitz that he explain who is protecting the fleet.

Toll's decision to tell the story of the run-up to this encounter from the Japanese point of view fleshes out an event that could devolve overmuch into a catalog of personal criticism. With most of their carrier fleet destroyed and the Allies creeping closer to the home islands of Japan, the increasing focus on suicidal attacks deserves, and receives, serious attention. Ritual suicide had long been associated with honor in the samurai tradition in Japan, bolstered by the religious fanaticism and nationalism that led young recruits to believe that they were serving a divine purpose, with an attendant reward, when they offered their lives. Toll picks apart this ideal as it applies to the kamikaze strategy within the Japanese military. He points out that if one had fought honorably, there was no obligation to perform suicide in the samurai tradition and, likewise, no dishonor to retreat or defeat. When mass armed suicide designed to cause maximum casualties became a clear military strategy, it was not without protest among some Japanese leaders, who saw it as being not only inhumane, but contrary to ancient principles of humility and respect for the enemy. By October 1944, however, the Japanese were running out of options and the kamikaze fleet was born, allowing Japan to fight on despite shortages of trained pilots, planes, ships, fuel, and hope.

Toll explicitly lays out two general schools of thought among both Allied leadership in the Pacific and among historians and strategists since. Adherents of the sequential approach, such as Halsey and Nimitz, saw victory as the result of one major tactical defeat of the Japanese at a time. The stone-skipping across the Pacific from Hawaii to Japan lends credibility to this view, as the Allies move clearly forward, clearing islands as they go. Others, such as Admiral King, believed in a more holistic, cumulative approach, destroying shipping, cutting supply lines, bombing cities and ports in Japan, and bringing the conflict to a close without necessitating the protracted and bloody fighting that would certainly follow an invasion of Japan. Toll manages to describe how both approaches worked to bring Japan to its knees, and in the end, an invasion of the Japanese home islands was not necessary.

The atomic bombs dropped on Hiroshima and Nagasaki are widely credited for ending the war, but at a terrible cost. Toll offers a more nuanced picture of the bombings themselves, particularly the problematic Nagasaki mission and the reaction in Japan to the bombs. Far from ending the war in a flash (as the casual student of history might assume), hard-liners continued to advocate for full national destruction rather than unconditional surrender (though Toll also points out that there was significant handwringing on both sides of exactly what "unconditional" meant), and coups erupted even after the emperor had accepted Allied peace terms.

Japan is doomed from the first by a deep underestimation of the character of the American people, believing them to be too soft to wage war effectively. In battle after battle, their error was proved. In his *New York Times* review, Mark Perry called this belief "the most egregiously false assumption in the history of warfare" and applauded Toll for "eloquently" proving this. In addition, Perry praised Toll's descriptions of the Japanese homeland and military culture and noted that he offers insight about the navy, "his true area of expertise as well as his enduring passion."

Despite some original thinking around the mindset of navy commanders, and some new insights into the evolution of kamikaze strategy, few would describe this tome as a light read at nearly one thousand pages. An anonymous reviewer for *Kirkus Reviews* concluded that it is "conventional but richly rewarding," while *Publishers Weekly* stated, "Written with flair and chock-full of stories both familiar and fresh, this monumental history fires on all cylinders." The US Naval Institute review noted that "discerning readers will not wish that Ian Toll's massive capstone to his Pacific war trilogy, about the war's final year, were a page shorter."

Author Biography

Ian W. Toll is a naval historian best known for his critically acclaimed *Six Frigates: The Epic History of the Founding of the U.S. Navy* (2008), which won the 2007 Samuel Eliot Morison Award and the William E. Colby Military Writers Award and appeared in the New York Times Editor's Choice list.

Bethany Groff Dorau

Review Sources

Jordan, Jonathan W. "'Twilight of the Gods' Review: A Blood-Soaked Peace." *The Wall Street Journal*, 28 Aug. 2020, www.wsj.com/articles/twilight-of-the-gods-review-a-blood-soaked-peace-11598623808. Accessed 21 Dec. 2020.

Perry, Mark. "How the U.S. Won the War against Japan." Review of *Twilight of the Gods: War in the Western Pacific, 1944–1945*, by Ian W. Toll. *The New York Times*, 28 Aug. 2020, www.nytimes.com/2020/08/28/books/review/twilight-of-the-gods-ian-w-toll.html. Accessed 21 Dec. 2020.

Rems, Alan. Review of *Twilight of the Gods: War in the Western Pacific, 1944–1945*, by Ian W. Toll. *U.S. Naval Institute*, Aug. 2020, www.usni.org/magazines/naval-history-magazine/2020/august/book-reviews. Accessed 21 Dec. 2020.

Steagall, Jason L. Review of *Twilight of the Gods: War in the Western Pacific, 1944–1945*, by Ian W. Toll. *Library Journal*, vol. 145, no. 8, Aug. 2020, p. 80. *Literary Reference Center Plus*, search.ebscohost.com/login.aspx?direct=true&db=lkh&AN=144664857&site=lrc-plus. Accessed 22 Jan. 2021.

Review of *Twilight of the Gods: War in the Western Pacific, 1944–1945*, by Ian W. Toll. *Kirkus Reviews*, 15 Apr. 2020. *Literary Reference Center Plus*, search.ebscohost.com/login.aspx?direct=true&db=lkh&AN=142684602&site=lrc-plus. Accessed 21 Dec. 2020.

Review of *Twilight of the Gods: War in the Western Pacific, 1944–1945*, by Ian W. Toll. *Publishers Weekly*, 1 Apr. 2020, p. 65. *Literary Reference Center Plus*, search.ebscohost.com/login.aspx?direct=true&db=lkh&AN=142790887&site=lrc-plus. Accessed 21 Dec. 2020.

The Undocumented Americans

Author: Karla Cornejo Villavicencio (b. 1989)
Publisher: One World (New York). 208 pp.
Type of work: History, memoir
Time: Present day
Locale: The United States

Karla Cornejo Villavicencio's The Undocumented Americans (2020) is an intimate portrait of the lives of the undocumented in America, especially those who, like Cornejo Villavicencio herself, were brought to the United States as children.

Karla Cornejo Villavicencio's *The Undocumented Americans* is an aptly named book. The individuals whose lives are described in Cornejo Villavicencio's affecting first book are American in the deepest of ways, even if their legal status does not reflect this shared identity. Cornejo Villavicencio writes from personal experience. Born in Ecuador in 1989, Cornejo Villavicencio's parents immigrated to the United States when she was just over a year old, leaving her behind while they established themselves. When she was around five years old, her parents brought her to the United States. Through insightful reporting, featuring investigations of dozens of starkly different lives, Cornejo Villavicencio weaves her own story into a tapestry of other biographical explorations to reveal the felt immediacy of life for the undocumented in America.

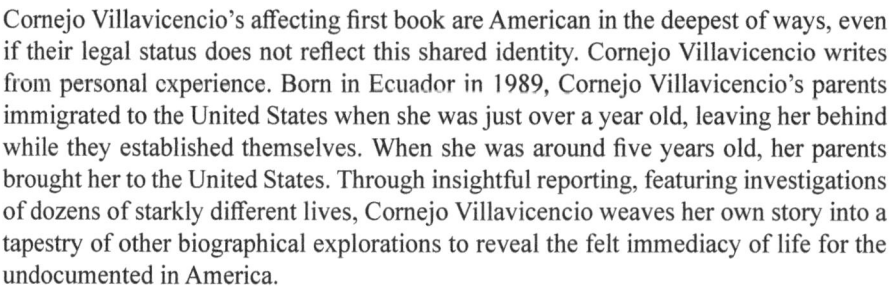

Cornejo Villavicencio grew up in the New York City boroughs of Brooklyn and Queens with her family, and it was there that she found a love for writing. She began by reviewing music for a local magazine and, along the way, she found success in academics, so much so that she achieved one of the most mythologized benchmarks of American success—acceptance to Harvard University. Having become one of the rarified few to achieve this level of recognition for her intelligence and academic skill, Cornejo Villavicencio nevertheless put her success on the line when, in her senior year, she penned an essay for the news website *The Daily Beast* in which she revealed that she was undocumented and reflected on the uncertainty of her future after graduation.

One of the great successes of Cornejo Villavicencio's groundbreaking book is that it does not conform to any generalized depiction of life as an undocumented American. To be certain, Cornejo Villavicencio's experience is not typical of undocumented immigrants. She is an overachiever by comparison to any group of Americans, documented or not, and her achievements have granted her a platform for discussing an issue that all too often is shaped by misconception and racial prejudice. As the author

Karla Cornejo Villavicencio

explains, there are many Americans who believe that by violating immigration law, the undocumented have made themselves criminals and thus should be treated as such. Others operate under the mistaken impression that immigrants bring crime and violence to America, a fear encouraged by political opportunists who stoke xenophobic fears and then offer themselves and their "hard line" immigration tactics as the solution to this illusory problem. There are also many Americans who object to immigration out of the belief that immigrants take opportunities and jobs away from them and their American-born progeny. Racism is a key factor, too, as some White Americans believe that the United States should remain a White-dominant country and oppose any of the various forces that increase the nation's ethnic and cultural diversity.

On the other side of the coin, many of those who support immigration and allowing undocumented migrants to have a legal path to citizenship portray individuals in this group in equally unrealistic, if more flattering, ways. In their zeal to defend the marginalized, some journalists and commentators are guilty of focusing only on the most outstanding examples of upstanding non-citizenship, those individuals whose achievements and experiences capture the injustice and tragedy of their shared civic limbo. Cornejo Villavicencio herself is an example of the kind of undocumented person frequently singled out by commentators from the left. She lived a life largely free from controversy or legal scandal, won acceptance to two of America's most elite educational institutions, and then became a National Book Award nominee and acclaimed essayist. Supporters of the undocumented have likewise created an illusion of the ideal non-citizen citizen—a person who is quiet, well-behaved, follows the rules, works hard, studies hard, and achieves despite lacking the advantages of wealth and inherited status. While such individuals make good fodder for those arguing the case for a path to citizenship, in *The Undocumented Americans*, Cornejo Villavicencio set out to create a more nuanced and realistic view. She avoids portraying the undocumented as heroes or villains and instead shows that they express and live the full spectrum of American life.

Over the course of six chapters, Cornejo Villavicencio tells the stories of individuals in diverse walks of life and various parts of the country. They are day laborers, housekeepers, construction workers, dog walkers, and many other roles. Cornejo Villavicencio explains that she wanted to tell the story of the "weirdoes we all are outside of our jobs." She explains further that her goal was to argue that it is not only the heroes whose lives are meaningful, but also the "randoms," or the various characters whose lives are just as interesting and valid of recognition. She wanted to display the value of individuals beyond what they do for a living, showing who they are in their daily lives, the images rarely seen in the profiles of immigrants used as arguments on the right or left. Along the way, Cornejo Villavicencio eviscerates the myths of the undocumented.

In her effort to cut through the politicized dialogue and explore the individuals caught in this political limbo, Cornejo Villavicencio employs a variety of techniques. On one hand, the book is very much a work of investigative journalism. Cornejo Villavicencio traveled the country to interview undocumented individuals living various kinds of lives. One part of the book sees her traveling to Flint, Michigan, a city that has become emblematic of governmental failure and negligence due to its lead-polluted waters. For Flint's undocumented, an already dire situation has become monstrous. Lacking the legal status to seek bureaucratic assistance, they are the ignored sufferers of a national tragedy. Cornejo Villavicencio uses their plight as a metaphor for undocumented people elsewhere, existing in a system willing to capitalize on their lives and labor but that ignores their needs and offers little to no support.

In another section of the book, Cornejo Villavicencio tells the story of a man, pseudonymized as Joaquín, who made the deadly and dangerous southern border crossing into the United States in 1998. His first job, working on a boat on the Hudson River, saw Joaquín unwittingly become a first responder after the 9/11 terrorist attacks, ferrying police, firefighters, and emergency workers across the Hudson every night for two weeks. Following this service, Joaquín and the other undocumented workers were summarily fired, without being given cause. Cornejo Villavicencio describes how Joaquín kept the identification badge he had been given, a keepsake to remember that he had been a first responder. The book also tells other stories of the hundreds of undocumented caught up in the 9/11 tragedy. A man called Rafael had been a firefighter in Mexico. Risking arrest or deportation, he showed his badge to firefighters on 9/11 and they suited him up to help. Rafael ran up and down the North Tower stairs countless times, at one point carrying a pregnant woman down twenty flights just before the North Tower collapsed. Rafael died ten years later, hospitalized with respiratory ailments from the toxic dust and smoke he inhaled on that fateful day.

From the heroism of undocumented Latinx first responders after 9/11 and Hurricane Katrina, Cornejo Villavicencio travels to Miami to uncover another frequently hidden side of immigrant culture—the various ethnic shops, bodegas, and alternative healers who bring elements of foreign culture into America's communities and serve as gathering points for immigrants, both documented and undocumented. She explores how an underground medical system—unofficial clinics and doctors operating illegally out of back rooms—is often the only option for the undocumented who cannot purchase health insurance and are barred from mainstream health care. Cornejo Villavicencio asks readers to imagine being forced to forego chemotherapy for herbal remedies when diagnosed with cancer, or to consider pregnant mothers unable to seek medical help when facing potentially deadly complications.

One of the most interesting aspects of Cornejo Villavicencio's book is how the author distorts the style of journalistic reporting. Unlike the detached commentaries that investigative journalists typically strive to achieve, Cornejo Villavicencio does not try to hide how deeply she became involved with the people she met and interviewed for her book. She expresses the frustration, fear, and anger that she feels at the situations she finds her subjects enduring and at the system that has left them to this ambiguous and often cruel fate. Many reviewers noted that Cornejo Villavicencio's willingness to violate the rules of journalism and to ignore the forced attempt at objectivity by getting personally involved with her subjects is what gives her exploration of the subject its real strength.

Another way in which Cornejo Villavicencio stretches the boundaries of traditional journalistic writing is through the inclusion of fictionalized passages, woven into the stories. The example most cited by critics comes when the author imagines the final moments of Ubaldo Cruz Martínez, a day laborer who drowned in his Staten Island basement during Hurricane Sandy. The interjection of fictional elements, poetry, and creatively written reimagined dialogues helps set Cornejo Villavicencio's memoir-cum-political dialogue apart from others seeking to explore the same subject. She artistically enhances the narrative, using her imagination and her potent, raw emotion to explore the subject in ways that more academic treatments cannot.

The fact that Cornejo Villavicencio faced this difficult reality herself is another part of what provides the book with such emotional heft. She describes how being abandoned by her parents in Ecuador left her, as doctors have told her, with mental illness due to her brain being stripped of dendrites. She imagines how the same has happened to the children separated from their parents under the Trump administration's controversial policies and pictures herself in a future alongside those children, becoming an "army of mutants" with minds stripped of branches.

The Undocumented Americans became a best seller after its release and won widespread praise from critics, many of whom wondered if it might help shift public opinion on the subject. In the *New York Times*, reviewer Caitlin Dickerson recognized that those who see undocumented immigrants as criminals who "put themselves in a vulnerable position and should be punished for breaking the law" might not be changed by reading Cornejo Villavicencio's work; however, Dickerson opined that these critics might find that the book awakens some interest in the lived experiences of the individuals after reading about their "interior details, flattering and unflattering." Writing in *Public Books*, Jeff Peer commented that literary journalism exists "so that readers without direct experience might begin to imagine all those unimagined existences, hear the voices of the voiceless." Whether this changes the realities for the subjects of such books is an open question, but Peer argued that such work is nonetheless essential because "we must have a record, a document of what has been done in our names."

As for Cornejo Villavicencio's writing skill, critics were likewise impressed. Alicia Mireles Christoff, writing in *The Common*, expressed amazement at the "nerve" and "inventiveness" of her work. Other reviewers similarly praised the sensitivity and humor with which she was able to approach her subject. Cornejo Villavicencio's nomination for the National Book Award, among the most prestigious literary awards in the world, is a testament to how well received *The Undocumented Americans* was among both critics and readers alike.

Author Biography
Karla Cornejo Villavicencio is an Ecuadorian-born American writer who became one of the first undocumented immigrants to graduate from Harvard University. Her work *The Undocumented Americans* was short-listed for the National Book Award in Nonfiction.

Micah L. Issitt

Review Sources
Christoff, Alicia Mireles. "Review: Dispatches from the Land of White Noise—The Undocumented Americans." Review of *The Undocumented Americans*, by Karla Cornejo Villavicencio. *The Common*, 27 Aug. 2020, www.thecommononline.org/review-dispatches-from-the-land-of-white-noise-the-undocumented-americans/. Accessed 4 Jan. 2021.
Dickerson, Caitlin. "This Is the Face of an Undocumented Immigrant. Don't Look Away." Review of *The Undocumented Americans*, by Karla Cornejo Villavicencio. *The New York Times*, 24 Mar. 2020, www.nytimes.com/2020/03/24/books/review/the-undocumented-americans-karla-cornejo-villavicencio.html. Accessed 4 Jan. 2021.
Luca, Cassandra. "'The Undocumented Americans' Refuses Stereotypes and Claims Its Own Space." Review of *The Undocumented Americans*, by Karla Cornejo Villavicencio. *The Harvard Crimson*, 27 May 2020, www.thecrimson.com/article/2020/5/27/the-undocumented-americans-book-review/. Accessed 4 Jan. 2021.
Muñoz, Daisy. "Book Review: *The Undocumented Americans* by Karla Cornejo Villavicencio." Review of *The Undocumented Americans*, by Karla Cornejo Villavicencio. *The Latinx Project*, 1 June 2020, www.latinxproject.nyu.edu/intervenxions/book-review-emthe-undocumented-americansem-by-karla-cornejo-villavicencio. Accessed 4 Jan. 2021.
Peer, Jeff. "Necessary Documents, Undocumented Americans." Review of *The Undocumented Americans*, by Karla Cornejo Villavicencio. *Public Books*, 10 Aug. 2020, www.publicbooks.org/necessary-documents-undocumented-americans/. Accessed 4 Jan. 2021.
Review of *The Undocumented Americans*, by Karla Cornejo Villavicencio. *Kirkus*, 15 Jan. 2020, www.kirkusreviews.com/book-reviews/karla-cornejo-villavicencio/the-undocumented-americans/. Accessed 4 Jan. 2021.

Untamed

Author: Glennon Doyle (b. 1976)
Publisher: Dial Press (New York). 352 pp.
Type of work: Memoir
Time: 2016–the present
Locale: Primarily Florida

Untamed is an intimate memoir of the lessons learned at the end of Glennon Doyle's marriage and the beginning of a new relationship and a new sense of self.

Principal personages
GLENNON DOYLE, a blogger and author, the narrator
ABBY WAMBACH, a retired professional soccer player, her romantic interest and later wife
CRAIG MELTON, her former husband and the father of her three children
CHASE, her son, the oldest child
TISH, her older daughter
AMMA, her younger daughter

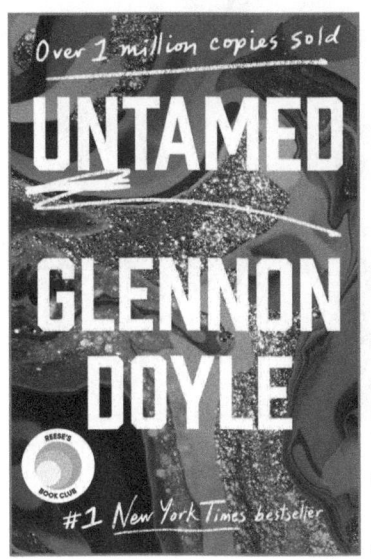

In a *New York Times* article, best-selling author Elizabeth Gilbert summed up the appeal of Glennon Doyle's writing as "intimate, funny, moving stories that will reflect light back on our own existence." This book, the third memoir and spiritual exploration by the author, joins *Carry on, Warrior: Thoughts on Life Unarmed* (2013) and *Love Warrior: A Memoir* (2016) in their exploration of the author's journey through addiction, alcoholism, eating disorders, spousal infidelity, motherhood, marriage, and finally—or, at least as of the publication of *Untamed* in 2020—true love. Doyle herself would agree that part of the secret of her happiness is that she has learned to trust herself, and if that means that she burns down a significant part of her life, like her first marriage, she knows what she rebuilds will be stronger.

The book begins with a story of a visit to the zoo where a cheetah who has been raised with a dog chases a stuffed animal as part of an educational demonstration. Doyle and her daughter Tish connect with the limitations of this animal's life—safe, well fed, and having only a dog as a role model, the cheetah is still restless, still has moments of being wild. Doyle uses this as her core metaphor for the experience of many women living in a patriarchy that denies women the understanding of their true nature and leaves them wondering why they are dissatisfied with their lives.

The central question in *Untamed* is how women can be "untamed" and escape from the internal and external cages of homophobia, racism, misogyny, and self-hatred. To

Glennon Doyle

employ a metaphor Doyle uses to describe why she wrote the book, she asks, "Where did my spark go at ten? How had I lost myself?" For Doyle, losing the spark led to years of pain resulting in addiction, a decades-long struggle with bingeing and bulimia, and a lingering feeling that something was terribly wrong with her marriage and her life. Doyle identifies ten as the age when boys and girls begin to fit themselves into the roles prescribed for them, whether or not they fit. For girls, this means becoming quiet, small, and compliant, according to Doyle. She identifies her eating disorder as her rebellion, where she "indulged my hunger and expressed [her] fury." Years of this behavior convinced her that she was crazy, another common message to disempower women. Returning to the cheetah metaphor, she writes, "I was just a caged girl made for wide-open skies." Yet such autobiographical details largely retread ground covered in her previous two memoirs, though perhaps with more compelling imagery.

What does all of this have to do with falling in love with another woman? Doyle identifies pursuing that attraction as the "first decision I made as a free woman." This freedom is internal, as she was certainly not free by external standards. Mother of three and married to former model Craig Melton, whose porn habit and repeated infidelities she had just exposed to the world in her best seller *Love Warrior*, Doyle was seen by many as a crusader for keeping complicated marriages together through love and forgiveness. While falling in love with Abby Wambach, Doyle felt for the first time that she was making a decision that went against all the messages and expectations that she had been trying to comply with her whole life. Through this transformative experience, Doyle felt that she had the opportunity to examine every aspect of her life, from how she interacted with her children to her relationship with religion and spirituality. She asks the age-old question of who she really is and explores what it had cost her to pretend to be someone else. "All of the things that make a woman human are a good girl's dirty secret," Doyle writes.

Doyle's rise to fame as a writer and inspirational speaker began slowly. The stay-at-home mom struggling to relate to other women's seemingly perfect lives started sharing her musings with the world in 2009. Doyle's honesty about the challenges of finding endless fulfillment as a wife and mother and her Christian worldview resonated with readers, and her *Momastery* blog took off. Within a few years, she made her first attempt to be "a reckless truth-teller," as she put it, in *Carry On, Warrior*, an inspirational story of how her deep faith in God, her strong family, and "senseless, relentless hope" helped her carry on despite the challenges in her life and her issues with illness, addiction, and depression. In her second book, *Love Warrior*, Doyle describes the fallout in her life and family after her husband admitted to multiple infidelities. Through separation and reconciliation, the book follows the couple's journeys of self-discovery as they learn to forgive each other and communicate honestly. *Untamed* recounts how that second book, proclaiming its message of faith, hope, and forgiveness in her marriage, was anticipated to be one of the biggest books of the year and poised to hit bookstores, with an extensive tour planned, when she met and fell in love with Wambach, a two-time Olympic gold medalist and captain of the United States women's soccer team, at an author event in Chicago.

Doyle had built a career on being relatable to middle-class Christian women, mothers in particular, and another woman might have kept this development to herself as her book about her marriage climbed the charts. Doyle, however, decided to be honest about the change in her life, risking the ire or confusion of her fan base. *Untamed*, as much as it is a book of inspirational advice about empowerment, is also an exploration of how doing this bold thing—entering openly into her relationship with Wambach—allowed Doyle to examine other assumptions she had made about herself. Doyle is unsparingly open about the pain and disruption that her relationship with Wambach and decision to divorce Melton caused with family, particularly her mother and her children. At times she felt as though the price of her happiness was too high. "Good mothers don't break their children's hearts in order to follow their own," she believed, as she relates in *Untamed*. She also relates her reexamination of what good parenting means and what it does not.

As Doyle has found love and a deeper knowledge of herself, she has moved from trying to be honest about a dishonest life to being willing to explore other painful, uncomfortable things. "We can do hard things" has become a motto of hers and is repeated throughout the book. Being strong and loving through this painful process seems to have led to a series of epiphanies about the experience of women in general, and this is also where the book has been most sharply criticized.

Some critics of *Untamed* have found fault with its quotable lines about power, freedom, and what Doyle calls "Knowing," the inner guide that she identifies as God. The idea that women have the power and freedom to become their true selves assumes that the constraints on them are surmountable and primarily internalized, which is certainly not a universal experience among women across race, class, and sexual orientation. Sarah Neilson, in her review for the *Seattle Times*, called Doyle to task for writing essentially "a self-help book for wealthy white women." While the book does "lightly" venture into the "complex territories of race, privilege, misogyny and capitalism," it ultimately "boomerangs back to the tired language of every affirmation book ever written." Even Neilson, however, acknowledged that the exploration of the tension between Doyle's Christianity and Christian fan base and her relationship with and eventual marriage to a woman is "unique and interesting." Notably, Doyle's coming out and same-sex relationship serve as the catalyst for the book but not its central conflict or lens, which may dismay readers who, like Neilson, wish that Doyle would reexamine heterosexist norms around family formation or parenting.

In addition, multiple Christian media outlets, perhaps predictably, have rejected the conclusions Doyle reached amid her spiritual explorations. On the Gospel Coalition website, songwriter and blogger Alisa Childers both affirmed Doyle's longing for something more but questioned Doyle's definition of freedom, arguing that "Doyle offers a counterfeit freedom that emancipates readers from right and wrong, objective truth, the Bible, and Christianity." Childers and others asserted that Doyle's "Knowing" is the untrustworthy and fickle self, not the divine, and thus saw Doyle's work as not just self-help but as a dangerous replacement of God with self. Others, however, may join *Autostraddle* reviewer Heather Hogan in applauding Doyle's efforts to grapple with her faith.

Ultimately, *Untamed* raises some provocative questions, regardless of one's opinion of her conclusions, and is thus well worth the read. Longtime fans of Doyle's writing may find fresh insights on a range of subjects in this latest installment of her personal and familial saga, while those who are less familiar with her story will likely enjoy her candid recollections and the romance at the center of the book. It is also sure to please devotees of the self-help genre.

Author Biography
Glennon Doyle is the author of the best sellers *Carry On, Warrior: Thoughts on Life Unarmed* (2013) and *Love Warrior: A Memoir* (2016). She is also the founding president and a board member of the nonprofit Together Rising, which supports the grassroots efforts of other women.

Bethany Groff Dorau

Review Sources
Childers, Alisa. "Untamed: The Gospel of Glennon Doyle." Review of *Untamed*, by Glennon Doyle. *The Gospel Coalition*, Crossway, 29 May 2020, www.thegospelcoalition.org/reviews/untamed-glennon-doyle. Accessed 19 Oct. 2020.
Egan, Elisabeth. "A Third Glennon Doyle Memoir? Yes, and Here's Why." Review of *Untamed*, by Glennon Doyle. *The New York Times*, 5 Mar. 2020, www.nytimes.com/2020/03/05/arts/untamed-glennon-doyle.html. Accessed 19 Oct. 2020.
Hogan, Heather. Review of *Untamed*, by Glennon Doyle. *Autostraddle*, 8 July 2020, www.autostraddle.com/glennon-doyles-untamed-a-gay-love-story-about-a-grown-ass-woman-who-does-what-the-fck-she-wants. Accessed 22 Oct. 2020.
Neilson, Sarah. "Is Glennon Doyle's New Memoir 'Untamed' Inspirational or Heavy-Handed?" Review of *Untamed*, by Glennon Doyle. *The Seattle Times*, 6 May 2020, www.seattletimes.com/entertainment/books/is-glennon-doyles-new-memoir-untamed-inspirational-or-heavy-handed. Accessed 19 Oct. 2020.
Review of *Untamed*, by Glennon Doyle. *Kirkus*, 15 Jan. 2020, www.kirkusreviews.com/book-reviews/glennon-doyle/untamed-doyle. Accessed 22 Oct. 2020.
Review of *Untamed*, by Glennon Doyle. *Publishers Weekly*, 23 Dec. 2019, www.publishersweekly.com/978-1-9848-0125-8. Accessed 22 Oct. 2020.

Unworthy Republic
The Dispossession of Native Americans and the Road to Indian Territory

Author: Claudio Saunt (b. 1967)
Publisher: W. W. Norton (New York). Illustrated. 416 pp.
Type of work: History
Time: Primarily 1820s and 1830s
Locales: Primarily the southeastern United States; Indian Territory (present-day Oklahoma); Washington City (present-day Washington, DC)

Claudio Saunt's exhaustively researched Unworthy Republic *details a national shame. An early nineteenth-century campaign, spearheaded by US president Andrew Jackson, resulted in the deportation of thousands of indigenous peoples from ancestral lands in the southeastern United States to wastelands west of the Mississippi River, an action that left permanent stains on American history.*

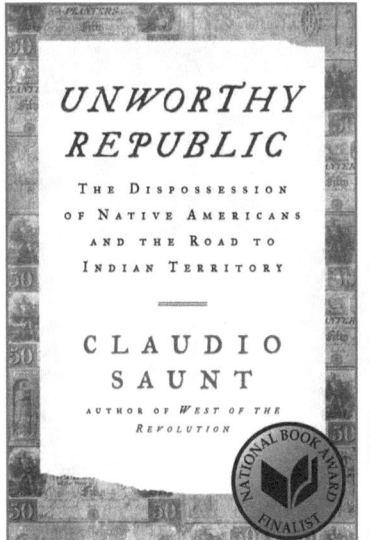

Principal personages
THOMAS JEFFERSON, the US president from 1801 to 1805
ANDREW JACKSON, the US president from 1829 to 1837
WILLIAM HICKS, a leader of the Cherokee Nation
JOHN ROSS, a leader of the Cherokee Nation
JOHN RIDGE, another Cherokee leader, a signer of the Treaty of New Echota
ELIAS BOUDINOT, the editor of the *Cherokee Phoenix* newspaper
ISAAC MCCOY, a White missionary and advocate for indigenous expulsion
THEODORE FRELINGHUYSEN, a US senator from New Jersey, an opponent of expulsion
GEORGE TROUP, the governor of Georgia in the mid-1820s
WILSON LUMPKIN, the governor of Georgia in the early 1830s
WILLIAM APESS, a Pequot activist

Fifty years after the Declaration of Independence spawned a revolution to gain freedom from Great Britain, America was greatly changed. The original thirteen colonies had grown into two dozen states, including two west of the Mississippi River (Louisiana in 1812, Missouri in 1821), which acted as a dividing line between regions of White settlement and those inhabited by indigenous peoples. The republic was big and bold enough to infringe upon the freedoms of large swaths of inhabitants who, in the minds of the all-White, all-male founders, were not created as equal as they. White

Claudio Saunt

women, for example, hardly counted as citizens, since unlike White men, they could not vote or hold office. Likewise, some two million individuals of African heritage lived in involuntary servitude, having inherited the chains of slavery from their captive forebears. Though the transatlantic slave trade was abolished in 1808, the internal industry thrived; every newborn child of an enslaved person was treated as property and increased the workforce of the enslaver.

Then there were the American Indians, the original inhabitants of the North American continent with whom the young country had initially formed nation-to-nation treaties and who would not officially become American citizens until 1924. It is their systematic suppression, against the backdrop of America at its half-century anniversary, that serves as the sharp focus of Claudio Saunt's meticulous and searing study *Unworthy Republic: The Dispossession of Native Americans and the Road to Indian Territory* (2020). The well-organized, well-documented work incorporates excerpts from contemporary publications, speeches, legislation, and letters that bolster the clear narrative prose throughout. Maps, drawings, illustrations, and some fifty pages of endnotes help reinforce the author's argument, which rests upon three sturdy historical pillars.

First, though colonists, beginning centuries earlier, had displaced indigenous peoples by various means (wars, introduced diseases, encroachment, dubious legal agreements, and so on), Saunt sets out to show the early-nineteenth-century removal effort was different—systematic, relentless, ruthless, an American first. The program was ultimately so successful it became the playbook for manipulating, moving, and controlling masses of people as employed by such aspiring colonial empires as the French in North Africa, the Russians in the Caucasus, and the Germans in Africa and later in Eastern Europe in the nineteenth and twentieth centuries.

Second, and more controversially, Saunt argues the expulsion of indigenous peoples need not have happened. He uses copious evidence to demolish some of the main myths used to prop up the notion that relocation was necessary and unavoidable, such as that the indigenous inhabitants and the White settlers could not coexist because the latter were purportedly "uncivilized." He contends that under more favorable circumstances—a few years' delay, or better overall luck—the exiles could have remained where they were indefinitely. But, as Saunt shows, it was not to be. Indigenous peoples, particularly those living in large sovereign nations in the southeastern United States, were targeted in state-sponsored schemes of mass expulsion. Tens of thousands of men, women, and children were uprooted from farms they had cultivated for generations in Georgia, Alabama, Mississippi, and Florida, as well as some areas of the

Midwest. Federal and state governments colluded in the passage of laws that reduced tribal rights. It was all part of a devious plan to coerce, defraud, trick, cheat, threaten, and summarily remove the recalcitrant victims. Exiles were forced to travel hundreds of miles west—on foot, on horseback, by wagon, or by steamboat—toward the vague promise of new lands to compensate for the loss of the old, ancestral lands. Many individuals (most often the sick, the very young, and the very old) died during the journey from exposure, starvation, disease, or outright murder. Their ordeal became known as the Trail of Tears.

Third, Saunt concludes his account by describing how the program began the rapid expansion of the nation to its eventual western boundaries. This was largely achieved by trampling indigenous peoples into submission. Mile by mile, desirable native territory was acquired by force or ruse, by hook or by crook. Military forts, established at the frontiers of newly acquired territory, kept the leading edge moving forward like a scythe. The defeated were moved from lands many people wanted—for their fertility, water sources, or other precious resources—onto lands nobody wanted.

The author begins the first of five parts by spotlighting a historical footnote character, Isaac McCoy. A self-educated missionary working among American Indians in the new state of Indiana and in Michigan Territory in the 1820s, McCoy had a brainstorm: the creation of an Indian paradise called Aboriginia, to be located west of the Mississippi River. The concept was akin to a plan that originated with Thomas Jefferson, the president who negotiated the Louisiana Purchase in 1803. Jefferson drafted legislation that would have provided federal power to trade indigenous-owned acreage east of the Mississippi for land in the vast new territory, but never followed through on it. The idea nevertheless gained popularity, and by the 1820s, American Indian lands had already been diminished by around 600,000 square miles. McCoy's efforts, as Saunt shows, helped generate vigorous debate about the pros and cons of expulsion, with such mealy-mouthed politicians as George Troup and Wilson Lumpkin arguing for deportation and eloquent indigenous advocates and allies, including Cherokee leaders William Hicks and John Ross, opposing them in an ultimately losing battle. The controversy—complicated by the discovery of gold on the Cherokee Nation's ancestral land in southern Appalachia—culminated in 1830 when, by a margin of just five votes, Congress passed the Indian Removal Act and President Andrew Jackson signed it into law. Saunt offers a window into the largely unremembered protest movement against the proposal and ably unveils the behind-the-scenes machinations that led up to that historic vote.

Though expulsion was ostensibly undertaken for humanitarian reasons, based on patently false claims from bigoted supporters that American Indians were lazy farmers and "impoverished drunks" doomed to imminent extinction, the real reason, as Saunt emphasizes, was more sinister. White Southerners (backed by Northern and British investors) wanted to expand operations, to increase profitable cotton-growing businesses run with unpaid slave labor. As Saunt succinctly expresses it, "Self-interest made it possible for these wealthy planter-politicians to convince themselves that it was best for African American slaves to be held close to their masters and for native peoples to be kept far way." They particularly eyed the fertile homelands of the Cherokees,

Chickasaws, Choctaws, Creeks, and Seminoles, where indigenous farmers—some of whom, emulating their White neighbors, owned enslaved Black people—had thrived for centuries. While some, like the Seminoles, resisted forced relocation, the majority of the eighty thousand people affected bowed to the pressure to leave.

The expulsions began in 1830 with the expulsion of the Choctaw Nation as a test case. According to the Treaty of Dancing Rabbit Creek (1830), Choctaw householders were to receive 640 acres apiece in Indian Territory, while children were granted lesser parcels. These terms were not honored, however. The expulsions were a disaster, with many deaths among the exiles. Despite the dismal results, the removal went forward apace.

The parsimonious federal government initially earmarked just $500,000 to feed, shelter, and transport eighty thousand indigenous exiles, who were treated more like livestock than humans, based on an estimate of a few dollars per person. Even operating on the cheap, such as providing spoiled meat or erecting open-air tents for shelter in freezing temperatures, the government wildly underestimated expenses. The removal would ultimately cost about $75 million to carry out.

It would cost the tribes considerably more. Traveling along nonexistent roads through swampy wilderness, or by steamboats that were floating deathtraps (especially during the cholera epidemic of 1832), the deportees left trails marked not only by tears, but by unknown numbers of bodies. Hundreds, perhaps thousands, fell dead along the way while trekking toward promised lands that proved to be vastly inferior to those they had left behind. Additionally, the new lands were measured and mapped by incompetent surveyors who lost rivers, misplaced mountains, and sent exiles to territories already occupied by Plains tribes who would not welcome thousands of strange newcomers. Saunt provides numerous details of the journey that are specific and heartbreaking and troubling; Saunt's work raises many questions about the ethical core, the true soul of the nation as perceived both by American citizens and by the world at large.

Unworthy Republic received almost universal critical acclaim and was short-listed for the 2020 National Book Award for Nonfiction. Caitlin Fitz, writing for the *Atlantic*, for example, stressed the far-reaching social implications that the work describes: "Saunt's greatest contribution is to weld the narrative of deportation to new histories of capitalism that emphasize slavery's centrality to national economic development" and "injects new insights about the development of American capitalism." The Minneapolis *Star Tribune*'s Chris Hewitt termed the book "quietly outraged," a readable history that "keeps track of the miscarriages of justice being perpetrated throughout America and its territories," with "vivid portraits of those who supported and opposed 'Indian removal.'" Jennifer Szalai, in her *New York Times* review, called *Unworthy Republic* powerful, lucid, and unflinching in demonstrating how "Indigenous people were caught in the teeth of a vast bureaucracy that combined penny-pinching austerity with terrible management, corruption and chaos on the ground." Several reviewers applauded Saunt for his careful investigation into and analysis of financial records, correspondence, and other primary sources in building his case, though Fitz did mildly fault the author for failing to incorporate additional historical evidence from anti-expulsion politicians in support of his contention that indigenous expulsion was not inevitable.

Readers will likely come away from *Unworthy Republic* not only better informed about the unjust manner by which the country expanded and what might have been instead, but also perhaps filled with more questions about the intersection of capitalism and racism and what needs to be done now toward justice and reconciliation.

Author Biography

Claudio Saunt teaches early American history at the University of Georgia. His previous nonfiction books include *A New Order of Things: Property, Power, and the Transformation of the Creek Indians, 1733–1816* (1999), *Black, White, and Indian: Race and the Unmaking of an American Family* (2005), and *West of the Revolution: An Uncommon History of 1776* (2014).

Jack Ewing

Review Sources

Fitz, Caitlin. "The People Who Profited Off the Trail of Tears." Review of *Unworthy Republic: The Dispossession of Native Americans and the Road to Indian Territory*, by Claudio Saunt. *The Atlantic*, May 2020, www.theatlantic.com/magazine/archive/2020/05/claudio-sant-unworthy-republic-trail-of-tears/609097. Accessed 21 Jan. 2021.

Hewitt, Chris. Review of *Unworthy Republic: The Dispossession of Native Americans and the Road to Indian Territory*, by Claudio Saunt. *Star Tribune*, 27 Mar. 2020, www.startribune.com/nonfiction-unworthy-republic-the-dispossession-of-native-americans-and-the-road-to-indian-territory-by-claudio-saunt/569156882. Accessed 21 Jan. 2021.

Romeo, Nick. "Illuminating Slave Owners' Crucial Role in the Expulsion of Native Americans." Review of *Unworthy Republic: The Dispossession of Native Americans and the Road to Indian Territory*, by Claudio Saunt. *The Washington Post*, 10 Apr. 2020, www.washingtonpost.com/outlook/illuminating-slave-owners-crucial-role-in-the-expulsion-of-native-americans/2020/04/09/9931aa04-5a6d-11ea-9000-f3cffee23036_story.html. Accessed 21 Jan. 2021.

Szalai, Jennifer. "'Unworthy Republic' Takes an Unflinching Look at Indian Removal in the 1830s." Review of *Unworthy Republic: The Dispossession of Native Americans and the Road to Indian Territory*, by Claudio Saunt. *The New York Times*, 24 Mar. 2020, www.nytimes.com/2020/03/24/books/review-unworthy-republic-claudio-saunt.html. Accessed 21 Jan. 2021.

Review of *Unworthy Republic: The Dispossession of Native Americans and the Road to Indian Territory*, by Claudio Saunt. *Kirkus*, 23 Dec. 2019, www.kirkusreviews.com/book-reviews/claudio-saunt/unworthy-republic. Accessed 21 Jan. 2021.

Review of *Unworthy Republic: The Dispossession of Native Americans and the Road to Indian Territory*, by Claudio Saunt. *Publishers Weekly*, 25 Feb. 2020, www.publishersweekly.com/978-0-393-60984-4. Accessed 21 Jan. 2021.

The Vanished Birds

Author: Simon Jimenez (b. 1989)
Publisher: Del Rey (New York). 400 pp.
Type of work: Novel
Time: Distant future
Locales: Various planets, space stations, and spaceships

In The Vanished Birds, *a solitary spaceship pilot adopts a nonverbal young boy with a strange power; the two become close, but their bond is challenged as they are drawn into corporate intrigue with implications for the fate of humanity as a whole.*

Principal characters

NIA IMANI, the captain of a transport ship
AHRO, a mysterious boy she raises
KAEDA, a man who lives on a remote agricultural planet
FUMIKO NAKAJIMA, a space station designer

The Vanished Birds begins with the story of Kaeda, a man who lives on Umbai-V, a planet designated as a "Resource World" for the intergalactic corporate empire Umbai. The planet's sole business is growing, harvesting, and processing a single plant's seeds; every fifteen years, transport ships arrive to collect the produce. The transport ships travel through "Pocket Space," which the book describes as creating "an imbalance of time." For observers on Umbai-V, the round trip to pick up and deliver the produce takes fifteen years, but for those on the ships, only eight months pass.

As a child, Kaeda meets the captain of one of these transport ships, Nia Imani. He is fascinated by her and the larger world that she represents, and ends up meeting her again every time she returns. When Kaeda is a young man, their relationship turns briefly romantic, but soon she must leave again, not to return for another fifteen years. Kaeda asks her to take him away with her, but she refuses. By the time of Nia's next visit, Kaeda has made a life with his childhood sweetheart, raising children with her and becoming a respected member of his community. However, Nia's presence reminds him of what he cannot have.

One day, Kaeda, now an old man, is present when a child is found in what seems to be the wreckage of a spaceship. When Nia next returns, he asks her to take the child, Ahro, whom he had sheltered for the last several weeks, with her. Ahro cannot, or does not, speak, but he loves music and is able to communicate somewhat by playing a flute. Nia agrees to escort the boy to the nearest space station.

At this point, the narrative jumps back almost a thousand years to tell the story of Fumiko Nakajima, a genius engineer contracted by Umbai to build space stations for humanity to move into after fleeing a dying Earth. Fumiko's romantic partner, Dana, objects to the project, believing that it would be better to focus on sustainable technology to improve the situation on Earth for as long as possible. The space stations, Dana argues, will be accessible only to the wealthy, while the majority of people will be left behind on Earth in an increasingly inhospitable climate. In the end, however, Fumiko still goes through with beginning the new job, choosing career over love. It is, in part, this decision that leads to the state of affairs of the story's "present day," in which Umbai controls a vast swath of planets along with their four space stations.

Fumiko remains alive for the next millennium, spending long periods of time in cryosleep. When Nia brings Ahro to the space station known as the Pelican, Fumiko meets him and becomes convinced that he has the power to "Jaunt," a sort of teleportation ability that Fumiko believes can be exploited to speed up space travel. She asks Nia to raise Ahro and keep him safe until he comes into his power, at which point she is to turn him over to Umbai for study. To do this, Nia must spend the next fifteen years living in "real time" rather than the accelerated timeline of Pocket Space.

The nature of Nia's job has long prevented her from forming any real human connections, and she is content with this solitary existence in which she owes nothing to anyone (besides, of course, her employer). However, she cannot help growing close to Ahro, who soon becomes a son to her in all but name. She begins to have doubts about the assignment Fumiko has given her, wondering if she can bring herself to condemn Ahro to a lifetime as a test subject. When Ahro's abilities finally manifest, Nia's crewmates wonder about their implications for the highly stratified society they live in. Perhaps, they think, this will upend the established order. "He might change the course of human history," one says.

Eventually, however, the corporation does get its hands on Ahro, allowing widespread access to his Jaunt ability. Far from putting an end to the status quo, it just allows Umbai new avenues for exploitation. Umbai-V, for example, becomes a tourist destination, with disastrous effects for its economy and culture. The ramifications are only somewhat explored, however, as the narrative scope narrows down to Ahro and Nia's frantic attempts to find one another again. This focus dominates the final chapters of the book, leading to a bittersweet conclusion.

On a surface level, *The Vanished Birds* draws on the "space freighter" subgenre of science fiction (perhaps best exemplified by the television series *Firefly*, which ran from 2002 to 2003). The setting of a cargo ship crewed by a ragtag bunch of misfits is a familiar one, and like many of the entries in the subgenre, the crew have various personality clashes but ultimately form strong bonds. The novel's strongest inspiration, however, is most likely Alfred Bester's *The Stars My Destination* (1956). The protagonist of that novel, Gully Foyle, possesses the power to "space-jaunte," teleporting great distances across the cosmos. As with Ahro, Foyle's powers draw the attention of corporate interests who hope to be able to make use of them commercially. Foyle, however, manages to get the better of them and jauntes away to live a peaceful life, keeping the secret of space-jaunting out of the hands of people who would use it poorly.

The Vanished Birds shares with *The Stars My Destination* a concern with the injustices of capitalism and overly powerful corporations. But *Birds* is, perhaps, somewhat more cynical in its exploration of the possibility of escaping or changing the oppressive society in which one lives. The novel posits a future in which little has changed for the better in over a thousand years. "Life has changed," the narration says at one point, "but not our capacity for absurd cruelties."

However, *The Vanished Birds* is not without hope. It does suggest that, although humanity has taken quite some time to learn from its mistakes, it might yet do so. In addition, the novel finds a redemptive beauty in the realistically portrayed bonds people form with one another—often despite themselves. Nia and Ahro are the primary example of this, but Nia's crewmates during her fifteen years raising Ahro also become a kind of family, and these themes are echoed in the stories of a number of secondary but strong minor characters.

Critical response to *The Vanished Birds*, with its compelling plot and well-drawn characters, was largely positive, with many reviewers hailing it as an extremely promising debut for a new author. The beauty of the prose and the overall literary feel of the book were particularly praised. Paul Di Filippo, writing for *Locus* magazine, for example, noted that "Jimenez's sentences are beautifully, strikingly crafted" and he compared the "rich sensory embedding of the action" to the work of seminal science-fiction author Samuel Delany. Another element that many reviewers appreciated was the warmth and humanity of the characters—including those that are fairly minor—and their relationships. An anonymous reviewer for *Kirkus* praised the way that, despite the novel's epic scale in terms of both space and time, it "always anchors itself in human connection." The reviewer then added, "Even characters whose lives are glimpsed only in passing, as waypoints along Nia's time-skipping journeys, are fully realized and achingly alive on the page." Samantha Nelson, writing for the AV Club website, concurred, writing, "Jimenez knows just how to give each supporting character enough space to make them feel essential to the story and Nia's makeshift family."

In addition, a number of reviewers found the book's predictions of the future chillingly plausible. Its depiction of an Earth rendered uninhabitable by global warming and a future firmly in the grip of powerful, amoral corporations and severe income inequality is timely and resonated with many critics. Michael Graves, for example, writing for the website of the Lambda Literary Foundation, said that the book "reads like a premonition." This effect is made all the more powerful by Jimenez's ability to create and depict this future world well enough and in such an engaging way as to fully immerse the reader.

Several reviews also had some criticisms of the book, most commonly that the ending felt rushed and perhaps overly narrow in scope. Nelson wrote that the final chapters of the book hasten to "heighten the drama . . . leaving little time for denouement." Di Filippo noted this as well, stating that "the final fifty pages or so cram in an entire revolution in civilization, as well as the culmination of all the personal quests." For most, however, this was a minor detraction from an otherwise enjoyable experience.

Despite these small flaws—which are perhaps not surprising in a highly ambitious work from a first-time novelist—*The Vanished Birds* is a remarkable novel. It is a powerful example of the opportunities that science fiction allows for commentary on the problems of the present day, but it is not a cold and cerebral work of allegory; it delivers its message by keeping the reader emotionally invested in the characters and their connections to one another.

Author Biography

Simon Jimenez has had his work featured in such publications as the online literary magazine *Canyon Voices* and *Nothing Short Of* (2018), an anthologized collection of flash stories. *The Vanished Birds* is his first novel.

Emma Joyce

Review Sources

Di Filippo, Paul. Review of *The Vanished Birds*, by Simon Jimenez. *Locus*, 16 Jan. 2020, locusmag.com/2020/01/paul-di-filippo-reviews-the-vanished-birds-by-simon-jimenez. Accessed 29 Nov. 2020.

Graves, Michael. "*The Vanished Birds* Is a Well-Crafted Science Fiction Debut." Review of *The Vanished Birds*, by Simon Jimenez. *Lambda Literary*, 9 July 2020, www.lambdaliterary.org/2020/07/vanished-birds. Accessed 29 Nov. 2020.

Nelson, Samantha. "*The Vanished Birds*' Bittersweet Love Stories Span Time and Space." Review of *The Vanished Birds*, by Simon Jimenez. *AV Club*, 14 Jan. 2020, aux.avclub.com/the-vanished-birds-bittersweet-love-stories-span-time-1840857390. Accessed 29 Nov. 2020.

Review of *The Vanished Birds*, by Simon Jimenez. *Kirkus*, 14 Oct. 2019, www.kirkusreviews.com/book-reviews/simon-jimenez/the-vanished-birds/. Accessed 29 Nov. 2020.

Review of *The Vanished Birds*, by Simon Jimenez. *Publishers Weekly*, 14 Aug. 2019, www.publishersweekly.com/978-0-593-12898-5. Accessed 29 Nov. 2020.

The Vanishing Half

Author: Brit Bennett (b. 1990)
Publisher: Riverhead Books (New York). 352 pp.
Type of work: Novel
Time: ca. 1940s–1990s
Locales: Mallard, Louisiana; New Orleans, Louisiana; Los Angeles, California

The Vanishing Half *relates the story of Black twins born in the fictional town of Mallard, Louisiana, in the mid-twentieth century. After leaving Mallard at sixteen, one twin chooses to live her life passing as a White woman, while the other returns to their hometown, resulting in an exploration of identity and a growing awareness of how their decisions affect the next generation.*

Principal characters

DESIREE VIGNES, Stella's twin sister
STELLA VIGNES SANDERS, Desiree's twin sister
JUDE WINSTON, Desiree's daughter
KENNEDY SANDERS, Stella's daughter
REESE CARTER, Jude's friend and then lover
EARLY JONES, Desiree's lover; a bounty hunter

In *The Vanishing Half*, author Brit Bennett draws on two long-standing literary traditions, the literature of racial passing and colorism and the literature of twins, to explore the theme of identity. Racial passing, a term historically associated with the United States, is when a person of one racial identity or background is accepted and "passes" as a person from a different racial group. From the beginning of the Antebellum period (late eighteenth century) through the end of the Jim Crow era (1964), racial passing was most associated with Black Americans either trying to escape slavery, or, after emancipation, avoiding the dangers and legal consequences of racism by passing as White. The complexities and emotional impact of racial passing have been addressed in moving literary classics such as *Passing* (1929), by Nella Larsen (1891–1964), which portrays the difficulties and often tragic consequences of the action. Similarly, Charles W. Chesnutt (1858–1932) depicted both passing and colorism—the prejudice, often within a racial group, which prizes people with lighter skin over those with darker skin—in many of his short stories, including "The Passing of Grandison" (1899).

Bennett's other central focus, the special connection between twins, has been seen in literature since antiquity. *The Vanishing Half* echoes themes expressed in Greek mythology through Castor and Pollux, the sons of Leda, who share an incredibly strong bond. Parallels can also be drawn to William Shakespeare's (1564–1616) comedic play *Twelfth Night* (ca. 1600–1602), in which the twins Sebastian and Viola rely on the use of disguises and subterfuge to hide their identities. While Bennett draws heavily from these literary traditions, she questions and offers an in-depth exploration of identity with a contemporary twist.

Bennett begins exploring the theme of identity at the outset of the novel, setting much of it in the fictional town of Mallard, Louisiana. The town is indistinguishable on most maps because of its small size and mysterious origins, adding a light touch of magical realism to the story. Several generations of twin protagonists Stella and Desiree Vignes's family lived in Mallard, and the town was founded by Alphonse Decuir, their great-great-great grandfather, who was the son of a white slaveholder and an enslaved woman. He made Mallard a haven for light-skinned African Americans. People in town compare themselves to each other and judge each other based on the color of their skin. The lighter their skin, the more they are respected and admired.

Brit Bennett

Both Stella and Desiree have very light skin, and when they are young, they, too, are admired. Their mother hopes they will marry light-skinned boys in town to perpetuate their heritage. Because of their light skin, Desiree and Stella seem to live a charmed life in some ways. But they traumatized when they witness their father's tragic death early on, and as their mother struggles as the sole provider for the family, they are forced to leave school and work at the age of sixteen. Once they are in the work force, they realize how little their light skin helps them in the wider, White world outside of Mallard. Their first employers are White and take advantage of them, prompting Desiree and Stella to flee Mallard and start new lives in New Orleans. They also come to realize that Mallard carries its own prejudices, particularly when Desiree returns to Mallard with her dark-skinned daughter Jude, who is continually ostracized and ridiculed for her skin color. The twins may be light-skinned, but they come to understand that they will suffer the consequences of racism, colorism, and discrimination, despite their mother's fantasy that staying in their small town and being light-skinned is all they need to live a good life.

As the twins try to make new lives for themselves, they realize they are limited to certain low-paying jobs because of their race in 1950s New Orleans, and they make pivotal, life-altering decisions that impact their identities as individuals and as twins. Stella decides she must strike out on her own, and rather than facing Desiree and explaining her decision, she leaves a note. Desiree is devastated, believing herself to be the adventurous twin and Stella to be the shy and less adventurous one. After Stella leaves, Desiree will spend much of the rest of her life thinking about Stella and searching for her. Desiree's identity as an individual and as a twin is constantly in question. She thinks about her past with Stella, their relationship, and everything they shared, including witnessing their father's death, and while she is eventually able to move on with her life—marrying a dark-skinned man, giving birth to Jude, and then returning to Mallard—Desiree often appears in limbo emotionally, waiting for her twin to return. She even allows her bounty hunter boyfriend, Early Jones, to search for her sister in the hope that they will be reunited.

Stella, on the other hand, chooses to live as a White woman, eventually moving to Los Angeles. She marries a White man, gives birth to a daughter who has lighter skin than her own, and keeps her past in total secrecy. Stella leaves her entire family behind to live the life she has chosen. She has brief moments where she thinks of the past, but she values her new life as a White woman above all else. Indeed, she does everything in her power to keep her identity safe and her past a secret, including ignoring the blatant and pronounced racism against a Black family who move in across the street. In Bennett's portrayal of the twins' different choices and paths, she examines the ways people reinvent themselves and the consequences of that reinvention, both for themselves and the people they love.

Bennett also delves into the theme of identity through the novel's secondary characters, including Early Jones and Reese Carter. Early becomes Desiree's lover after she leaves her husband and returns to Mallard. Early and Desiree first met as teenagers, when he spent a summer working the local orchards picking fruit. The pair met secretly because Early was dark-skinned, a migrant worker, and Desiree's mother put a stop to them seeing each other. When Early was very young, his parents, who were burdened with too many children, gave him to an aunt and uncle, and he never saw his parents again. That abandonment affected him deeply. He lives a transient life as a bounty hunter, sleeping in his car and moving from job to job, until one of those jobs allows him to reconnect with Desiree. Their relationship evolves slowly and carefully. Early becomes Desiree's confidant about her missing sister and a surrogate father-figure for Jude when Jude allows it. Early supports Desiree emotionally as no other man in her life has done. Although he thinks he will never settle down and believes his identity is that of a drifter, he eventually moves into the family home with Desiree and shares her life. He is able to reinvent himself as the man he wants to be.

Similarly, Reese Carter starts as Jude's college-aged friend and their relationship evolves into love. Reese, who was assigned female at birth, started life as Therese Anne Carter, and when his family would not accept him as a son, he left his Texas home and slowly shed his female identity by cutting his hair, binding his chest, and changing his clothes. As he becomes comfortable in his gender identity and expression, he and Jude become closer, share more of their lives and their past, and choose a life together. Both Reese and Early reinvent themselves in positive ways, becoming truer versions of themselves, whereas Stella's reinvention is fraught with erasure as she tries to eliminate her past rather than incorporating it into her present life and future.

Several critics also compared Bennett's writing style, narrative structure, and thematic approach with that of Toni Morrison's classic novels *The Bluest Eye* (1970), *Sula* (1973) and *Tar Baby* (1981). Bennett uses, as Morrison often did, multiple point-of-view narrators, with several characters relating different parts of the story. Most chapters are narrated by either Desiree, Stella, Jude, or Kennedy, but there are also sections narrated by Early and Reese, providing readers with a wide range of perspectives on identity. Most effective are the chapters where mother and daughter struggle to understand each other. Kennedy, who has been an attention seeker much of her life, continually hopes her mother will notice her and reveal her true self rather than keep secrets about her past. Jude has different struggles with her mother. She repeatedly asks Desiree to leave Mallard since her light-skinned peers make her feel unwelcome and unappreciated because of her dark skin, and while Desiree acknowledges Jude's pain and agrees to think about it, they never move. When Jude leaves for college, she wants a different life than the one her mother seems content to live in Mallard, yet Jude loves and respects her mother, and they have a much closer relationship than Kennedy has with Stella. Stella's reluctance to discuss her past and her secrets, to essentially hide part of her identity, causes a significant rift between her and her daughter. As Heller McAlpin noted in a review for NPR, "Bennett is interested in the unanticipated consequences of life-changing decisions."

Critics overwhelmingly praised *The Vanishing Half*—which earned a spot on the long list for the National Book Award and reached number one on the New York Times Best Sellers list—and its author more generally. Writing for the *New York Times*, Parul Sehgal called Bennett a "remarkably assured writer." McAlpin argued that *The Vanishing Half* was "an even better book, more expansive yet also deeper" than Bennett's acclaimed debut novel, *The Mothers* (2016). Many reviewers particularly appreciated the questions Bennett raises about racial identity and bigotry. Most readers will be enthralled with the depth, complexity, and emotional impact of Bennett's characters as they explore their identities.

Author Biography
Brit Bennett is the award-winning author of the *New York Times* best-selling novel *The Mothers* (2016), for which she was named to the National Book Foundation' 5 Under 35 list of promising young authors. She has also had essays published in the *New Yorker*, the *Paris Review*, and other prestigious publications.

Marybeth Rua-Larsen

Review Sources
Grant, Colin. "The Vanishing Half by Brit Bennett Review—Two Faces of the Black Experience." Review of *The Vanishing Half*, by Brit Bennett. *The Guardian*, 23 June 2020, www.theguardian.com/books/2020/jun/23/the-vanishing-half-by-brit-bennett-review-two-faces-of-the-black-experience. Accessed 23 Sept 2020.
McAlpin, Heller. "'The Vanishing Half' Counts The Terrible Costs of Bigotry and Secrecy." Review of *The Vanishing Half*, by Brit Bennett. *NPR*, 3 June 2020,

www.npr.org/2020/06/03/868197705/the-vanishing-half-counts-the-terrible-costs-of-bigotry-and-secrecy. Accessed 23 Sept 2020.

Page, Lisa. "Brit Bennett's 'The Vanishing Half' Is a Fierce Examination of Passing and the Price People Pay for a New Identity." Review of *The Vanishing Half*, by Brit Bennett. *The Washington Post*, 18 June 2020, www.washingtonpost.com/entertainment/books/brit-bennetts-the-vanishing-half-is-a-fierce-examination-of-passing-and-the-price-people-pay-for-a-new-identity/2020/06/01/6a63f890-a436-11ea-b473-04905b1af82b_story.html. Accessed 23 Sept 2020.

Resnick, Sarah. "Brit Bennett Reimagines the Literature of Passing." Review of *The Vanishing Half*, by Brit Bennett. *The New Yorker*, 15 June 2020, www.newyorker.com/magazine/2020/06/22/brit-bennett-reimagines-the-literature-of-passing. Accessed 23 Sept 2020.

Sehgal, Parul. "Brit Bennett's New Novel Explores the Power and Performance of Race." *The New York Times*, 26 May 2020, www.nytimes.com/2020/05/26/books/review-vanishing-half-brit-bennett.html. Accessed 23 Sept 2020.

Vesper Flights

Author: Helen Macdonald (b. 1970)
Publisher: Grove Press (New York). 320 pp.
Type of work: Essays, nature, environment
Time: 2010–20
Locales: The United Kingdom and the United States

Vesper Flights is a collection of essays on a variety of topics related to the natural world. It is British writer and naturalist Helen Macdonald's second book.

When Helen Macdonald published *H Is for Hawk* (2014), she worried that no one would like the book because of how it amalgamated genres. On the surface, that work is a memoir about Macdonald's experience raising a goshawk named Mabel while grieving the sudden death of her father. However, given the myriad tangents that she goes on as the book unfolds, it could also be classified as a work of nature writing or even a partial biography of the author T. H. White. Although this patchwork-like quality had the potential to be a disaster, it ultimately works thanks to the simple fact that Macdonald is an exceptional writer. With astute insights into the world and compelling storytelling, it is not surprising that *H is for Hawk* quickly became an international best seller, transforming Macdonald into a literary celebrity in the process.

Macdonald's follow-up nonfiction book, *Vesper Flights* (2020), is likely to please the fans that she gained from her triumphant breakthrough. A collection of forty-one essays, some new and some previously published across the past decade, *Vesper Flights* is decidedly not a memoir, but it still has many of the qualities that make *H Is for Hawk* great. The author again puts both herself and her most intimate thoughts on the page while examining the significance of the natural world around her. *Vesper Flights* also has a similar sense of melancholy as its predecessor, although it is much more subdued. Where *H Is for Hawk* is about grappling with personal loss, it can be argued that *Vesper Flights* is about humanity's collective loss of the natural world as a result of capitalism and climate change.

Macdonald's examination of these destructive forces is subtle but omnipresent throughout the collection, existing on the edges of nearly everything she writes. Whether it is witnessing a meadow from her childhood being destroyed or weeping when a beleaguered swan sits down next to her, Macdonald is always noting the steady erosion of environmental conditions. And while she is completely honest about the direness of the situation, at one point even calling it an "apocalypse," what makes

Vesper Flights such a rewarding read is that she never suggests that it is completely hopeless. In her essay "Symptomatic," she writes that humans must speak up and fight for the environment, "Even if change seems an impossibility. For even if we don't believe in miracles, they are there, and they are waiting for us to find them."

Indeed, what makes *Vesper Flights* particularly enjoyable is that so many of the things that Macdonald writes about feel miraculous. She is the kind of naturalist who marvels at everything around her, making even the smallest events feel profound. In the essay titled "Ants," for example, Macdonald writes about the time she pulled off the road to witness the mating ritual of a winged ant colony. She describes how the queen ant mates only once in her potentially thirty-year lifetime, collecting sperm from different mates all at once and them storing them to use in future years. In order for this ritual to take place, there must be pockets of warm air for the queen ant and the drones she mates with to float up in. While most readers are likely not inherently interested in the topic of ant reproduction, they will find themselves in awe of how intricate and fascinating the process really is.

Helen Macdonald

Another example of how Macdonald makes nature riveting is found in the titular essay, "Vesper Flights." In it, she regales her readers with details about the seemingly supernatural lives of swifts. From the time that they leave their nests, swifts spend almost no time on the ground and instead eat, mate, and even sleep while flying. Sometimes they can get up to 10,000 feet in the air—so high that they can see the curve of the Earth and the formation of weather patterns below. Macdonald's love and enthusiasm for creatures such as these birds ultimately proves to be contagious throughout the book.

Macdonald's writing style in *Vesper Flights* is variable, and therefore difficult to classify. In part, this is a result of the fact that each of the essays within the collection were written over a ten-year timeline and many were intended for different publications. Consequently, they have different tones and perspectives. "In Her Orbit," for example, is a profile that Macdonald wrote about astrophysicist Nathalie Cabrol and her search for habitable environments that are similar to Mars. It is one of the book's longest essays and feels more formal and detached than most of the other works, though it is still highly engaging. Many of the book's other essays are quite short, sometimes only two or three pages in length, and focus on singular subjects or experiences. On the surface, the range of topics that Macdonald covers is quite broad. There are essays on everything from her New Year's tradition of walking in the woods alone, to the effects of Brexit, to the arrival of a new species of birds to London. Upon closer inspection, however, it becomes clear that all of her essays share a signature blend of scientific facts with introspection. Furthermore, these works successfully contextualize the significance of natural forces and what they mean for the planet.

Vesper Flights is about many things, but it is at its greatest when it focuses on the intersection of life that exists between animals and humans. Through Macdonald's eyes, these small interactions are some of the most important as they remind people of their place in the world and that there is something much bigger at play. She captures this important feeling in the brief essay "Nothing Like a Pig" when she writes about coming face to face with a captive boar that allows her to scratch its back. Their encounter is brief, but it reminds her of the innate intelligence that such creatures have. In "Nests," Macdonald again feels the overwhelming magic of the natural world when she holds a falcon egg up and clucks softly at it and the chick inside calls back. She also determines that she is not the only one with such experiences in "Inspector Calls," an essay about a young autistic boy named Antek who connects with her pet parrot.

By highlighting these small interspecies moments, Macdonald establishes how important it is for people to do whatever they can to protect the most vulnerable members of their surrounding environment. This message is especially evident in the fascinating piece "High Rise," which recalls her experience with ornithologist Andrew Farnsworth on top of the Empire State Building watching the migration of thousands of birds through the skyscrapers. While a breathtaking sight, it is also incredibly sad as many of the birds die because they are disoriented by the buildings and their lights. The essay ultimately functions as an important reminder of how humans have destroyed aspects of the natural world and therefore are responsible for saving it.

Reception of *Vesper Flights* was overwhelmingly positive, with several publications calling it one of the best books of 2020. Most critics were quick to praise Macdonald's elegant prose in particular. In his review for *USA Today*, Matt Damsker extolled the author's ability to balance the "cosmic and the common," remarking, "At its height, MacDonald's writing captures the inexpressible rhythm of being." It is true that one of Macdonald's strengths is somehow relaying the ineffable feeling of being alive. This is a notable skill, as it requires incredible finesse for a writer to capture that simple, pure, and universal feeling that is most comparable to being a child. In turn there is an honesty and bravery to her writing that proves to be immensely fulfilling. Meanwhile, other critics commended Macdonald for her ability to bring new depths to the naturalist writing genre. As Parul Sehgal wrote for the *New York Times*, Macdonald's writing "muddies any facile ideas about nature and the human, and prods at how we pleat our prejudices, politics and desires into our notions of the animal world. There's nothing of the tourist or bystander in her approach." In this way, *Vesper Flights* is a welcome addition to the genre that might best be compared to contemporary naturalist books like *The Soul of an Octopus* (2015), by Sy Montgomery, or Robert Macfarlane's *The Wild Places* (2007).

Vesper Flights is not without flaws, however. In his review for the *StarTribune*, Malcom Forbes noted that Macdonald's introduction "expresses the hope that her book might resemble a Wunderkammer, or cabinet of curiosities. This turns out to be a fitting comparison." Though this is in some ways part of the work's charm, it can also give the feeling of a random collection of topics and ideas that lacks a truly cohesive thematic backbone. Combine this with the fact that Macdonald often shifts her tone and tempo from essay to essay, and some readers may have a difficult time getting absorbed. For those that find the disparateness of the pieces to be jarring, it might be best to read the book in small increments rather than long sittings. But despite this critique, *Vesper Flights* is ultimately an informative and highly enjoyable work that can push readers' understanding of the world around them in new directions. As Michael Schaub wrote in his review for NPR, "What sets *Vesper Flights* apart from other nature writing is the sense of adoration Macdonald brings to her subjects." Anyone who is looking to cultivate a similar adoration will likely find this book to be deeply rewarding.

Author Biography
Writer and naturalist Helen Macdonald is the author of the nonfiction work *Falcon* (2006), multiple poetry collections, and numerous essays. Her memoir *H Is for Hawk* (2014) was an international best seller and won the Samuel Johnson Prize for Nonfiction and the Costa Book Award.

Emily E. Turner

Review Sources
Damsker, Matt. "'Vesper Flights' Review: Helen Macdonald Returns with Collection of Soul-Stirring Nature Essays." *USA Today*, 26 Aug. 2020, www.usatoday.com/story/entertainment/books/2020/08/25/vesper-flights-review-helen-macdonald-soul-stirring-nature-essays/5628244002/. Accessed 28 Jan. 2021.
Forbes, Malcom. Review of *Vesper Flights*, by Helen Macdonald. *StarTribune*, 21 Sept. 2020, www.startribune.com/review-vesper-flights-by-helen-macdonald/572181062/. Accessed 25 Jan. 2021.
Schaub, Michael. "'Vesper Flights' Offers Hope to a World in Desperate Need of It." Review of *Vesper Flights*, by Helen Macdonald. *NPR*, 29 Aug. 2020, www.npr.org/2020/08/29/906979271/vesper-flights-offers-hope-to-a-world-in-desperate-need-of-it. Accessed 25 Jan. 2021.
Sehgal, Parul. "Helen Macdonald's 'Vesper Flights' Sees Wonder—and Refuge—in the Natural World." Review of *Vesper Flights*, by Helen Macdonald. *The New York Times*, 18 Apr. 2020, www.nytimes.com/2020/08/18/books/review-vesper-flights-helen-macdonald.html. Accessed 25 Jan. 2021.
Review of *Vesper Flights*, by Helen Macdonald. *Kirkus*, 20 Apr. 2020, www.kirkusreviews.com/book-reviews/helen-macdonald/vesper-flights/. Accessed 25 Jan. 2021.
Review of *Vesper Flights*, by Helen Macdonald. *Publishers Weekly*, 23 Mar. 2020, www.publishersweekly.com/978-0-8021-2881-2. Accessed 25 Jan. 2021.

We Are Not Free

Author: Traci Chee
Publisher: Houghton Mifflin Harcourt (New York). 400 pp.
Type of work: Novel, history
Time: March 1942–March 1945
Locales: San Francisco, California; San Bruno, California; Newell, California; and Topaz, Utah

Traci Chee's young adult historical novel We Are Not Free *(2020) follows the experiences of Japanese Americans living on the West Coast during World War II. Fourteen young men and women from San Francisco describe what they lost when they were held in internment camps following the Japanese attack on Pearl Harbor.*

Principal characters
MASARU "MAS" ITO, 20, a serious college student
MINORU "MINNOW" ITO, 14, Mas' brother, a budding artist
SHIGEO "SHIG" ITO, 17, Mas and Minnow's well-liked brother
DAVID "TWITCHY" HASHIMOTO, 17, an energetic teenager
KEIKO KIMURA, 16, Twitchy's girlfriend
AMY "YUM-YUM" OISHI, 16, Shig's girlfriend, a pianist
HIROMI "BETTE" NAKANO, 17, Yum-yum's friend, who wears a blond wig
YUKI NAKANO, 14, Bette's sister, a softball star
FRANCIS "FRANKIE" FUJITA, 19, a long-haired troublemaker
STANLEY "STAN" KATSUMOTO, 18, a smart teen whose family owned a grocery in Japantown
MARY KATSUMOTO, 15, Stan's grumpy sister
TOM "TOMMY" HARANO, 16, a poet and music-lover
AIKO "IKE" HARANO, 13, Tommy's disobedient sister
KIYOSHI "YOSH" TANI, 16, a transfer from Los Angeles to Tule Lake

After a dedication to the author's grandparents (Margaret and Peter Kitagawa and Sachiko and Michio Iwata) and other people of Japanese heritage who inspired the story, the first thing a reader encounters in *We Are Not Free* (2020) is a "Character Registry." Fourteen main characters are listed as they might appear on a government form. Surnames are alphabetical, with given names and nicknames. Gender, age, address, and family number are included. This is a handy reference for keeping track of relationships that exist or develop throughout the story among the characters. It also hints at the dehumanizing bureaucratic treatment of American citizens that lies at the heart of the story.

We Are Not Free opens in March 1942, four months after the entry of the United States into World War II. Residents of Japantown, a long-established community of Japanese Americans in San Francisco, California, are nervous. Prominent local businesspeople with contacts in Japan have been arrested on suspicion of espionage and taken away. Assaults from *keto*—White inhabitants of other neighborhoods—are on the rise. They decorate houses and stores with cruel graffiti. They launch taunts, insults, and physical attacks against the Issei (first-generation Japanese) and their children, the Nisei, who were born in the United States and are American citizens. Young and old Japanese Americans alike worry what the future will bring.

Traci Chee

Their fears prove to be well-founded. In April, a Civilian Exclusion Order is issued by the US army, affecting more than 100,000 people living along the North American West Coast. Persons of Japanese heritage are officially considered "enemy aliens." They are to be excluded from cities like San Francisco (now designated a military zone). Soon, under the auspices of the War Relocation Authority (WRA), they will forcibly be taken away by armed soldiers and confined in internment camps for an indefinite period.

In the brief time before the roundup begins, well-maintained Victorian homes in Japantown are sold for whatever pittance a merciless buyer's market will yield. Mom-and-pop businesses must be liquidated overnight at huge losses. Family heirlooms and other precious possessions acquired over decades are discarded or marked down to bargain prices. Individuals are allowed to take what they can carry: two suitcases apiece. As painful as such sacrifices are, the greatest felt loss is the ability to come and go at will. The deprivation of freedom—as it might be for anyone wrongfully imprisoned—is an outrage, but one the Japanese American community is powerless to do anything about. The idea of freedom, and what it means to be an American, will become constant, common refrains among the multiple narrators of *We Are Not Free*.

Though the community as a whole draws closer together in unity against the unfairness of their predicament, the situation affects different individuals in different ways. Some retreat internally and stoically adapt, practicing *gaman*, or perseverance. Others, going stir-crazy, act out. The youthful individuals at the center of the story represent nine different families. They contribute varied perspectives in usually first-person, present-tense fashion. Each character, whose personality is revealed in the narration, advances the timeline by several months, highlighting events significant to the group. Each adds to the Japanese American youth community's collective experience:

the overnight transformation from typical children of ordinary families into criminals worthy of incarceration. The teens' stories overlap because most grew up in the same neighborhood. As their ordeal drags on over weeks and months, they become better acquainted. Their accounts are enhanced by visual markers that reinforce the subject matter, such as newspaper clippings, vintage photographs, postcards, drawings, maps, posters, documents, and other memorabilia.

The novel begins with the viewpoint of Minoru "Minnow" Ito, who is fourteen years old at the beginning of the story. He is small, shy, sensitive, and especially observant because he is deeply interested in art. He carries a sketchbook everywhere and fills it with drawings of people and landmarks in the neighborhood. By his own admission, Minnow sometimes gets "so wrapped up in a drawing that I get transported onto the paper." Like any kid brother, he greatly admires older siblings Shigeo ("Shig") and especially Masaru ("Mas"), who he views as a superhero like in the comics. Minnow serves as initial spokesperson for the people affected by the upheaval, and he introduces many characters who become more prominent later in the novel.

By turns, other residents of Japantown take up the narration and give different perspectives on life in the internment camps. For example, Shig's musical girlfriend, Amy, called Yum-yum, tells about the facilities at Tanforan, where the community is first transported. The former racetrack is now outfitted with barbed wire and guard towers. Captive families are boarded in 180-square-foot horse stables that stink of manure. Stalls contain only Army cots, so prisoners have to build furniture out of scrap lumber for what will become a five-month stay. At night, the young people exercise their scant liberty, flaunting camp rules to prowl the grounds, play silly games, drink contraband liquor, and pair off to neck in the shadows.

Hiromi "Bette" Nakano narrates details of the evacuation of prisoners by train from Tanforan to Topaz, Utah. A large compound featuring dozens of barracks, still under construction, the facility at Topaz is situated on a bleak, treeless plain. There, Frankie Fujita in early 1943 reports the news of US president Franklin D. Roosevelt's plan to form an all-Japanese combat team. Everyone seventeen or older is required to swear loyalty to the United States by signing a form expressing willingness to serve on combat duty in American military forces. Those who sign also have to renounce fealty to the Japanese emperor. The form creates a psychological barrier that causes the beginning of the disintegration of the group of youngsters. Stan Katsumoto, whose family refuses to sign, discusses the bitter division in the Japanese American community generated by the loyalty question. He wonders how a negative response will affect his aspiration to attend college.

Possibilities open up for those who agree to swear loyalty. Bette considers resettling in New York City, where a married older brother resides. Shig contemplates moving to Chicago. Aiko Harano notes that several young men from the group—Mas, Frankie, and Twitchy—who took the oath have been accepted as candidates for the Japanese 442nd Regimental Combat Team. One by one they leave for basic training. Families that refuse to sign are shipped out. (Children younger than seventeen, for better or worse, must abide by their parents' decision, and their inability to have a say in their destiny creates further disharmony.) They end up at isolated Tule Lake

Segregation Center in northern California near the Oregon border. The facility, built to hold 18,000 people, boasts greater security in confining those still under government control. Fences are higher and topped with barbed wire. Guard towers are taller. A half-dozen tanks mounted with machine guns maintain order.

We Are Not Free follows each of the splinter groups. Children left behind at Topaz from families that signed the loyalty oaths (the "Yes-Yes" crowd) are granted greater liberties. Yuki Nagano, for instance, is a member of a girls' team permitted to leave the compound to play softball against a White high school (though they are still subject to blunt prejudice in the nearby rural town). Bette and Shig leave to pursue opportunities in fresh, free non-coastal urban environments. The outcasts (the "No-Nos"), revolt against harsh conditions at Tule Lake and are punished. The new soldiers of the all-Japanese unit suffer indignities during training at Camp Shelby, Mississippi. When they are ready, the soldiers are shipped overseas to risk their lives. The unit fights with great courage on the European front of the war and earns a disproportionate number of military decorations for its efforts.

Author Traci Chee uses frank language and discusses mature concepts to explore the historical events that are very personal. As she writes in the author's note near the end of the book, "This history is my history." Remarkable insights are put into the mouths of babes. Especially lyrical passages are attributed to young Tommy Harano, who wrestles with the contradictions of being both Japanese and American. The story provides intimate glimpses of a culture that seems foreign to White society. In the course of the story, readers are introduced to aspects of Japanese culture: foods, traditions, vocabulary, family structure. At the same time, *We Are Not Free* demonstrates the multitude of similarities among humans that transcend ethnicity and time period. Adolescents of all origins are quite alike, the author demonstrates. They share the same emotions, doubts, and anxieties. They have identical hopes and fears for the future.

We Are Not Free was selected from among more than 1,500 entrants as a finalist for the National Book Award for Young People's Literature. Critics across the board were similarly impressed. Alice Cary of *BookPage*, for example, called the novel "a captivating portrait of teens . . . their yearnings, heartbreaks, fear and anger ring true on every page." The anonymous reviewer for the *Smithsonian Asian Pacific American Center* wholeheartedly agreed, noting that the author's "effortless amalgamation of history and fiction becomes spectacular storytelling that is both illuminating and immersive." Other reviewers used such phrases as "an unforgettable must-read," "emotionally compelling," and "stunning, important."

Chee's work is part of a growing body of literature that deals with the significant stain that the internment of Japanese Americans during World War II left on national history. Some of the many fictional examples for comparison might include Julie Otsuka's *When the Emperor Was Divine* (2002), John Hamamura's *Color of the Sea* (2006), and Stanley N. Kanzaki's *The Issei Prisoners of the San Pedro Internment Center* (2009). For those interested in delving further into the subject, as is likely to be the experience of readers once finished with Chee's engaging novel, the author provides a helpful list of books and websites.

Author Biography
Traci Chee became a best-selling author with an acclaimed young-adult fantasy trilogy consisting of *The Reader* (2016), *The Speaker* (2017), and *The Storyteller* (2018), which posit a world without books.

Jack Ewing

Review Sources

Cary, Alice. Review of *We Are Not Free*, by Traci Chee. *BookPage*, 1 Sept. 2020, bookpage.com/reviews/25496-traci-chee-we-are-not-free-ya. Accessed 14 Dec. 2020.

Dumas, Bryan. Review of *We Are Not Free*, by Traci Chee. *Historical Novel Society*, May 2020, historicalnovelsociety.org/reviews/we-are-not-free/. Accessed 14 Dec. 2020.

Harlan, Jennifer. "Teenagers in Turmoil." Review of *We Are Not Free*, by Traci Chee. *The New York Times*, 10 Oct. 2020, www.nytimes.com/2020/10/10/books/review/young-adult-crossover-fiction.html. Accessed 14 Dec. 2020.

Kwong, DeHanza. Review of *We Are Not Free*, by Traci Chee. *School Library Journal*, 1 Apr. 2020, www.slj.com/?reviewDetail=we-are-not-free. Accessed 14 Dec. 2020.

Review of *We Are Not Free*, by Traci Chee. *Smithsonian Asian Pacific American Center*, 29 Aug. 2020, smithsonianapa.org/bookdragon/we-are-not-free-by-traci-chee-in-shelf-awareness/. Accessed 14 Dec. 2020.

We Are Not from Here

Author: Jenny Torres Sanchez
Publisher: Philomel Books (New York). 368 pp.
Type of work: Novel
Time: Present day
Locales: Guatemala, Mexico, southwestern United States

A harrowing tale based on contemporary events, We Are Not from Here *(2020) tells of three Guatemalan teens who flee the violence of their hometown and head north. Relying on outdated information and rumors, they travel via a network of trains called "La Bestia," hoping for possible sanctuary in the United States.*

Principal characters

PULGA GARCIA, a fifteen-year-old boy who lives with his widowed mother
PEQUEÑA, a seventeen-year-old who has an infant son and is like a cousin to Pulga
CHICO, a thirteen-year-old orphan who lives with Pulga and is like a brother to him
REY VILLA, an adult ex-convict and gang leader
NESTOR VILLA, Rey's younger brother, a classmate of Pulga's and a bully
DON FELICIO, an elderly store proprietor and parent of an adult son living in the US
DOÑA AGOSTINA, the wife of Don Felicio

In interviews, young-adult author Jenny Torres Sanchez has often talked about feeling like an outsider when she was growing up. Her heritage made it seem she was living between two worlds. While she was born in the Brooklyn borough of New York City, she was the child of recent immigrants: her mother was from Guatemala and her father from San Salvador. New arrivals often stand out in American neighborhoods, and because they look or sound different from locals, may generate a range of reactions—curiosity, suspicion, fear, prejudice—among residents. Sanchez, as she matured and began writing, drew upon the discomfort she felt as a child to help motivate those who populate her stories. Her well-received novels about youthful protagonists, besides dealing with typical teenage angst and self-doubt, have gained a reputation for presenting plausible, character-building tests that would challenge the will of anyone, young or old.

Her debut novel, for example, *The Downside of Being Charlie* (2012), revolves around the titular hero's desperate attempt to overcome an eating disorder, complicated by his mother's deteriorating mental stability. *Death, Dickinson, and the Demented Life of Frenchie Garcia* (2013) is a personal study of a young woman overcoming grief following the sudden suicide of her secret crush. Later novels explored family tragedy (*Because of the Sun*, 2017) and the lingering aftereffects of a brutal assault (*The Fall of Innocence*, 2018).

With her fifth novel, *We Are Not from Here* (2020), the author has expanded her scope to international proportions with a plot that reflects actual conditions present in the Western Hemisphere in the early decades of the twenty-first century. The story, divided into five parts, involves three young people linked by tragedy who run from violence and intimidation toward a more positive future.

We Are Not from Here begins in Puerto Barrios, a large city in eastern Guatemala along the Gulf of Honduras on the Caribbean Sea. (The city is also the hometown of Sanchez's mother in real life.) In the 2010s, Puerto Barrios became notorious for having one of the highest murder rates in one of the world's most violent countries. Much of the violence was the result of clashes between rival drug traffickers in territorial disputes. Frequent shootouts among competing gangs have resulted in the deaths of many innocent victims. The tropical climate, widespread poverty, and a profusion of firearms wielded by criminals with little to lose combine to make Puerto Barrios a dangerous city—and also to drive the plot in Sanchez's novel.

The story is told by two alternating first-person, present-tense narrators. One is Pulga ("Flea"), a physically slight but agile and mentally alert fifteen-year-old boy. He lives in a small house with his hardworking mother and aspires to become a musician like his late father, a bassist killed years earlier in a car crash while living and working in California. Pulga, thinking of the future, collects information about people who have attempted to travel to the United States, where he has an aunt he has never met. Chico, whose mother was gunned down in the streets, lives with Pulga and his mother. A big, chubby, slow-thinking boy, Chico once knocked out Nestor Villa, a school bully who was tormenting Pulga. The incident attracted the unwelcome attention of Nestor's older brother Rey, a scar-faced gang leader who learned new criminal skills while serving time in an American prison. Deported upon his release, Rey operates out of Guatemala City and commands a crew of thuggish subordinates.

The other narrator is Pequeña ("Little One"), an attractive, petite young woman who has vivid dreams; she experiences visions and sometimes hallucinates. She believes she is protected by an angel, La Bruja. Pequeña is Pulga's cousin, but not by blood. When first introduced, she is about to give birth at home, assisted by an "aunt," Tía Lucia, and by Pulga's mother, Consuelo. Pequeña, whose real name is Flor, seems strangely indifferent to her newborn son.

The action of the novel quickly accelerates when Pulga and Chico visit Don Felicio's nearby store to obtain firecrackers to celebrate the birth of Pequeña's unnamed baby. While inside, the boys witness a terrible crime involving the Villa brothers. Though the boys then run home, the Villa brothers, suspecting Pulga and Chico know what happened, threaten them at gunpoint. Afterward, the Villas involve the boys in a drug deal, so they cannot mention what occurred at the store without implicating themselves in multiple crimes.

Meanwhile, Pequeña is reluctant to breastfeed her newborn child. The reason becomes obvious when Rey Villa arrives outside her bedroom window. His eyes gleam with pride: he is the father of the baby. Months earlier, he saw Pequeña on the street, became attracted to her, and began stalking her. One night he climbed into her bedroom window and raped her at knifepoint, threatening to kill her family if she made any noise during the assault. After the birth, Rey becomes attentive to Pequeña, visiting her often when the members of her extended family are absent. He gives her money, which she hides away. Rey even gives her a large diamond ring. He tells her the next day he will come for her and take her home with him. However, she instinctively knows that when Rey tires of her, when she loses her looks and her figure changes following further pregnancies, she will be discarded.

Pulga and Pequeña come to an identical conclusion at the same time: they have to escape from Puerto Barrios immediately or "something bad will happen." Chico, who is helpless on his own, agrees to flee with them. They all load backpacks with clothing, food, water, and other items. The boys head for the local bus terminal, vowing never to return, because they know Rey would kill them. Pequeña stops first at a pharmacy to see Leticia, a former beauty, who in her mid-twenties looks old and tired after giving birth to an illegitimate son by a boyfriend who deserted her. Leticia, sympathetic to Pequeña's plight, allows her to purchase several items—including a razor and a switchblade knife—on credit, against store policy. When Pequeña shows up to meet the boys at the bus station, she is dressed like a man, with her hair razored short, because she feels safer concealing her gender. They buy tickets for the first leg of their journey. Their goal is the United States border, more than two thousand miles away.

The three companions ride to Guatemala City, then board another bus to Tecún Umán, on the southwest coast of the country. They cross the Suciate River by raft into Mexico, then make their way to Ciudad Hidalgo, a city in central Mexico where they stay at a shelter run by a priest, Padre Gilberto, and a kindly woman named Marlena. Ultimately, they pay to ride in vans with other migrants. Their trip is continually interrupted by checkpoints manned by police or other authorities, forcing the passengers to bail out and hide. Finally, the three travelers arrive at a train yard, run by the Ferromex railway system. They wait until the time is right, then run to catch a train moving north, a perilous undertaking. They scramble on top of boxcars (or crowd within, when doors are carelessly left unlocked). Over the following days and weeks, the trio of youngsters, in company with other individuals and families, run a dangerous gauntlet. They avoid kidnappers, immigration officials, border patrol, and bandits. They encounter local hostility toward immigrants. They travel through severe weather, from freezing rain to blazing sun, clinging by their fingernails, trying not to fall off the fast-moving train—as they follow a torturous path leading, they hope, toward freedom and safety.

We Are Not from Here is a worthy addition to the growing body of Latinx immigrant literature. Though the author's intentions are different, the subject matter overlaps with such novels as Valeria Luiselli's *Lost Children Archive* (2019), about the fate of border-crossing children, and with nonfiction accounts like Oscar Martínez's *The Beast: Riding the Rails and Dodging Narcos on the Migrant Trail* (2013). Though intended for young adults, Sanchez's novel pulls no punches in describing the harsh realities and visceral experiences of growing up in a bleak world of limited possibilities, which engenders the need to escape. Many reviewers praised the novel for its exploration of these truths, and it is through her descriptions of this dangerous journey that Sanchez's writing particularly excels. She clearly has great compassion for her characters and writes from a place of deep understanding—her own family in Guatemala witnessed and lived through many of the same tragedies that are central to the novel's characters. As Paola Mendoza wrote in a review for the *New York Times*, "She infuses this tragic tale with the love and dignity her characters demand. It is clear she knows the territory." Critics also applauded Sanchez's talent for creating a genuinely gripping read. As the *Kirkus* reviewer stated, "Sanchez delivers a brutally honest, not-to-be-missed narrative enriched by linguistic and cultural nuances in which she gracefully describes the harrowing experiences the young people endure after making the choice to survive." Likewise, Autumn Allen, writing for *BookPage*, commended Sanchez in a starred review for her "stunning, visceral and deeply moving read."

The tone of the work is set at the start. A brief prologue describes how the blood of the murdered turns brown as it seeps into the soil. This underlines one theme: the randomness and finality of violence. Pulga and Pequeña—despite her sometimes-magical thinking—are realists, "We are small people," Pequeña notes. "The world wants to crush us." Meanwhile, Pulga muses, "Living on this land is like building a future on quicksand." Though downbeat, the novel contains a thread like a ray of sunshine. The sense of community—that allowed strays like Chico and Pequeña to be embraced as part of a family—exists in many places. As the teens learn on the road, there are generous, selfless humans willing to encourage and assist the youngsters in their quest. Sanchez's authenticity allows readers to empathize with their plights.

Author Biography

A former English teacher, Jenny Torres Sanchez published her first young-adult novel, *The Downside of Being Charlie*, in 2012. Her third novel, *Because of the Sun* (2017), received a Florida Book Award. *We Are Not from Here* (2020) is her fifth novel.

Jack Ewing

Review Sources

Allen, Autumn. Review of *We Are Not from Here*, by Jenny Torres Sanchez. *BookPage*, June 2020, bookpage.com/reviews/25157-jenny-torres-sanchez-we-are-not-from-here-ya#.X026DSFMGUk. Accessed 10 Sept. 2020.

Mendoza, Paola. "Brave Teenage Refugees Seek a Home of the Free." Review of *We Are Not from Here*, by Jenny Torres Sanchez. *The New York Times*, 27 June 2020, www.nytimes.com/2020/06/27/books/review/we-are-not-from-here-jenny-torres-sanchez.html. Accessed 10 Sept. 2020.

Paz, Selenia. Review of *We Are Not from Here*, by Jenny Torres Sanchez. *School Library Journal*, 1 Mar. 2020, www.slj.com/?reviewDetail=we-are-not-from-here. Accessed 10 Sept. 2020.

Review of *We Are Not from Here*, by Jenny Torres Sanchez. *Kirkus*, 26 Feb. 2020, www.kirkusreviews.com/book-reviews/jenny-torres-sanchez/we-are-not-from-here/. Accessed 10 Sept. 2020.

Review of *We Are Not from Here*, by Jenny Torres Sanchez. *Publishers Weekly*, 8 Apr. 2020, www.publishersweekly.com/978-1-9848-1226-1. Accessed 10 Sept. 2020.

We Have Been Harmonized
Life in China's Surveillance State

Author: Kai Strittmatter (b. 1965)
First published: *Die Neuerfindung der Diktatur: Wie China den digitalen Überwachungsstaat aufbaut und uns damit herausfordert*, 2018, in Germany
Translated from the German by Ruth Martin
Publisher: Custom House (New York). 368 pp.
Type of work: Current affairs, history, technology
Time: Primarily 2010s
Locale: China

Kai Strittmatter's detailed report about life in an increasingly powerful Communist country, with massive access to data about almost all its citizens, is a long-overdue wake-up call about the dangers of surveillance everywhere.

German journalist Kai Strittmatter is a recognized expert on China. In the preface to *We Have Been Harmonized: Life in China's Surveillance State*, he lays out the background that gives him such authority on the subject. He began studying China in the 1980s and moved there as a correspondent in 1997. After spending time in Turkey from 2005 to 2012, he returned to China until late 2018. He authored several previous books on the country, demonstrating a deep understanding of Chinese culture, politics, economic issues, and more. He also witnessed firsthand many significant—and often worrisome—developments in Chinese society in the first decades of the twenty-first century. *We Have Been Harmonized*, which was revised and updated for the 2020 US edition, serves as Strittmatter's warning about growing totalitarianism in a country he knows all too well.

While Strittmatter focuses on contemporary China, he provides enough historical context that readers less familiar with the country will not feel lost. Indeed, early on he delves back thousands of years to provide evidence that twenty-first-century concerns over fake news and leaders willfully ignoring reality are hardly new—Chinese rulers have manipulated facts for thousands of years. Most relevant, however, is the much more recent history of China's Communist rulers. Mao Zedong, chair of the Chinese Communist Party (CCP) and founder of the People's Republic of China in 1949, created an entire authoritarian system that continues to bear his name. Maoism was touted as a way to create a nation with genuine social and economic equality. Mao showed how communication was key to control, with his collection of quotations known as the *Little Red Book* becoming a symbol of the regime. The promises of progress and equality did not exactly come to pass, however. China remained an impoverished country, ruled by an all-powerful dictator. Dissent was crushed before it could even be expressed.

Only after Mao died and China gradually opened its economy to the world did the country grow more prosperous. Strittmatter notes how many Western observers assumed that these economic changes would eventually but inevitably lead to a more liberal political system as well. This hope was buoyed by apparent signs over the decades of "reform movements, original debates, surprising experiments, and brave taboo-breakers" in China and even within the CCP itself. Yet even as the Chinese economy boomed in the 1990s and into the twenty-first century, tracking to soon become the largest in the world, real democracy failed to find a foothold.

Kai Strittmatter

Skeptics began to fear that the Western dream of Chinese liberalization might be nothing more than a dream. China, they worried, might become a rich and powerful nation but not one that would play by the globalists' rules. Critics also noted how developments in Western society were playing into China's hands: allowing jobs and entire industries to shift to China could alienate large segments of Western populations, leaving them open to populist and autocratic leaders of their own. (At several points Strittmatter skewers US president Donald Trump as representative of this kind of opportunism.) The resulting global political instability would only further allow Chinese officials to justify their authoritarian policies. And, crucially, technological advances would give the dictatorship more powerful means of control than ever.

Strittmatter describes in great, convincing, and frightening detail how this is exactly what has happened. The China of optimistic Westerners' dreams is fast disappearing, replaced by a dictatorship in some ways even more terrifying than Mao's. Mao, after all, ruled over an impoverished land that he managed to keep impoverished by trying, ineffectively, to make it rich. But Mao's present heir, Xi Jinping, is a dictator far more powerful, both at home and abroad, than Mao could ever have hoped to be, thanks to China's newfound economic heft. Indeed, Strittmatter argues that Xi's regime is a far greater threat to global democracy than any other power, including that of similarly autocratic Russian leader Vladimir Putin. After becoming CCP chair in 2012, Xi quickly consolidated power to a degree unmatched since Mao. He also led a major buildup China's army, navy, air force, space force, and other levers of power.

Closely attuned as he is to Chinese culture, Strittmatter does not blame the Chinese people for their state's shift from authoritarianism to totalitarianism. He points to Taiwan and Hong Kong as examples of how Chinese people have prospered under democratic freedoms, enjoying good incomes as well as free thought and open debate. Unsurprisingly, both places have drawn the wrath of the Communist regime in China now—behavior predicted by some of the same skeptics who doubted the wisdom of relying on capitalism to bring democracy. For Xi and his supporters, Taiwan and Hong Kong risk exposing the fact that the CCP is not the only path to prosperity, and therefore cannot be tolerated. Similarly, China's ambitions to assert its power in the South China Sea and elsewhere serve to maintain and increase its economic and political control both domestically and abroad.

While Strittmatter is clear and urgent in his warning of China as a growing global threat, his true focus in *We Have Been Harmonized* is, as the subtitle suggests, life within China. Xi's government may seek to expand its influence beyond its present borders as much as possible, but inside those borders, it has succeeded in creating a powerful and still-growing surveillance state. Strittmatter convincingly suggests that Xi has far more control over other humans than practically anyone else on earth, starting with his own citizens. On the other side of the coin, the Chinese people have less real freedom today than they have ever had, even during the darkest days of the Cultural Revolution of the 1960s and '70s. This is enabled above all by cutting-edge information technology, from ubiquitous surveillance cameras and facial recognition programs using artificial intelligence to internet censorship and data harvesting. It is increasingly difficult in contemporary China to do almost anything in private.

One of Strittmatter's most chilling examples of the surveillance state is the Chinese government's development of "social credit" scores. In a growing number of areas, Chinese citizens are monitored in practically every way imaginable and are given these scores based on various factors intended to gauge their loyalty to the regime. Anyone with a good score can live a reasonably comfortable (if shockingly unfree) life; anyone with a low score can be penalized in increasingly onerous ways. In many ways China has come to resemble nothing so much as the society described in *Nineteen Eighty-Four*, George Orwell's famous, grimly prophetic 1949 novel. This is all the more remarkable considering that China was still a relatively poor country in the actual year 1984. The rapid transformation it has seen in only a few decades underscores the potential for the Communist regime to take its totalitarianism even further as technology continues to improve.

Strittmatter also shows how the West bears a good deal of the blame for China's surveillance state. Western technology companies, in general—and giants such as Apple and Google in particular—have helped create a digital landscape in which collection of personal data is the norm. Indeed, such companies have often cooperated closely with the Chinese government, helping to rob ordinary Chinese citizens of what few freedoms they may once have enjoyed. Even the internet itself, once naively assumed to be an instrument encouraging real freedom and allowing open discussion and debate, is now largely controlled by a few monopolistic megacorporations that are more than willing to determine what can and cannot be said or even thought. Strittmatter further suggests this erosion of freedoms affects not only China, but also the United States and other Western countries and indeed nations around the world. And China's technological savvy allows it to exploit the situation, selling surveillance equipment and other devices meant to monitor and record practically everything and raking in huge profits.

We Have Been Harmonized describes, in bleak detail, a nightmare that has already arrived in China and seems right around the corner for much of the West as well. This is, for all kinds of reasons, a truly terrifying book. Throughout, Strittmatter clearly urges readers to take seriously a threat that has been building for years. "China is working to create the perfect surveillance state," he warns. "And this China wants to shape the rest of the world in its own image." He is not idly stirring controversy or fearmongering: he backs up his claims with careful reporting and solid evidence. His urgent tone may at times come across as combative, presenting himself as one who has all the answers and disdaining those who might offer different interpretations, but his arguments are ultimately highly convincing.

The critical reception of *We Have Been Harmonized* was highly positive, with reviewers agreeing that Strittmatter presents a compelling and troubling portrait of China. It received starred reviews from *Kirkus*, *Publishers Weekly*, and *Library Journal*, for example. Writing for the *Guardian*, John Naughton called it a "remarkable book" and noted, "The more one reads, the more pressing one conclusion becomes: almost everything we knew about contemporary China is wrong." By beginning to correct perceptions of one of the world's chief powers, Strittmatter may help us reckon with the future of both China and the rest of the world. One thing seems certain: the Chinese government will be watching.

Author Biography

Kai Strittmatter is a German journalist who has specialized in covering China. He is the author of various books on the country and its culture, including guidebooks designed to introduce the nation to Western tourists.

Ruth Martin is a freelance translator specializing in German to English translation. She has worked with many publishers on a wide range of literary projects.

Robert C. Evans, PhD

Review Sources

Li, Nigel. Review of *We Have Been Harmonized: Life in China's Surveillance State*, by Kai Strittmatter. *The Taipei Times*, 27 Feb. 2020, www.taipeitimes.com/News/feat/archives/2020/02/27/2003731689. Accessed 30 Jan. 2021.

Naughton, John. Review of *We Have Been Harmonized: Life in China's Surveillance State*, by Kai Strittmatter. *The Guardian*, 30 June 2019, www.theguardian.com/books/2019/jun/30/we-have-been-harmonised-life-china-surveillance-state-kai-strittmatter-review. Accessed 30 Jan. 2021.

Temple-Raston, Dina. "Surveillance, Reeducation and the Office of Honesty: How China Tames Its People." Review of *We Have Been Harmonized: Life in China's Surveillance State*, by Kai Strittmatter. *The Washington Post*, 13 Nov. 2020, www.washingtonpost.com/outlook/surveillance-reeducation-and-the-office-of-honesty-how-china-tames-its-people/2020/11/12/075dbfae-1e13-11eb-90dd-abd0f7086a91_story.html. Accessed 30 Jan. 2021.

Wallace, Joshua. Review of *We Have Been Harmonized: Life in China's Surveillance State*, by Kai Strittmatter. *Library Journal*, 1 Oct. 2020, www.libraryjournal.com/?reviewDetail=we-have-been-harmonized. Accessed 30 Jan. 2021.

Review of *We Have Been Harmonized: Life in China's Surveillance State*, by Kai Strittmatter. *Kirkus*, 17 June 2020, www.kirkusreviews.com/book-reviews/kai-strittmatter/we-have-been-harmonized/. Accessed 30 Jan. 2021.

Review of *We Have Been Harmonized: Life in China's Surveillance State*, by Kai Strittmatter. *Publishers Weekly*, 17 June 2020, www.publishersweekly.com/978-0-06-302729-9. Accessed 30 Jan. 2021.

Weather

Author: Jenny Offill (b. 1968)
Publisher: Alfred A. Knopf (New York). 224 pp.
Type of work: Novel
Time: 2016
Locale: Brooklyn, New York

Weather, a novel written in fragments, is an exploration of how people love and protect each other during unstable times. Protagonist Lizzie Benson is a university librarian and also works as an assistant for a climate change expert, answering increasingly troubling emails from podcast listeners. While raising her son and supporting her troubled brother, Lizzie attempts to hold onto hope as she deals with the ever-approaching catastrophe of climate collapse and the 2016 US presidential election.

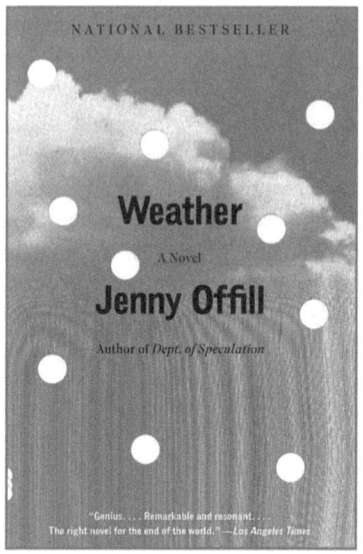

Principal characters

LIZZIE BENSON, a university librarian who also works for Sylvia
BEN, Lizzie's husband, a classicist turned educational video game designer
HENRY, Lizzie's brother, a recovered addict who often relies on Lizzie
SYLVIA, a climate expert and podcast host
CATHERINE, Henry's girlfriend, who is an advertising executive
ELI, Lizzie and Ben's son

Weather is the third published novel by American writer Jenny Offill. With her previous novel, *Dept. of Speculation* (2014), Offill developed a fragmented style that allowed her to unfold her plotline alongside quick asides and offhand observations. In that critically acclaimed work, Offill conjures a story about a marriage that has begun to crack following the birth of a baby and midlife disappointments. The chapters switch perspective between the protagonist who tells the story in the first person, to a woman speaking directly to her distant husband. Blending these voices, *Dept. of Speculation* collages its way through a funny, sometimes painful tale. *Weather* evolves Offill's fragmented style. Told from protagonist Lizzie Benson's point of view, the novel marries the day-to-day experiences of Lizzie's roles as a mother, wife, sister, and university librarian with her growing fears about the effects of climate change on the world, the 2016 US presidential election, and her family, who live in Brooklyn, New York.

Jenny Offill

At the novel's outset, Lizzie is working at the university library—the same university where the reader is told she was once a promising graduate student but never finished her dissertation, which was titled "The Domestication of Death: Cross-Cultural Mythologies." She has since abandoned academic aspirations and is a fixture of the library's staff. Her husband, Ben, a trained classicist, has similarly abandoned his academic pursuits and now designs educational video games. Lizzie's brother, Henry, is a regular presence, often enlisting Lizzie to help him work his way out of depressive states. As a recovering addict, Henry is frequently at the top of Lizzie's mind.

The plot of *Weather* takes something of a meandering approach, with the story taking a special interest in inaction versus strong forward motion. By juxtaposing the mundane against the massive issues of climate change and political tumult, Offill uses this structure to support social commentary. The reader sees Lizzie at her job at the library connecting with her regular patrons, taking a car service run by a man named Mr. Jimmy who has lost his other drivers and customers to a new app, sometimes taking the bus, helping her son with his homework, taking walks with her brother, and going to a meditation class she hates. She also answers letters for Sylvia, her former dissertation advisor who has hired Lizzie to correspond with people who write in response to her podcast, *Hell and High Water*. Those letters create an opening for Offill to introduce the reader more explicitly to the pervading anxiety of climate change and its ramifications. Sylvia, who once felt a passion for addressing the climate crisis, has grown weary of the topic and the letters she is receiving. However, taking on this responsibility leaves Lizzie with an enormous sense of impending doom, no matter the ridiculous nature of the correspondence. In one relatively grounded letter, a listener writes, "What are the best ways to prepare my children for the coming chaos?" Lizzie's response reads, "You can teach them to sew, to farm, to build. Techniques for calming a fearful mind might be the most useful though." Other emails delve deeper; for example, "How is the goodness of God manifested even in the clothing of birds and beasts?"

The fears begin to pervade Lizzie's life. Meeting with Sylvia in New York, she mentions she hopes to buy land in a colder climate, so her and Henry's children would have somewhere to live. (Sylvia's response that the only safe option is to become very rich is another example of the sharp social criticism offered throughout.) Yet climate change is just the beginning of the complex, often interconnected worries that emerge for Lizzie and the other characters. At one point Lizzie notes that she does not tell Ben about the letters she answers, saying, "He would not be pleased by the nature of these questions. He's already worried the evangelicals are trying to take over everything. In cahoots, of course, with the Jews for Jesus." The issues presented both sympathetically reflect and somewhat parody the concerns of many progressives in the 2010s, with the lines between valid fears and paranoia blurring. But ultimately there is one key theme that carries through *Weather*: how does a person protect the people they love when the future is anything but certain? When Sylvia questions whether Lizzie actually believes she can protect her children far in the future, Lizzie's reaction is telling: "I look at her. Because until this moment, I did, I did somehow think this."

Lizzie turns from anxiously facing climate collapse to obsessing over survivalist techniques, learning things like how to create a lamp from a can of tuna—in oil, not water—or how chewing gum can come in handy in a crisis. In one comical scene, as she runs to catch the bus, out of breath before she reaches it, Lizzie realizes no matter the preparation, she is not cut out for the end times. And of course, planning is not the same as acting—Lizzie's efforts do little to change the outcome of the future she fears. Ben, on the other hand, largely chooses to ignore the issue all together. His mind is on the outcome of the 2016 presidential election between Hillary Clinton and Donald Trump, though the candidates are never named.

Weather's tone allows Offill to approach the topics of despair, protection, impending doom, and love with a comedic air even in the face of horror. For example, when an older professor who has attended a talk at the university is handed a card by a student asking him to take stock of his privilege, he asks Lizzie, "What do you think this is?" She thinks to herself, "The future?" At other moments, Offill inserts jokes into the flow of the narrative. The variation in style and content speaks to the existential despair Offill's characters are experiencing. (To add to the list, Henry has a child with and marries his girlfriend, Catherine, only to relapse under the pressure of fatherhood. He ends up on Lizzie's couch.)

Complementing this tone and contrasting with the weighty problems at hand are the everyday frustrations of the main characters. Eli has a crush on a girl at his school and wants to lock down summer play dates, but Lizzie does not know her mom. Lizzie and another mom work to actively avoid each other, hiding out in coffee shops and hardware stores. When Lizzie cannot handle another conversation with Mr. Jimmy, she takes public transportation. The resistance to a traditional narrative works particularly well when the readers encounter Lizzie in her day-to-day actions, as if the text is mimicking the scattered way one's brain approaches the overwhelming realities of modern life.

Offill uses Lizzie's sharp observations to bring up other broad social issues, such as gentrification, privilege, wealth, and responsibility. At one point Lizzie says of the mother Nicola, whom she is outrunning, "She had this way that she would talk about our zoned elementary school, in one breath praising the immigrant kids who went there and in the next talking about the tutors she'd hired to get her son out of it. Strivers, she called them. Like they were all cleaning chimneys or selling papers hot off the press."

While the novel works well in many ways, the structure does sometimes feels obtrusive in a way *Dept. of Speculation*'s use of fragmented texts avoided. For one,

Weather can lose focus or just feel tiring as Lizzie is attempting to bring humor to a situation. The dry approach also becomes a bit claustrophobic during the more intense scenes between Lizzie and Henry.

Weather received wide-ranging praise upon its release, with positive reviews published in *BookForum*, *The New York Times*, *The Nation*, and *NPR*, among other places. In her review for *BookForum*, critic Christine Smallwood noted, "*Weather* captures something essential about a contemporary mood, a kind of pre-traumatic stress caused by the threat of what we know and don't do anything about." Writing in *The Guardian*, Kate Clanchy wrote, "Perhaps all our clever chat, like all Lizzie's talk, will get us nowhere. It's an alarming prospect—reading *Weather* made me grind my teeth at night, just like its narrator—but it is certainly a brilliant exemplar for the autofictional method. Offill pulls us in close in order to make us worry about things outside us; mirrors the self to show us what we are selfishly ignoring."

Published ahead of the 2020 US presidential election and in the midst of climate disasters like devastating wildfires in California and an unprecedented hurricane season, *Weather* finds itself speaking directly to its time, with characters dealing with many of the same anxieties of its audience. While *Dept. of Speculation* was relatable because of its explorations of familiar relationships, *Weather* speaks to a different, less tangible aspect of human existence, providing a moment for contemplation while being entertained by Offill's always shining prose.

Author Biography
Jenny Offill is the author of the novels *Last Things* (1999), a *New York Times* Notable Book of the Year and a finalist for the *Los Angeles Times* First Fiction Award, and *Dept. of Speculation* (2014), which was short-listed for the Folio Prize, the PEN/Faulkner Award, and the International Dublin Literary Award. She also published several children's books.

Melynda Fuller

Review Sources
Clanchy, Kate. "Weather by Jenny Offill Review—Wit for the End Times." Review of *Weather: A Novel*, by Jenny Offill. *The Guardian*, 13 Feb. 2020, www.theguardian.com/books/2020/feb/13/weather-by-jenny-offill-review. Accessed 24 Sept. 2020.

Jamison, Leslie. "Jenny Offill's 'Weather' Is Emotional, Planetary and Very Turbulent." Review of *Weather: A Novel*, by Jenny Offill. *The New York Times*, 7 Feb. 2020, www.nytimes.com/2020/02/07/books/review/weather-jenny-offill.html. Accessed 24 Sept. 2020.

McAlpin, Heller. "Stormy 'Weather' Captures Our Anxious Age with Bracing Wit." Review of *Weather: A Novel*, by Jenny Offill. *NPR*, 11 Feb. 2020, www.npr.org/2020/02/11/804579851/stormy-weather-captures-our-anxious-age-with-bracing-wit. Accessed 24 Sept. 2020.

Smallwood, Christine. "Meditations in an Emergency." Review of *Weather: A Novel*, by Jenny Offill. *BookForum*, www.bookforum.com/print/2605/jenny-offill-s-novel-of-the-barely-bearable-present-23833. Accessed 24 Sept. 2020.

Review of *Weather: A Novel*, by Jenny Offill. *Kirkus*, 11 Nov. 2019, www.kirkusreviews.com/book-reviews/jenny-offill/weather-offill/. Accessed 26 Oct. 2020.

When Truth Is All You Have
A Memoir of Faith, Justice, and Freedom for the Wrongly Accused

Authors: Jim McCloskey (b. 1943) with Philip Lerman (b. 1956)
Publisher: Doubleday (New York). 320 pp.
Type of work: Memoir
Time: 1940s–present day
Locales: United States, Canada

When Truth Is All You Have *is a memoir about Jim McCloskey and his efforts with Centurion Ministries, an organization he founded that works to exonerate innocent men and women who have been imprisoned for crimes they did not commit.*

Principal personages
JIM MCCLOSKEY, the founder of Centurion Ministries, an advocate for innocent prisoners
JORGE "CHIEFIE" DE LOS SANTOS, the first prisoner he helped to free
PAUL CASTELEIRO, a lawyer who worked with him
KATE GERMOND, his colleague
CLARENCE BRANDLEY, a death-row prisoner he helped to free

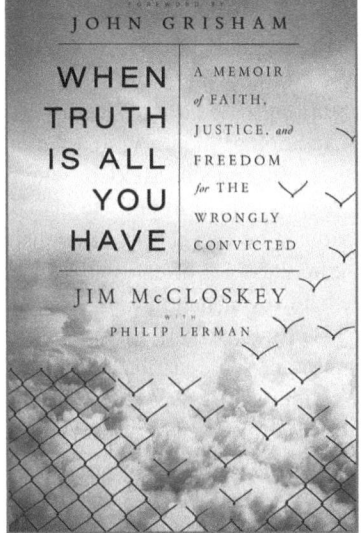

In the forward to *When Truth Is All You Have: A Memoir of Faith, Justice, and Freedom for the Wrongly Accused*, the best-selling novelist John Grisham tells readers that getting an accused prisoner exonerated by the courts is "virtually impossible" and "takes an advocate who is tireless, fearless, and dedicated to justice." Grisham describes Jim McCloskey—a former business consultant who founded Centurion Ministries in 1983 to free people who had been wrongly convicted of crimes—as someone who aptly fits this description. In an introductory author's note, McCloskey himself prepares readers for the content, stating, "My goal in writing this book it to provide readers with a glimpse into the world of the wrongly convicted. I hope to offer insight into our nation's criminal justice system: how it serves and doesn't serve those who are falsely accused of crimes." The rest of the book tells the stories of prisoners McCloskey worked with, but sprinkled throughout these stories, he shares glimpses of influential moments in his own personal life.

Those personal moments from McCloskey's life include snapshots of his childhood and family life, his military service, his years as a businessman, and his relationships. He does not shy away from revealing his own weaknesses, some of which helped him understand his clients better. For instance, he learned that his own prejudices could influence his perception of a person when he asked his mentor at Trenton State

Prison, "Who *was* that Black guy screaming at me?" He was quickly informed that the prisoner was, in fact, White. This experience taught him the unreliability of eyewitness. The other strictly personal chapters provide flashbacks to different parts of his life, starting with an introduction to his parents. In another memory, he tells of a summer visit to Tijuana, Mexico, where he and two friends landed in jail. He also discusses the women he loved, past relationships, and the emptiness he often felt. Those experiences, however, taught him lessons he took into his mission to save the wrongly accused. For instance, he contributes "the feeling of having faith when reason fails" to his father. He learned "how easy it is to find yourself behind bars, and how easy it can be for nice White college kids with connections to get out of that scrape." He watched his military superiors "blatantly fabricating reports," which "steeled me for what was to come."

Jim McCloskey

What was to come would be his ministry with prisoners across the United States and in Canada. The stories McCloskey shares are often heartbreaking and consistently maddening. He begins with the story of Jorge "Chiefie" de los Santos, the first prisoner McCloskey helped while he was still a student at Princeton Theological Seminary. McCloskey met de los Santos while serving as a ministerial intern at Trenton State Prison. The internship started with a cardinal rule: "don't get involved, under any circumstances, in any way, shape, or form, with any of the inmates' cases or their personal lives." By his second day, McCloskey had already broken that rule with de los Santos, whose personality and honesty about his past appealed to the minister. McCloskey learned that de los Santos had been arrested for a murder that he claimed he had not committed. Ironically, McCloskey did not believe de los Santos's accusations of a crooked criminal justice system at first, but eventually, he was won over. A lengthy personal investigation into the case set McCloskey off on the path that would determine the work he would do for the rest of his life. After helping free de los Santos from prison with the aid of a local lawyer, Paul Casteleiro, McCloskey founded Centurion Ministries—the first organization of its kind in the world—and soon took on more cases. The first was the case of Rene Santana, a prisoner McCloskey had met while working with de los Santos. Santana was accused of the robbery and murder of a Newark gambler. Once again, McCloskey jumped into the investigation, working with Santana's lawyer to prove the man's innocence. While laboring to free Santana, McCloskey took on the case of Nate Walker, a young Black man who had been accused of raping and kidnapping a White woman.

Those cases are followed by Clarence Brandley's story. Brandley, a Black man, was on death row for the 1980 rape and murder of a White high school student in

Texas. Brandley, a janitor at the high school, was arrested almost immediately because he had found the girl's body. There was little evidence against Brandley, but racial injustice was at work. Less than a month before Clarence was to be executed, McCloskey's team won him a reprieve. Even though he had been found innocent, it took another two years before Brandley was freed from prison, highlighting yet another issue with the system that had wrongly accused him.

Throughout the rest of the memoir, McCloskey shares the stories of many more inmates. Some of them were innocent and freed; some were guilty, and Centurion dropped their cases. Among the many successes mentioned are Darryl Burton, who served twenty-four years, and Joyce Ann Brown, who had been imprisoned for eight years before McCloskey and his team took her case. Other successes include the Savannah Three (Mark Jones, Kenneth Gardiner, and Dominic Lucci), Mark Schand, Richard Miles, and Willie Green. One memorable case is that of Roger Coleman, who had been accused of raping and murdering his sister-in-law. Centurion did as much as they could to get the courts to reexamine the case, but Coleman's case was never completely solved, and McCloskey began to suspect Coleman's involvement.

Through the narratives of the prisoners' lives and McCloskey's investigations into their crimes, many issues in the criminal justice system are exposed. At the close of the book, McCloskey points out the wrongs he perceives in the system in his epilogue: a rigid system resistant to change, widespread perjury, insufficient forensic evidence, unreliable eyewitnesses, racial disparities, false confessions, and misconduct in the courts, to name just a few. He prefaces those ongoing problems with a positive note on what has changed for the better in the system, including DNA testing and an increased interest in the innocence movement, which led to a National Registry of Exonerations. He cites the organization's findings that in thirty years (from 1989 to 2019), over 2,500 individuals, including 123 death-row inmates, had their convictions overturned and that two-thirds of the states had passed legislation for restitution to the wrongly convicted for their years of unjust incarceration. McCloskey finishes his epilogue with a list of policy changes that he believes would further improve the system, including electing district and state attorneys who have proven records that show they care about wrongful convictions, mandating proper storage and management of evidence in all levels of police departments, and changing unfair policies about appeals.

Though the prisoners' stories are the focus of much of the book, McCloskey also talks about his journey in faith. Early in the book, he writes that it is the story of "how I learned to look that evil in the eye and still understand that there is good in the world. And how, if you allow it, you can become a catalyst for that good." Despite his desire to maintain his faith in God, he is honest in the struggles that he experienced at different points in his life and how they tested that faith. Though this doubt centered on his religious experiences, he also shares how his faith in the justice system was undermined as he encountered injustice at all levels—from police officers to judges. In addition to faith, McCloskey encourages readers to maintain hope and ends the book with an invitation "to walk beside us, when you can, in whatever way you can. Because the justice system is not just. But it could be."

The critical reviews of *When Truth Is All You Have* have uniformly lauded the work that McCloskey has spent his life doing. Barbara Bradley Hagerty, the *Washington Post*'s reviewer, called the book "a riveting and infuriating examination of criminal prosecutions" that "upends our naïve and complacent view of prosecutions," but also commended it as "full of drama and hope." Anitra Gates stated in *Library Journal* that "McCloskey and Lerman's natural storytelling style make this an enjoyable read even when addressing tough subjects. This will be essential for collections focused on social justice, the wrongly convicted, and spiritual transformation." In addition to commenting on McCloskey's work, the review in *Publishers Weekly* called the author "an engaging narrator" and applauded his inclusion of "both successes and heartbreaking losses." Indeed, *When Truth Is All You Have* makes one rejoice in the successes of McCloskey's work and desire to fight along with him when reading of the failures.

Author Biography
Jim McCloskey is the founder of Centurion (formerly Centurion Ministries). His life work has been investigating the cases of wrongly accused men and women and helping free them from jail. He formerly served in the military in Japan and Vietnam and was a successful businessman.

Philip Lerman has cowritten several nonfiction books and authored his own memoir about becoming a parent. He has also worked as a television producer and was the national editor of *USA Today*.

Theresa L. Stowell, PhD

Review Sources
Gates, Anitra. Review of *When Truth Is All You Have: A Memoir of Faith, Justice and Freedom for the Wrongly Convicted*, by Jim McCloskey and Philip Lerman. *Library Journal*, 1 June 2020, www.libraryjournal.com/?reviewDetail=when-truth-is-all-you-have-memoir-of-faith-justice-and-freedom-for-the-wrongly-convicted. Accessed 23 Nov. 2020.
Hagerty, Barbara Bradley. "Taking on the Hardest Cases—without DNA—and Setting the Innocent Free." Review of *When Truth Is All You Have: A Memoir of Faith, Justice and Freedom for the Wrongly Convicted*, by Jim McCloskey and Philip Lerman. *The Washington Post*, 7 August 2020, www.washingtonpost.com/outlook/taking-on-the-hardest-cases--without-dna--and-setting-the-innocent-free/2020/08/06/9bea85ac-a042-11ea-b5c9-570a91917d8d_story.html. Accessed 2 Nov. 2020.
Review of *When Truth Is All You Have: A Memoir of Faith, Justice, and Freedom for the Wrongly Convicted*, by Jim McCloskey and Philip Lerman. *Kirkus*, 29 Mar. 2020, www.kirkusreviews.com/book-reviews/jim-mccloskey/when-truth-is-all-you-have. Accessed 23 Nov. 2020.
Review of *When Truth Is All You Have: A Memoir of Faith, Justice, and Freedom for the Wrongly Convicted*, by Jim McCloskey and Philip Lerman. *Publishers Weekly*, 20 Apr. 2020, www.publishersweekly.com/978-0-385-54503-7. Accessed 23 Nov. 2020.

Wilmington's Lie
The Murderous Coup of 1898 and the Rise of White Supremacy

Author: David Zucchino (b. ca. 1951)
Publisher: Atlantic Monthly Press (New York). 448 pp.
Type of work: History
Time: Primarily 1898
Locale: Wilmington, North Carolina

This historical investigation by David Zucchino looks at the Wilmington coup, a White supremacist assault on the then majority-Black city of Wilmington, North Carolina, in 1898.

Principal personages
ALFRED MOORE WADDELL, a former Confederate, a leader of the White supremacist insurrectionists in Wilmington
ABRAHAM GALLOWAY, a Black resident of Wilmington who held state office after the Civil War
JOSEPHUS DANIELS, a White newspaper editor who helped instigate the White supremacist riot in Wilmington
ALEXANDER "ALEX" MANLY, a Black newspaper editor who defended consensual mixed-race relationships

Wilmington's Lie (2020), a history of the 1898 Wilmington, North Carolina, race riot, is one of a number of prominent books seeking to contribute to the public debate over the ongoing influence of racism in American life and politics. Pulitzer Prize–winning journalist David Zucchino uses Wilmington's fraught history to explore the way that lies fueled White supremacy in the past and continue to do so in the present. *Wilmington's Lie* also contributes to the recent debate about the rise of domestic terrorism in the United States. Just as in the early 2020s, American domestic terrorists in the 1890s tended to be White supremacists, and the factors that led to the now-infamous Wilmington massacre of 1898 are strikingly similar to the contemporary rise of White supremacist terrorists.

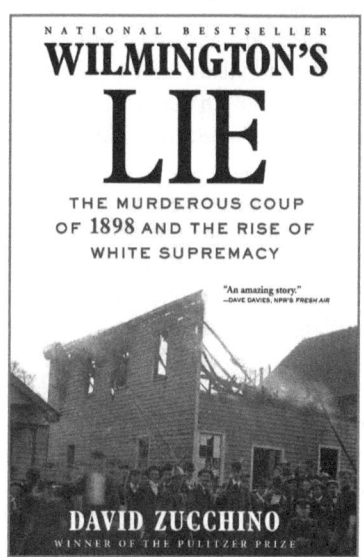

Zucchino has previously explored difficult questions about racism and racist ideology. In his first nonfiction book, *The Myth of the Welfare Queen* (1997), Zucchino exposes the racial stereotype of the "Black welfare queen" who games the system to fraudulently claim tax revenues set aside to help the less fortunate, tracing how this mythological problem resulted from centuries of misinformation about Black work ethic, intelligence, and commitment to other supposed American ideals. In *Wilmington's Lie*, his third book, Zucchino explores the lies that undergird White supremacy itself: that different races have different value and a legitimate racial hierarchy of value exists, and that Black people are dangerous and/or sexually deviant. Both lies were and remain essential to the big lie of White supremacy: the myth that the White race is special or more suited to leadership than other races are.

In the first part of the book, Zucchino describes the history of North Carolina and Wilmington from the end of slavery leading into the 1890s. Readers may be surprised to learn how the small city of Wilmington had unexpectedly evolved into a functional multiracial community where emancipated African Americans and their descendants had begun to achieve some measure of citizenship and prosperity. By the late 1890s around 56 percent of residents were Black, and the city's growing port shipping business created enough revenues that members of the city's Black population had entered the middle class. Moreover, Black Americans were taking a leading role in the community. Zucchino devotes a great deal of time to the story of one such figure: Abraham Galloway, who had escaped slavery, served as a Union Army spy, and was twice elected to the state senate representing North Carolina in the 1860s. The little city also had a number of Black business owners, police officers, and officers of the courts. The achievements of Black Americans in the city were publicized and celebrated thanks to the city's Black newspaper, *The Record*.

David Zucchino

Zucchino describes how White supremacists felt extremely threatened by the mere existence of Wilmington, as the city was rapidly becoming a concrete refutation of the lies underlying their philosophy. In their cowardice and jealousy, White people circulated claims that the Black men of Wilmington were sexual deviants who were violently violating White women. As Zucchino explains, students of history will find lies like this throughout American history. Lies about sexual violence were especially common right before White mobs attacked communities of color. Accusations of sexual violence or debauchery are effective because they arouse both sexual jealousy and provide a ready-made excuse for violence. Claiming that members of a target race or group are rapists gives people who have violent feelings of animus against them justification to attack members of that group and to believe that they themselves are not villains, but heroes defending the vulnerable from danger.

In refutation of hate speeches given by White supremacists claiming that Black men were raping or abusing White women in Wilmington, Alexander Manly, the editor for the *Record*, stated accurately that there were relationships between Black men and White women in Wilmington but that they were consensual. He also called attention to the hypocrisy of White men, who had long been raping and impregnating Black women but disdained the possibility that White women might find Black men desirable. Manly's article inflamed White sexual insecurities and jealousies and inspired calls for Manly to be lynched.

White sexual jealousy and fear became a tool for conservative White politicians seeking to regain control of the state from the Republican Party, then the more socially progressive of the major political parties. White supremacist politicians alleged that voters had to return their party to power, or else sexual assault and job theft committed by upwardly mobile Black men would spread. As Zucchino ably demonstrates, there was no evidence of widespread lawlessness or sexual violence, however. In the absence of legitimate arguments for their return to power, the conservative political establishment in North Carolina launched a propaganda campaign. Josephus Daniels, publisher of the state's most influential newspaper, ran exaggerated and fraudulent stories about Wilmington's political incompetence and Black violence, clearly violating journalistic ethics. A former Confederate colonel, Alfred Moore Waddell, helped to organize a series of campaign rallies and encouraged White supremacists to use violence to prevent Black citizens from voting in upcoming elections. Zucchino also delves into the stories of other White supremacists who fomented unrest in the lead-up to the election and coup, including their rivalries and alliances.

Even with months of propagandizing, the conservatives would still likely have lost the election, but they did not let their lack of popular support stop them. When Election Day came, armed White militias "defended" polling places against Black citizens seeking to vote, threatened the lives of Black leaders, and openly stuffed ballot boxes. A coalition of conservative, White supremacist groups essentially stole the election through outright fraud, disenfranchisement, and intimidation across the state. However, their offenses did not stop there.

Within days of the stolen election, in which White supremacists reclaimed control of the state legislature, Waddell announced a "White Declaration of Independence" and armed White men calling themselves Red Shirts attacked the city of Wilmington and its Black neighborhood of Brooklyn in particular. Buildings and homes were burned and destroyed. Black politicians and their White allies were forced to resign from office at gunpoint. White supremacists appointed themselves to fill the vacancies left by the forced resignations, with Waddell assuming the mayorship. Thousands of Black residents and some progressive Whites were driven from the city and into the swamps and forests to escape the violent mobs. The violence lasted for days, with between sixty and three hundred Black residents left dead in the streets.

In the wake of the coup, the White supremacist–controlled press celebrated it as a return of "law and order," and the county quickly began imposing a new series of laws that were essentially meant to keep Black Americans abased. Voting law statutes and economic policies guaranteed that Black residents would find it difficult to regain power, while appointed heads of state branches worked to undermine those Black Americans who had already won a share of independence or property ownership. More than a half-century of oppression followed in the wake of the violent 1898 coup that returned White supremacists to power in North Carolina.

In the final third of the book, Zucchino describes the aftermath of the coup. No one was ever punished for the crimes committed in Wilmington, and in fact, many of the leaders—including instigator Josephus Daniels—went on to have flourishing, high-profile political careers in state and federal government for many years. For decades, the history of the coup was reframed as a heroic response to a Black "race riot" by the Red Shirt attackers, who had patriotically defended the city against a surge in Black violence. Generations of schoolchildren were poisoned by this legacy of lies and hatred, never learning the truth about Wilmington and some of the historic leaders of their state.

The book's epilogue brings the story of Wilmington back to the present day, exploring how similar lies are being used to disenfranchise Black voters, to foment racial jealousy and animus, and to train children to embrace the fundamental tenets of White supremacy. These are the same basic lies that fueled slavery and Black disenfranchisement after the end of Reconstruction. Interestingly, many modern American readers would consider the likes of Daniels and Waddell to be not just domestic terrorists, but traitors as well. The advancement of the Black residents of Wilmington, from slavery and poverty to leadership, is emblematic of what can occur in a democratic society if members are given a chance to prove themselves to the people, the ultimate source of power in a true democracy. Readers will walk away from *Wilmington's Lie* with the realization that the coup in Wilmington revealed that North Carolina, and perhaps the nation at large, was not really a democracy at all. The Wilmington Red Shirts violated the principles of the Constitution and democratic ideals stretching back to Democritus: they installed an authoritarian government in place of the democratically elected one, and the organs of the state did not punish them or prevent that from happening. If anything, they were rewarded for defending the system that undergirded America's democratic mythos, a system of privilege, power, manipulation, and propaganda that served the White upper class and no one else.

Critics were overwhelmingly positive in their assessments of David Zucchino's latest exploration of race and power in America. For the *Washington Post*, historian Louis P. Masur called the book "deeply researched and relevant." *New York Times* critic Eddie S. Glaude Jr. described it as "brilliant" and lauded Zucchino for avoiding "overwriting" the scenes of violence and drama that he depicts and for keeping his moral judgement distant as he builds the history of racism and the lies told to justify it. Several reviewers found the second part of the book to be particularly riveting and cinematic in quality. Zucchino's years as a journalist serve him well when he turns his eye toward historical subjects, as he ably depicts events much as a reporter covering a warzone does, with enough detachment to allow readers to form their own emotional conclusions. Yet it is clear throughout that Zucchino has no sympathy for the betrayal of democracy or for the use of lies to perpetuate the myths of racial animus and White supremacy. He is equally clear in his belief that these same consequential forces are still fueling racism in twenty-first-century America.

Author Biography
David Zucchino is a journalist and former war correspondent who won the 1989 Pulitzer Prize in Feature Writing for his coverage of South African apartheid and was a finalist for another five Pulitzers. He also previously published *The Myth of the Welfare Queen* (1997) and *Thunder Run: The Armored Strike to Capture Baghdad* (2004).

Micah L. Issitt

Review Sources
Adams, Michael Henry. "Wilmington's Lie Review: Race, Outrage and the Roots of Modern Inequality." Review of *Wilmington's Lie: The Murderous Coup of 1898 and the Rise of White Supremacy*, by David Zucchino. *The Guardian*, 8 Feb. 2020, www.theguardian.com/world/2020/feb/08/wilmingtons-lie-review-david-zucchino. Accessed 25 Jan. 2021.
Bordewich, Fergus M. "'Wilmington's Lie' Review: An American Tragedy." *The Wall Street Journal*, 3 Jan. 2020, www.wsj.com/articles/wilmingtons-lie-review-an-american-tragedy-11578067530. Accessed 24 Jan. 2021.
Glaude, Eddie S., Jr. "When White Supremacists Overthrew an Elected Government." Review of *Wilmington's Lie: The Murderous Coup of 1898 and the Rise of White Supremacy*, by David Zucchino. *The New York Times*, 7 Jan. 2020, www.nytimes.com/2020/01/07/books/review/wilmingtons-lie-david-zucchino.html. Accessed 26 Jan. 2021.
Masur, Louis P. "How a Mob Turned a Diverse City into a White-Supremacist Bastion." Review of *Wilmington's Lie: The Murderous Coup of 1898 and the Rise of White Supremacy*, by David Zucchino. *The Washington Post*, 23 Jan. 2020, www.washingtonpost.com/outlook/how-a-mob-turned-a-diverse-city-into-a-white-supremacist-bastion/2020/01/23/f7bc101c-2356-11ea-86f3-3b5019d451db_story.html. Accessed 25 Jan. 2021.
Timpane, John. "'Wilmington's Lie': This Little-Known 1898 Coup in North Carolina Had an Ugly Legacy." Review of *Wilmington's Lie: The Murderous Coup of 1898 and the Rise of White Supremacy*, by David Zucchino. *Inquirer*, 12 Feb. 2020, www.inquirer.com/arts/books/wilmingtons-lie-david-zucchino-book-review-20200212.html. Accessed 28 Jan. 2021.

Yellow Bird
Oil, Murder, and a Woman's Search for Justice in Indian Country

Author: Sierra Crane Murdoch (b. ca. 1987)
Publisher: Random House (New York).
  400 pp.
Type of work: Miscellaneous
Time: 2011–19
Locale: North Dakota

Investigative journalist Sierra Crane Murdoch's Yellow Bird: Oil, Murder, and a Woman's Search for Justice in Indian Country *is an investigative story about a true crime that took place on an American Indian reservation and the efforts of Lissa Yellow Bird to investigate the crime.*

Principal personages
KRISTOPHER CLARKE, a.k.a. *KC*, an employee of the Blackstone oil trucking company who disappeared from the Fort Berthold Indian Reservation
LISSA YELLOW BIRD, an amateur detective who investigated his disappearance
JAMES HENRIKSON, his friend, one of the owners of Blackstone
SARAH CREVELING, Henrikson's wife and business partner
JILL WILLIAMS, Clarke's mother
TEX HALL, the tribal chairman of Fort Berthold at the time of Clarke's disappearance
SIERRA CRANE MURDOCH, the narrator, a reporter who covers the investigation

Yellow Bird: Oil, Murder, and a Woman's Search for Justice in Indian Country is the first book from reporter Sierra Crane Murdoch. It won praise not only for Murdoch's clear skill as an investigative journalist, but also for the ways in which she integrates the central true-crime story into the broader story of the neglect of American Indians and the ways in which indigenous communities continue to be exploited, ignored, and marginalized. The crux of *Yellow Bird* is a presumed murder that happened in 2012. That year, a twenty-nine-year-old White oil worker named Kristopher Clarke, or KC as friends and family knew him, went missing, and his body was never found. He had last been seen on the Fort Berthold Indian Reservation in North Dakota.

Murdoch gradually introduces readers to a little bit of background on the Fort Berthold reservation, which has been set aside for the use and continuation of the Three Affiliated Tribes, or the Mandan, Hidatsa, and Arikara Nation. The reservation has a long history, having been established in 1870 as part of the 1851 Treaty of Fort Laramie that saw Mandan, Hidatsa, Crow, Blackfeet, Assiniboine, Dakota Sioux, and some Cheyenne and Arapaho bands relocated from their traditional territories in the northern Great Plains to reservation lands. Since then, the US government has periodically taken land from the Three Affiliated Tribes for economic exploitation. Most dramatically, this occurred in the mid-1950s with the creation of the Garrison Dam, which created Lake Sakakawea partially on the land controlled by the tribes. The lake flooded villages and important farmland utilized by members of the community, decimating the local economy.

The reservation had the fortune and misfortune of being located right next to one of the largest deposits of shale oil in the United States, a geological feature known as the Bakken Formation. The Bakken oil boom, which ramped up in the 2010s, transformed the economy of the region and created numerous jobs, but also caused a whole host of problems, including oil spills and polluted waterways. For some of the American Indians living on land near the Bakken oil fields, the boom was a boon, but for others, it was a bust. Social scientists noted an intense increase in crime and drug use in many of the towns surrounding Bakken and that American Indians were especially hard hit by the crime wave.

The true-crime tale the Murdoch narrates is related to the tumult that came to Ford Berthold during the oil boom. It was at the height of the boom that Clarke went missing while working for Blackstone, a White-owned company that had recently come to take part in the area's oil-shale industry. Murdoch had already been visiting the reservation and studying the impact of the oil boom on the reservation's residents when Clarke went missing. She had been examining one major factor in the crime wave that spread through the area: the police force of the Three Affiliated Tribes, which had sole jurisdiction on the reservation, had been stymied in its efforts to combat the crime wave because reservation law officials had no jurisdiction over the White individuals who came onto reservation land and commit crimes. When Clarke went missing, Murdoch decided to follow the crime, hoping to explore the way that the boom and arrival of White criminals had affected the reservation.

This is how Murdoch met Lissa Yellow Bird, an Arikara woman with a complicated past. Many critics and readers alike noted that Yellow Bird makes for a fascinating figure, akin to the antihero characters found in certain works of fiction. To start, Yellow Bird, who is recovering from multiple drug addictions, had spent two years in prison for possession of methamphetamine. The mother of five children by five different men, Yellow Bird struggled to find stability for herself and her family, rotating through a variety of jobs, including stripper, bartender, carpenter, and welder, among others. She obtained a degree through the University of North Dakota's criminal justice program and became, essentially, a private detective specializing in tracking missing people. She searches for answers on what happened to the missing White man who disappeared on reservation land, and Murdoch records her relentless efforts.

Yellow Bird is the star of Murdoch's fascinating true-crime investigation, serving as both the primary personage and a lens for Murdoch's deeper investigation into the lives of American Indians on the reservation. Writing in the *Los Angeles Times*, Carolyn Kellogg said, "Lissa Yellow Bird is one of the most fascinating characters I've ever read about—and she's a real person. She has been a terrible mother, a rebellious daughter, a drug addict, a drug dealer, a prisoner. She has also been the opposite of each of those things: devoted, attentive, sober, free." As Murdoch explores Yellow Bird's story, she also uncovers the story of Yellow Bird's family and of the longer history of how the Arikara, Hidatsa, and Mandan people were subjected to exploitative policies and marginalized by indifference and negligence. Murdoch explains how this largely forgotten enclave of American Indians only became of interest to the broader nation with the discovery of oil on and hear their lands. From that point on, their lives were shaped by the greed and indifference of White-owned corporations.

To understand the central crime under investigation—the disappearance of Clarke—Murdoch takes readers through a complicated system of contractors and explains the difficult administration and bureaucratic processes needed to do business on tribal lands. This is how Clarke ended up working for his friend James Henrikson, the owner of an oil trucking company contracting with a tribal leader. Murdoch first came to North Dakota to study how the oil boom changed the culture of the reservation, and over years working with Yellow Bird, she exposed a system of bribery going on beneath the surface of tribal and oil-industry society.

Clarke's truck was found off the reservation, abandoned but unlocked, and Clarke was nowhere to be found. It was Yellow Bird who first latched onto the case, rather than Murdoch. Yellow Bird found a plea posted to Facebook by Clarke's mother, Jill, with whom she connected, and soon began working intensively on the case. Murdoch details aspects of Yellow Bird's subsequent investigation showing how Yellow Bird's own complicated history enabled her to become a unique kind of detective, as Kellogg noted. Because of her familiarity with the criminal justice system, Yellow Bird was able to navigate the bureaucracy between government offices. As a former criminal, she was able to understand and navigate the criminal networks in the underbelly of her society. As a member of the Three Affiliated Tribes, she was able to access both tribal information and members of the tribal bureaucracy.

At times, Yellow Bird's investigative methods could be unorthodox. At least once in the investigation, she assumed a fake identity and participated in catfishing through social media. It did not take her long to suspect that Henrikson and his wife, Sarah Creveling, were behind Clarke's disappearance. As Yellow Bird uncovers, the duo had already committed a number of financial and other misdeeds, and Clarke was on the verge of defecting to a rival company and bringing business with him—a clear threat to Henrikson and Creveling's operations on the reservation.

Yellow Bird quickly discovers her main suspects, but the problem becomes how to find enough evidence to lead to their arrest. Working with Jill Williams, Yellow Bird then utilizes a wide variety of methods, some questionable, to pressure Henrikson and to build suspicion among the public and the administration. The tactics work, and the information that Yellow Bird gives to law enforcement is instrumental in the arrests made in the case and subsequent trial. Along the way, Yellow Bird and Murdoch also reveal the way that the tribal government had itself fallen victim to greed and vice and had failed to protect the interests of the tribe amid the opportunities of the oil boom.

In an author's endnote, Murdoch is careful to explain that as a White writer, she could not deliver a view from within the Indigenous society she was covering. To this end, she wrote the book from the first-person perspective, attempting to be open and honest about the story being told by a White woman about an American Indian woman. She also included Yellow Bird and her family in the editing process, allowing them to choose how much of their story and what details could be shared. Murdoch wanted to provide Yellow Bird with some voice in how her own story was created and distributed, and Yellow Bird, to her credit, did not object to being depicted in her complicated multitudes, as both villain and hero.

Murdoch's *Yellow Bird* received widespread praise from critics, who called the book a success as a true-crime mystery and praised Murdoch's skill and sensitivity in her depiction of Yellow Bird's complicated life and history. Reviewers did note some criticisms, however. The details of Henrikson and Creveling's crimes were covered in tremendous detail in the popular press, and as *Bismarck Tribune* critic Steve Wallick noted, *Yellow Bird* adds little to what has already been described of the crime and subsequent trial. It also hews closely to its subject and touches on but does not delve into the epidemic of missing and murdered American Indian women, particularly in the Bakken region, as David Treuer (Ojibwe) pointed out in his *New York Times* review. Nonetheless, the story serves as a fascinating, if limited, exploration of how greed and corruption damage communities and societies. As Murdoch herself noted, while Clarke's death was on one hand the result of one person's greed, it also exemplifies the general selfish dehumanization of others that can result from broad economic changes that transform, and often damage, entire communities.

Author Biography

Sierra Crane Murdoch is a journalist and essayist whose work has appeared on *This American Life*, *The Atlantic*, *The New Yorker*, *Harper's*, and *High Country News*. She was a Middlebury Fellow in Environmental Journalism, a MacDowell Fellow in Literature, and a visiting fellow in investigative reporting from the University of California, Berkeley.

Micah L. Issitt

Review Sources

Greenberg, Susan H. "Unburying the Truth." Review of *Yellow Bird*, by Sierra Crane Murdoch. *Middlebury Magazine*, 21 May 2020, middleburymagazine.com/review/unburying-the-truth. Accessed 16 Nov. 2020.

Kellogg, Carolyn. "Review: True Crime on the Reservation, Starring an Unlikely Amateur Sleuth." Review of *Yellow Bird*, by Sierra Crane Murdoch. *Los Angeles Times*, 19 Feb. 2020, www.latimes.com/entertainment-arts/books/story/2020-02-19/review-true-crime-on-the-reservation-starring-an-unlikely-amateur-sleuth. Accessed 16 Nov. 2020.

Treuer, David. "An Oil Boom, a Missing Body and a Native Woman's Quest to Find It." Review of *Yellow Bird*, by Sierra Crane Murdoch. *The New York Times*, 25 Feb. 2020, www.nytimes.com/2020/02/25/books/review/yellow-bird-sierra-crane-murdoch.html. Accessed 16 Nov. 2020.

Wallick, Steve. "'Yellow Bird' a Worthwhile Story of One Woman's Search." Review of *Yellow Bird*, by Sierra Crane Murdoch. *Bismarck Tribune*, 22 Mar. 2020, bismarcktribune.com/entertainment/books-and-literature/yellow-bird-a-worthwhile-story-of-one-woman-s-search/article_a18e4ec7-d288-5cef-aee9-ea3621695f88.html. Accessed 16 Nov. 2020.

Category Index

Biography
Agent Sonya: Moscow's Most Daring Wartime Spy (Macintyre), 10
Dancing at the Pity Party: A Dead Mom Graphic Memoir (Feder), 116
The Dead Are Arising: The Life of Malcolm X (Payne), 125
Hidden Valley Road: Inside the Mind of an American Family (Kolker), 250
His Very Best: Jimmy Carter, a Life (Alter), 260
Hitler: Downfall 1939–1945 (Ullrich), 269
Inge's War: A German Woman's Story of Family, Secrets, and Survival under Hitler (O'Donnell), 329
The Last Negroes at Harvard: The Class of 1963 and the 18 Young Men Who Changed Harvard Forever (Garrett and Ellsworth), 377
Nobody Will Tell You This but Me: A True (as Told to Me) Story (Kalb), 442
Pelosi (Ball), 480
The Price of Peace: Money, Democracy, and the Life of John Maynard Keynes (Carter), 494
The Rise and Fall of Charles Lindbergh (Fleming), 532
The Splendid and the Vile: A Saga of Churchill, Family, and Defiance during the Blitz (Larson), 582

Current affairs
The Address Book: What Street Addresses Reveal about Identity, Race, Wealth, and Power (Mask), 1
Death in Mud Lick: A Coal Country Fight against the Drug Companies That Delivered the Opioid Epidemic (Eyre), 139
Eat the Buddha: Life and Death in a Tibetan Town (Demick), 177
Five Days: The Fiery Reckoning of an American City (Moore with Green), 206
Is Rape a Crime?: A Memoir, an Investigation, and a Manifesto (Bowdler), 348
Paying the Land (Sacco), 475
Race against Time: A Reporter Reopens the Unsolved Murder Cases of the Civil Rights Era (Mitchell), 508
The Second Chance Club: Hardship and Hope after Prison (Hardy), 541
Stamped: Racism, Antiracism, and You (Kendi and Reynolds), 591
Those Who Forget: My Family's Story in Nazi Europe (A Memoir, a History, a Warning (Schwarz), 620
We Have Been Harmonized: Life in China's Surveillance State (Strittmatter), 685

Education
The Last Negroes at Harvard: The Class of 1963 and the 18 Young Men Who Changed Harvard Forever (Garrett and Ellsworth), 377

Environment
Paying the Land (Sacco), 475
Vesper Flights (Macdonald), 671

Essays
Brown Album: Essays on Exile and Identity (Khakpour), 67
Fight of the Century: Writers Reflect on 100 Years of Landmark ACLU Cases (Chabon and Waldman), 201
A History of My Brief Body (Belcourt), 265
Hood Feminism: Notes from the Women That a Movement Forgot (Kendall), 299
Intimations (Smith), 338
Just Us: An American Conversation (Rankine), 358
Vesper Flights (Macdonald), 671

Graphic nonfiction
Almost American Girl (Ha), 20
Dancing at the Pity Party: A Dead Mom Graphic Memoir (Feder), 116
Dragon Hoops (Yang), 168
Paying the Land (Sacco), 475

History
The Address Book: What Street Addresses Reveal about Identity, Race, Wealth, and Power (Mask), 1
Agent Sonya: Moscow's Most Daring Wartime Spy (Macintyre), 10
A Black Women's History of the United States (Berry and Gross), 52
Caste: The Origins of Our Discontents (Wilkerson), 76
Death in Mud Lick: A Coal Country Fight against the Drug Companies That Delivered the Opioid Epidemic (Eyre), 139
Eat the Buddha: Life and Death in a Tibetan Town (Demick), 177
Fight of the Century: Writers Reflect on 100 Years of Landmark ACLU Cases (Chabon and Waldman), 201
Hitler: Downfall 1939–1945 (Ullrich), 269
Inge's War: A German Woman's Story of Family, Secrets, and Survival under Hitler (O'Donnell), 329
The Last Negroes at Harvard: The Class of 1963 and the 18 Young Men Who Changed Harvard Forever (Garrett and Ellsworth), 377
One Mighty and Irresistible Tide: The Epic Struggle over American Immigration, 1924–1965 (Yang), 460
Paying the Land (Sacco), 475
The Price of Peace: Money, Democracy, and the Life of John Maynard Keynes (Carter), 494
A Promised Land (Obama), 499
Race against Time: A Reporter Reopens the Unsolved Murder Cases of the Civil Rights Era (Mitchell), 508
Reaganland: America's Right Turn 1976–1980 (Perlstein), 513
The Splendid and the Vile: A Saga of Churchill, Family, and Defiance during the Blitz (Larson), 582
Stamped: Racism, Antiracism, and You (Kendi and Reynolds), 591
Supreme Inequality: The Supreme Court's Fifty-Year Battle for a More Unjust America (Cohen), 605
Those Who Forget: My Family's Story in Nazi Europe (A Memoir, a History, a Warning (Schwarz), 620
Twilight of the Gods: War in the Western Pacific, 1944–1945 (Toll), 643
The Undocumented Americans (Villavicencio), 648
Unworthy Republic: The Dispossession of Native Americans and the Road to Indian Territory (Saunt), 657
We Are Not Free (Chee), 675
We Have Been Harmonized: Life in China's Surveillance State (Strittmatter), 685

CATEGORY INDEX

Wilmington's Lie: The Murderous Coup of 1898 and the Rise of White Supremacy (Zucchino), 699

History of Science

Some Assembly Required: Decoding Four Billion Years of Life, from Ancient Fossils to DNA (Shubin), 572

Law

A Knock at Midnight: A Story of Hope, Justice, and Freedom (Barnett), 372

Supreme Inequality: The Supreme Court's Fifty-Year Battle for a More Unjust America (Cohen), 605

Medicine

Death in Mud Lick: A Coal Country Fight against the Drug Companies That Delivered the Opioid Epidemic (Eyre), 139

Hidden Valley Road: Inside the Mind of an American Family (Kolker), 250

Memoir

Almost American Girl (Ha), 20

Apple (Skin to the Core) (Gansworth), 34

Brown Album: Essays on Exile and Identity (Khakpour), 67

Counterpoint: A Memoir of Bach and Mourning (Kennicott), 107

Dancing at the Pity Party: A Dead Mom Graphic Memoir (Feder), 116

Dirt: Adventures in Lyon as a Chef in Training, Father, and Sleuth Looking for the Secret of French Cooking (Buford), 154

The Dragons, the Giant, the Women (Moore), 173

A History of My Brief Body (Belcourt), 265

Hollywood Park (Jollett), 279

Inge's War: A German Woman's Story of Family, Secrets, and Survival under Hitler (O'Donnell), 329

Is Rape a Crime?: A Memoir, an Investigation, and a Manifesto (Bowdler), 348

Just Us: An American Conversation (Rankine), 358

A Knock at Midnight: A Story of Hope, Justice, and Freedom (Barnett), 372

The Last Negroes at Harvard: The Class of 1963 and the 18 Young Men Who Changed Harvard Forever (Garrett and Ellsworth), 377

Memorial Drive: A Daughter's Memoir (Trethewey), 401

Nobody Will Tell You This but Me: A True (as Told to Me) Story (Kalb), 442

A Promised Land (Obama), 499

Race against Time: A Reporter Reopens the Unsolved Murder Cases of the Civil Rights Era (Mitchell), 508

Recollections of My Nonexistence (Solnit), 523

The Second Chance Club: Hardship and Hope after Prison (Hardy), 541

Sigh, Gone: A Misfit's Memoir of Great Books, Punk Rock, and the Fight to Fit In (Tran), 554

The Smallest Lights in the Universe (Seager), 568

Those Who Forget: My Family's Story in Nazi Europe (A Memoir, a History, a Warning (Schwarz), 620

The Undocumented Americans (Villavicencio), 648

Untamed (Doyle), 653

When Truth Is All You Have: A Memoir of Faith, Justice, and Freedom for the Wrongly Accused (McCloskey with Lerman), 695

Miscellaneous
DMZ Colony (Choi), 164
Yellow Bird: Oil, Murder, and a Woman's Search for Justice in Indian Country (Murdoch), 704

Music
Counterpoint: A Memoir of Bach and Mourning (Kennicott), 107

Nature
Entangled Life: How Fungi Make Our Worlds, Change Our Minds & Shape Our Futures (Sheldrake), 187
Owls of the Eastern Ice: A Quest to Find and Save the World's Largest Owl (Slaght), 470
Vesper Flights (Macdonald), 671

Novel
Afterlife (Alvarez), 6
All the Devils Are Here (Penny), 15
Anxious People (Backman), 24
Apeirogon (McCann), 29
The Bear (Krivak), 38
Black Sun (Roanhorse), 47
Blacktop Wasteland (Cosby), 57
The Book of Longings (Kidd), 62
A Burning (Majumdar), 72
Cemetery Boys (Thomas), 81
The City We Became (Jemisin), 85
Cleanness (Greenwell), 94
Code Name Hélène (Lawhon), 98
Conjure Women (Atakora), 103
Crooked Hallelujah (Ford), 112
Deacon King Kong (McBride), 120
A Deadly Education (Novik), 130
Dear Edward (Napolitano), 135
The Death of Vivek Oji (Emezi), 144
Devolution: A Firsthand Account of the Rainier Sasquatch Massacre (Brooks), 149
The Discomfort of Evening (Rijneveld), 159

The Eighth Life (for Brilka) (Haratischvili), 182
The Evening and the Morning (Follett), 192
Fair Warning (Connelly), 196
A Girl Is a Body of Water (Makumbi), 211
The Glass Hotel (Mandel), 215
A Good Neighborhood (Fowler), 220
Grown (Jackson), 225
Hamnet (O'Farrell), 235
Harrow the Ninth (Muir), 240
Hench (Walschots), 245
Hieroglyphics (McCorkle), 255
Home before Dark (Sager), 284
Homeland Elegies (Akhtar), 289
How Much of These Hills Is Gold (Zhang), 304
Hurricane Season (Melchor), 309
Interior Chinatown (Yu), 334
The Invisible Life of Addie LaRue (Schwab), 343
Jack (Robinson), 353
Kim Jiyoung, Born 1982 (Nam-joo), 367
Leave the World Behind (Alam), 382
Long Bright River (Moore), 387
A Long Petal of the Sea (Allende), 391
The Lost Book of Adana Moreau (Zapata), 396
Mexican Gothic (Moreno-Garcia), 406
The Mirror & the Light (Mantel), 411
Miss Benson's Beetle (Joyce), 416
Moonflower Murders (Horowitz), 420
The Mountains Sing (Mai), 425
My Dark Vanessa (Russell), 429
The New Wilderness (Cook), 433
The Night Watchman (Erdrich), 438
Not So Pure and Simple (Giles), 447
The Only Good Indians (Jones), 465
Piranesi (Clarke), 485
Real Life (Taylor), 518
The Searcher (French), 537
Shuggie Bain (Stuart), 550
The Silent Wife (Slaughter), 559

CATEGORY INDEX

Sisters (Johnson), 564
The Southern Book Club's Guide to Slaying Vampires (Hendrix), 577
Squeeze Me (Hiaasen), 587
Summer (Smith), 596
The Sun Down Motel (James), 601
Swimming in the Dark (Jedrowski), 610
They Went Left (Hesse), 615
The Thursday Murder Club (Osman), 625
Tigers, Not Daughters (Mabry), 630
Tokyo Ueno Station (Miri), 635
Transcendent Kingdom (Gyasi), 639
The Vanished Birds (Jimenez), 662
The Vanishing Half (Bennett), 666
We Are Not Free (Chee), 675
We Are Not from Here (Sanchez), 680
Weather (Offill), 690

Novella
If It Bleeds (King), 319
The Office of Historical Corrections (Evans), 456
Ring Shout (Clark), 528

Poetry
Apple (Skin to the Core) (Gansworth), 34
Beowulf: A New Translation (Anonymous), 42
DMZ Colony (Choi), 164
Guillotine (Corral), 230
Homie (Smith), 294
Just Us: An American Conversation (Rankine), 358
Obit (Chang), 451
Postcolonial Love Poem (Diaz), 489

Science
Some Assembly Required: Decoding Four Billion Years of Life, from Ancient Fossils to DNA (Shubin), 572

Short Fiction
Hitting a Straight Lick with a Crooked Stick (Hurston), 274
I Hold a Wolf by the Ears (van den Berg), 314
In the Valley (Rash), 324
The Office of Historical Corrections (Evans), 456
The Secret Lives of Church Ladies (Philyaw), 546

Sociology
The Address Book: What Street Addresses Reveal about Identity, Race, Wealth, and Power (Mask), 1
Caste: The Origins of Our Discontents (Wilkerson), 76
Death in Mud Lick: A Coal Country Fight against the Drug Companies That Delivered the Opioid Epidemic (Eyre), 139
Is Rape a Crime?: A Memoir, an Investigation, and a Manifesto (Bowdler), 348
A Knock at Midnight: A Story of Hope, Justice, and Freedom (Barnett), 372
The Second Chance Club: Hardship and Hope after Prison (Hardy), 541

Technology
We Have Been Harmonized: Life in China's Surveillance State (Strittmatter), 685

Verse novel
Clap When You Land (Acevedo), 90
Kent State (Wiles), 363
Punching the Air (Zoboi and Salaam), 504

Title Index

The Address Book: What Street Addresses Reveal about Identity, Race, Wealth, and Power (Mask), 1
Afterlife (Alvarez), 6
Agent Sonya: Moscow's Most Daring Wartime Spy (Macintyre), 10
All the Devils Are Here (Penny), 15
Almost American Girl (Ha), 20
Anxious People (Backman), 24
Apeirogon (McCann), 29
Apple (Skin to the Core) (Gansworth), 34

The Bear (Krivak), 38
Beowulf: A New Translation (Anonymous), 42
Black Sun (Roanhorse), 47
A Black Women's History of the United States (Berry and Gross), 52
Blacktop Wasteland (Cosby), 57
The Book of Longings (Kidd), 62
Brown Album: Essays on Exile and Identity (Khakpour), 67
A Burning (Majumdar), 72

Caste: The Origins of Our Discontents (Wilkerson), 76
Cemetery Boys (Thomas), 81
The City We Became (Jemisin), 85
Clap When You Land (Acevedo), 90
Cleanness (Greenwell), 94
Code Name Hélène (Lawhon), 98
Conjure Women (Atakora), 103
Counterpoint: A Memoir of Bach and Mourning (Kennicott), 107
Crooked Hallelujah (Ford), 112

Dancing at the Pity Party: A Dead Mom Graphic Memoir (Feder), 116
Deacon King Kong (McBride), 120

The Dead Are Arising: The Life of Malcolm X (Payne), 125
A Deadly Education (Novik), 130
Dear Edward (Napolitano), 135
Death in Mud Lick: A Coal Country Fight against the Drug Companies That Delivered the Opioid Epidemic (Eyre), 139
The Death of Vivek Oji (Emezi), 144
Devolution: A Firsthand Account of the Rainier Sasquatch Massacre (Brooks), 149
Dirt: Adventures in Lyon as a Chef in Training, Father, and Sleuth Looking for the Secret of French Cooking (Buford), 154
The Discomfort of Evening (Rijneveld), 159
DMZ Colony (Choi), 164
Dragon Hoops (Yang), 168
The Dragons, the Giant, the Women (Moore), 173

Eat the Buddha: Life and Death in a Tibetan Town (Demick), 177
The Eighth Life (for Brilka) (Haratischvili), 182
Entangled Life: How Fungi Make Our Worlds, Change Our Minds & Shape Our Futures (Sheldrake), 187
The Evening and the Morning (Follett), 192

Fair Warning (Connelly), 196
Fight of the Century: Writers Reflect on 100 Years of Landmark ACLU Cases (Chabon and Waldman), 201
Five Days: The Fiery Reckoning of an American City (Moore with Green), 206

A Girl Is a Body of Water (Makumbi), 211
The Glass Hotel (Mandel), 215
A Good Neighborhood (Fowler), 220
Grown (Jackson), 225
Guillotine (Corral), 230

Hamnet (O'Farrell), 235
Harrow the Ninth (Muir), 240
Hench (Walschots), 245
Hidden Valley Road: Inside the Mind of an American Family (Kolker), 250
Hieroglyphics (McCorkle), 255
His Very Best: Jimmy Carter, a Life (Alter), 260
A History of My Brief Body (Belcourt), 265
Hitler: Downfall 1939–1945 (Ullrich), 269
Hitting a Straight Lick with a Crooked Stick (Hurston), 274
Hollywood Park (Jollett), 279
Home before Dark (Sager), 284
Homeland Elegies (Akhtar), 289
Homie (Smith), 294
Hood Feminism: Notes from the Women That a Movement Forgot (Kendall), 299
How Much of These Hills Is Gold (Zhang), 304
Hurricane Season (Melchor), 309

I Hold a Wolf by the Ears (van den Berg), 314
If It Bleeds (King), 319
In the Valley (Rash), 324
Inge's War: A German Woman's Story of Family, Secrets, and Survival under Hitler (O'Donnell), 329
Interior Chinatown (Yu), 334
Intimations (Smith), 338
The Invisible Life of Addie LaRue (Schwab), 343

Is Rape a Crime?: A Memoir, an Investigation, and a Manifesto (Bowdler), 348

Jack (Robinson), 353
Just Us: An American Conversation (Rankine), 358

Kent State (Wiles), 363
Kim Jiyoung, Born 1982 (Nam-joo), 367
A Knock at Midnight: A Story of Hope, Justice, and Freedom (Barnett), 372

The Last Negroes at Harvard: The Class of 1963 and the 18 Young Men Who Changed Harvard Forever (Garrett and Ellsworth), 377
Leave the World Behind (Alam), 382
Long Bright River (Moore), 387
A Long Petal of the Sea (Allende), 391
The Lost Book of Adana Moreau (Zapata), 396

Memorial Drive: A Daughter's Memoir (Trethewey), 401
Mexican Gothic (Moreno-Garcia), 406
The Mirror & the Light (Mantel), 411
Miss Benson's Beetle (Joyce), 416
Moonflower Murders (Horowitz), 420
The Mountains Sing (Mai), 425
My Dark Vanessa (Russell), 429

The New Wilderness (Cook), 433
The Night Watchman (Erdrich), 438
Nobody Will Tell You This but Me: A True (as Told to Me) Story (Kalb), 442
Not So Pure and Simple (Giles), 447

Obit (Chang), 451
The Office of Historical Corrections (Evans), 456

TITLE INDEX

One Mighty and Irresistible Tide: The Epic Struggle over American Immigration, 1924–1965 (Yang), 460
The Only Good Indians (Jones), 465
Owls of the Eastern Ice: A Quest to Find and Save the World's Largest Owl (Slaght), 470

Paying the Land (Sacco), 475
Pelosi (Ball), 480
Piranesi (Clarke), 485
Postcolonial Love Poem (Diaz), 489
The Price of Peace: Money, Democracy, and the Life of John Maynard Keynes (Carter), 494
A Promised Land (Obama), 499
Punching the Air (Zoboi and Salaam), 504

Race against Time: A Reporter Reopens the Unsolved Murder Cases of the Civil Rights Era (Mitchell), 508
Reaganland: America's Right Turn 1976–1980 (Perlstein), 513
Real Life (Taylor), 518
Recollections of My Nonexistence (Solnit), 523
Ring Shout (Clark), 528
The Rise and Fall of Charles Lindbergh (Fleming), 532

The Searcher (French), 537
The Second Chance Club: Hardship and Hope after Prison (Hardy), 541
The Secret Lives of Church Ladies (Philyaw), 546
Shuggie Bain (Stuart), 550
Sigh, Gone: A Misfit's Memoir of Great Books, Punk Rock, and the Fight to Fit In (Tran), 554
The Silent Wife (Slaughter), 559
Sisters (Johnson), 564
The Smallest Lights in the Universe (Seager), 568

Some Assembly Required: Decoding Four Billion Years of Life, from Ancient Fossils to DNA (Shubin), 572
The Southern Book Club's Guide to Slaying Vampires (Hendrix), 577
The Splendid and the Vile: A Saga of Churchill, Family, and Defiance during the Blitz (Larson), 582
Squeeze Me (Hiaasen), 587
Stamped: Racism, Antiracism, and You (Kendi and Reynolds), 591
Summer (Smith), 596
The Sun Down Motel (James), 601
Supreme Inequality: The Supreme Court's Fifty-Year Battle for a More Unjust America (Cohen), 605
Swimming in the Dark (Jedrowski), 610

They Went Left (Hesse), 615
Those Who Forget: My Family's Story in Nazi Europe (A Memoir, a History, a Warning (Schwarz), 620
The Thursday Murder Club (Osman), 625
Tigers, Not Daughters (Mabry), 630
Tokyo Ueno Station (Miri), 635
Transcendent Kingdom (Gyasi), 639
Twilight of the Gods: War in the Western Pacific, 1944–1945 (Toll), 643

The Undocumented Americans (Villavicencio), 648
Untamed (Doyle), 653
Unworthy Republic: The Dispossession of Native Americans and the Road to Indian Territory (Saunt), 657

The Vanished Birds (Jimenez), 662
The Vanishing Half (Bennett), 666
Vesper Flights (Macdonald), 671

We Are Not Free (Chee), 675
We Are Not from Here (Sanchez), 680